CONTINENTAL LIAR

From the State of Maine

James G. Blaine
MAINE HISTORIC PRESERVATION COMMISSION

CONTINENTAL LIAR

From the State of Maine

JAMES G. BLAINE

Neil Rolde

Down East Books

Camden, Maine

Down East Books
An imprint of Globe Pequot

Distributed by NATIONAL BOOK NETWORK

First Edition: January 2007
First Down East Books edition: July 2023

Copyright© 2006 by Neil Rolde

Library of Congress Cataloging-in-Publication Data
Rolde, Neil, 1931-
  Continental liar from the state of Maine : James G. Blaine/ by Neil Rolde. - 1st ed.
      p. cm.
  ISBN-13: 978-1-68475-129-7 (pbk. : alk. paper)

  1. Blaine, James Gillespie, 1830-1893. 2. Statesmen-United States-Biography.
3. Cabinet officers-United States-Biography. 4. Legislators-United States-
Biography. 5. United States. Congress. House-Speakers-Biography. 6. United
States. Congress. Senate-Biography. 7. United States-Foreign relations-
1865-1898. 8. United States-Politics and government-1865-1900. 9. Maine-
Biography. I. Title. II. Title: James G. Blaine.
  E664.B6R65   2006
  973.8'6092-dc22
  [B]
                              2006024305

Designed on Crummett Mountain by Edith Allard, Somerville, Maine
Layout by Nina DeGraff, Basil Hill Graphics, Somerville, Maine
Copyediting by Judith Robbins, Whitefield, Maine

∞™ The paper used in this publication meets the minimum requirements of American National Standard for Information Sciences-Permanence of Paper for Printed Library Materials, ANSI/NISO Z39.48-1 992.

DEDICATION

This book, the eleventh I have had
published, is dedicated to Carlotta, whose
mother called her Lola, and who, to the rest
of us, is known as Carla, my wife of forty-six-
plus years. Her patience with the scribbling I
do has been both an inspiration and a goad.
Whenever I tell her I have finished a piece of
writing, she smiles and says, "Wonderful.
When are you starting the next one?" That
role in my output, that silent, tolerant whip,
must be highlighted and celebrated.

Flag used in James G. Blaine's 1884 presidential campaign
MAINE STATE MUSEUM

CONTENTS

INTRODUCTION

J AMES G. BLAINE has been largely forgotten. Mention his name and you will receive a few sniffs of remembrance only from some of our more American history-minded citizens—"Oh, yes, the continental liar from the State of Maine"—that's generally the first blurt, the rhyming tag with Blaine that his political enemies enduringly pinned to his persona. Musing further, "Didn't he almost become...?" In Maine the pause might be followed by "governor"—while others, Down East and elsewhere, would know the correct answer: president of the United States! Further digging into memories of school lessons long past might elicit the exclamation: "Rum, Romanism, and Rebellion!" These three alliterative words—not from Blaine but from a prejudiced Protestant preacher—doomed his 1884 campaign for the White House. Blaine lost New York State by 1,047 votes and with it, the electoral college.

His career in national politics, begun as a congressman in 1862, did not end with that defeat. He was still a headline-maker and a force in Republican politics until almost a decade later, when he died of a lingering kidney disease on January 27, 1893.

This talented if flawed political figure, who has been called an "amiable Richard Nixon," was once Speaker of the House of Representatives, presiding during most of the Reconstruction years. He also became a U.S. senator, not by popular election but as the choice of the Maine legislature, where he had served as speaker. That was the way things were done in those days. Both before and after his run for the presidency, separate U.S. presidents had made him secretary of state, which was considered then the preeminent cabinet post. Modern evaluations of his two foreign policy tenures treat Blaine as the "father" of American overseas expansion.

Moreover, Blaine was once a best-selling author, penning a two-volume work of more than 1,000 pages called *Twenty Years of Congress*. It was a tribute to his national fame as a politician that such a ponderous tome sold so well and, not incidentally, engendered added publicity for his eventual presidential run. He was the subject of numerous books, a whole shelf-load of mostly hurriedly thrown-together campaign biographies, extolling his virtues. On the opposite side was the novel, *Democracy,* famous in its day, in which he was pilloried and caricatured. Its initially anonymous author turned out to be Henry Adams of Boston, the brilliant curmudgeon great-grandson of John Adams, and grandson of John Quincy Adams, and a fierce Blaine-hater. Tongues wagged all over official Washington, speculating about who might have created the villainous character of Senator Silas P. Ratcliffe, so obviously patterned on James G. Blaine.

Democracy, published in 1880, a year when Blaine was seeking the G.O.P. nomination, is still read in our time. At least, a new paperback edition was reissued in 1961. The last two full biographies about Blaine came out in the early 1930s, one by a Columbia University professor, David Saville Muzzey, and another by a distinguished journalist and politician, Charles Edward Russell, who wrote for the *New York Herald* and twice was a candidate for governor of New York on the Socialist ticket. Even the earlier puff pieces about Blaine were the work of serious writers. In 1884, when running for president, his Boswells were people such as Russell H. Conwell, the president of Temple University, famed as a lecturer, as well; and H. J. Ramsdell, a noted *New York Tribune* contributor, who collaborated with Ben Perley Poore, the dean of nineteenth-century Washington reporters. Following Blaine's death, a slew of books appeared. One deserving special attention was by a nationally known feminist author, Gail Hamilton, the pen name of Mary Abigail Dodge of Hamilton, Massachusetts, who was the cousin and bosom friend of Blaine's wife Harriet, practically a member of the Blaine family, and a sometime ghostwriter for the candidate himself. Her opus of 800-plus pages, released two years after Blaine's death, is a hodgepodge of material, full of totally uncritical hero worship, but absolutely invaluable for its treasure trove of letters that only an intimate could have collected. I use quotations from this source frequently. Just as helpful are the letters of Mrs. Harriet Blaine, lovingly collected after her death by her youngest daughter, Harriet Blaine Beale.

The Blaine marriage lasted for more than forty years and was universally deemed to be a close, loving alliance, despite the hurly-burly of their hectic lives. In death today, James Gillespie Blaine and Harriet Stanwood Blaine lie side by side in Maine atop one of Augusta's various hills. Simple metal markers label the illustrious couple, whose bodies were brought from Washington, D.C., in 1920 and reburied in a quiet, lovely garden designed by the Olmstead firm, America's foremost public landscapers at the time. The family aspect of Blaine's life has been absent from most of the books that were written about him before and after his death, except for his wife's volumes of letters and the monumental if disorganized work of Gail Hamilton. This book attempts to fill those gaps, trying to bring not only James G. Blaine to life, but shining as much light as archival material permits on the web of influences, both political and personal, that surrounded him. He was not only a world-famous public figure, but a husband, a father (to six surviving children), a grandfather, a sibling, a son, a friend, a neighbor, and an aspiring young American whose inconceivable success contained elements of Greek tragedy in its almost tragic denouement. A recent column in the New York *Times* referred to James G. Blaine as "Obscure as Ozymandias,"[1] the ultimate poetic symbol of triumph and power turned to ashes. But, all in all, he was a fascinating human being.

My own curiosity about James G. Blaine began through repeated visits to his former home in Augusta, Maine. It is most commonly called the Blaine House and serves as the residence the state offers Maine governors during their terms. This rambling mansion, built in 1833 by a retired sea captain, lies directly across the street from the state capitol building in which the legislature and the governor's office are housed. In 1967 I went to work as an assistant to Governor Kenneth M. Curtis, who would hold staff meetings upstairs in one of the private rooms adjacent to his family's quarters before departing for the statehouse each morning.

The downstairs, with its sunroom, parlor, and living room, was open to the public at certain hours, and governors also hosted events there, such as Christmas parties, to which friends and supporters would be invited, and benefits for non-profit organizations.

Harriet Blaine Beale, that same youngest daughter who had assembled her mother's letters, donated the property to the state. She had done it as a mother herself, in memory of her only child, Walker Blaine Beale, just out of Harvard, who had been killed in battle in France in 1918. Before going overseas, he had become the actual owner of the Blaine House and let the state use the premises for the war effort. Mrs. Beale made the gift final in 1920, when Governor Carl Milliken took possession.

In those years of my working for Governor Curtis, James G. Blaine was not much of a presence. There were some memorabilia on the premises—yellowing pictures, a bust, framed letters, his desk—and the name had rung a bell from my intensive American history classes. Although I played pool in his billiard room and tennis on a court erected at the Blaine House long after his death, I was as oblivious of this giant of American politics as most Americans still are today. Besides, he was a Republican, and in the Maine of the late 1960s and early 1970s, I was an ardent Democrat (still am) and part of a movement to undo the G.O.P. hegemony that Blaine, himself, had helped to foster in his adopted state.

He was originally "from Away" (Pennsylvania), like me (Massachusetts), but that didn't stop either of us from getting elected to the Maine House of Representatives. So in later years, as a representative, my visits to the Blaine House were usually on more formal occasions arranged by whichever governor—Democrat, Republican, or Independent—occupied this handsome structure. After I left public service, one of those governors—Independent Angus King—asked me to co-chair a group called Friends of the Blaine House, a citizen organization dedicated to raising funds for improvements to the historic site.

As I became more involved, I realized that the public needed to know more about the man who had given the building its name, had renovated it, brought presidents to it, and had nearly become president himself. One of the activities the Friends of the Blaine

House initiated was hiring an intern to do some studies of James G. Blaine, particularly scanning back issues of the local newspaper, the *Kennebec Journal*, of which he had become the editor and co-owner in 1854, and amassing all references to him.

Thirty years after the young Pennsylvanian arrived in the small state capital of Augusta where his wife had been raised, Blaine found himself running for president of the United States at the head of a political party—the Republican Party—that had not even existed before.

Now there was a story that should be told again, utilizing all the new materials and knowledge the intervening century and a half might have unearthed since the early 1850s.

In 1905 another of Blaine's biographers—a second cousin by marriage and a lifelong friend—Edward Stanwood, posed a key question about his esteemed relative, who had been the most famous and infamous American politician of his day. "Is his influence permanent or transitory?" Would he end up as a "demigod of American history" or would his legacy be "evanescent"?[2]

The latter seems the case. Even in Maine, there isn't a statue of him. Prominent fellow Maine Republicans of the period—Thomas Brackett Reed and Joshua Chamberlain—have been accorded that honor by posterity. Blaine's worst rival in the national Republican Party, New York's Roscoe Conkling, is thus memorialized in downtown Manhattan's Madison Square Park, and at the same site, in bronze, stands President Chester A. Arthur, who fired Blaine as secretary of state and whom Blaine, in turn, denied reelection by capturing the G.O.P. nomination in 1884.

A quarter of a century after Stanwood posed his questions, Charles Edward Russell initially proffered an answer. He wrote tht the Republican icon had struck him as "almost a phenomenon, a rare product of that mingling of sentiment and shrewd materialism, of wisdom, acquisitiveness, and idealism, of the main chance and devotion to the republic, that seem to be distinctively American."[3] But by the end of his study, this unabashed socialist was expressing the thought that if Blaine had "been content to remain poor, he would have been one of the greatest forces ever known in American history."[4]

Is this dichotomy between wondrous promise and meager delivery the reason why James Gillespie Blaine has been so neglected, and is this unspoken unplanned, and even unexpected judgment warranted?

We shall see.

1. Column by Thomas Frank, the New York *Times,* editorial page, August 15, 2006.
2. Edward Stanwood. *James Gillespie Blaine* (Boston: Houghton Mifflin and Company, 1905), page 362.
3. Charles Edward Russell. *Blaine of Maine, His Life and Times* (New York: Cosmopolitan Book Corp., 1931), Prefatory Note (no page number).
4. Russell, page 432.

ACKNOWLEDGEMENTS

An author is always offered helping hands in the formation of a book. My gratitude is therefore expressed to the following individuals.

Most especially first to Earle G. Shettleworth, Jr., Director of Maine's Historic Preservation Commission. It is doubtful whether this book could have been written—certainly not as it came out—without his tireless support. My mail was continually filled with material he would send me from the vast collections at his disposal in Augusta. His interest in the subject of James G. Blaine and the progress of my work literally paralleled my own.

On a trip to Blaine's home area in Pennsylvania, I received wonderful cooperation from Norma Ryan, the mayor of Brownsville, Barry Blaine ("maybe a relative"), the Brownsville town librarian and Anna Mae Moore, the librarian at Washington and Jefferson College, Blaine's alma mater. In Washington, D.C., Don Ritchie at the U.S. Senate Historical Office was marvelously cooperative, and there was efficient help at the U.S. Senate Library and the Library of Congress. I am beholden to Sam Spencer of Portland for arranging my visit to Blaine's Dupont Circle home in D.C., which his family owns, and to Richard Holderman for showing me around that impressive edifice.

In Maine, a whole host of people supplied information and assistance. My son-in-law Craig Annis was again my computer guru, librarians Bill Barry, Nick Noyes (at the Maine Historical Society), Tom Gaffney (at the Portland Public Library), and Annie Cough (at the Maine State Library) made my life easier. Tony Douin at the Maine State Archives was his usual knowledgeable self. Kerck Kelsey took extra time to share his information on Israel Washburn, Jr. Ted Laitala, Lee Webb, and Virginia Spiller provided interesting tidbits related to Blaine. Deanna Bonner-Ganter at the Maine State Museum graciously gathered picture material for me. Sue Hinkley gave me a copy of her work on Luther Severance. I would like to thank Mike Zoglio of Tower Press in Doylestown, PA, for expeditiously forwarding me a hard-to-find biography of the mysterious and alluring Mrs. Elizabeth Bigelow Lawrence. And finally, as always, plaudits for my great editor-publisher, Jennifer Bunting, and the incomparable crew at Tilbury House.

Augusta Postmaster Joseph Manley made the announcement:
"Mr. Blaine is nominated!"

ONE

TIME OF TRIUMPH

T APPROXIMATELY 4:30 P.M. on Friday, June 5, 1884, the definitive news reached Augusta, Maine that its leading local citizen, the Honorable James G. Blaine, had become the national Republican Party's nominee for president of the United States. Edward G. Mason, then a non-voting-age student in Augusta's Dirigo Business College, has left posterity a sprightly memoir of what happened next in Maine's state capital.[1]

People had been gathering downtown on Water Street, fronting the west side of the Kennebec River, ever since it had been learned the balloting in far-off Chicago at the G.O.P. convention would begin that morning. The focus of attention was the post office, where Postmaster Joseph Manley, Blaine's closest political associate in Maine, had arranged to display telegraphic bulletins as soon as they were received from the Windy City. The suspense for the swelling partisan crowd, which had already filled the whole street by noon, was intense. Twice before, in 1876 and 1880, Maine's favorite son had also been an odds-on bet to win the nomination, only to see his and his followers' hopes thwarted by a combination of intra-party political enemies and circumstances.

The first ballot announcement, greeted by loud cheers, had Blaine in a lead over his closest opponent, incumbent President Chester A. Arthur, by close to 60 votes, but still short of the 400-plus needed for a majority. On the second ballot, his plurality increased by 15 votes. From a chair now placed in front of the post office, the handsomely moustachioed Joe Manley eventually read out the third ballot result—25 more votes still for Blaine, ever nearer to victory. The throng went wild.

Then, before the fourth ballot was known, or at least made public, a group of men began to string a flag rope across Water Street from the post office to the building opposite. Joe Manley's electrifying announcement followed: "Mr. Blaine is nominated." Five minutes later, he and his crew had a mammoth banner strung up, proclaiming: "OUR NEXT PRESIDENT, JAMES G. BLAINE."

"Bells, factory whistles, tin horns, and human voices were reinforced by a small cannon, pressed into service for the occasion," Mason wrote. The loudest noise of all, the "deep bass" of the Allen Publishing House steam siren, joined the din and folks pointed out that Mr. Allen, himself, the wealthy publisher, was a staunch Democrat and, for the time being, at least, had joined his fellow Augustans in the "general rejoicing."

The students in Mason's school, instead of going back to their classes, rushed out into the crush of celebrating Blaine enthusiasts. Mason described that his only impression of the ensuing two or three hours was "of being swept along in a dense moving mass of humanity and of shouting myself hoarse." Other Augusta schools had emptied and hundreds of youth were cruising the streets, the boys tooting tin horns and adding to the scene of happy delirium that their local hero had finally won his party's highest prize and was, they were certain, en route to the White House.

The Republicans in the rest of the state weren't far behind. By ten o'clock that night, trains had rolled in from Bangor and Portland and other parts of Maine and a huge delegation, accompanied by five blaring bands, had marched up the hilly path to the stately Blaine home, where it lay in the shadow of the dignified, Bulfinch-designed capitol building. The great man himself was waiting, having much earlier received the first news of his triumph while resting in a hammock slung between two apple trees on the front lawn (in those days, candidates did not attend conventions). His daughter Margaret ("Maggie"), after receiving a message on the family telephone (one of the few in Maine, if not the country) had rushed out to the reclining figure, crying: "Father, Father, you have won!" and soon the incipient procession of well-wishers from Water Street had surrounded the house. Noted for his oratorical ability and personal magnetism, the veteran politician had graciously acceded to demands for a speech but made it a brief one, expressing his gratitude for their support, longtime loyalty, and affection.

James G. Blaine receives the official word of his nomination from ex-U.S. Senator John B. Henderson of Missouri, who had served as the presiding officer at the G.O.P. convention in Chicago. Son Walker stands behind his father, holding the document containing Blaine's equally official acceptance.
CONWELL'S *LIFE AND PUBLIC SERVICE OF JAMES G. BLAINE*

Nominee James G. Blaine, standing in the doorway of his Augusta home, addressing one of the crowds that assembled to greet him and hear his words.
CONWELL'S *LIFE AND PUBLIC SERVICE OF JAMES G. BLAINE*

Pictured in another very popular illustrated periodical of the period,
Frank Leslie's Illustrated Newspaper, *were these two scenes in*
Augusta, Maine, from the day Blaine captured the 1884 G.O.P.
presidential nomination; upper left, Margaret (Maggie) Blaine learns
by telephone (one of the first in Maine, if not the country) of her
father's victory; the other is the scene at Blaine's home, when he
came out to speak to his local supporters.

When the late-evening parade arrived at the same destination, among its far greater numbers were many who had been at the previous talk, so now the clamor arose for a much lengthier peroration and Blaine graciously acceded.

It had started to rain. Lightning and thunder gave way to a real torrent, but the crowd stood and listened, enraptured.

"I recall the scene very vividly: the commanding figure and strong face of Maine's best loved son," Mason continued. Other images had stuck with him, too: the "upturned faces" of the cheering audience lit intermittently by lightning flashes; the downpour seen through the "overspreading boughs of the trees on the Blaine lawn," and the off-key singing of a quartet from Bangor of an improvised song, with encores demanded despite its "limping rhythms"; the third time, Mrs. Blaine asking for it as a special favor. When Blaine included a reference to the inclement weather, someone in the dark cried out, no doubt in a thick Maine accent, drawing general laughter and thunderous applause: "We been waitin' fer this show-ah fer eight yee-ahs."

These impromptu celebrations were only the beginning. Almost at once, the move to immortalize the great man commenced. Biographers arrived, as if by magic. The *Kennebec Journal*, the Augusta-based newspaper where Blaine had begun his career in Maine as an editor and part-owner, printed a warning: "Do Not Purchase Any Biography of the Hon. James G. Blaine but the One Published at His Own Home."

And who was to be the publisher? Why, none other than Mr. E. C. Allen, the Democrat who had allowed his publishing house whistle to be tooted, celebrating Blaine's victory. Now, he had moved quickly to cash in on that event.

The writer for this July-scheduled volume was to be "Colonel Russell H. Conwell...an author of much note and literary reputation," and he had already reached the Maine capital. Before long, the possibility of a blockbuster bestseller-in-the-making was being trumpeted—tremendous advance sales nationwide, amazingly so in the Mississippi Valley—with predictions of "the largest sale of any biography ever put into the American market." Publisher Allen announced he was mailing out 30,000 circulars a day.

Conwell was also an ordained Baptist minister. Presently Augustans were to read in the *Kennebec Journal* that the Reverend Mr. Conwell would preach on Sunday, and that his sermons in Philadelphia drew such crowds that tickets had to be issued.

A Reverend Mr. Cressey was likewise reported in Augusta, seeking material for a life of Blaine.

H. J. Ramsdell, the reporter, who had previously worked as a clerk in the U.S. Senate when Blaine was a member, now huddled with the candidate at his home and he, too, with his cohort Ben Perley Poore, produced a Blaine book. *Coming into Maine,* as well, was a Mr. W. E. S. Whitman, who wrote under the name Tobey Candor, sent by a western publishing company. He immediately hired a local stenographer, Miss Mae Wadsworth, to assist him.

Another writer and future Blaine biographer present was not identified in the press by her pen name of Gail Hamilton. She was instead "Miss Dodge." In her massive biography, she has only a brief aside about this post-convention period that she, herself, witnessed. The feature she most remembered was the railway car, "festooned and bannered and blazoned" of the California delegation to Chicago that had continued on to Augusta. She wrote that "the novel spectacle of a gala train bearing California to Mr. Blaine's home in spontaneous good-will added a touch of romance to the general satisfaction."[2]

Edward Mason saw that train rolling in, bearing "a fine picture of Blaine serving as a headlight," profuse in its display of red, white and blue bunting, carrying gigantic banners proclaiming: "CALIFORNIA: JAMES G. BLAINE, OUR NEXT PRESIDENT." The renowned Chandler's Band of Portland, the National Soldiers' Home Band of Togus, and the Pullen Band of Augusta serenaded them. Among the more memorable speechifiers at the depot was a Judge Knight of California (Mason called him "a fine-appearing man and brilliant orator") and the "beloved" ex-vice president of the United States, Maine's own Hannibal Hamlin. In introducing Hamlin, it was remarked that in 1860, Illinois and Maine had furnished the G.O.P. presidential ticket and that in 1884, this was happening again, but reversed: Maine and Illinois, since Blaine's running mate was to be Senator John A. Logan from the Land of Lincoln.

*The arrival of the California delegates at the Augusta railroad
station on June 6, 1884.*
MAINE HISTORIC PRESERVATION COMMISSION

Logan, too, put in an appearance at Augusta. The former Civil
War general, who had been on William Tecumseh Sherman's staff
and was a darling of the Grand Army of the Republic veterans, arrived without much advance notice. Only a sparse crowd greeted
him. Walker Blaine, the candidate's oldest son, was waiting in a
barouche to transport the distinguished visitor to the Blaine family's manse. From among the onlookers, an old soldier, once allegedly of Logan's command and "considerably the worse for liquor,"
according to Mason's eyewitness account, caused a momentary
commotion by pumping "Jack's" hand again and again, while expressing delight in seeing him once more. Actually, Logan's full
nickname was "Black Jack," or "the Black Eagle of Illinois," due to
the remarkable deep black color of his eyes and hair and a rather
swarthy complexion.

He stayed long enough to visit the Old Soldiers Home at nearby
Togus and receive the cheers of 900 aging veteranss. A trip to Bangor and Ellsworth with Blaine and U.S. Senator Eugene Hale followed, but Logan then received news that his wife was ill in D.C.
and he hurried back to the capital.

Next in Augusta appeared the official delegation from the Republican Party, informing the designee of his nomination. Their chief spokesman was a distinguished former senator who had been the presiding officer at the Chicago convention. He was John B. Henderson, a Missourian, born in Virginia but a solid Union man during the Civil War, credited with helping to keep his border state out of the Confederacy and, in his days in Washington, D.C., an author of the Thirteenth Amendment that had ended slavery. Out of office because he had failed to vote for the impeachment of Andrew Johnson, General Henderson, as he was known—he'd been a Missouri militia brigadier—was a highly respected member of the Republican establishment.

The day was hot and the participants were out on the Blaine lawn, under the shade of some spreading elms. A semi-circle had been formed, composed of the "committee" that had accompanied Henderson from Chicago and assorted guests. It included one representative from every state and territory in the nation, plus an envoy from the District of Columbia. "Mr. Blaine, your nomination for the office of the President of the United States by the National Republican Convention recently assembled at Chicago is already known to you," Henderson began. His short address, political but low key, stressed party unity and party programs. Blaine was assured that the primary contest had been "free of any taint of bitterness" and that his selection "was but a truthful reflection of an irresistible popular demand."

The Chicago platform was reiterated, citing some motherhood and apple pie examples such as "economy and purity of administration" and "protection of citizens, native and naturalized, at home and abroad"; and some actual substantive program proposals such as "the prompt restoration of the navy" and "preservation of public lands for actual settlers." The address ended with the encomium that the twenty-three-year-old Republican Party had built a "new republic—a republic far more splendid than that originally designed by our fathers" and it would soon be the nominee's opportunity, as "architect in chief" to continue "this grateful work."

Blaine, a tall, stately man with lustrous dark eyes, his hair, moustache, and ample beard once almost as black as Logan's but now snowy white, listened impassively, arms across his chest, staring at the ground. Walker stood alongside him. When it was time for the candidate to respond, the twenty-eight-year-old son, who had been his father's assistant in his days as secretary of state under Garfield, handed over a manuscript. Quite uncharacteristically— he was a great off-the-cuff speaker—Blaine read from it.

The document was short and to the point, expressing the usual gratitude for the honor bestowed upon him and awe at the immense responsibility. Blaine then announced that a "more formal acceptance" would be forthcoming at another time. By this, he meant the practice of candidates in that era of issuing official acceptances of their party's positions in formal manifestoes. On occasion, candidates had disavowed a few of the planks. Blaine assured his listeners that the ideas of the convention had his "heartiest sympathy" and "unqualified approval." Then, hoping to make his guests feel right at home in Maine during their stay, he invited them into his home for a reception, followed by lunch at a neighbor's, and followed, in turn, by a train ride to Portland, a mass rally, and further travel south to D.C. for the same sort of ceremony with vice presidential nominee Logan.

It had been a heady several weeks for James G. Blaine. Some 3,000 telegrams of congratulation had poured into the Augusta household. One, in particular, must have haunted him. It certainly had touched Mrs. Blaine, to whom it had been addressed. The words were unemotional and almost totally non-political:

"The household joins in one great thanksgiving. From the quiet of our home we send the most earnest wish that, through the turbulent months to follow and in the day of victory, you may *all* be guarded and kept."

The wire had been sent from Cleveland, Ohio, and was signed Lucretia R. Garfield.

What memories must have been stirred! Horrid visions first. That nightmare scene within the women's waiting room entrance to the Baltimore and Potomac railroad station in Washington, D.C.: the president of the United States—his closest political if not personal friend, James Abram Garfield—shot in the back, bleeding on the marble floor. The two of them had taken that shortcut toward the train platform side by side. The president was on his way to a reunion at his alma mater, Williams College in Massachusetts, and in a holiday mood. Then bullets started flying, one almost grazing Blaine. After suffering for almost three months, Garfield died, essentially of blood poisoning and from poor medical attention.

If Blaine carried on with those doleful thoughts, he might have remembered that the dead Garfield's oldest sons, Harry and James, a year apart in age, were now students at Williams and had sent him congratulations on his nomination separately from their mother. The sad irony that this honor should now be his, rather than the start of their father's re-election campaign, would not have been lost on the candidate as he pondered these communication from the Garfield boys and "Crete," as the late president had called his wife, picturing her at home in Cleveland with her younger children, Abram, Irvine, and Mollie.

Blaine was a people person. His talent for recalling names was legendary and one of his greatest political strengths. He was similarly a devoted family man. A sketch done by one of the artists the national magazines had sent to Augusta showed him stretched on his front lawn hammock, surrounded by his six children: the sons, Walker, Emmons, and James Jr.; and his daughters, Alice, Maggie, and young Harriet. No doubt, during the posing for that conventional portrait of a successful politician and his good-looking off-spring, there must have been more than a moment of remembrance for the seventh Blaine child, Stanwood, who died at the age of three in Philadelphia before his parents' move to Maine in 1854.

As he lounged in his hammock once his children and the artist had dispersed, James G. Blaine's stream of consciousness could have taken him in many directions.

Needless to say, the approaching campaign would have been on his mind. He did not see it as an easy win. This man was an astute, but also intuitive, analyzer of the American political scene; he had been ever since childhood. It was conventional wisdom that his not-yet-chosen Democratic opponent would be the new and rapidly rising governor of New York State, Grover Cleveland, a tough foe, and he knew he could not win without New York. But his fear was even more than tactical. There were unseen rhythms

A famous drawing of Blaine in his hammock on the lawn of the family house in Augusta, surrounded by members of his family and household. The paper in his hand was the dispatch informing him of his nomination on June 5, 1884.
CONWELL'S *LIFE AND PUBLIC SERVICE OF JAMES G. BLAINE*

among the electorate and it might just be that the Democrats' time had come. The Republican Party, which he, himself, a former Whig, had played a strong role in creating, had been on a continuous win streak since 1860. This had to end sometime. They'd just barely scraped by in 1876 and Rutherford Hayes, or his handlers, had made a devil's bargain with the ex-Confederates and the South had been lost ever since. Garfield had been lucky to win in 1880. And had he lived? Well, the man had been popular and catching on.

All was not serene within the Republican Party, Blaine well knew. He'd been reading the newspapers. His internal opponents, calling themselves "Independents," had already held a gathering in Boston to organize. They were Brahmins, mostly—President Eliot of Harvard, Codman, Higginson, Weld, Hoar—cold-roast Boston's finest. The New York aristocracy was planning to do the same. But at least young Theodore Roosevelt, the rising G.O.P. star in the Empire State, who had moved heaven and earth to keep him from getting the nomination in Chicago, had declared he'd stick with the ticket.

There was also a lot of talk about the Irish Catholic vote coming over to him. In Maine, there'd always been plenty of "Blaine Democrats." The *Kennebec Journal* had quoted a Philadelphia Irishman as saying, "Why, for every vote that he may lose from the independent kickers, he can get two from Irish Democrats right in New York and Massachusetts where he will need them most." As secretary of state, he had pressured the British on the Irish question and, although it wasn't widely known, he never tried to hide the fact that his mother had been a devout Irish Roman Catholic, while he had been raised in his father's Presbyterian faith.

Those religious matters were a two-edged sword, like public funds for parochial education, to which he'd been strongly opposed. Then, thinking of the worrisome problem of New York State again, what of Roscoe Conkling, its Republican boss? Four years ago, Conkling had helped Garfield win. What would he do now? He could be a formidable friend, or a formidable enemy. And the mental image of that curly haired, pompous egoist from Utica brought a host of painful recollections, dating back to their first cataclysmic confrontation during a congressional debate in 1866.

That having Logan on the ticket might help was a counter-thought. "Black Jack" had been with Conkling in 1880, trying to win a third term for Grant. This time he'd made the difference at Chicago, delivering his Illinois votes to the Blaine forces on the fourth ballot. The army boys liked him, but Sherman hadn't cared for him as a subordinate. "Cump" Sherman—William Tecumseh—had told him so. They'd known each other as kids. *Now, there was a set of coincidences!* Blaine's mind went back to a period spent in southern Ohio, in the small county seat of Lancaster, visiting his relatives, the Ewings. Their big house on the hill flashed before his eyes again. Practically next door lived the Sherman family. Mr. Sherman had died young, leaving ten children. Thomas Ewing, Sr., the famed lawyer, Whig politician, and cabinet officer under Presidents Zachary Taylor, W. H. Harrison, and John Tyler, had agreed to adopt one Sherman child to relieve the beleaguered widow. Which one? "Take Cump!" the family cried. "He's the smartest." Also, the fact he was the most troublesome went unmentioned. It was not surprising that Ewing got him into West Point.

Wonder of wonders, "Cump" was now the country's ultimate military hero, general of the army, and married to Blaine's own dear cousin Ellen, Squire Ewing's daughter. Her three brothers had all become Union generals during the war, and Tom Jr., Blaine's closest friend during that Ohio interlude, had been elected to Congress, too, but as a Democrat! Blaine couldn't have known that one day Tom Jr. would be one of his pall bearers. And Cump's younger brother, John Sherman, U.S. senator, then secretary of the treasury, had been a rival of his old acquaintance in Ohio, Jim Blaine, for the presidency in 1880. The winner, Garfield had been John Sherman's campaign manager before becoming the "dark horse" whom Blaine had eventually crowned with his support when he, himself, couldn't prevail. These swirling bits of true history and odd turns of fate seemed like fiction when you put them all together.

Thinking of Garfield, Blaine would remember that Lincoln, too, had been shot, and the awful period afterward, of which he, himself, had been a part in Washington: Reconstruction. Andrew Johnson. Impeachment. Ku Klux Klan! And the Civil War earlier. And slavery. The incredible panorama of events against which his own political career had been built.

From his hammock, Blaine could gaze across an Augusta street to the promontory overlooking the Kennebec River that had originally been Weston's Hill. The judge who'd owned it had donated that land to the State of Maine, newly broken off from Massachusetts, for its state capitol site. Since 1832 the massive, domed, grey granite capitol had housed the government in which James G. Blaine had begun to make his name.

He had lived thirty years in this city of Augusta, having been only twenty-four years old when he'd arrived. It had to seem like a miracle. In this provincial place, this "tiny Rome" (it had seven hills and was spread along a good-sized river), he had risen to a height beyond his own imagining. Whatever the perils ahead, he could become the president of the United States! The topmost prize of American public life was in literal reach! Fame, he had already. Lasting fame was a distinct possibility.

Autobiography at such times would be only natural. James G. Blaine, in his hammock, given a few more solitary moments, might very well think back to the child he'd been in another hilly, riverside town in nineteenth-century America, in this case, in western Pennsylvania.

1. Edward G. Mason. "The Presidential Campaign of 1884 in Mr. Blaine's Home City," *New England Magazine*, May 1901.
2. Gail Hamilton. *Biography of James G. Blaine.* (Norwich, CT: The Humphrey Bill Publishing Company, 1895), p. 573.

Two

WESTSYLVANIA

HAD A PLAN TO CREATE a fourteenth colony to add to our original thirteen states-to-be succeeded, James G. Blaine would have been a *Westsylvanian*, instead of a *Pennsylvanian*. The attempt was made in October 1775, in the form of a petition to the Continental Congress from 2,000 male settlers in the Central Appalachian Mountains, then the outermost boundary of the "American" thrust west. These were James G. Blaine's father's people—the Scots-Irish, a breed apart, who, having fled Scotland for Ireland when persecuted for their Presbyterian religion, then left Ireland for America. They had never much liked being part of William Penn's Quaker domain in Pennsylvania and they wanted their own province—we were not yet calling ourselves states—which wouldn't just be the southwest corner of Pennsylvania, but would also include all of present-day West Virginia, a piece of Kentucky, and slivers of Ohio, western Maryland, and Virginia.

The delegates in Philadelphia from the two existing rebellious provinces most affected—Pennsylvania and Virginia—made short work of these pretensions. They pigeonholed the petition in committee and it never saw the light of day.

Yet Westsylvania—at least as a tourist entity—still lives. An organization calling itself the Westsylvania Heritage Corporation depicts the concept as "a new idea based on an old story" in a glossy quarterly publication issued from their Pennsylvania headquarters. "Today Westsylvania, the historic name for the Central Appalachian region that's not quite 'Mid-Atlantic' and not quite 'Midwest' has been revived,"[1] the promoters declare. Blaine country lies in the upper quadrant of the rectangularly shaped ghost province overlaid on a contemporary map. For the exact center of our subject's heritage, focus on the separate towns of Brownsville and West Brownsville, facing each other across the Monongahela River, 30 miles south of Pittsburgh.

James G. Blaine might just as easily have been able to label himself a Pittsylvanian if another proposed designation for this part of the United States had taken root. This thought takes us back to the French and Indian Wars, when William Pitt the Elder was the prime minister of Great Britain. Where three mighty rivers—the Monongahela, the Allegheny and the Ohio—still meet today, the French had erected Fort Duquesne, but once the British army regulars, with their American auxiliaries, had captured that redoubt, it became Fort Pitt in honor of the inspiring English leader. Eventually the site evolved into the metropolis of Pittsburgh.

As school children we learn about the ancient battles in this region primarily because George Washington was involved. On the outskirts of Blaine Country, near Uniontown, lies the grave of General Edward Braddock, the pigheaded British commander who refused to accept Washington's advice about how to fight Indian-style. Nearby is Fort Necessity, which Washington was obliged to surrender to the French. A Blaine ancestor, James G.'s great-grandfather Ephraim, was not simply a participant in these hostilities. He also became an intimate friend and comrade-in-arms of Washington during the Revolution.

Consequently, young Jim Blaine, growing up in Pennsylvania, could have bragging rights because of a highly prestigious forebear, who had come to America as a four-year-old child, developed into an Indian fighter, then a wealthy squire, a county sheriff, a militia colonel, and the quartermaster who fed Washington's troops at Valley Forge. In later life the grown-up, famous James G. Blaine might well have read with interest noted Boston historian Francis Parkman's *The Conspiracy of Pontiac*, detailing the heroics of a "Lieutenant Blane" in thwarting the attack of rebellious Ottawas, Delawares and Shawnees on Fort Ligonier in the aftermath of the French defeat in North America.[2] That courageous young officer would assuredly have been Ephraim Blaine, the founder of the family's fortune.

There were all sorts of stories to tell about Colonel Ephraim. During the time of Valley Forge, he is described as incessantly traveling "Back and forth from Carlisle [the Pennsylvania town where he lived] to Valley Forge, from Valley Forge to Carlisle"—a distance of 100 miles. "Night and day, every mill that he owned, every mill that he could control or influence, was kept running to feed the soldiers."[3] To pay for these provisions, he dug into his own pockets—dug deeply, it appears. Pennsylvania was to reimburse him with separate payments of $1 million and $750,000, immense sums then.

That Ephraim was effective in his efforts is borne out by a statement of Washington's biographer James Thomas Flexner, who wrote, "Valley Forge was the very image of misery only during the first two of the Army's six months there."[4] and that by February 1778, the supply of food was sufficient, if hardly of gourmet quality.

Ephraim Blaine's support of Washington was also political. That same fateful February 1778 witnessed the "Conway Cabal," an attempt by several high-ranking officers and politicians to replace Washington as commander-in-chief with General Thomas Conway. Blaine was one of those who alerted the Washington forces of the fact that Conway was badmouthing the Virginian and he helped assure that the plot would fizzle.

With the end of the American Revolution and the advent of independence, Ephraim Blaine and George Washington could also exchange notes on an interest they jointly shared—land speculation—especially where it involved western Pennsylvania. Washington bought many acres there. He had also been given lots in a town not far from the Brownsville-West Brownsville area that became Washington, Pennsylvania, and the county in which it was located was likewise named for him. Both places could boast they were first in the nation to so honor the father of our country. Ephraim Blaine made purchases of property in the same region, but kept his family home farther east at Carlisle on a 600-acre estate he'd named Middlesex; in addition, he kept a winter domicile in Philadelphia, the U.S. capital, where he hobnobbed with President Washington and other notables. On occasion, the president would come to visit him in Carlisle.

In the annals of the Blaine family, one of those visits came during an incident of some importance in American history. It is known as the Whiskey Rebellion and represented the first major challenge to the fledgling government formed under the U.S. Constitution. Taxes imposed on homemade liquor by Treasury Secretary Alexander Hamilton had fomented the uprising, which some have dubbed a Presbyterian or Scots-Irish affair, since the local economy in those parts of Appalachia depended on the distilling expertise the settlers had brought with them from Ulster. Federal troops had to be called out to suppress the uprising, whose epicenter was the very town of Washington, Pennsylvania, where an agitator named David Bradford had led an attack on the U.S. mail. The president, en route to join his soldiers, spent the night at Ephraim Blaine's manorial home in Carlisle. He did not need to travel any farther. Word came to him at Middlesex that the insurrection had been crushed and its fomenters arrested.

Washington County's next threat came from the south. At a time when there was no separate West Virginia, the State of Virginia claimed it and only relented after the drawing of the westward extension of the Mason-Dixon line. More than a century later, James G. Blaine, with his extensive knowledge of his home area's history, could point out the exact boundary along the Monongahela that marked the Virginia claim.

So it was at Washington County, Pennsylvania, not Virginia, that James G. Blaine was born. The town—they use the term borough in Pennsylvania—was West Brownsville. The date was January 31, 1830.

If you go to West Brownsville today, the roadside plaque marking his birthplace is on Railroad Street, a somewhat truncated main drag. Parallel to this brief thoroughfare between the roadway and the western bank of the Monongahela, there are indeed train tracks but no sign of rolling stock. In the twenty-first century, given the dilapidated look of the surrounding buildings, we would immediately designate this locale a depressed area, supposing the fault to lie in the playing out of the coal mines in the neighboring hills.

But directly across the Monongahela, in the sister borough of Brownsville, you learn there are also other reasons for the downturn that has given these communities their Rust Belt appearance, which local groups are trying to counteract with renewal projects.

Historically, Thomas Brown, a pre-1770 settler, gave his name to both locations and he is remembered mainly as the area's first tavern owner. Prior to Brown, the east side community was known as Redstone Old Fort. The hilly site of that fortification is "accredited to mound builders," i.e., early Indians. In 1747 a Delaware chief, Nemacolin, led a white frontiersman, Michael Cresap, from Maryland across the Alleghenies to this setting on the banks of the Monongahela, which is the "...western end of Nemacolin's trail," according to a DAR historical tablet. Atop the hill above, an impressive building, Nemacolin's Castle, now operated as a museum, was built by the Bowman family of coal barons who were descendants of Jacob Bowman, an Indian trader at the primitive fort.

The local guidebooks insist there is "Lots of history in Brownsville."

Yet no open public mention of James G. Blaine.

In Brownsville, itself, no plaque has been erected by the Pennsylvania Historical and Museum Commission to celebrate this illustrious native son. There is one for hometown boy Philander Knox, only three years younger than Blaine, who, like him, held the positions of U.S. senator and secretary of state, and for John Brashear, a local astronomer and educator.

But not until you cross one of the two bridges to West Brownsville is the name Blaine embossed anywhere.

His black and gold-lettered plaque on Railroad Street reads:

> James G. Blaine
> Born January 31, 1830, on this site
> of Pennsylvania pioneer ancestry.
> Washington College graduate. Moved
> to Maine in 1854. Served the nation
> as member of Congress, party leader and
> Secretary of State.

It has been posted on a grassy plot next to a modest, clapboarded house that decidedly is not early nineteenth century. In fact, *A Traveler's Guide to Historic Western Pennsylvania* specifically states: "The Blaine homestead is no longer standing."[5] It may well be questioned if "this site," so close to the river was *the* site.

Off Railroad Street is a rough, steeply inclined road snaking up into the hills. It is Blaine Boulevard and it rises up to "Blainesburg," as the locals refer to what was once the extensive property of the Blaine farm.

Seemingly, the name Blaine has not been entirely erased from the region's memory. People do recall something about James G., but not always clearly. A retired barber lived opposite Nemacolin's Castle when I visited it, and I struck up a conversation with him on his front porch. When I mentioned James G. Blaine, he perked up and pointed to a church steeple in the distance, exclaiming: "Yeah, he's buried up there at St. Peter's."

"Not James G. Blaine," I rejoined. "No, he's buried in Augusta, Maine."

"No, no," he argued back. "There's this big stone monument up there. It says Blaine on it."

"Listen, mister," I insisted. "I worked in Augusta, Maine, for years. I've stood right at his grave, which is next to his wife's, the two of them in a sort of garden known as the Blaine Memorial."

"Well, who's that at St. Peter's?"

"His mother, for one thing. St. Peter's is Catholic and she was a devout Catholic. And his father's grave, too. The father converted on his deathbed."

I didn't add that also buried in the plot was a sister, Elizabeth. My listener's nods showed I'd already won my point.

At this juncture the Pennsylvania pioneers on both sides who sired James G. Blaine deserve a capsule genealogy.

It begins with Colonel Ephraim, who in 1765 married Rebecca Galbraith, of impeccable Scots-Irish, Presbyterian ancestry. Two boys were produced, James and Robert, and this earlier James became James G. Blaine's grandfather. His grandmother was Margaret Lyon and their son, Ephraim Lyon Blaine, fathered James G. Blaine—plus nine other children. Blaine's Catholic mother, Maria Louise Gillespie, was the daughter of Neal Gillespie, Jr., yet another Scottish immigrant from Northern Ireland, but one whose family had kept their Catholic faith.

Needless to say, this mere cold recital of who begat whom conceals a good deal of human interest content.

Colonel Ephraim's two boys, James and Robert, went into business with him. James's first bride was Jane Hoge, whose father had preceded Colonel Blaine as sheriff of Cumberland County, and the young businessman's education entailed several trips abroad, including one for "special professional training" in Bordeaux, France. A prominent Pennsylvania judge has left us a word picture of this promising, gilded youth, that: "James Blaine, at the time of his return from Europe, was considered to be among the most accomplished and finest-looking gentlemen in Philadelphia."[6] But, alas, tragedy soon struck. Upon coming home from an extended business trip to New Orleans, James discovered his pregnant bride had died and been buried the day before. He ordered the body exhumed, looked upon her for the last time, had locks of her hair removed and then entwined with his own in ten rings he commissioned to be made and distributed. The gravestone at Carlisle still records in couplets the untimely passing of James's twenty-four-year-old love.

> Reader behold and drop a tear
> Beauty's remains lie bury'd here
> But Heav'n which lent the transient boon
> Hath bid her sun go down at noon...."[7]

Yet James's deep melancholy didn't endure overly long. His next love story reads like an English romantic novel. In the Blaine household, caring for James's mother who had become an invalid, was a young relative, very much a member of the family. When and how she finally caught cousin James's eye is hard to say. She certainly attracted George Washington's attention, for when he was a guest at Middlesex during the Whiskey Rebellion, he particularly praised her "flannel cakes" and asked for the recipe. That was in September 1794, and the following January, James and Margaret Lyon were joined in matrimony.

A month later, their happiness was clouded when Rebecca Galbraith Blaine passed away. The old colonel, now a widower, was actually not that old—fifty-three years of age—and, he, too, like his son, did not linger long in taking a second wife. The widow Sarah Postlethwaite Duncan had been married to one of his friends, John

Duncan, killed in a duel where the colonel had been his second.

Also named Ephraim was the son born to this older couple. Had he lived, he would have been the uncle of James G. Blaine's father Ephraim Lyon, although actually younger than his nephew. Unfortunately, as a toddler he drowned by tumbling into the mill raceway on the Middlesex estate when no one was watching him.

In February 1804, the colonel died. His widow, the former Mrs. Duncan, promptly left Carlisle for their townhouse in Philadelphia, where she remained the rest of her life. Her stepson James also left Carlisle about this time with his second wife Margaret, young Ephraim Lyon, and daughter Jane, but they headed west. Their first long-term stop was Brownsville, where James owned land. He opened a store and kept it for ten years, then went to Sewickley, a future suburb of Pittsburgh on the Ohio River, then southward to Washington County and its shire town of Washington. Gail Hamilton has written that "...the Blaines seem to have considered all Pennsylvania as their natural home and heritage, and wherever James Blaine went he could feel that the feet of his father had trodden the path before him."[8]

This Pittsylvania country was still rough, but growing. The Brownsville-West Brownsville area was a key choke point on the way west, a river ford bridged by a ferry, and a favored destination. Pioneers, crossing over Indian trails and atrociously rutted roads from the east, could embark here on flat boats and float down to the Mississippi and its whole lower length to New Orleans. The first such craft had left Redstone Old Fort in 1782. The first steamboat to reach the Louisiana city, the *Enterprise*, was built and launched in Brownsville in 1814. With an endless stream of customers needing supplies and nourishment, the way-station flourished. A favorite saying, still repeated wryly in local historical literature, is that "Pittsburgh might amount to something if it weren't so close to Brownsville,"

The National Road was opened in 1818, following Nemacolin's path out of western Maryland, and went right through Brownsville en route to Wheeling, then in Virginia. The concept behind it was George Washington's—to tie the western territories as states to the United States. "They hang upon a pivot," he put it. "The touch of a feather will turn them any which way." He didn't live to see the famous thoroughfare constructed. It was highly controversial—many people thought it unconstitutional for the federal government to build interstate highways. To mollify the states, permission was sought to traverse their boundaries. Pennsylvania agreed only after wringing a concession that the route would run through Brownsville and—most appropriately—Washington, Pennsylvania.

This latter municipality had been developed by David Hoge, the father of James Blaine's unlucky first wife. It was he who had made a present to his good friend George Washington of several lots in the town. Eventually, the president donated one of them back to the locals for a school. It became Washington College.

The Blaine family would have a close connection with this educational institution. Ephraim Lyon Blaine attended as a student, matriculating in 1807. Later he lived and worked and held political office in Washington and enrolled his son James Gillespie at his alma mater, of which he was a trustee, when the boy was but thirteen years old.

The Gillespie family lived in West Brownsville. Maria Louise Gillespie, whom Ephraim Lyon married in a Catholic ceremony, was considered the most beautiful woman in Pennsylvania at the time. A friend wrote jokingly: "The Duke of Sewickley, late Middlesex, it is said, will take a wife from the backwoods and has selected Maria Gillespie as the object."[9]

The bride was hardly an uncouth peasant maid. Her father, Neal Gillespie, Jr., was a man of considerable means, since he owned the ferry that crossed the river between the two Brownsvilles, as well as the many-acred "Indian Hill farm" in West Brownsville, which included a noted landmark mass of overhanging rock known as Krepp's Knob.

How unusual was this inter-faith marriage during that era? Over the years, various claims have been made about how the couple coped. One version has it that the boys were brought up Presbyterian, the girls in the Church of Rome. Another has it that all the children were raised Protestant. A Catholic publication, however, maintains all were baptized in their mother's religion.

The father, Ephraim Lyon Blaine. Scion of a successful Scots-Irish family that had emigrated to Pennsylvania in the eighteenth century, he experienced financial problems in his later years. Nevertheless, he was elected to a county office and he thoroughly imbued his son James with his Whig party philosophy. Accused during an election of being a Roman Catholic (because he had married a Catholic woman), he produced a testimonial from a local priest that not only was he not a Catholic but in the writer's opinion was not fit to be a member of any church.
HAMILTON, *Biography of James G. Blaine*

The mother, Maria Louise Gillespie, once called the "prettiest woman in Washington County" (Pennsylvania). She remained a devout Catholic throughout her life and saw to her husband's conversion on his deathbed, an act that her son, James Gillespie Blaine, refused when he, himself, was dying.

HAMILTON, *BIOGRAPHY OF JAMES G. BLAINE*

The 1830s, when James G. was growing up, had not yet seen that paroxysm of anti-Catholicism in the U.S. culminating in the Know Nothing movement of the 1850s. The emigration of Catholics from Ireland was still a trickle prior to the potato famine. Individual gentrified families like the Gillespies and their relatives the Boyles could be tolerated, even allowed to enter the melting pot. Roman Catholic services were being held in Brownsville as early as 1800, with a brick church accommodating a flock until it accidentally burned in 1842 and was replaced three years later by the present-day St. Peter's.

The lucrative ferry originally run by the father of Neal Gillespie, Jr., had been owned by Michael Cresap, the pioneer who had trekked into this region with Nemacolin. The Indian Hill estate had been the land of Indian Peter, a friendly Native American, and all of its 339 acres had been signed over to the Irishman by the indigene's children. Two Catholic aunts of Mrs. Ephraim Lyon Blaine had married into distinguished Ohio families in the shire town of

Birthplace of James G. Blaine
MAINE HISTORIC PRESERVATION COMMISSION

Lancaster, thereby establishing that connection later to play a transforming role in the life of young Jim Blaine.

One can imagine that his childhood on the banks of the Monongahela in the 1830s and early 1840s must have had a Mark Twainish aura. James Gillespie Blaine, brainy kid that he was, would have been far more Tom Sawyer-ish than Huck Finn-ish. The Blaines, if not quite as aristocratic or rich as in the era of Colonel Ephraim, were most definitely highly respectable folk. No snob, though, young Jim entered into all the local pastimes and mischiefs of his contemporaries, but exhibited an entrepreneurial temperament. His older brother Ephraim loved to fight. Jim didn't, but he could hold his own when forced to put up his fists. He was tall, lanky, a bit awkward and self-conscious. When he was bad, his mother would make him wear one of his sister's dresses for punishment. One day, eager to join his playmates, he simply hiked up a too-long skirt and ran.

As befitted a rural area of that era, education was fairly rudimentary. Aunt Tilly (Matilda) Dorsey conducted a "Select Summer School" at Krepp's Knob and she was a strict disciplinarian. Asked if she ever had to "whip" Jim Blaine, she unhesitatingly answered yes. The short version was that she had forbidden the children to go to a large blackberry patch near the school because of the poisonous copperhead snakes that infested it, and one day when she was absent, they all disobeyed her, including Jim, and all had to be spanked. The stretched-out anecdote has Jim Blaine a perpetual scamp of a blackberry picker, bringing fruit into class and flinging it at his schoolmates. To discourage him, Aunt Tilly had told the snake story, which failed to frighten the intrepid boy. After another berry-picking foray, he hit the dozing Aunt Tilly in the nose, awakening her with a start.

"Did you shoot that berry?" she demanded.

"No, I shot *you*" was the reply.

Despite her urge to laugh, Aunt Tilly had no choice but to pull the offender across her knee and paddle his bottom with a book.[10]

Two other things the teacher remembered about the most famous graduate of her institution were that he was good at spelling and his shoes never had dust on them; they were always shined.

Gail Hamilton added another learning ingredient: "He had also the liberal education of the National Road on which the Blaine and Gillespie homes were located."[11]

Her meaning was that the National Road opened a portal to the wider world. James G. Blaine spoke of his awe when illustrated English newspapers were brought to his home via the traffic on the National Road and his father read them aloud to the family. The Blaines were hardly just a bunch of provincials in the near-wilderness. By age seven, young Jim was a fiery Whig, like his father. When he was eleven, his great Whig idol, Henry Clay, rode through Brownsville. Everyone knew about it, since Clay suffered an accident coming down a hill to the waterfront landing. More of an indignity than an injury, Clay had been tossed out of his carriage when a wheel hit a rut, landing on his head in the mud. Yet James G. Blaine never lost his hero-worship of the famed Kentuckian.

Two years earlier, in the winter of 1839, the boy made his memorable trip to Lancaster, Ohio, and came into the presence of a man as imposing as Henry Clay. Thomas Ewing, Sr., was a Whig politician, too, a U.S. senator and a cabinet officer, under presidents William Henry Harrison, John Tyler, and Zachary Taylor. A friend of Clay and Daniel Webster, he was their equal in intellectual stature and, as a big, dominating man, probably surpassed them in physical stature. Blaine was to write of him: "I can truly say that I never met one who impressed me so profoundly."[12] In the museum at Lancaster dedicated to his even more renowned son-in-law General William Tecumseh Sherman, there is a bust of Thomas Ewing, Sr. One is reminded at once of Julius Caesar, remembering that Caesar, too, like Ewing, was bald—but with the attractive baldness of a man of power. Supposedly, while that likeness was being sculpted, the artist asked Ewing his ethnic origin. "Norman English" was the answer, but the sculptor shook his head and said, "No, Etruscan."

"Why Etruscan?"

"Well, you doubtless remember, Mr. Ewing, that the Etruscans were the first inventors of the dome...and you have the finest dome I have ever modeled."

One of Ewing's nicknames was the "Old Salt Boiler," because

he'd made his first money employed at a salt works. He told a tale of how he'd gotten seriously ill from exposure to the process, but didn't call a doctor. Instead, he took a copy of *Don Quixote* from the library and "laughed myself well in about ten days."

Thereafter, he studied law in Lancaster under General Philemon Beecher, who had married a Gillespie and, in turn, he was to marry Marie Boyle, whose mother was also a Gillespie.

One of the reasons young Jim Blaine was sent to live temporarily with his Ohio cousins was the private school attended by the sons of Thomas Ewing, Sr. Its master was a well-bred Englishman, William Lyons, the younger brother of Lord Alfred Edward Lyons, a hero of the Crimean War. Not quite the star pupil, Jim Blaine came in second to cousin Thomas Jr. for scholastic honors, and the prize was a portrait of the winner painted by the teacher, himself. A favorite family story was that when Thomas Sr. left to join President Harrison's cabinet, his office, where the portrait of his son had proudly hung, was rented to a pair of dressmakers and they used the picture as a pincushion, thoroughly ruining it.

When school ended, the cousins Jim Blaine and Hugh and Thomas Ewing, Jr., went on several trips. One was to visit another set of cousins, the Denmans, who had two boys of similar age, and they all enjoyed several weeks of royal fun. On another occasion, the lads were allowed to drive a horse and carriage by themselves to Columbus, the state capital, some thirty miles from Lancaster. Hugh, the oldest, was in charge. Colonel John Noble, a friend of the elder Ewing's, took charge of the boys in Columbus and saw that they had a wonderful time in the big city. One event, however, almost marred their carefree enjoyment, and it was due to Jim Blaine's already well-developed sense of political partisanship.

This incident had its inception en route to Columbus. Passing through the village of Greencastle, eight miles from Lancaster, they drove by a Democratic enclave where a Van Buren flag (this was during the election of 1840) was flying from a newly erected pole. A few "loco focos" (the nickname for ardent Democrats) were in view, and Jim Blaine made a derisive gesture at them. Hugh Ewing, despite his father's Whig affiliation, was offended. He told his Pennsylvania cousin that such things weren't done in Ohio and reflected badly on his father and family. Unrepentant, young Blaine argued his right to free speech. "Don't do it again," Hugh warned him. "I will do it again on the way back" was the reply that drew the retort, "If you do, I will put you out of the buggy."

That is precisely what happened on the ride home. Left to walk eight miles to Lancaster, Jim Blaine opted to head for yet

Thomas Ewing, Sr., the squire of Lancaster, Ohio. He was James G. Blaine's cousin by marriage and an influence on him because of his political successes— U.S. senator, secretary of the treasury under Presidents William Henry Harrison and John Tyler, and secretary of the interior under President Zachary Taylor. Upon the death of his close friend and neighbor, fellow lawyer Charles R. Sherman, he adopted one of the ten children left fatherless and that child was William Tecumseh Sherman who, in turn, married Ewing's daughter Ellen and thus became, in effect, a relative of Blaine's.
HAMILTON, *BIOGRAPHY OF JAMES G. BLAINE*

another Gillespie relative's house two miles nearer Lancaster than the Ewing home. Here, Hugh and Thomas Jr. caught up with him, the boys reconciled, and the whole affair remained a secret until they could no doubt laugh about it in their later years.

During the Lancaster stay Jim Blaine met some of the Sherman kids who lived two doors away. "Cump," William Tecumseh, was a cadet at West Point, but must have come home on leave for he has left a word picture of "Jim Blaine and Tom Ewing, two boys, cousins, as bright and handsome as ever were two thoroughbred colts in a blue-grass pasture of Kentucky."[13] John Sherman, the other famous brother, also later wrote of Blaine, "I have known him since he was a lad, living with his uncle [sic] Mr. Ewing of Ohio...and while I was older than the boy [by seven years] I saw a great deal of 'Jim,' as we called him."[14]

For Jim Blaine, nine to ten years old, the experience had to be a seminal event of his young life. If nothing else, he had a glimpse of others whose families were of mixed religious backgrounds, where Catholics and Protestants mingled. And Tom Ewing, Jr., his special buddy, then came to stay with him in West Brownsville for an entire school year. Among other activities, the two cousins organized a debating society and received some early practice in the give-and-take of argument. For sheer recreation, the inseparable pair trotted and galloped around the Pennsylvania countryside on two of Ephraim Lyon's "dappled grey and splendid" horses, on one occasion riding as far as Virginia.

In 1842 Jim Blaine's father entered politics. Running as a Whig in a Democratic district, he was elected prothonotary of Washington County, a kind of clerk or courts. It was said of Ephraim Lyon Blaine, who had the reputation of being a spendthrift, that when he arrived at the county seat in the town of Washington to assume office, the horses pulling his carriage were shod in silver. A fellow townsman thus described him: "I remember yet his courtly air as he came up the street, his bow so elegant and noticeable...but he made the money fly."[15] Gail Hamilton writes of "a generous disposition, abounding hospitality, expensive tastes without the frugality which naturally attends the slow accumulation of fortune...."[16]

Some accounts of his election claim that the key to his success was the tongue-in-cheek testimonial given him by his friend Father Murphy, the resident Catholic priest in Brownsville. His opponents were attacking him for secretly being a Catholic, a charge that could have sunk his campaign.

The response from Father Murphy was, "This is to certify that Ephraim L. Blaine is not now and never was a member of the Catholic Church; and furthermore, in my opinion, he is not fit to be a member of any church."

Voters often appreciate a good laugh and Ephraim Lyon apparently rode into office on the force of their chuckles.

Soon, the Blaines went off to live in Washington town, the father because of his job, and son Jim, since he was now ready to enroll in the academic institution with which his family had been connected for many years.

Today we would find it odd, if not impossible, that Jim Blaine was only thirteen years old when he entered Washington College.

---

1. *Westsylvania Stories*. Hollidaysburg, PA; Summer 2004, p. 5.
2. Francis Parkman. *The Conspiracy of Pontiac: The Indian War After The Conquest of Canada,* vol. 2 (Boston: Little Brown and Co., 1890, reprint 1969).
3. Hamilton, p. 15.
4. James Thomas Flexner. *Washington, The Indispensable Man* (Boston: Little Brown and Co., 1969), p. 117.
5. Lois Mulkearn and Edwin V. Pugh. *A Traveler's Guide to Historic Western Pennsylvania* (Pittsburgh: University of Pittsburgh Press, 1954), p. 328.
6. Hamilton, p. 37.
7. Ibid., p. 40.
8. Ibid., p. 52.
9. Ibid., p. 53.
10. James P. Boyd. *Life and Public Services of James G. Blaine: The Illustrious American Orator, Diplomat and Statesman* (Publishers Union, 1893).
11. Hamilton, p. 63.
12. Letter of condolence from James G. Blaine to his cousin Ellen Ewing Sherman, 5 November 1871, upon the death of her father.
13. Hamilton, p. 78.
14. Brownsville (Pennsylvania) *Clipper,* 2 February 1893.
15. Hamilton, p. 72.
16. Ibid., p. 72.

THREE

FORMATIVE YEARS

W HILE STILL RELATIVELY young, Jim Blaine and his cousin Tom Ewing, Jr., had talked about going on to college. This was an age when not many Americans even advanced beyond grammar school. As it turned out, Ewing went away to more exclusive Brown University in Providence, Rhode Island, and Blaine stayed nearer home. Was cost, masked by family sentiment, the consideration for his going to Washington College? The Blaine family finances weren't what they used to be, Jim once admitted to a college classmate, although the Blaines weren't exactly poverty-stricken.

The borough (today it's a city) of Washington, Pennsylvania, was a cozy enough setting for the underage student. A house on South Main Street, near the campus, bears a plaque that commemorates James G. Blaine's "temporary" stay during his undergraduate years. Did his county clerk father also live with him? Had mother Maria and the many Blaine siblings come from West Brownsville? The biographers are silent on these points. According to Gail Hamilton, that "still standing quaint and comely" abode had once belonged to the elder James Blaine, as well as to David Bradford, the infamous Whiskey Rebellion insurrectionist.

Today, Blaine's alma mater is Washington and Jefferson College. Started in the 1790s and receiving its official charter in 1806, Washington College later merged with Jefferson College of the neighboring town of Cannonsburg in 1865, long after James G. Blaine had left its original portals. His graduation was in 1847.

Another Blaine relative connected to Washington College was John Hoge Ewing, Jim's uncle by marriage, who had wed his father's sister, Ellen Blaine. It remains unclear if this Ewing was related to the Ohio Ewings. A Whig politician like Thomas Ewing, Sr., he, too, served in D.C.—one term as congressman from March 1845 to March 1847—while his nephew was still an undergraduate. Highly revered, John Hoge Ewing was a Washington College trustee for fifty-three years and the institution's president when it became Washington and Jefferson.

Also living in this local Ewing household was the widowed matriarch of the family, Margaret Lyon Blaine, who had come to live with her son-in-law after his wife's death in 1834. The college boy never failed to first pay his respects to his grandmother when he visited Uncle Ewing's home before going off to consort with a group of cousins near to his own age.

The adult James G. Blaine considered his uncle more than just a relative. "*We were friends* in the highest, broadest best sense," he wrote in an 1887 letter. "I can even now feel the thrill of pleasure I felt when at the closing examinations of my first year in college he spoke to me so approvingly and encouragingly of the examination I passed and of my conduct for the year."[1]

John Hoge Ewing, who had personally known giants like Clay, Webster, and Calhoun, most certainly further honed the interests of a youth already seasoned in Whig politics and public affairs.

Another relative in the vicinity was "Uncle Will," his mother's brother William Louis Gillespie. He has been described as "a gloved iconoclast," but in reality, he had been a candidate for the priesthood who deserted that vocation for a beautiful woman. Will, in Gail Hamilton's eyes, was "the dreamy and perhaps somewhat disappointed uncle who had not fulfilled the career which his friends wished."[2] This uncle and nephew were also close. On visits to Indian Hill, Will would use his clerical training to grill the boy in Greek and Latin, and afterward they'd go off into the woods together, hunting and fishing.

They were in touch by letter, too. One from Will to Jim, when the boy was in his junior year, upbraided him for not writing more, yet thanked him as the only relative who ever sent him newspapers. His sole news was about "the fun I have with long-faced Democrats," teasing them because of their problems selling wool due to a Whig-inspired tariff. Wishing news of Washington College, he asked how many graduates they had and who the Presbyterians' pastor was and noted that this Protestant cleric must assuredly get "astride of the old Pope and "hammer away at his seven heads and ten horns."[3] The still religious Will then brought up the subject of the Trinity and young Jim's "wild and infidel views" on it.

When he could get away from class, Jim Blaine would go shooting with a local black man, Randolph Tearle, said to be the most skilled hunter in the entire county. The "bushy-tailed fox" was their favorite game. An awed classmate remarked "there is not a rock or stump on these hills that Blaine doesn't know."

Washington College in the 1840s was all male and small (Blaine's class had thirty-three members), composed primarily of similar youngsters, offspring of middle-class families who had done well in the fast-growing western sections of the nation. Jim Blaine had friends like Tom Searight of the well-known local Pennsylvania Searights who had run a tollhouse on the National Road since 1835, and "Countie" or "Count" James Murray Clark, with whom he and Searight had discussions about setting up a law firm—Searight, Clark, and Blaine—following graduation. These two would-be partners, by the way, appear to have been Democrats, not Whigs.

Because of its National Road location, the school, itself, was wont to receive political luminaries on their way back and forth from the nation's capital. Men like Henry Clay, Thomas Hart Benton, Thomas Ewing, Sr., and John J. Crittenden would sometimes give talks to the students. President James K. Polk stayed on campus, en route to his inauguration in 1845, and John Quincy Adams spent three days at Washington College visiting one of the teachers. The college boys boasted that the eloquence of *their* president, the Reverend Doctor David M. McConnaughey, easily surpassed that of the former U.S. president.

Others stars of the faculty included the grandson and biographer of a signer of the Declaration of Independence, Richard Henry Lee, professor of rhetoric; Nicholas Murray, professor of language; W. P. Aldrich, professor of math and chemistry; and Robert Milligan, professor of English literature. And along with President McConnaughey, these four signed a flattering assessment of "Mr. James G. Blaine" and the work he had done in his college career. The report is loaded with compliments: "...a very punctual, orderly, diligent, and successful student...always respectful and becoming a gentleman...propriety of conduct and pleasing manners...his talents, literary acquirements, dignity, decision, fidelity, and prudence...will make him a great teacher..." plus, as if for some further laudatory icing on the cake, "He is of one of the most respected families of Washington County...." They also mentioned that he shared "first honor" in his class with two other young men, Tom Porter and John Hervey.

In extracurricular affairs, Jim Blaine gravitated toward debating. One of his classmates, William H. M. Pusey, the outgoing head of the Literary Society (a major debating club) has described how Jim Blaine came to see him and, with a slight stutter, said: "B...bill, I would like to be president of the Literary, Can you f...fix it for me?" Pusey was not encouraging. Blaine had never debated, despite being a member of the group, and besides, he knew nothing about parliamentary procedure. The rebutting reply was: "I can c...commit *Cushing's Manual* to memory in one night." And since he did so, Pusey fixed it for him at the next meeting. Some of the topics with which he and his fellows grappled were:

1. Should criminals be condemned to death because of circumstantial evidence?

2. Is the extent of territory more dangerous to our government than party spirit?

3. Do signs of the times indicate the downfall of our republic?

4. Should the United States agree to the right of mutual search [on the high seas] between herself and England?

A debate in which Blaine notably failed to participate was to speak in the affirmative on the question, "Were monasteries productive of more evil than good during the Middle Ages?" His Catholic heritage and his desire to play it down may well have been the motivating factors.

Excerpts from his college reading list clearly reveal young Blaine's historical and political bent. *History of Rome* by Oliver Goldsmith, Day's *Historical Collections of Pennsylvania, The Life and Speeches of Henry Clay,* de Tocqueville's *Democracy in America,* and Thier's *History of the French Revolution*. In between, he read popular novels like *Oliver Twist* and the works of Sir Walter Scott.

A few months shy of his eighteenth birthday, this "weedy, loose-jointed" youngster from West Brownsville whom classmates called "Nosey Blaine," because of his long nose, found himself out in the world, needing to seek his own fortune.

His first choice was to go to Yale and study law. But Ephraim Lyon revealed to Jim there wasn't enough money to send him. Or so a number of his biographers have intimated. His own view of the matter was put forth in a letter to his college buddy "Count" J. M. Clark, once he had ventured forth and landed a job.[4]

Illustrated here, at an early age, is an example of a trait of James G. Blaine's that blossomed in his later political life—the knack of a putting a gloss on negative matters and doing it with a show of utmost sincerity. The line between a seeming truth and the exact truth habitually became drawn very finely.

Blaine wrote Clark that his father had suffered financial losses by endorsing (presumably for financial loans) "men who deceived him." Nevertheless, Ephraim Lyon was now back on his feet, the family had a "sufficiency," and "pap," who wished to help all his children, wanted him, James, to enter the professions, either law or medicine. "It was altogether my own doing that I came away from home," he insisted, "and I believe it was for my good that I have done it. Whenever I choose however to return, father is willing to render me all the aid in his power." But the problem with doing that, Blaine argued, was if he studied for a profession, like going to Yale law, when he'd finished, he'd have exhausted his inheritance and "not have much more than will buy me a library"[5]

One wonders how much exact truth there was in all of this attempt to justify why, after graduation, he had gone to Kentucky and was starting as an assistant teacher of languages at the Western Military Institute in Georgetown, Scott County, twelve miles from Lexington.

His explanation to Clark had been posted from Kentucky. In a letter around the same time to Tom Searight, he again showed his talent for putting a slick polish on defending himself and/or his actions. He was embarrassed that the military academy, using its promotional material, had him graduating "Number 1" in his Washington College class, He knew he would be criticized, since the claim was false—he had shared that honor with Tom Porter and John Hervey. But the fault wasn't his. Mr. McKennan, one of their professors at Washington, had included the incorrect reference as part of his letter of recommendation and WMI Superintendent Colonel Thurston F. Johnson had picked it up and had it printed.

"My classmates who may happen to see it will think that I am taking a great stiff out here in Kentucky, just because I happened to get a share of the first honor," Jim Blaine wrote Searight. He added that the Count had mentioned receiving one of these military academy catalogues, but this couldn't be, or else it was mailed "when I was asleep, for I determined long ago not to send one to Washington without preceding it with this explanation."[6]

Both Searight and Clark were a year behind Blaine at Washington College. They were still undergraduates, finishing their senior year, hearing from their "elder" comrade who was most likely their own age rather than that of his classmates.

In the bevy of private letters that Blaine family member Gail Hamilton was able to collect and publish in 1895, a large packet came from those early days in Kentucky. Certain ironies are reflected in them. For example, Blaine told Count Clark, "When I leave my present situation I don't think I shall ever look for another, but I shall return to old Pennsylvania. The longer I am away the more I feel attached to her.... I can never nor shall I ever be anything else in feeling than a Pennsylvanian...."[7]

"Blaine of Maine" could not remotely be imagined then, although he did express a thought that his destiny might lie elsewhere than his native state. The instrument of that destiny was not far off, as it happened. He wrote to Tom Seawright, "We have some of the prettiest girls about here that ever lived in the world. They beat the Washington girls all hollow, one always excepted. I am in love with about a half dozen, and the only difficulty I have is to decide between them, and it is no easy matter, I assure you."[8]

It is impossible to discern if the one exceptional beauty in Washington was so in Jim Blaine's eyes or referred to a sweetheart of Tom Searight's. In any event, the lusty young college grad soon found himself involved with a fellow teacher, a certain Miss Harriet Stanwood, who was an instructress at the affiliated female seminary run by Colonel Johnson's wife, twenty miles away from Georgetown in the town of Millersberg. She was not a Kentucky belle, however; she was just the opposite—a sharp-tongued, highly intelligent Yankee descendant of New England Puritans, whose family, originally from Massachusetts, had now been ensconced for several generations in the city of Augusta, capital of the relatively new state of Maine.

Life at the Western Military Institute seemed agreeable enough to "Professor" Blaine at the moment. His popularity among the 150 cadets was high. Only slightly older than most, he knew them all and often called them by their first names. The majority were from the South, many the sons of slave owners, and a pecking order existed. Blaine once intervened when one of the poorer students, John F. Edwards, knocked down a snobby classmate who had insulted his mother, and he saved the boy from expulsion. Blaine taught preparatory courses in Latin and Greek and a class in elementary algebra. Patterned on West Point and the Virginia Military Institute, with graduates of both among its faculty, WMI intended to become "*the* military school of Kentucky."

The new Washington College graduate had gotten his job by pure lucky chance. While in Lexington, boarding with a Mrs. McKee, he first heard of the school—"just got into a buggy and drove down one morning"—applied for a position and was accepted the next day.

Why he had gone to Lexington, Kentucky, was most likely hero worship of Henry Clay, whose hometown it was. On November 13, 1847, two weeks after his arrival, he stood in the Lexington marketplace, notebook in hand, heard the "Great Commoner" speak against the Mexican War, jotted down his words, and, allegedly, twenty years later, could still recite them by heart.

As a Whig in those days, Blaine was against U.S. expansion, a position he would later reverse as secretary of state. Politics was ever on his mind. His missives to his Democratic college friends were full of the astute analyses that were to make him such an accomplished politician in the future.

His roommate Forbes, professor of mathematics at WMI, was, he wrote Clark, a loco-foco Democrat, a "real James K. Polk man." He added that the Democrats ("your party") would have a hard time picking a candidate to replace Polk in 1848, that Zachary Taylor's "stock has been rising," and that he, himself, might like to see Buchanan (James Buchanan, a Pennsylvania Democrat) rather than General Taylor (a fellow Whig) as president, if it were not that Buchanan had been too close to the Polk Administration. Polk's strong pro-slavery stance went unmentioned. Kentucky then was a slave state. Even Henry Clay, deviser of the Missouri Compromise and soon to engineer another Civil War-averting agreement in 1850, owned slaves. The Bluegrass State, Blaine noted, would be holding a convention the following summer to decide whether to continue or to abolish slavery. His judgment on the matter was, "Kentucky has been ruined by slavery—her soil and climate won't admit of it—she is too far north."

Blaine's correspondence in those days was sprinkled with political pronouncements on every level of government. It could be the machinations of the Pennsylvania State Legislature, or a cryptic reference to an action of the Ohio Legislature, or how Polk beat Clay in Scott County (site of WMI), but Taylor carried it for the Whigs four years later, or hailing a strictly local vote at home that stopped an attempt to split up Washington County.

In April 1849, as the time neared for that convention on slavery in Kentucky, Blaine penned his detailed outlook to Tom Searight. He described Henry Clay as strong for emancipation and colonization (sending Blacks to Liberia) but that "the day has long since gone when Henry Clay's will was law in Kentucky." Scott County was sending its most able man, a lawyer, James I. Robinson, to head its delegation. He was an outright slavery man and so would be two-thirds of the delegates. Echoing a Southern viewpoint, Blaine laid the blame on the "ultra course" of the abolitionists in the North for so inflaming the "public pulse of Kentucky."

Did these words mean Blaine was pro-slavery? Columbia University Professor David Muzzey thought so and expressed this opinion in his 1934 biography. To back up his charge, he included an anecdote culled from the biography of an ex-U.S. senator from

Iowa, George Wallace Jones. It alleges that when Blaine was speaker of the U.S. House in 1875, Jones went back to D.C. on a lobbying trip and met Blaine, who said to him, "Do you not recall my having been introduced to you in 1850 by Mr. Clay at Blue Lick Springs, Kentucky? I educated your sons Charles and William at the Western Military Institute."

The blunt old senator was said to have replied, "Well, you played the Devil educating them, for you made the two of them secessionists."[9] Author Muzzey wrote that the speaker curtly changed the subject, as a sign of Blaine's pro-Southern proclivities. Similar charges were later hurled by Democrats in Maine, who alluded to their nemesis's prior residence in Kentucky.

There is room for other thoughts. In 1850, whether he lived in the North or the South, James G. Blaine would not have felt too kindly toward abolitionists. They were too radical for conservative-minded Whigs. Besides, his hero Henry Clay was working hard at the time for a compromise that would contain slavery (the Whig position), not eliminate it. As for the Senator Jones story, parts of it seem apocryphal. Muzzey gives the impression that Senator Jones was a strong Union supporter, annoyed that his sons had become pro-South and blaming Blaine. Left out of the tale are the facts that Jones was a Democrat, a great friend of Jefferson Davis, and that his continued correspondence with the rebel president in 1861 caused his arrest for disloyalty and imprisonment for sixty-four days, until released by order of President Lincoln. Finally, that meeting of Blaine's with the senator took place at Blue Lick Springs, Kentucky, which presents another bit of confusion to the historian.

A few of Blaine's biographers have placed the Western Military Institute at this scenic site in Kentucky's Nicholas County, rather than at Georgetown in Scott County, at least forty miles away. But an extant letter signed "J. G. Blaine," in his own handwriting, clearly identifies Georgetown as the town in which he taught.

In that instance, the young "professor" was seeking a distinguished speaker for a school event at WMI—after their first choice fell ill. Second choice was Robert Jefferson Breckinridge, then Kentucky's general superintendent of schools, a "big name," member of one of the state's most illustrious families. The topic, Blaine wrote, was the "Common School," the highly controversial issue of free public and secondary education. He added, "The Georgetown people have long been expecting an address from you upon this subject and I think there could be no time more favorable than the present. I am instructed to tender you the invitation in behalf of the Faculty and the Literary direction of the Military Academy and the citizens of the town." Apologizing for the late notice, Blaine finished flatteringly, "but we are well aware that you require no time to prepare for such an occasion."[10]

No older than twenty, Blaine was already showing his smoothness. He also invited Breckinridge to choose the most convenient hour for his lecture and offered to have a carriage waiting to take him to Georgetown from Lexington.

Although mature beyond his years on political matters, Blaine at times was still the one-year-out-of-school graduate, nostalgic for the carefree college days he had just left, reminiscing on paper to his pen pals, "...do you remember that night...that you stole one of the pillows off of Briceland's sofa and hung it up on Creigh's awning post? ...do you remember...the day on which we first wore the striped velvet vests with the red buttons? ...do you mind that awful cold night that we went to Caldwell? Mayor Johnson was in his shirtsleeves and I lost my old cap that was so h_____ ugly?" Antics and high jinks—the stuff of reunion conversations.

Yet all at once, following these rather sophomoric reminiscences, James G. Blaine was married! The date given for his and Harriet's nuptials was June 30, 1850. Ever since 1849, Blaine had been looking for an opportunity to leave WMI. The resignation of Colonel Johnson and crisis conditions at the academy gave him his chance. Thomas Ewing, Sr., had been named to President Taylor's cabinet and Blaine thought of enlisting his cousin's help to apply for a clerkship in the Department of the Interior, but nothing came of the idea. Yet by 1851, he was gone from Kentucky, and a year later he arrived in Philadelphia, not only with a wife, but also with a child, to teach at the Pennsylvania Institute for the Blind.

In point of fact, his prediction had rung true that he would head back to Pennsylvania from below the Mason-Dixon line as soon as possible. The other surmise—that his real destiny might nonetheless lie elsewhere—was just over the horizon. The couple's stay in Philadelphia proved relatively short—less than two years.

1. Hamilton, p. 82.
2. Ibid., p. 79.
3. Ibid., p. 80.
4. Ibid, p. 86—JGB to J. M. Clark, 2 December 1847.
5. Ibid, p. 87.
6. bid., p. 92—JGB to Tom Searight, 14 January 1848.
7. Ibid., p. 88.
8. Ibid., p. 92.
9. David Saville Muzzey. *James G. Blaine: A Political Idol of Other Days* (New York: Dodd, Mead and Company, 1934), p. 19.
10. JGB to R. Breckinridge, July 1 (no year date, but probably 1849).

FOUR

PULLING UP ROOTS

AT CHRISTMASTIME, 1852, James G. Blaine received a holiday letter from his widowed mother, then living in the small borough of Elizabeth, Pennsylvania, on the Monongahela, not far from Pittsburgh. She was thanking her "Jimi" for the Xmas gift he had sent her, worrying maternally that he had no vacation from the school for the blind and religiously about how he was spending his Sundays, "Not I fear, as I wish in attending church...."[1]

Some family news was that "your Uncle Willie" was set on going west and she hated the idea of being separated from her only brother. Also, that "Little M. and A. are dressed this day for the first time in their new frocks that you sent them...." The picture of these young nieces is then completed with, "A. says her Uncle Jim dress is the prettiest one she has and wishes very much you could see how beautiful she looks in it. She knows you would think her almost as pretty as Stannie...." "Stannie" undoubtedly was Uncle Jim's wife Harriet Stanwood. The couple's child, born the previous year, had the first name of Stanwood, but it's unlikely the above comment referred to a male baby. At the time, mother and son were apparently staying with her family in Augusta, Maine, where Stanwood had been born, while husband Jim remained in Philadelphia.

"Do you have no idea of visiting us before July? Oh, it seems so long to wait till then," was a last motherly pull on Blaine's heartstrings, but it does appear he waited until summer vacation to be with her. Several letters sent to Tom Searight in July and August 1853 were postmarked Elizabeth. His plans, he told Tom, were to leave Elizabeth for Philadelphia by August 7, then go to New England, and return to Philadelphia by September 1.

This trip to see his lonely, widowed mother brings up an apparent family mystery. His father had been dead a little more than three years and the date generally given for Ephraim Lyon's death is June 28, 1850. Jim Blaine is described at the funeral and the burial in St. Peter's Catholic churchyard in Brownsville and depicted with the beard that would later become one of his trademarks. Yet two days after Ephraim's demise, June 30, 1850, this same young man with the same dark fledgling facial hair was definitely, by his own account, in Georgetown, Kentucky, marrying Stannie.

The most cogent explanation for such an odd set of circumstances has come from Maine historian H. Draper Hunt in his book *The Blaine House, Home of Maine's Governors*.[2] It is based upon the notion that Blaine, learning his father had passed away, knew he would have to go to Pennsylvania and feared he might have to stay in West Brownsville and take care of Ephraim Lyon's tangled affairs. Two days after the sad event he and Harriet, who had become secretly engaged, were married in Kentucky with only a few "chosen and trusted friends" present. Blaine, himself, years later, explained, "It being very doubtful if I could return to Kentucky, I was threatened with an indefinite separation from her who possessed my entire devotion. My one wish was to secure her to myself by an indissoluble tie against every possible contingency in life." He was also to confess that a "secret marriage" suggested by the "ardor and inexperience of youth" was an act of folly.

These ex post facto remarks were made in response to a political crisis the long-ago secret marriage had caused when he was running for president in 1884. There had been a second marriage, dated in March 1851, and legally registered in Pennsylvania. The problem for the Blaines in that regard was the timing of Stanwood's birth, which was only three months later. "Shotgun wedding" became a war cry for the Democrats when Blaine's convoluted story didn't seem to pass the straight-face test—that because their Kentucky marriage a year earlier hadn't been registered, he and Harriet had gone through a second wedding in Pennsylvania. It was turned by his foes into another Blaine lie.

Not for another thirty-three years, however, would this discrepancy be noticed and no one conceivably could have predicted Jim Blaine would one day run for the top office in the United States. Then, he was simply another young, married college grad about to change jobs, who had taken a few law courses from a Kentucky judge, and whose future was anything but secure or predictable.

In Philadelphia, after all, he spent time initially in the law office of Theodore Cuyler before answering an ad for a teacher's position at the Pennsylvania Institute for the Blind. The need for a steady salary had to be the main factor. Impressed by his memory and

The Institution for the Blind in Philadelphia where Blaine—newly married, and prior to leaving for Maine—taught. Coincidentally, his opponent in the 1884 presidential campaign, Grover Cleveland, also once taught in a school for the blind as a young man.
MAINE HISTORIC PRESERVATION COMMISSION

knowledge of history and politics, Dr. William Chapin, the school's principal, hired Blaine from among forty applicants.

Almost immediately, Blaine was made principal of the boys department. He taught literature and science and, as at WMI, was a great favorite of the students. He read aloud to the children from Dickens, particularly from a book he much liked called *Charcoal Sketches*, and it always set them laughing. He arranged spelling bees. He would even encourage the boys to argue with him.

Michael M. Williams, a homeless blind boy and subsequent school employee, has left some memories. "Everybody loved Mr. Blaine and his wife," Michael wrote, and he was particularly close to the pair. Mr. Blaine had made a deal with him, which was to ring the bells for assembly and dismissal, a faculty chore that Blaine detested, and Mrs. Blaine found Michael helpful, too. She had become her husband's assistant and when it was her turn to read aloud to the classes, she would put little Stanwood in Michael's lap. The affection between Michael and the Blaines even endured a bawling-out the former once received for messing up Professor Blaine's math questions.

Other facts about Blaine from that period were that he was not a professing Christian, did not offer prayers at meals, and only conducted prayer services from printed forms. Another quirk was his dislike of rising early to get to class on time. He was often seen rushing down steps two at a time, "coat and vest in one hand and collar in the other." One incident was often told long afterward. It appears he wasn't the sole person who hated to get out of bed. There were always a few students late for breakfast, and when half a dozen failed to arrive on time one morning, Blaine locked them in their dorm. Managing to unscrew the lock, they rushed to the dining hall only to find the tables had been cleared and they had to go to class hungry. This happened only once.

As a parting gift to the institution, Blaine presented essentially the first book he ever wrote. It bore the title *Journal of the Pennsylvania Institution for Instruction of the Blind, from its Foundation, compiled from Official Records, by James G. Blaine, 1854*. He'd done it all on his own, without a word to anyone until he had a finished manuscript. His history was compiled from the "minute books of the Board of Managers," starting with the school's inception until his departure on November 23, 1854. The board's members were so delighted by his unexpected gift that they appropriated $100 to reward him for his effort.

Principal William Chapin, in an interview years later, said, "the book illustrates the character of the man in accurate mastery of facts and orderly presentation of details," and reported it still in continual use for reference and being kept up to date. Allowing Mrs. Blaine and the couple's two-year-old son to live at the school, he added, was the only exception the board had ever made to its rules. His final judgment on Blaine remained, "If he was a young intellectual giant then, we may presume those powers are now somewhat colossal."[3]

But why did James G. Blaine, at the age of twenty-four, leave a comfortable position where he had become an acknowledged success and which, in addition, would have allowed him to remain in his purportedly beloved Pennsylvania?

Was it the death of little Stanwood? This tragic happening seemingly occurred in Philadelphia, for cousin Edward Stanwood speaks of the child's body transported to Augusta for final burial.[4] No cause is cited, but the impact on the young parents may well be imagined. Harriet, in particular, would have had no compunction about leaving the City of Brotherly Love.

Also playing a key role in the Blaines' departure was a fortuitous meeting on a train at the end of one of Blaine's vacation trips to the Maine capital. On board was a Mr. John Dorr and the two struck up a conversation. They were soon talking business, and that business was the newspaper business. Dorr had been a partner in the *Kennebec Journal*, the most prominent Whig newspaper in the state. Its history went back to 1825 when two young journalists working in Washington, D.C., Luther Severance and Russell Eaton, went north to begin the enterprise. Dorr had come aboard in 1839, after Eaton had left and Severance had run the paper alone for six years. Now, Luther Severance was gone, temporarily at least to Hawaii as the U.S. commissioner to the island kingdom, a political ambassadorial post given him by Whig President

Zachary Taylor. In addition to serving as the *Kennebec Journal* editor, Severance had been a state legislator and a U.S. congressman, and although their contact upon his return was brief, he would have a strong influence on James G. Blaine. The transplanted Pennsylvanian's second piece of preserved writing, in fact, is an extensive memorial piece about Luther Severance.

There was a looming vacancy in the *Kennebec Journal*'s editorial department and John Dorr thought the young man he met on the train would be perfect for the job. Most importantly, he was a staunch Whig. His writing experience might be skimpy—he had done a few columns for the *Philadelphia Inquirer*—yet he was obviously bright, well-up on national politics, college-trained, and married into a prominent Augusta family. One of the lures Dorr dangled was the changing political climate in Maine, ordinarily a Democratic state. Maine people were upset about the potential spread of slavery, especially since the recent passage of the Kansas-Nebraska Act, and were also strongly in favor of prohibition. The Democrats were on the wrong side of both those powerful issues. If the Whigs were to control the next legislature—and those prospects looked good—the state's lucrative printing contract would go to the *Kennebec Journal*, no longer to its Democratic rival, *The Age,* and the Whig publication's financial prospects would soar. Dorr was not only offering Blaine a job; he was also inviting him to buy into the newspaper and become a working partner.

Blaine's new family connections made this deal possible. Two of his brothers-in-law, Jacob Stanwood and Eben C. Stanwood, had become prosperous merchants in Boston and they lent him the money needed in order to cash in on this "opportunity." Also brought into the transaction was Joseph Baker, a local lawyer, who'd been serving as interim editor since the spring of 1854.

On November 10, 1854, Baker and Blaine were listed on the masthead as the new "Editors and Proprietors."

Added below was a message to "Patrons of the Journal" from the previous owner, W. H. Simpson, who wrote, "Mr. Baker is well-known to the readers of the Journal" while, he admitted, "Mr. Blaine comes upon us comparatively a stranger." However, not to worry.

"It is but just to say that he is a gentleman of decided talent, of liberal education, extensive travel, and acquainted with public men and measures of this country."[5]

A broadside from the new owners, themselves, followed:

OUR FUTURE COURSE

We shall cordially support the Morrill or Republican party, the substantial principles of which are, as we understand them, Freedom, Temperance, River and Harbor Improvements within constitutional limits, Homestead for freemen, and a just administration of the public lands of the states and the nation— We shall advocate the cause of Popular Education as the surest safeguard for our Republican institutions and especially the common schools of the state and city.[6]

Having baldly stated their politics (note the use of Republican party instead of Whig), they promised to devote "a large share of attention" to the business interests of the State of Maine, Kennebec County, and the city of Augusta; to print "Religious Intelligence of all kind"; to keep the price of the paper the same as before; and to continue to do job printing.

Left unstated was that with Anson P. Morrill elected Maine's first Republican governor, the *KJ* would be doing the state's considerable printing.

The Stanwood family had been in Maine since 1822, arriving only two years after Maine had split off from Massachusetts. A residence of more than three decades doesn't make you exactly a native in Maine, though. But they were certainly of Yankee Puritan heritage, descended from one Phillip Stainwood, who had emigrated to Gloucester, Massachusetts, in 1652. As Stanwoods, one branch moved to Ipswich in 1723. Harriet's father, Jacob Sr., a wool merchant, left for Maine when he was thirty-seven years old. Twice married, he fathered ten children, of whom Harriet was the ninth, and the seventh by his second wife, Sally Caldwell of Ipswich, before his sudden death from a heart attack in 1845. Ties to their Massachusetts roots, especially in Essex County, gave the Stanwoods a somewhat more cosmopolitan outlook than many of their Augusta neighbors. Still, their unmistakable Yankee Puritan background had to be something new for the young Pennsylvanian. These people were palpably different from those of his own Scots-Irish country—Anglo-Saxon as opposed to Celtic. Even their principal church was different—Congregational as opposed to Presbyterian. But Jim Blaine was nothing if not adaptable. Meeting all these Maine folks at their own levels in his amiable, ingratiating fashion, he found himself accepted. He could even draw a parallel between the physical setting of Augusta and the environs of Brownsville-West Brownsville. Both were hilly communities; both bordered a good-sized, bridgeable river; both were bustling, growing, and yet not far removed from their original rural settings; and, furthermore, both had been sites of dramatic action during the French and Indian wars. Augusta was actually much older; the first settlement there had been a Pilgrim trading post, established not long after the Plymouth landing in 1620. The beaver furs Edward Winslow had traded for corn with the local Abenaki Indians and sent back to England had helped enormously to pay off the colony's debt.

Blaine surely heard how the first "murders" (of white men) in Maine took place at *Cushnoc*, the original name for Augusta, in an exchange of deadly rifle shots when a rival shipload of fur traders tried interloping on the Pilgrims' territory. He would have learned, too, how Augusta was chosen to be Maine's permanent capital, moved from Portland, and how Portland had fought to keep on trying to get it back even after the state capitol building had been constructed overlooking the banks of the Kennebec River. The partisan overtones of that battle would have been mentioned. Augusta had been chosen for the honor due to its Democratic political leanings. Nearby Hallowell, a bustling port, had been the first choice of the search committee, but the Jeffersonian Democrats who had brought statehood to Maine, rejected it as too Federalist. Following that, a noted Democrat, Judge Nathan Weston, offered a plot of his land in Augusta as the site for a capitol building.

The grandson of this judge, Melville Weston Fuller, a Bowdoin graduate and attendee at Harvard Law School, was no less of a Democrat and Blaine's chief enemy in Augusta from 1855 to 1856. He was editor of *The Age*, that ferociously Democratic opponent of the *Kennebec Journal*. Veteran members of the legislature recall those two slim young men in the halls of the statehouse, acting as their own reporters. Who would have guessed that one day Fuller would be chief justice of the United States, and Blaine—well, Blaine would almost be president!?

A battle of young Titans was averted when Fuller, just months after his election as president of Augusta's city council and appointment as city solicitor, abruptly pulled up stakes, left his native hearth, and migrated permanently to Chicago. An unhappy love affair has been a major speculation for this abrupt move, and another, that *The Age*, having lost its state printing and advertising contract, had seen its profitability diminished.

It is certainly true that the *Kennebec Journal* had seen its margins go up. Blaine later boasted, "Was I not then State printer, making $4,000 a year and spending $600, a ratio between outlay and income which I have never since been able to establish and maintain."[7] The savings that resulted from this *ratio* were wisely invested—in Pennsylvania coal lands that increased in value exponentially with the growth of Pittsburgh and the steel industry.

But all that was far in the future.

What Augusta did for the carpetbagger from Pennsylvania in those early years was give him a taste of earning money and doing so—quite legitimately—via the political process and contacts he could make in that arena. It's to be doubted if, in transporting himself and his wife northward, he had thoroughly scouted the political possibilities open to him. Yet he could hardly have found a better time to arrive in the city of Augusta and the state of Maine.

The catalyst for an immense change in the political climate of Maine and most of the northern United States had been the passage of the Kansas-Nebraska Act, which was signed into law by President Franklin Pierce on May 30, 1854. In Maine the issue was particularly galling because the new law effectively repealed the Missouri Compromise by which Maine had become a separate state in 1820. The federal government's part of the thirty-four-year-old bargain was to allow no slavery north of a line equivalent to the southern boundary of Missouri, and now this agreement had been brutally violated. Henceforth, as Northern anti-slavery forces charged, slavery could be installed anywhere in the country. Worse still, the hated Fugitive Slave Law, by which all Americans were made accomplices in the return of escaped slaves, was stringently tightened, with severe punishments for those who helped slaves seek freedom in Canada and no legal safeguards for anyone accused.

This crisis split political parties. The Whigs, already in decline, accelerated toward their ultimate disappearance. The other major party, the Democrats, began to lose its rank-and-file anti-slavery members in large numbers and some prominent leaders in the North. Meanwhile, a new party, destined to be called Republicans, was forming.

A Maine man, Whig Congressman Israel Washburn, Jr., had played a leadership role in this latter effort. The very night he and his allies lost their last chance to stop the Kansas-Nebraska Act by eleven votes in the U.S. House, Washburn held a meeting at his quarters in D.C. More than thirty angry Whigs and Free-Soil Democrats attended and the talk was centered on starting a new party. It was Washburn who suggested the name Republicans. A little more than a month later, on July 6, the official Republican Party was apparently launched at Jackson, Michigan. Maine's first Republican caucus has been accredited to the small Franklin County town of Strong. The movement, wherever it sparked, caught fire immediately. By September in that wild year of 1854, Maine was electing a Republican governor, even before James G. Blaine arrived.

Anson Peaslee Morrill of Readfield, the man who cracked open the Democrats' almost total stranglehold on Maine's gubernatorial seat, had been a Democrat. Under that party's rubric, he had been elected to the legislature, made sheriff of Somerset County, and given the lucrative patronage plum of state land agent. He originally bolted in 1853, and the issue for him then allegedly was prohibition or the insertion at the Democratic state convention of a plank in the party platform against it. Running for governor as a combined prohibition and Free Soil candidate in 1853, Anson Morrill was unsuccessful. But what a difference a year made!

In 1853 Morrill had come in third in a four-man race with 11,058 votes. The September 1854 vote (Maine elected its governors every year and held its balloting, except for president, in September, ahead of the rest of the country) was also a four-way split. Morrill—now the "Republican"—had 44,852 votes, only 985 shy of an absolute majority. His closest opponent, the "regular" Democrat and five-time former governor Albion Parris had 28,896. But since there was no plurality voting in Maine at the time, the legislature had to decide on the winner and narrowly chose Morrill. He lost the house by ten votes—to a Whig—then won all thirty-one votes in the senate. The *Kennebec Journal*, James G. Blaine, Editor, ran the headline on January 12, 1855: "ANSON P. MORRILL ELECTED GOVERNOR FOR THE CURRENT POLITICAL YEAR."

It was also reported that Blaine had a new partner, the Reverend John L. Stevens, who was leaving the Universalist ministry to plunge into partisan politics, partly at the urging of his close friend, governor-elect Morrill. The departing co-owner, Joseph Baker, who simply wanted to attend to his law practice, underlined the paper's purpose by wishing Blaine and Stevens "abundant success advocating the principles of Right and Republicanism."

Those two men went right at it. Their columns seethed. Wearer of the cloth or not, John L. Stevens could be venom-tongued. Yet most likely, it was Blaine who referred to their opposition as "two defunct political schools—straight-out Whiggery and Nebraska "loco-focoism"; i.e., his former Whig comrades who wouldn't become Republicans and the always disliked Democrats, characterized by him as "the pro-slavery and rum party of the day."

His ire, expressed here in 1855, derived from enemy press attacks on Governor Morrill's maiden speech to the legislature. In a battle of words, the *Kennebec Journal* called *The Age* "our savage neighbor," its "vulgarity unredeemed by wit," and the names it called Morrill "epithets current only in the dirty dialect of Five Points" (an Irish Catholic immigrant slum in Portland).

This last reference brings up a ticklish point: the anti-Catholicism then rampant in the U.S. and Maine under the name of Americanism or the American Party, or colloquially, the Know-Nothing movement, because its adherents, when asked what they were about, only answered, "We know nothing."

What position did James Gillespie Blaine take, half Scots-Irish Catholic, his own father converted to that religion on his deathbed, his mother still practicing that faith, a cousin a nun, respected relatives, even siblings, devout Catholics? To read his writings in the *Kennebec Journal*, you'd never guess his background. On December 1, 1854, one *KJ* editorial explicitly stated that the "three greatest evils of the times and the worst foes of our liberties" were "SLAVERY, RUM, and FOREIGNERS." It had to have been written by Blaine, since John L. Stevens had not yet joined the paper.

This apologia for anti-Catholicism, despite demonstrated outrages in Maine such as the burning of a Catholic church in Bath and the tarring and feathering of a priest in Ellsworth, began in the *Kennebec Journal's* columns under the title of "Native Americanism and Slavery." Starting it off, Blaine quickly tried to debunk an expressed fear about anti-Catholics, i.e., "the feeling of opposition to Catholics and foreigners will become so predominant in their minds that they will consider slavery a minor evil." Of the 10,000 Free-Soilers who voted for Anson P. Morrill (who strongly supported the Know-Nothings), a large proportion belonged to the "secret order," Blaine wrote. They came from the anti-slavery wings of the Whig and Democratic parties. "These men"—the Know-Nothings and others who cooperated with them—"constitute the true democratic Republican party of 1854. They are the party of Progress and Reform."

Thus did Blaine welcome an element of Protestant intolerance into the composition of the new party he was helping to form. The Know-Nothings did not last long as an independent force. But their ghosts, in a sense, have haunted the G.O.P. almost to this day, lending it the aura of the white, Anglo-Saxon, Protestant party, and, in Blaine's case, doing more than haunting him in his future quest for the presidency.

In the matter of his own personal religion, Blaine certainly did follow the maxim of when in Rome upon his arrival in Augusta. Throughout New England, the establishment church in almost every community had been inherited from the Puritans. The First Parish Congregational Church was the place you wanted to be if you were an ambitious young man. Edward Stanwood described

Blaine as a "convinced believer in the Presbyterian creed"[8] and the excuse that might be offered for Blaine's switch from his childhood faith was that Presbyterians were as scarce as hen's teeth in Maine and, besides, resembled the Congregationalists in belief. Still, there was something inevitable about finding James G. Blaine in Augusta's First Parish Congregational Church, where he soon became one of its pillars.

"The Puritan church [in Augusta] was Federalist and Whig," wrote a biographer of Melville W. Fuller.[9] "Democrats were made uncomfortable in the Congregational church and many of them joined the Episcopal...." In actuality, some of those Democrats, like the Fullers and members of their family, the Westons, had been pushed out in the 1830s for tolerating dancing in their home. The stern Calvinist Reverend Benjamin Tappan literally put these distinguished citizens, including Judge Weston, on trial; his grandson, the future chief justice, then an infant, although baptized a Congregationalist, all his grown life stayed an Episcopalian.

When James G. Blaine joined the Augusta First Parish, the Reverend Tappan had retired. His son-in-law, the Reverend Edwin B. Webb had taken his place. He was only a few years older than Blaine and the two of them became fast and lifelong friends. They have been described walking arm-in-arm in deep discussion "many, many a night" on State Street, one of Augusta's main drags, or sitting upon the stone steps of the capitol, which borders that thoroughfare—this at a time before Blaine bought his "mansion" in the same area. In those early years in Augusta, he and Harriet and the first of their brood of new children were boarding in the old Stanwood home at 22 Green Street, about half a mile away from Weston's Hill. Living with them were the two oldest of Harriet's unmarried sisters, Aunt Caddy and Aunt Susan.

These maiden ladies soon had nephews to fuss over: Robert Walker Blaine, born in 1855, always known as "Walker," and possibly named after a Blaine brother-in-law whose surname was Walker; and Williams Emmons Blaine, born in 1857, always known as "Emmons," and indisputably named for the Honorable Williams Emmons of nearby Hallowell, a former state senator and judge, and the best friend of Blaine's late father-in-law, Jacob Stanwood, Sr.

Drawing of the Kennebec Journal's *building in Augusta, Maine, as it was when Blaine served there as co-owner and editor, starting in 1854 and lasting until he sold his share in this newspaper and printing enterprise. The* Kennebec Journal, *then a thrice-weekly publication, still exists in the present as a daily.*
MAINE HISTORIC PRESERVATION COMMISSION

The swift acceptance of the Blaine family included the most prominent of Democrats, former U.S. senator James Bradbury. This beloved old gentleman taught a Sunday school class that Blaine attended, and upon the birth of each of the Blaine children, Bradbury, also a neighbor, would send over a silver bowl his family had owned for 150 years to be used in the baptism ceremony.

Although Senator Bradbury never changed his party allegiance, other prominent Maine Democrats in these years were leaving to become even more prominent Republicans. Anson Peaslee Morrill was a prime example and he was soon followed by his brother, Lot Myrick Morrill, who not only was a Democratic state senator but chairman of the Democratic State Committee. The prize catch of all was the undisputed most popular politician in Maine, the Jefferson-Jackson party's U.S. senator, Hannibal Hamlin. An elaborate scheme was being devised, probably with the help of Blaine and his partner John L. Stevens, who had been made chairman of the Republican State Committee, to induce Hamlin to leave Washington and run for governor on the Republican ticket. Then, after his sure victory, he would resign, the Republican-dominated legislature would send him back to D.C. as a G.O.P. senator, and his place as chief executive would be filled by that other convert, Lot M. Morrill.

During the years at the beginning of the 1850s, Maine's Republican hegemony was by no means guaranteed. Blaine, Stevens, and company had a taste of that in 1856 when Governor Anson P. Morrill was not re-elected for a third term. One of the party's major winning issues—prohibition—had backfired on them because of a dramatic and fatal incident in Portland.

Maine was the pioneer state in the Union to outlaw the manufacture and consumption of alcoholic beverages. Nationwide, even worldwide, prohibition was known as "The Maine Law." The man behind this development was a feisty Portland ex-firefighter named Neal Dow and in 1856, he was the city's highly controversial mayor. When a riot developed over a cooked-up charge that Dow hypocritically and illegally had the city buy liquor for "medicinal" purposes, he had it quelled by ordering the militia to fire into the crowd. One man was killed, others wounded, and the repercussions allowed a coalition of Democrats and "Straight Whigs" to elect a governor, Democrat Samuel Wells. Blaine and Stevens soon felt the pinch when they lost their contract with the state and their machinations began—successfully as it turned out—to bring the Republicans back into statewide power.

In 1856, the national Republican Party made its first attempt to run a candidate for the U.S. presidency. The twenty-six-year-old James G. Blaine has been described at this time as "the party's leading publicist and errand boy." Perhaps for the latter reason, he won a coveted spot as one of the G.O.P. delegates to their initial national convention. It was to be held in Philadelphia, and he could tell these non-cosmopolitan Mainers that he knew Philadelphia. Furthermore, he was soon making all the arrangements for the Maine delegation at the American Hotel, "because it is much used for political conventions."

He was much more than just a "go-fer," however. Party brass consulted him and sought his political opinions, as Congressman Israel Washburn, Jr., did in a letter about what role the Know-Nothings might have in the Republican campaign. Other heavy hitters like U.S. senators William Pitt Fessenden and Hannibal Hamlin were in touch with him, too.

The candidate the Republicans selected for president was John C. Fremont of California, a military figure and well-known explorer of the West—a he-man type who might have been attractive to one so young as Blaine. But this political neophyte showed a conservative streak, opting for Supreme Court Justice John McLean of Ohio as his candidate on the very grounds that McLean had conservative Whig antecedents. Once Fremont gained the nomination, needless to say, Blaine stumped hard for him.

Blaine's prestige had been enhanced no end in Philadelphia, not only due to his usefulness, but because he had been selected as one of the three secretaries of the convention. Back home from Philadelphia, these secretarial skills of the Augusta journalist were soon much in demand. Mini-conventions were being held to choose Republican candidates for local and congressional office. At the state senate convention for Kennebec County, Blaine was made temporary secretary and put in charge of credentials. At another meeting, this time for picking county-wide candidates, such as sheriff and county commissioner, he again was made secretary. The Fourth District Congressional Convention, held in Waterville, saw him on a three-man committee to report, and no doubt *write*, "Resolutions." James G. Blaine had become the Maine G.O.P.'s *indispensable* man.

On July 11, 1856, the state's Republicans held a massive gathering of 1,200 delegates, called "the most energetic, enthusiastic political meeting ever held in Maine." Hannibal Hamlin unanimously received their nomination for governor. He had finally defected from the Democrats in the most dramatic fashion possible—declaring his apostasy in a bravado speech on the floor of the U.S. Senate.

During the spirited campaign that ensued, Blaine's very first public utterance was reported to have occurred at a mass meeting of Franklin County Republicans in the city of Farmington. This area included the birthplace of the Maine G.O.P. and a large crowd had assembled to hear not James G. Blaine, a member of the audience, but one of their heroes, U.S. Senator William Pitt Fessenden, who had made the switch from Whig to Republican. In this instance, once Fessenden failed to appear, calls went out for that "young Blaine feller from Augusta," reputed to have given "some good talks at some o' the caucuses."

Other accounts of his maiden address to a political rally placed Blaine in the farm town of Litchfield in his own Kennebec County. Wherever it happened, he was said to have wowed his audience with the following story. A New Hampshire farmer was trying to sell one of his horses as a racehorse. Because of its supposed speed, he wanted $500. A jockey tried out the steed, then offered $75. After a few moments' thought, the seller finally said, "It's a devil of a drop, but I'll take it." Those rural crowds roared their appreciative laughter and Blaine, who was said to have been terrified of public speaking, was an instant hit on the political circuit.

Success upon success followed for the Maine Republicans. They easily took back the governorship in September when Hamlin swamped Wells, the Democratic incumbent. Although Fremont didn't win the presidency, he carried Maine by far more than the 20,000 votes Blaine had predicted. The Republicans swept the state's congressional seats and the legislature.

The slavery issue had come to be the dominating factor. On the national scene, the Know-Nothings, spurning a Republican alliance, had run their own candidate, ex-President Millard Fillmore, and he had done very poorly. Civic warfare had erupted in Kansas between Free-Soilers and pro-slavers determined to turn the new state their way. The *Kennebec Journal* continually carried ads soliciting "Bread and clothing for Kansas." Its columns rarely failed to thunder against the "Border Ruffians," the pro-South guerrillas infiltrating from Missouri. Blaine, who was secretary of the

"Meeting for the Aid of Kansas Sufferers," took to calling Maine Democrats "Border Ruffians."

Not only in Kansas were Americans coming to blows over this issue. Right in Boston, Blaine's own brother-in-law, Jacob Stanwood, Jr., had been set upon in a hotel lobby in a totally unprovoked attack by a North Carolinian named Bushrod W. Vicks, who beat him with a cane. It was almost a replica of a far more infamous assault on the floor of the U.S. Senate, where a South Carolinian, Congressman Preston Brooks, savagely caned Massachusetts Senator Charles Sumner for an anti-slavery speech he had made. Editor Blaine, writing about both incidents, revealed that what "ruffian Vicks" obviously didn't know was Stanwood's previous longtime sympathy with the South as a conservative Whig, and hopefully now those Whigs who still tried to excuse the South might "be disposed to admit that the Black Republicans [a name fastened on them by their opponents] are doing battle against a tyranny as inexorable as ever cursed the earth." Then, Blaine went on to vituperate, "Preston Brooks has received thirteen canes and two services of plate, to say nothing of the bouquets, the compliments, and the kisses for his chivalrous assault on Mr. Sumner. We expect nothing else than that Bushrod W. Vicks will be sent to Congress by a grateful constituency for his manly courageous attack on Mr. Stanwood...."[10]

Politics did not take up all of Blaine's attention during these hectic years between 1854 and 1857, unless you count any activity of his as pointed toward the career goal he ultimately pursued, even teaching Sunday school for his friend Reverend Webb and raising money for the church. Consider the Sunday school teaching. In his campaign hagiography, Russell H. Conwell has him doing mission work in Augusta's worst slum, the "People's Hall," which the author likened to the notorious "Devil's Half-acre" of Bangor, where woodsmen and sailors indulged their taste for liquor and wild women. "The entire moral atmosphere of People's Hall and its surroundings were changed," Conwell would have us believe, by Blaine's lecturing.[11]

Similarly, Blaine's panegyric to Luther Severance was no doubt heartfelt, a tribute to a much-admired, older role model—editor, office holder, and diplomat—who had recently died of cancer and been mourned and lionized by the city of Augusta. But publishing a memoir of Severance under his by-line could also be seen as a clever political act on Blaine's part.

Ostensibly, James G. Blaine was still a newspaperman. And he was even thinking of moving up in the profession. On August 10, 1857, he wrote to his mother, "In case Walker gets through his sickness comfortably and H. [Harriet] and the baby remain in good condition, it is not improbable that I shall go to Portland in a few weeks to edit a daily paper."[12] The big-time—at least in Maine journalism—was beckoning. The owner of the *Portland Advertiser*, Republican Congressman John M. Wood, wanted Blaine for his editor-in-chief and was willing to pay him $2,000 a year, then the largest salary offered a Maine editor. Also, Blaine could continue to keep his family in Augusta and spend his weekends with them. It was an offer James G. Blaine could not refuse.

1. Maria Gillespie Blaine to James G. Blaine, Christmas Eve 1852, as quoted in Hamilton, p. 96.
2. H. Draper Hunt. *The Blaine House, Home of Maine's Governors* (Augusta, ME: Friends of the Blaine House, 1994), p. 5.
3. Boyd, p. 82.
4. Edward Stanwood. *James Gillespie Blaine* (Boston: Houghton, Mifflin and Co.), 1905, p. 29.
5. *Kennebec Journal*, 10 November 1854, p. 2, col. 2.
6. Ibid.
7. As quoted in Stanwood, p. 43.
8. Stanwood, p. 37.
9. Willard C. King. *Melville W. Fuller, Chief Justice of the United States, 1888–1910* (New York: The MacMillan Company, 1950), p. 13.
10. Hamilton, p. 118.
11. Russell Conwell. *Life and Public Service of James G. Blaine* (Augusta, ME: E. C. Allen and Co., 1884), p. 89.
12. JGB to Maria Gillespie Blaine, 10 August 1857; Hamilton, p. 129.

FIVE

~~~

ELECTED

A S MAINE'S HIGHEST-PAID professional journalist in the years
1857–58, James G. Blaine faced a personal dilemma. A letter to his mother, during the Christmas season of 1857,
outlined the problem. Should he relocate to Portland, as his em-
ployers at the *Portland Advertiser* were lightly but persistently pres-
suring him to do? "I spend about one-half the week in Portland and
the remainder at home," he wrote his "Dear Ma," and he could get
a large part of his editorial work done without having to be in the
newspaper office. He had thought "a good deal about moving" but
didn't think he would. "Rents are enormously high and expenses
of living higher in every way than here." Although Portland, with a
population of about 30,000, was a beautiful city with many attractive places to live, he admitted, "I think, however, that upon the
whole I prefer the quiet and refinement of Augusta."

His election in September 1858 as one of two state representatives from Augusta did make a difference in his situation vis-à-vis
the Portland daily. He now had to pay for a substitute while the
legislature was in session, plus provide three leading editorials or
letters to the editor each week. A new contract in 1860 required
him to produce three leading editorials *and* one letter each week
while serving, and receive no more than $12 a week in pay. Behind
the scenes a strong effort was underway to pressure Blaine into re-
suming his full-time position. On August 15, 1860, Blaine received a
letter from Senator William Pitt Fessenden, who was a Portland resident. Part threat, part plea, Fessenden's missive informed Blaine
that "The publishers and owners of the *Advertiser* have made up
their minds, at last, that they must adopt a new system." Cutting
to the chase, he then demanded, "Now, can you and will you
become identified with Portland?"[1] If so, Fessenden intimated, he
could get him the permanent editorial job.

James G. Blaine at twenty-eight. This was four years after he arrived in Maine and was beginning to make a name for himself. He had been elected that year to the Maine legislature from Augusta and, despite his young age, was becoming a force in the Maine Republican party. In 1858 he was still also serving as editor of the Portland Advertiser, *following his work on the* Kennebec Journal. *The beginning of the Civil War two years later found him as an indispensable aide to Governor Elihu Washburn's war effort, although he has been pictured in that era as having no beard.*
HAMILTON, *BIOGRAPHY OF JAMES G. BLAINE*

That Blaine's final answer was no certainly wouldn't have surprised anyone. In the 1860 session of the legislature, the two-term representative from Augusta had to fight off one of those stubborn—if sporadic—attempts by Portland legislators to remove the capital back to their city. The pretext in 1860 was that Portland was building a new city hall, which could easily be expanded to house state government. Gail Hamilton has emphasized that his brief flirtation with Portland did not in any way "invalidate the vigor with which, whenever an attempt was made to take away the capitol from Augusta and give it to Portland, he opposed it tooth and nail"[2]

Even before his first election, James G. Blaine was almost a quasi-legislator, considering the time he spent in the statehouse, on Republican politics, and on special legislative-style missions. In this latter regard, the dry language of a report in *Maine Public Documents 1859, Legislature* masks a state government scandal that Blaine quietly helped repair. The governor at the time was Lot M. Morrill, and his response to a legislative resolve creating a commissioner to investigate conditions at the state prison was to appoint Blaine to that temporary post. The job paid $4 a day plus expenses, and he had to report back by February 1, 1859, and cover three issues: enlargement of the facility at Thomaston, payment of debts "long since contracted," and determination of whether the system of labor and discipline there could be run on a self-sustaining basis.

Later, as a freshman member of the house, Blaine heard Governor Morrill refer to his finished report in the chief executive's message of February 11, 1859.

No punches had been pulled. The governor quoted language such as: "The dilapidated condition of some of these buildings is a public disgrace." Overcrowding was a distinct problem. So was the prison's large annual deficit. Plans for spending $13,000 on reconstruction were shown to be woefully inadequate and would require anywhere from $70,000–$80,000.

Not mentioned by the governor was more damning information that Blaine had dug up regarding a plethora of "bad management, wastefulness, and 'cooked' accounts." Overpayments were so bad that the cost of feeding the prisoners, if divided by the number of prisoners, would come to an obscene figure. Blaine's report also contained cost comparisons with other state prisons. The upshot was a swift change of wardens and managers.

The other Augusta representative elected with Blaine in 1858 was William T. Johnson, another of those Republicans with Democratic antecedents. Johnson had once published the *Bangor Democrat* and in Augusta, published *The Age* and not until 1856 did he sell *The Age* to the Fullers. Because he had served as clerk of the house in 1842, 1843, and 1844, knew so many of the representatives, and had the necessary administrative skills and experience, he was made speaker for the year 1859.

Blaine would not lag far behind him in being voted into the presiding officer's spot. Nor, in this, his first run for office, had he lagged far behind the veteran Johnson's vote—a difference of only twenty-seven votes, and an easy win for them both over two Democrats. One wonders if Blaine, given his omnivorous interest in politics, took note of an item printed in the Augusta paper on November 5, 1858, following the elections in the rest of the country. From New York State it was reported: "Utica, Nov. 2. Roscoe Conkling, Republican, is elected to Congress in the 20th District." Who could have dreamed of the future clash in Congress that was in the making? As the story goes, Conkling, a bruiser of a man and a boxer, had been recruited in part to prevent future physical attacks by Southerners, like that of "Bully" Brooks on Senator Sumner. In 1858 the Maine Republicans, despite such great progress in a very short time, were not quite completely entrenched. Neal Dow's debacle in Portland had hurt them statewide, notwithstanding the *Kennebec Journal's* spin on that incident as "the deliberated plan preconcerted by the rum party, with the design of breaking down the authority of Mayor Dow." Now, suddenly, during Blaine's first term in the legislature, another scandal broke, also connected to Neal Dow, and one that loomed as an even more significant detriment for the new party in power.

State treasurers in Maine were then and still are elected by the majority party in the legislature. Benjamin D. Peck owed his job of managing the state's finances to the Republican sweep that accompanied Hannibal Hamlin's victory in September 1856. The Reverend Mr. Peck—he was an elder of an obscure Protestant denomination—had also been editor of a publication, the *Maine Temperance Watchman,* and had even more clout from his being head of the Temperance Watchman's Control Committee, commanding a "Brotherhood" of 5,000 "dries" and Know-Nothings. Out on the campaign trail, Peck, often in concert with Neal Dow, fulminated against "Rum, Hunkerism, Catholicism, and Corruption." In

1857 he began his work at the state treasury, and right off the bat ignored a state law passed in the previous session that made it illegal for the state treasurer to lend state funds to private citizens.

Allegedly on the advice of Neal Dow, who told him just to get good security for the loans, Peck kept giving out sums to individual borrowers, most of whom were cronies of his. Dow, himself, took out a loan of $8,000, which he subsequently paid back. A rather dicey moment for Peck occurred in October 1858 when a Republican congressman-elect, Daniel E. Somes from Biddeford, went bankrupt still owing money to the state.

It helped Peck that Dow had been elected to the legislature in 1858 and made a member of the finance committee. After a perfunctory look at Peck's department, that body gave the state treasurer's office a clean bill of health.

But finally the roof fell in on Peck. Along with several Bangor businessmen, he sank a good deal of state money into timberlands and a sawmill project in Canada. The Bangor investors had provided worthless personal notes and bills embezzled from the Norumbega Bank. When this institution collapsed in October 1859, Peck's outlay of $100,000 was revealed. Also exposed was Neal Dow's new debt of $11,500.

On January 2, 1860, Governor Lot M. Morrill proclaimed State Treasurer Benjamin D. Peck to be a public defaulter and the Republican legislative leaders, covering themselves, rushed to create a "Joint Select Committee on the Defalcation of Benjamin D. Peck." Blaine was chosen to head its contingent of house members and doubtlessly instructed privately to orchestrate the smart political moves that would prevent the scandal from exploding.

Right away, Blaine, his co-chair State Senator Josiah H. Drummond, and another house member rushed to Bangor to interview Peck, who had been jailed in connection with the Norumbega Bank collapse. The special Select Committee also worked fast to lay its hands on Peck's papers, some of which had already had been spirited away by Neal Dow.

Yet, before long, the Drummond-Blaine leadership was to be accused of dragging its feet. "Where is its report?" complained the *Bangor Daily Union,* whose editor Marcellus Emery was a well-known Democrat. Emery baldly charged the investigation would be spun out to the next legislature "in order that the Black Republican party may not have the damning record to contend against during the Presidential campaign [of 1860]." Furthermore, the *Bangor Daily Union* charged, "Peck had used thousands of dollars of the State's money in the Congressional Campaign of 1858." Several instances and amounts were cited, including loans to congressman-elect Somes.

One can sense how astute a politico James G. Blaine could be in his reaction to this inflammatory charge. Editor Emery was hauled up before the committee and forced to admit his information was all "mere rumor." Next came a strong denial from Republican Congressman James S. Pike of the Sixth District that Peck had ever sent him $1,000, as had been reported by the press. The committee apologized for the lateness of its report and offered the excuse that its fifty sessions had produced a hundred pages of testimony. Because the committee took on an appropriately stern tone of disapproval and began by acknowledging that "Public confidence has been shocked by the shameless defalcation of the Treasurer," Neal Dow, whose dreams of eventual high office in the state had been shattered by the revelation of his role, grumped that it was a "malignant report."

Lost in the general obfuscation of a drama thus artfully strung out was the fact that Peck never did go to jail over his deliberate lawbreaking. except for a few days in connection with the Norumbega Bank failure. Nor did the state receive all its money back until years later, thanks to a vigorous effort by Attorney General Thomas Brackett Reed.

For deftly shoving this matter under carefully stage-managed wraps, freshman Representative Blaine received a fitting reward. The party leaders made him chairman of the Republican State Committee in place of John L. Stevens, with whom they weren't happy. Tactfully, Blaine let his friend and former business partner finish out the campaign year on a winning note before he firmly took over the reins in 1859, so firmly he didn't relinquish them until 1881.

Re-elected easily in 1859, James G. Blaine gathered ever more political experience, learning to deal with the threats and opportunities offered by the constant play of events within a legislative and political ambiance. In short, he was on his way, before the age of thirty, to becoming a pro, and the presidential election of 1860 gave him a real chance to prove his mettle.

At the Republicans' Philadelphia convention in 1856, Abraham Lincoln of Illinois had come in second during the balloting for vice president, while losing to William Dayton of New Jersey. There is no indication that Lincoln attended this first of the new party's major gatherings. But Blaine was present and the name Lincoln would certainly have stuck in his mind. Two years afterward, the *Portland Advertiser* sent him on assignment to cover one of the Lincoln-Douglass debates in Illinois. The young reporter/politician came away singularly impressed by his fellow Republican's performance.

Participating in another G.O.P. convention, this time in Chicago in May 1860, and with Lincoln a contender, Blaine had decided to back the lanky lawyer. His "druthers," he said, would have been Maine's own William Pitt Fessenden, and as state party leader, he worked hard to convince the Portlander to run as a favorite son. Some speculation is that Blaine, being Machiavellian, was merely seeking to keep a majority of the Maine delegation from voting on the first ballot for William Seward. Fessenden declined to speak at public meetings in the state to generate support, however, and the effort totally floundered, whereupon Blaine went full out, trying to break away Seward votes for Lincoln.

He also traveled to Chicago with the delegation, although not an official member of it. As an active lobbyist for Lincoln, he sought to convince his fellow Maine Republican party leaders that Seward might carry Maine but could not carry the country. Governor Lot M. Morrill was a special target of Blaine's and on the train ride out west, he did manage to convince the state's chief executive to back the "Railsplitter."

A letter of Blaine's tells of this episode in his own words. "Governor Morrill and myself worked hard for Lincoln from the time we reached Chicago and you may depend we feel no little gratification from the result. All the way out in the cars I tried to persuade Lot that Lincoln was the man, but he would not believe it until after he reached Chicago." They siphoned off a mere six out of Maine's sixteen votes, but even this small undermining of the Northeast's expected almost uniform support for Seward had a strong psychological effect. Following Lincoln's win, Hannibal Hamlin's nomination as vice president had to have been a surprise, although it was interpreted as a move to reward Maine's effort. More likely, balancing Lincoln, the Midwesterner and former Whig, with Hamlin, the former Democrat and a New Englander, outweighed any other consideration. Blaine, in his letter about the G.O.P. conclave, called Hamlin "a lucky man," explaining, "He always turns up on the winning side and the very fact he is on the ticket is a good augury of success."

The recipient of that letter is not identified. Its date was May 20, 1860, and the postmark, Springfield, Illinois. "I came here yesterday from Chicago," Blaine wrote, "in coming with the committee appointed by the National Convention to notify Mr. Lincoln of his nomination." A tremendous crowd met the group at the depot, conducted the visitors to the Chenery Hotel, "treated [us] to a handsome supper" and then, at Lincoln's home, the chairman, a Mr. Ashmun from Massachusetts made the formal presentation. Lincoln responded with his formal acceptance, "a most admirable, pertinent and brief speech," in Blaine's words. Blaine's reporter's eye was out for details during the reception where everyone met the candidate and his wife. Mary Todd Lincoln was described as "a very lady-like and quite good-looking person." Honest Abe, it seemed, was a good deal handsomer than his caricature in the newspapers. "While a very awkward-looking man, you realize at once that it is the awkwardness of genius rather than any proof of the lack of it."[3]

John L. Stevens was supposedly so upset by his candidate Seward's loss and Blaine's role in undermining the New Yorker in favor of Lincoln that he turned on him rather viciously back in Maine. The alleged dialogue was: "Here, you have got your man [Lincoln]. Now, take your d____d paper [the *Kennebec Journal*] and run it."[4]

To be sure, three years earlier Blaine had ceased being Stevens's partner in the ownership and management of the Augusta paper. Stevens had his own partner, John S. Sprague. But in December 1859, Blaine did publicly announce his resignation from the *Portland Advertiser*. It is possible he resumed some editorial duties at the *KJ*. Gail Hamilton swore he did, "much, it must be admitted, to Mr. Blaine's satisfaction, since it left him free to resume and use the *Journal* battering ram through the Lincoln campaign."[5]

Blaine worked like a demon to get Lincoln and the whole Republican ticket elected in Maine that fall. By then, he had fully taken over the Republican State Committee from John L. Stevens and was completely in charge of local and national campaigns in the state. Even prior to leaving for Chicago, he had organized a Republican Club in Augusta and become its president. Every Thursday evening these activists met in the hall on top of Deering and Turner's Store and Blaine would whip up the enthusiasm of the mostly young men present with bristling attacks on Democrats, especially Stephen Douglass, whom he saw as their opponents' prime candidate against Lincoln and whom he assailed as the politician "foremost in striking down the Missouri Compromise." Under his guidance, other such clubs began forming across the state.

He was also finding out what internal party politics could be like. There was a real shocker at the G.O.P. district nominating conventions for Congress. All six incumbent Republican congressmen were denied re-election! Some big names, like Anson P. Morrill, Frederick Pike, and Samuel Fessenden (brother of the U.S. senator) went down. Most vocal was Congressman Freeman H. Morse of Bath who bitterly blamed Blaine, although the rotation of seats among counties—an old Maine tradition—was probably the biggest reason for this unpleasant surprise. Trying to placate Morse, Blaine promised to find him a sinecure in D.C. if the G.O.P. won the national election. Morse's snide response was that he'd rather "go fishing for a living...than to gain a place by any of the Augusta junto."

The results of the September and November Maine elections made this bickering fade. Blaine led his party to impressive victories. In the governor's race, Lot Morrill hadn't sought re-election—his eye was on the U.S. senatorial seat, which would be vacated if

Hannibal Hamlin were elected vice president—and Congressman Israel Washburn, Jr., was persuaded to leave Washington and become the Republican standard bearer. He won easily in September, chalking up a margin of 17,000 votes. The G.O.P. possession of the Maine State Legislature was extraordinary: in the house, 127 Republicans versus 24 Democrats; in the state senate, percentage wise, they were even more dominant.

Maine's September Republican triumph spun off spontaneous public celebrations in New York and Illinois. The Lincoln campaign saw it as an excellent sign for their prospects. And despite poor weather in November, holding down voter turnout, Maine gave the G.O.P. a 24,000-vote advantage in capturing the state's eight electoral votes.

As the chief engineer of these campaigns, directing funds, arranging speakers, assisting candidates in the petty details of politicking, James G. Blaine had earned tremendous respect among his peers. His judgment might be resisted, but he was in the driver's seat as head of the Republican State Committee.

This had to be a heady time for the thirty-year-old Pennsylvanian. On top of his political triumph, the father of two had become the father of a third child. His two boys, Walker and Emmons, "...two as beautiful children as in the fondness of my heart I could possibly desire," were thriving and now the first girl, Alice, had appeared. He had no way of knowing his brood would eventually double to six, three of each sex, but a happy, fulfilling family life, thanks to Harriet, was something he could take for granted. They were still living at the Stanwoods' old home on Green Street, in a seven-room section of that big house, with the added luxury of built-in help from the maiden aunts and a domestic servant or two. Best of all, James G. Blaine had the freedom to concentrate heavily on his budding political career.

Right from the start, he had tricky issues to deal with in Augusta. The Lincoln-Hamlin victory did, indeed, leave a U.S. Senate seat to be filled by the votes of the Republican legislative majority. Lot M. Morrill had the edge, but at the start there were other candidates. The strongest would have been Israel Washburn, Jr., the governor-elect, had he stayed in the race. The stubbornest was Freeman H. Morse, the disgruntled ex-congressman. Blaine's vote was not recorded, yet arguably he would have gone for Morrill, his companion in the Lincoln fight and the odds-on favorite.

Another dicey problem was how to handle "personal liberty laws." Simply put, "personal liberty laws" were measures passed in Northern states to stymie the Fugitive Slave Act, that much-hated piece of federal legislation aimed at recapturing escaped slaves. Because Blaine had been elected speaker of the house by his colleagues when the legislature convened in January 1861, he became a key player, along with Governor Washburn, in a subtle drama connected with efforts to mollify the South and keep the slave states infuriated by Lincoln's election from seceding.

Blaine's role in these maneuverings just prior to the Civil War was, to state it charitably, extremely agile. Maine's first personal liberty law, "An Act Further to Protect Personal Liberty" had been passed in 1855. It forbade sheriffs, jailers, judges, and others, from helping to capture or detain fugitive slaves or return them to their owners, and the penalty for non-compliance was a $1,000 fine and/or a possible jail term. But deeming even this measure too weak, Maine lawmakers two years later toughened it by allowing county district attorneys to provide legal assistance to escaped slaves at state expense and forbidding local sheriffs to hold such prisoners in their jails or municipal judges to hear such cases.

Under federal law, these state-mandated obstructions were clearly unconstitutional. Southerners were livid about this Northern form of nullification. Having attained enough power to control the federal Congress, executive, and judiciary, the slave owners weren't about to let "States Rights" in the North trump their efforts to maintain slavery in its full rigor. Southern demands that all Northern personal liberty laws be repealed had been a strong issue during the 1860 presidential campaign. Lincoln's victory threatened that effort, but some Republicans were uncomfortable with the charge of "unconstitutionality," as well as willing to placate the Southerners so stirred up by Lincoln's triumph.

In Maine, Democratic newspapers like the *Eastern Argus* argued that repeal "would have a decided effect to allay excitement in the South and would very much strengthen Mr. Lincoln's hands in meeting the revolutionary movements." The Republican organs were either opposed outright to repeal—like the Blaine-connected *Kennebec Journal* and *Portland Advertiser*—on the grounds of protecting trial by jury and the writ of habeas corpus, or only willing to swap repeal for softening of the Fugitive Slave Act. The issue was clouded by Lincoln's action on December 30, 1860, when the president-elect took the position that "all unconstitutional state laws should be repealed" to help preserve the federal Union.

One may speculate that a bit of a charade was concocted in Maine. It was known that Governor Washburn and U.S. Senators Fessenden and Morrill, were not in favor of repeal nor did it seem likely the G.O.P. rank and file would support any move that drastic.

Thus, when the legislature opened on January 3, 1861, Governor Washburn's address asked for a "candid examination of the laws of the State." If any were in violation of the U.S. Constitution, they should be repealed. However, he insisted, to repeal laws just to make a concession was unthinkable. Less than a month later, in his new capacity as speaker of the house, James G. Blaine formally requested the Maine Supreme Court to review Maine's personal liberty laws as to their constitutionality. "But he (Blaine) assured Governor Washburn that he could check the repeal movement quietly but effectively." So wrote Michael Winters Whalon in his dissertation "Maine Republicans, 1854-1866: A Study in Growth and Political Power."[6]

In their decisions, the eight justices of the Maine Supreme Court were all over the place—presenting five different opinions regarding the four laws on the Maine books. On two of the four, they were unanimous there was no unconstitutionality. On another, the no vote was 5-3. The only one to receive an opposite majority opinion, 5-3, was the statute that prohibited a state official from aiding a federal marshal.

Legislative votes were finally taken in March 1861. The Maine Senate did support repeal, so the final drama was in the House. As if to continue his camouflage in high style, Speaker Blaine came down from the rostrum to argue for repeal. His eloquence usually carried all before him. But not in this case. The honor went to Representative William H. McCrillis of Bangor who spoke for an hour against repeal. The final vote was 47 in favor of repeal and 67 opposed and 37 not voting, thus bearing out Blaine's boast to Washburn that he would kill the thing "with relative ease."[7]

It was a moot issue, anyway. Coddling the South was no longer an urgent matter. Seven Southern states had already seceded. Fort Sumter was under siege in Charleston Harbor. Within three days, if he could get to Washington, D.C., safely, Abraham Lincoln would take his place as the president of the United States.

---

1. Hamilton, p. 125.
2. Ibid., p. 124.
3. Ibid., p. 129.
4. Ibid.
5. Ibid., pp. 129–30.
6. Michael Winters Whalon. "Maine Republicans, 1854–1866: A Study in Growth and Political Power." (Lincoln, NE: University of Nebraska, Ph.D. dissertation), p. 94.
7. Ibid.

SIX

CIVIL WAR

W HEN GOVERNOR ISRAEL WASHBURN, JR., addressed the Fortieth Maine Legislature on January 3, 1861, he had other issues to discuss in addition to personal liberty laws and attempts to avoid secession.

There was still a need to look at the state prison, he told the lawmakers. Also, the northeast corner of the state—Aroostook County, in particular—had to be developed and tied closer to the rest of Maine. To settle those unpopulated spaces, some of it very good farmland, he suggested bringing over Norwegian farmers who, he said, were used to weather so cold they would think the land on the Canadian border "tropical." (In time, it was the Swedes who were actually brought in). A railroad to Aroostook seemed necessary, too.

Almost four months later, on April 22, he summoned the legislators again to focus on preparing Maine for war. Eight days previously, Fort Sumter had surrendered. Already, Lincoln's call was out for troops to subdue the seven Southern states that had seceded (four more would join them) and the Northern states were rallying to the cause. Justifying this special meeting of the legislature, Washburn reported "a requisition has been made upon me by the president of the United States for a portion of the Militia of this State, to aid in suppressing" what he characterized as "a combination too powerful to be suppressed by the ordinary course of judicial proceedings." By this he meant the actions of South Carolina, Georgia, Alabama, Florida, Mississippi, Louisiana, and Texas in defying the laws of the United States.

His peroration ended with a demand for bipartisanship and unity. Washburn was short (five foot, six inches), bespectacled, dynamic, and stirring words spilled easily from this son of a prolific

Livermore, Maine, farm family that sent four of its offspring to Congress. "Then the divisions of party will disappear from amongst us, and the names by which we have been recognized will be forgotten and all will be known as patriots and defenders of the Union...and this Union is to be defended and the Constitution preserved, not by Democrats, not by Republicans, but by men who love their country—and all men of whatever party, who are for the government and will stand by it, and fight for it as brethren."

On cue, as soon as the governor had finished and he and his retinue had retired, up stood Representative Albert Gould, the Democratic leader of fewer than twenty-five elected members and asked for unanimous consent "to introduce a resolution which I doubt not will meet a response in every heart...." His words were stirring, too: "...in imitation of our Fathers, 'we pledge our lives, our fortunes and our sacred honor' to the preservation of that Government which they committed to us that we may transmit it unbroken to our children."

The *House Journal* then records, "The Convention, by rising, signified unanimously the passage of the resolve."

Another example of this type of accord was the warm reception given Democrat Dr. B. F. Buxton of Warren when he resigned from the house to become the surgeon for a regiment of volunteers. It was Buxton who, at the beginning of the session in January before the war started, had been the token opponent the minority had put up, as was traditional, to challenge James G. Blaine for speaker. He'd gotten 23 votes to 121 for Blaine. A well-respected man, Buxton often served as speaker pro-tem, presiding over the house when Blaine was absent or wished to step down from the rostrum to speak.

The Democrats in Maine, as at the national level, soon split into two camps—"War Democrats," like Buxton, and those who supported a negotiated peace with the South and duly received the unflattering nickname of "copperheads," after those poisonous reptiles Blaine had known in Appalachia. Sensing an opportunity to deepen the rift, Blaine, in 1862, converted his Republicans into the Union party, amalgamating with those Democrats who supported Lincoln's policy of not yielding to the Confederacy.

But why didn't Blaine follow Dr. Buxton's example, give up his seat, and volunteer for the Yankee armed forces? He was just thirty years old. Forever his defender, Gail Hamilton explained, "Concerning Mr. Blaine, there was never any question of his battlefield. The soldiers themselves drafted him into the support and sustenance of the army...."[1]

Or at least as Governor Washburn's right-hand man, Blaine was soon traveling the eastern half of the North, in the capacity of a quartermaster general—shades of his great grandfather—supplying the arms, uniforms, and gear the Maine regiments needed. As for the draft law, his compliance was perfectly legal: he paid a substitute to take his place in the ranks. After the war, when chided by opponents for his failure to fight, he was unapologetic, except, he said, for having hired a Democrat who promptly deserted.

This entire supply operation was a hasty, hurry-up improvisation. Troops needed to be raised immediately and sent south, if nothing else, to protect Washington, D.C. Governor Washburn had to make snap decisions and his first official act in a military capacity came when Albert W. Paine, a Bangor lawyer, telegraphed him and asked what to do about a company of volunteers in that city who had formed spontaneously. Washburn telegraphed back, "Rendezvous the troops and the State will pay."

Yet someone had to find the rifles, the clothing, the tents, and all the other equipment this body of soldiers would need—a task made more difficult in that every other Northern state faced the same task and there were only so many suppliers. In Maine's case, Washburn instinctively turned to James G. Blaine.

On April 25, 1861, three days after the legislature's joint convention in Augusta, Blaine was in Boston. He telegraphed Maine Militia General Davis Tillson, "Will forward the blankets by tonight's boat. Overcoats and pants will be ready by Monday. Look out for shirts that will arrive in Portland." On the road right afterward, Blaine reached Springfield, Massachusetts, on April 26. His message read, "380 Minie Rifles will be in Portland tomorrow evening. I will be in Boston at 2 P.M." From there, this string of telegrams continued. The first, still on April 26, was, "350 rifle muskets have gone down on the afternoon train. Have telegraphed to

Springfield for the remaining 30." On April 27 Blaine imparted the further intelligence that "800 revolvers, 250,000 percussion caps, 24,000 Colts cartridges go down by express this afternoon."

These exchanges between Maine's man in the field and Augusta at the end of April and beginning of May 1861, continued apace because, as usual, nothing went according to plan. Blaine was staying at Boston's Tremont House when he learned that only 464 overcoats, 826 pants, and 74 infantry caps and coats had been received in Maine up until 11 A.M., Monday, May 1. He fired back that all the caps had been sent on Monday and the rest of the overcoats by "car and boat."

Because of these foul-ups, Blaine informed Governor Washburn it was best for him to stay in Boston until the following week. On April 27 the harried speaker of the house on assignment was seeking the chief executive's advice on which steamship line to use, Fall River or Stonington, for shipping material north 1,600 flannel shirts and drawers—and, did Washburn want blankets from a manufacturer named Burleigh of Berwick, Maine? Let him know at the Tremont House. "You have no idea of the competition here in all kinds of manufactured goods…Tents for the 1st. Regiment have to be supplied in Maine. There are none in Massachusetts."

Politics, too, intruded. Governor John A. Andrew of Massachusetts was urging a steamship of Maine troops to appear in Boston the following Monday night and join Massachusetts troops, both to go to Annapolis, Maryland, "as a measure of safety." (Maryland's loyalty was seriously in doubt and, indeed, Massachusetts troops, marching through Baltimore en route to D.C. later, engaged in a firefight with Confederate sympathizers.) Were this done, Blaine advised Washburn, he, himself, should come to Boston with the detachment and gain political points by standing next to Governor Andrew and jointly addressing the assembled men in arms. "Answer immediately," Blaine urged.

Glitches also occurred in his contacts with the governor. An annoyed Blaine fired off a telegram to Washburn on April 29, saying he had started negotiating with the Stonington Line, only to find out that a Captain Gardiner had started contracting with the Fall River Line. "How is this?" he snippily demanded.

But the biggest aggravation Blaine had to suffer concerned a Lieutenant Cartwright, whom he was recommending for a position with the Maine forces. On April 24, already in Boston, he had telegraphed Governor Washburn: "Lieutenant Cartwright of this city is most experienced in the Army-drill and such a man as he would be invaluable in training our new recruits. If desired, his services are at your call. You can telegraph me in regard to this matter. I advise you to secure him."

Less than a week later, on May 1, a letter Blaine sent Washburn on the Cartwright matter had a decidedly unhappy tone. The governor was reminded Lieutenant Cartwright belonged to "one of the most respected and wealthy families in Boston" and he, Blaine, "was surprised at the [poor] reception given him in Augusta." Having been told by the governor's office to "Have Cartwright or some other good officer for drilling come here immediately," he had had the young officer hurry off to Maine. The next sentence tells the rest of the story: "I was very greatly surprised and mortified last evening by the sudden and unceremonious return of Lieutenant Cartwright from Augusta." For emphasis, Blaine added the matter was of "no small chagrin to him." Yet the final paragraph showed the politician still at work. "I shall be at home as soon as you receive this letter probably and if anything can be done to relieve the awkwardness of matters as they stand, I shall ask as a personal favor to me that it be done."[2]

There had always been some underlying tensions between Blaine and Washburn, despite the conventional picture of them as a closely working pair of allies, not only at the opening of the Civil War but in Republican affairs even prior to the conflict. One of Washburn's biographers, Gaillard Hunt,[3] made it obvious he wasn't fond of James G. Blaine. Hunt saw him as deceptive, self-serving, unscrupulous, and, most damning of all, an obstacle to Israel Washburn, Jr.'s, rise to the highest echelons of the Republican Party.

Hunt dwells on Blaine's penchant for secrecy in written documents and includes samples, like one going back to the 1856 presidential campaign: "Please destroy the Fremont letter." And he includes an elaborate flim-flam concocted by Blaine, spelled out in a letter to Washburn, also in 1856. Blaine, then still the young editor at the *Kennebec Journal*, was trying to get a letter sent to him in confidence placed in Horace Greeley's *New York Tribune*, and he didn't want it revealed he had "outed" a private letter. The substance of the maneuver had to do with an attack, which would be reprinted in Maine, on local "Straight Whigs" who had refused to join with Republicans. For author Hunt, the real substance was Blaine's Machiavellian instincts.

With another of Blaine's communications to Washburn of that period, Hunt had an even better, less complicated example of perceived skulduggery. He printed in full a letter of Blaine's dated December 16, 1857, and accompanied its inclusion with these prefaced remarks: "He [Washburn] was still cooperating in a general way with Blaine; but if he did not form a high opinion of the rising young editor, he had reason. The session [in Congress] had hardly begun when he received the following communication."[4]

It concerned a nephew of Harriet's. The boy wanted an appointment to West Point and there was a vacancy. Would Washburn appoint him? The aspirant had spent the past summer and autumn in Greenville, Maine, then part of Congressman Washburn's district and, as Blaine put it, "He is therefore a quasi if not an entirely bona fide resident...." Blaine had added, "I am willing to do anything to secure the place for him either in the way of buying off all rivals at any reasonable price or complying with any conditions that may possibly be linked with success...." A sum of $300 or $400 was mentioned. Author Hunt's stated conclusion was, "It cannot be denied that the letter leaves on the reader's mind an ugly impression of Mr. Blaine," and laconically, he continued, "Mrs. Blaine's nephew was not nominated for West Point by Washburn."

From then on, according to Hunt, there was one thing after another, including the charge that Blaine didn't initially support Washburn for governor in 1860, instead backing Abner Coburn, the richest man in Maine, albeit lukewarmly; and that after Washburn's easy victory for the nomination at the Republican Convention, Blaine then turned his back on Washburn's ambition to have the U.S. Senate seat vice president-elect Hamlin would vacate. "He [Washburn] did not become a candidate for the Senate but he would have done so had the times been more propitious. They were not so, Morrill and Blaine being in league, and Blaine being the chairman of the Republican State Committee."[5]

Not mentioned by Hunt is the fact that a year before, Hannibal Hamlin had pulled off a similar stunt—coming from D.C. to run for governor, serving but a short time, then getting himself elected to the U.S. Senate. This transparent place-swapping had drawn severe criticism. For Washburn to do so again could have hurt the Republicans and been fodder for opponents and Washburn was no fool. He deferred to Lot Morrill, probably telling himself he could try for the big prize in Washington at a later date.

Hannibal Hamlin was Maine's most popular politician throughout Blaine's early years in the Pine Tree State. Initially a Democrat, he made a dramatic switch to the Republicans on the floor of the U.S. Senate, the critical issue for him being slavery. He was then chosen to run with Lincoln and became his first vice president. Off the ballot in 1864, he returned to Maine and the U.S. Senate and teamed up with Blaine to control the Republican party Down East.
RIDPATH, *LIFE AND WORKS OF JAMES G. BLAINE*

Beyond any doubt, Governor Washburn leaned heavily on Blaine to backstop his own energetic contributions to Maine's war effort. A long letter of October 1861 from the governor in Augusta to Blaine in D.C. not only details the bewildering minutiae the chief executive had to deal with all across the board but how his partnership with Blaine worked, for example:

"Stoves are now much needed, as cold weather is coming on. Telegraph me—remember the net expense will not exceed, hardly come to, $3.50, including stove and pipe."

"Advise me of the proper steps to draw money for payment of the horses and clothing."

"Cavalry regiment is full, though about 100 men have not yet come into camp. I can move it in two weeks if it only has arms. Can you get them?"

"Will you see how Colonel Berry is satisfied with the arms of his regiment...?"

"I would like to have you visit all our Maine camps and report conditions."

A typically political request concerned a Colonel Marshall of the Seventh Maine. His forces had constructed a fort in Baltimore and Washburn thought it would be "exceedingly gratifying to the people of this State and particularly to Mrs. Marshall" if the fort could be named for Colonel Marshall. "Will you speak to the Secretary about it?" That is, to Secretary of War Simon Cameron.

Political favors, patronage, promotion—the onset of war certainly tended to increase the opportunities. Blaine, thwarted in the case of Lieutenant Cartwright, did much better with another of his military recommendations to Governor Washburn. He had met West Pointer and career officer Oliver Otis Howard of Leeds, Maine, when the latter was on pre-war duty at the Augusta Armory and Blaine was still an editor. They became strong friends once Blaine became speaker of the Maine House and sponsored a bill to allow children who lived on the arsenal grounds to go to "common" (public) schools in the state. While still speaker, in the middle of May 1861, Blaine sent his friend Howard a short telegram: "Will you, if elected, accept the colonelcy of the Kennebec Regiment?" Telegraphing back, Howard, then teaching at West Point, answered yes, and was informed on May 29 that he'd been unanimously chosen to head Maine's Third Regiment. Off to Augusta hurried Howard and he was soon meeting in the State House with Washburn and Blaine.

In Howard's autobiography, published after his distinguished career as "the praying general" of the Civil War and western Indian fighting, and, most of all, in consideration of his service to ex-slaves as head of the Freedmen's Bureau during Reconstruction (Howard University is named for him), there is an exceptionally good physical description of Blaine at this period.

The youthful colonel—he had just been promoted from lieutenant—was taking his seat in Governor Washburn's office when, in his words, "a young man with a brisk, business-like air opened the door and entered without ceremony...." After some dialogue, a full description ensued:

"This energetic visitor was James G. Blaine. One could hardly find a more striking character. His figure was good—nearly six feet and well-proportioned; his hair, what you could see of it under his soft hat pushed far back, was a darkish brown. It showed the disorder due to sundry thrusts of the fingers. His coat, a little big, was partially buttoned. This, with the collar, shirt front and necktie, had the negligée air of a dress never thought of after the first adjustment. His head was a model in size and shape, with a forehead high and broad, and he had, as you would anticipate in a strong face, a large nose. But the distinguishing feature of his face was that pair of dark grey eyes, very full and bright. He wore no beard, had a slight lisp in speech with a clear, penetrating nasal tone. He excelled even the nervous Washburn in rapid utterance.... Such was Blaine at thirty years of age."[6]

Note Blaine is pictured here as beardless—a temporary interval, most likely, in the usual appearance he projected, both before and after 1861.

With or without masculine adornment, this thirty-year-old was now a major player in Maine politics. If not exactly on an even plane with the party big-wigs, including Washburn, who had helped make him party chief, he had advanced considerably upward in the intervening three years. He and Washburn were working pretty much as equal partners in an exhausting war effort that gave Maine the distinction of raising more men per capita for the Union forces than any other state. At the same time, Blaine was becoming a fixture in other parts of the country, gaining national stature and, to an extent, acting like a congressional member in his contacts with people like Secretary of War Cameron.

William Pitt Fessenden, distinguished Portlander, who was a U.S. senator from Maine and later one of Lincoln's secretaries of the treasury. This ramrod-stiff Yankee lawyer served as a mentor to Blaine in his early years and was a staunch help to him in building the Maine Republican party. Fessenden's prestige diminished after he voted against impeaching President Andrew Johnson.
RIDPATH, *LIFE AND WORKS OF JAMES G. BLAINE*

As we have seen, he was not above a little nepotism. In a letter to Senator William Pitt Fessenden, a frequent collaborator, he asked help with the Senate Committee on Military Affairs for his brother-in-law Robert G. Walker of Pennsylvania, whose promotion to brigade commissary was pending before that body. He had heard it might be opposed. Although Walker had voted for Douglass in 1860, Blaine assured Fessenden he hadn't voted Democratic since and was "as thoroughly loyal as any member of our Senate...a man of stainless honor and ex-member of General Butterfield's staff in Virginia where he'd almost been killed at Chickahominny." A word from Fessenden to Senator Wilson "would settle the matter in Walker's favor without delay."

Fessenden, as he did in various other instances, presumably supported Blaine's request. The other U.S. senator, Lot Morrill, and Maine's six congressmen do not seem to figure in Blaine's correspondence as he shouldered these duties for the state, and one may well ask, where was Vice President Hamlin? Not in Washington most of the time, it seems.

It is a known fact that this premier Maine politician and federal officeholder spent a good deal of the Civil War in Kittery, Maine, as an enlisted man as a member of a coastal artillery detachment defending the shores of his native state against an enemy who never came. His patronage from the Lincoln administration was close to nil. The sole cabinet officer allowed New England, whom Lincoln let him pick, was Gideon Welles of Connecticut, secretary of the navy, an old curmudgeon who then ignored his benefactor whenever the question arose of contracts for Down East shipbuilders. Blaine, the staunch Lincoln supporter from the very start, conceivably had better entrée in D.C. and certainly more verve, ambition, and drive than other party big shots who might not have yet seen him as a serious rival.

Some historians argue that Blaine's next move—going to Congress—resulted from a memorable speech on the war effort he gave to the Maine House of Representatives. By then, he was serving his second term as speaker. In Augusta, it was universally granted that he had been fair in the rough and tumble of a seemingly endless debate, which in Maine always has to be kept decorous. Quick wit is a must in the job, as well as poise, patience, a thorough grounding in the rules of parliamentary procedure, and a firm grasp of how to move the session along. By all accounts, Blaine scored high in all these categories and, to a degree, it was all the easier for him in that he had overwhelming majorities—even approaching 5-1. At the same time, he had to know how to keep his troops together. His renowned speech on March 7, 1862, included by biographer Conwell in its entirety of twenty-eight pages, was a brilliant example of why thirty-two-year-old James Gillespie Blaine was seen by his G.O.P. colleagues in Augusta as the person these mostly older men all respected, admired and leaned on for leadership.

The scene in the house that day followed a seven hour monologue spread over two days by the Democratic floor leader, Albert Gould. As a dramatic response, signaling a strong rebuttal, Speaker Blaine laid down his gavel, summoned a colleague to take his place, descended from the rostrum and took a seat assigned to him in the chamber. He then stood up and asked to be recognized to address the House. The speaker pro-tem responded, "The Chair recognizes the gentleman from Augusta." All eyes would have been on that tall, erect-standing figure who, apparently, at the time wore no beard but projected a weighty sense of confidence and command. And like every good politician, he started off with a bit of humor.

"Mr. Chair. The first hour of the seven which the gentleman from Thomaston has consumed I shall pass over with scarcely a comment," Blaine commenced. A knowing smile would have gone through the Republican ranks, accompanied by an exchange of winks. They had an idea of what was coming. And here Blaine gently chided his opponent for having, in his long-winded speech, brought before them "in violation of parliamentary rules," a quarrel he was conducting with a fellow Democrat, E. K. Smart, now a state senator. To characterize his position on that affair, Blaine cited what he called a Grub Street couplet, "apt if not elegant," which went:

> For the matter of that I don't care a toss-up
> Whether Mossup kicks Barry or Barry kicks Mossup.

The Republicans must have howled and the speaker pro-tem would have had to rap his gavel for order, while Blaine stood with a poker face. When the hullabaloo subsided, he gravely warned Representative Gould that Colonel Smart could be "quite as valiant an adversary as he would care to encounter."

"Without further delay on matters personal," Blaine immediately continued, and the serious discussion began on the issue at hand. It was about war powers, most specifically about a resolution the Maine House was considering to "provide for the confiscation of estates, real and personal, of rebels, and for the forfeiture and liberation of every slave claimed by any person who shall continue in arms against the authority of the United States...." It was in protest of this item that Gould, although a supporter of the war, had risen and harangued the members for the equivalent of close to a full working day.

Gould's arguments were not included in Conwell's book. But Blaine's refutation strategy against them was: first, to prove that Congress, under the war power granted it by the Constitution could adopt any such resolution; and second, that it was expedient to do so.

Apparently, Gould had insisted only the president had the war power, not Congress. Blaine's opening retort was, "Could argumentative nonsense go farther?" One can almost sense those old Yankee G.O.P. members, sitting back in their seats, eagerly anticipating the "humdinger" or "ripsnorter" that Jim Blaine was about to unleash on poor Gould.

Sure enough, it *was* a masterful speech. It was full of American history—quotes from Alexander Hamilton and Patrick Henry during the shaping of the Constitution, erudition writ so large by Blaine that he could even, without batting an eye, drop the name of Vattel, (actually Emerich de Vattel), a Swiss philosopher and jurist, who had devised a famous definition of civil war.

This was done to counter Gould's objection that the present conflict in the United States was not a civil war.

"What kind of a war, then?" Blaine wondered aloud.

Gould rose from his seat and answered, "A domestic war," and was greeted by hoots of laughter.

Blaine proved himself devastating in situations like this, ad-libbing, "Well, Mr. Chairman, we shall learn something before this discussion is over. Domestic war! I have heard of domestic woolens, domestic sheeting, and domestic felicity, but a 'domestic war' is something entirely new under the sun. All the writers of international law that I have ever read speak of two kinds of war, foreign and civil. Vattel will, I suppose, have a new edition with annotations by Gould, in which 'domestic war' will be defined and illustrated as a contest, not quite foreign, not quite civil...."[7]

Whether true or not that this particular performance had gained him the congressional nomination, the idea of his going to Congress would have seemed a no-brainer to his contemporaries in the Kennebec District.

Two years earlier, in June 1860, they had already been after Blaine, but we find him writing to former Governor Anson P. Morrill who was seeking that same seat in Congress for himself. Morrill was informed, rather cryptically by Blaine that "the opportunity to set matters right in Monmouth occurred early and naturally." What Blaine wanted Morrill to know was how he had put down a boomlet for himself from Monmouth, a neighboring town to Augusta, and he enclosed correspondence from a George H. Andrews of Monmouth offering Blaine every Republican vote in the town, and Blaine's own gracious refusal based on the fact that "ex-Governor Morrill deserves the nomination.... You can readily see how unbecoming it would be in a man of my years to contest the nomination with him, even if I personally desired to do so."[8]

Smart politics. Two years later, Anson Morrill decided not to run for re-election. The Republicans needed a strong candidate. James G. Blaine was the obvious and unanimous choice of the district convention. On July 8, 1862, Blaine officially became the G.O.P. candidate. As expected, he had little trouble winning the September general election, Two months later, the D.C.-bound politico-elect, who didn't have to report for more than a year, took another first step in his life. He bought a home.

The location was interesting. In a sense, he was putting himself in the limelight almost perpetually by living across the street from the edifice where Maine's government was centered. Almost every day since he'd arrived in Augusta, he'd been looking at the structure erected at that intersection by a retired ship's captain named James Hall in 1833, one year after the state house had been constructed. By the time Blaine sought to buy it, the place had changed hands, ending up as the property of a rich Augusta merchant, Greenwood Child. And it was from his son, J. Rufus Child, that Blaine received his warranty deed in exchange for $5,000 from "said Harriet S. Blaine, her heirs and assigns forever...."

The source of that five grand was never stipulated, but the house was Harriet's, a birthday present from her loving husband.

The deed referred to it as Captain James Hall's "Mansion House," which may explain why "the Blaine Mansion" is one of the terms Mainers use to refer to their governors' official residence. Draper Hunt calls the original dwelling "box-like" and "stately" and Blaine's external additions, which included a replica of the front section, have changed its shape but not its elegance. A portico, a porch, an open veranda with a balustrade, a cupola with windows—all these frills were tacked on by the Blaines, along with many interior changes, among them Blaine's real pride, the billiard room with its floor of alternating light and dark planks. Today, the house is painted white, with black shutters, and flanked by a white picket fence. An 1887 photo shows darker exterior paint.

All this transformation was not done overnight. But when the Blaine family, now expanded to five, moved from the old Stanwood place on Green Street, they were entering their "home," no matter how many other buildings they were to own. Walker was seven, Emmons was five, Alice a baby of two. "It was a house for children," Draper Hunt has written,[9] and he has included a paen from young Harriet, the last to be born in its confines: "Augusta stood for freedom, for a large old yard with apple trees and a butternut tree in the corner, and a vegetable garden at the back. It stood for a stable with horses and a pony; it stood for the kindest neighbors in the world, whose front doors were never locked and whose cookie jars were never empty and for a household of aunts who were only waiting to welcome and spoil us."[10]

"Father" was often absent, headed to Washington, D.C., mostly after having established this "anchor to windward," to which he

An etching of the Blaine home in Augusta. This corner of State and Capitol Streets still marks the heart of Maine's governing complex, with the State House and adjoining buildings directly opposite. In 1919 Blaine's youngest daughter, Harriet Beale, gave the state the "mansion" in memory of her son, killed in World War I, and since 1920 it has been the official gubernatorial residence.
Conwell's *Life and Public Service of James G. Blaine*

returned again and again. He was "the sun around which his children revolved," joyously greeting him at the Augusta station on his return from "away," and clinging to him on the trip home while, inveterate gladhander that he was, he waved to any and all constituents encountered during that ride through the capital city.

This commute of Blaine's back and forth between Maine and the outside world commenced in earnest with the start of the Thirty-eighth Congress in early December of 1863.

1. Hamilton, p. 130.
2. All the preceding telegrams and correspondence are from a collection at the Maine State Archives, Augusta, Maine.
3. Gaillard Hunt. "Israel, Elihu, and Cadwallader Washburn" in *American Biography* (New York: The MacMillan Company, 1925).
4. Ibid., p. 54.

5. Ibid., p. 106.

6. Oliver Otis Howard. *The Autobiography of O. O. Howard,* vol. 1 (New York: Baker and Taylor Company, 1907), pp. 114–15.

7. Conwell, p. 108.

8. Hamilton, p. 137.

9. Hunt, p. 16.

10. Ibid.

SEVEN

OFF TO CONGRESS

IN ACCEPTING HIS congressional nomination, James G. Blaine unequivocally announced, "If I am called to a seat in Congress, I shall go there with a determination to stand heartily and unreservedly by the administration of Abraham Lincoln. In the success of that administration, under the good providence of God, rests, I solemnly believe, the fate of the American Union."[1]

Those with a jaundiced view of Blaine might claim this was his usual opportunism, clinging to the coattails of a popular president. His defenders could retort that it was just the opposite, an act of courage, since Lincoln's star was fading fast in the summer of 1862. The Union had little to show for its massive effort to curb the South's rebellion. "We were the war party with nothing to show but a list of defeats," Blaine's fellow Republican from way Down East, James S. Pike, was quoted as saying. The 1862 elections in the fall were to show G.O.P. weaknesses everywhere in the North.

It could be asserted that in tying his political career to Lincoln's, Blaine had demonstrated an admirable sense of loyalty and consistency. He had battled for underdog Lincoln at the 1860 convention. In the charade of the personal liberty law, he had publicly fallen on his sword for the president's position. Now, when mutters were already starting within the party about replacing Lincoln in the coming 1864 election, he was once again sticking his neck out for Honest Abe.

One result turned out to be that he was brought directly to the president's attention. Maine, with its early September voting, would be crucial in any reelection campaign. Lincoln consulted his vice president, asking Hamlin "...to pick out some bright, likely young man to look out for delegates in Maine and keep a weather eye out for squalls in New England."[2]

No better choice could be made, Hannibal Hamlin responded, than the freshman Congressman James G. Blaine, who was also chairman of the Maine Republican State Committee. "...Mr. Hamlin had already recognized him as a coming leader of brilliant gifts with a special talent for organization," Hamlin's grandson wrote.[3] Lincoln was pleased by the suggestion and told the vice president to have Simon Cameron and himself "fix it up." Reputedly, as a quid pro quo, at Hamlin's urging, a bit of patronage was also secured—that army paymastership for Blaine's brother-in-law.

In the two Maine elections of September and November 1862, Blaine's mettle as a political organizer was severely tested. Albert Gould's temerity in challenging those Republican resolutions in the Maine House was an indication of what lawmakers were hearing back home—a thoroughgoing war weariness. Although the state's Democrats remained split, Peace Democrats now outnumbered War Democrats by more than 3-1.

Moreover, the problem for Blaine was compounded by the fact that Israel Washburn, Jr., had decided not to run again for governor. Washburn claimed he was exhausted by his herculean exertions in rallying Maine to the colors during his two one-year terms. While his absence made it possible for Blaine at last to put forward his friend, millionaire Abner Coburn, for the post, Coburn was a totally uncharismatic candidate. That the 1862 governor's race in Maine has been deemed a "dull campaign" may have had much to do with this self-made lumber baron's lack of personality. He won, but only by 4,000 votes—12,000 fewer than Washburn's previous majority.

Worse still, in the November campaign, a Democrat was elected to the U.S. Congress, ending the Maine G.O.P. monopoly on seats in D.C. Excuses for Lorenzo D. M. Sweat's victory over John Goodwin in the First District were immediately forthcoming, conceivably orchestrated by Blaine: Goodwin hadn't worked and the lack of patronage at the Navy Yard in Kittery had also contributed. As for Blaine's own election, he had no trouble whatsoever and could point out, as well, that the Republicans had done far more poorly elsewhere than in Maine: fifty congressional seats lost and their margin reduced to twenty.

We have a portrait, in James G. Blaine at this stage of his life, of a type familiar on the American scene: the young man in a hurry, rising inexorably to the top of his profession thanks to his talent, extraordinary energy, ruthlessness, and single-minded devotion to his goal. Yet there is a softer side to this picture.

It is not surprising that Gail Hamilton would want to humanize her hero. And she does so through his own words in a selection of letters from this period, when he was just starting his national political career. They show the family man—brother, sister, father, son—enmeshed in the lives of his dear ones, not just scheming to get ahead politically. Or as the authoress puts it, "His letters to his mother and sister are continuous—almost always accompanied by some little 'gift' or 'remembrance' or proposal of pleasure which he begs them to accept. In his occasional journeys he remembers not only the Great Hearts but the Little Hearts to be gladdened by news from him; and printed letters to the children are scattered all along the way."[4]

One example was a note in May 1859 to his sister, otherwise unidentified but likely Elizabeth, two years older than himself and married to career soldier Major Robert G. Walker, the brother-in-law he had helped. "You and Ma could not do me a greater favor than to send me all your family letters from Lancaster, Washington, Pennsylvania, and wherever else you may think worthwhile. I am so far out of the circle of my 'kith and kin' that I hear no more of them than though I was in Siberia.... I hope to be able to make a visit to Philadelphia within the year, but at what time I cannot now say.... Emmons is now nearly two years old, a perfect rogue. Walker sedate and sober...."

Then, there were these epistles to the Little Hearts:

"MY DEAR WALKER: [he was six-years-old] I received your nice little note this morning. I shall long keep it as the first letter written to me by my darling little son. I saw Abraham Lincoln at the White House, and I heard that his children are sick with the measles. Kiss dear little Alice for Papa."

Four-year-old Emmons had apparently—with help from Mama—sent his letter, too. Walker was to read Papa's response to him, which included, "When I come home we will get the express wagon out of the barn, and have it nicely fitted up for you and Walker to ride in next summer." Next, the perhaps obligatory, "Kiss Alice for me."

On this same trip, Blaine visited West Point (he had been appointed to the U.S. Military Academy Board of Inspectors) and another missive to Emmons to be read by Walker described the school to a four year old. "MY DEAR EMMONS: There are a great many boys and young men here learning to be soldiers. When they drill they have a splendid band of music and 30 musicians. A man walks at the head of the band with a large gilt staff in his hand, with which he directs them how to play. He wears a very big hat with four very large feathers in it. They call him the Drum Major.... I don't think you ought to whistle at the table, but you can do so in the front yard."

The grown-up six-year-old Walker received an even more sophisticated message. Blaine delved into U.S. history, telling his little son that Union troops in Mississippi had captured the home of "Jeff Davis" and found a letter there from ex-President Pierce informing Davis that Northerners would help Southerners fight the Republicans. "I send you an exact copy of it. Keep it carefully. Love to Emmons and the Palace."

Other views of the Blaine household were to come from Thomas H. Sherman, James G. Blaine's long-time secretary. He starts his book, *Twenty Years With James G. Blaine*,[5] with a vivid description of the nation's capital at the start of the Civil War in 1861, when Blaine had first begun his quartermaster's jaunts to the capital.

"Washington...was a squalid, unattractive town," Tom Sherman flatly stated. Pennsylvania Avenue was poorly paved. Army wagons and artillery would sink in the mud or become clouded by dust. There were stepping stones across gutters. Water pumps and public dippers were available for drinking with the warning that it was wise to take half a wine glass of brandy and then the water, when the temperature soared to 100 degrees. Since the water was piped from the Potomac, it was as brown as ale. Cows, pigs, and hens ran loose in the streets, which were lit by feeble gas lamps. Many of the whites refused to ride in omnibuses and street-cars with blacks. These native whites, Sherman recorded, were "almost wholly" in sympathy with the South. The flags of the Confederate Army could be seen across the Potomac.

At the time, Sherman, a telegraph operator, was working for Western Union, in charge of several branch offices. In this role, he later met Congressman Blaine, made an impression, and eventually, once the Maine man was elected Speaker and could hire an assistant, went to work for him.

By the time the Thirty-eighth Congress did convene and Blaine took up a more extended residency in D.C., Republican prospects were somewhat brighter than they had been in November 1862. A number of factors were involved.

One was the Emancipation Proclamation announced by Lincoln on September 22, 1862, but not put into effect until early in 1863. Although far from universally well-received at first in the North, the strategy of freeing the slaves was ultimately to prove quite useful to the Union as a political and propaganda tool, particularly in its influence overseas where its popularity helped keep British and French leaders from recognizing the Confederacy.

But more important still was the incontestable Northern victory at Gettysburg in the summer of 1863. While continuing to present a threat, even to Washington, the Confederacy had reached its "high water mark" militarily, and once Lee retreated southward, the rebels began banking on their survival through a triumph at the polls, by depriving Abraham Lincoln of re-election in 1864.

At home in Maine, before heading to Washington to take up his congressional duties, James G. Blaine had a lot to worry about. Getting Lincoln back in office was absolutely crucial to the war effort. Dumping Abner Coburn, his protégé, so to speak, as governor, was another must. No better illustration of Coburn's ineptitude can be found than the scathing sketch presented by a Maine enlisted man from Saco, John W. Haley, in his wartime diary. After the ex-lumber baron on a trip to Virginia addressed the Seventeenth Maine, Haley wrote:

"Governor Coburn is, without exception, the most wretched speechmaker that ever punished the cushion of the Governor's chair. What sin have we committed that we should be so punished and on the eve of battle, too? He acted more like a great blubbering school boy than like the Governor of Maine. The sum total of his remarks was the sum of all flattery, piled so thick it fell off in great chunks."[6]

Nevertheless, Blaine had to maneuver delicately to persuade his friend, the governor, to step down after only a one year term in office. Coburn's wealth had certainly been of considerable worth in financing the Maine G.O.P., if not also a personal boon to Blaine, himself. The man might be crude and clueless but he was also a decent person, noted for his philanthropies. How Blaine convinced him to step aside and still remain cooperative has never openly been discussed.

Quite possibly, the strategy Blaine employed for the 1863 campaign in Maine might have done the trick. The Republicans needed camouflage, he argued, as he moved literally to change the G.O.P.'s name to the Union party and encompass the War Democrats in their fold. Furthermore, the Union party should have a War Democrat head up its ticket. And he had just the man for the job! Blaine turned to Samuel Cony, from a distinguished Augusta family, a former mayor of the city and a state treasurer, who had recently achieved great popularity as assistant paymaster-general of Maine by loaning money to soldiers from his own private fortune. Since these War Democrats now physically intermingled with the Republicans at the Union party convention, Blaine shrewdly arranged that the old Democratic war horse, E. K. Smart, moved Coburn *not be nominated*, thus keeping his own hand hidden. Blaine not only benefited by Cony's smashing victory over pacifist Bion Bradbury by almost 18,000 votes, but he also gained an important personal supporter in Cony's son-in-law Joseph Manley, who, in time, became his indispensable right hand man.

When Blaine appeared, therefore, in the House chamber of the Congress on December 7, 1863, he was already considered a man to watch.

There were 183 men in the Thirty-eighth Congress, hailing from twenty-four loyal states. Of this number, no more than about a dozen achieved the dreams of fame and glory all elected officials entertain on winning office and some only through a notoriety they wouldn't have welcomed. Two of the latter were Oakes Ames of Massachusetts, censured by the House for his part in the infamous Credit Mobilier scandal of 1872, which involved the attempted bribery of congressmen with railroad company stock; and Schuyler Colfax of Indiana, who achieved the vice presidency of the United States but saw his career devastated by the same railroad scam.

Colfax, a fellow Republican, was speaker of the House when Blaine arrived. There is a story about Blaine's youth that when still a teenager in 1847, he learned Robert C. Winthrop of Boston, a Whig, had become a speaker of the House and told his classmates at Washington College he would someday hold the same position. That thought must have been in his mind as he observed Colfax in the role and, more than once, had to go to his rescue with the superior knowledge of parliamentary rules he'd picked up in Maine.

If a possible rival to his ambitions had appeared among those fellow House members of the Thirty-eighth, it was James A. Garfield of Ohio. Blaine's first comments about this Civil War general a year younger than himself, who arrived with a strong reputation gained from winning battles in Kentucky, were not entirely flattering. "He is a big good-natured man that doesn't appear to be oppressed with genius." In later years, however, they were to become allies and deep personal friends.

Both were also to be touched to a degree by the Credit Mobilier fiasco, Garfield more so than Blaine, who was allegedly confused (as an owner of the company's stock) with his brother J. E. Blaine (John Blaine). Neither of them really suffered long-term damage from this particular scandal.

All that unpleasantness was still well in the future when the honorable gentlemen of the Thirty-eighth gathered to do their work, with the end of the war still a year and a half away.

Traditionally, freshman legislators are supposed to be seen, not heard. Despite his advance billing as a savvy political operator in Maine and ex-speaker of his state's house of representatives, James G. Blaine was still a first-termer. Speaker Colfax appointed him to the Committee on Post Offices and the Committee on Military Affairs, two committees conducive to patronage opportunities but not exactly places where an ambitious newcomer could shine. However, later that same session, Blaine was made chair of a Special Select Committee, assigned to deal with the question of having the U.S. government assume the war debts of the loyal states.

So here was some red meat he could bring back to his constituents! His own experiences in equipping the Maine forces had shown him how much the war was costing the local taxpayers in his adopted state. That his position was to lead him to a clash on the House floor with the most intimidating of House leaders, the irascible, powerful Thaddeus Stevens of Pennsylvania, could only be a plus for Blaine if he carried it off with aplomb, which he did.

This collision was precipitated through a bill introduced by Stevens, chairman of the mighty Ways and Means Committee, to reimburse Pennsylvania for having to call out its militia to resist Lee's invasion of the state in the summer of 1863. Blaine objected to piecemeal legislation of this sort, citing the fact that Maine had been forced to spend its own money to protect the federal naval shipyard located at Kittery. He then had the temerity to offer his substitute for the veteran congressman's bill—establishing a special three person committee to add up the indebtedness of all the loyal states and report back their findings with a recommendation for what course to follow.

Needless to say, Blaine's course was to have the feds wholly absorb the states' costs. He was eloquent in his use of financial facts and historical precedent to promote the idea that the United States government could easily handle a war debt of $3 billion and the inclusion of $300 million to refund the states.

This was an age when congressmen didn't have ghostwriters to do their speeches and not much in the way of research assistance; consequently Blaine's marshalling of statistics and history to bolster his arguments presaged the always impressive scholarship in his public remarks. He contrasted the country's war debt, predicated on ending the war in July 1865, with the U.S. war debt at the time of the American Revolution and Great Britain's war debt during the Napoleonic struggle. In both cases, the Union's $3 billion represented a far lower percentage of national assets. His careful presentations drew grudging compliments from Thaddeus Stevens, whom he continued to oppose. In one other notable incident in the final December 1864 meeting of the Thirty-eighth, Blaine boldly trumped Stevens's attempt to have Congress actually *set* the value of a dollar. Before the veteran legislator knew it, Blaine had gotten Stevens's measure tabled, using almost reckless language like "absurd and monstrous" in characterizing the Pennsylvanian's attempted action. Stevens chalked up young Blaine's triumph as due to his personal magnetism. His actual words were, "The House being magnetized by the excited manner of the gentleman from Maine, became alarmed and immediately laid the bill on the table without its being presented, and without a single member having had an opportunity to read a word of it."[7] From that moment on, the term magnetism stuck to Blaine for the remainder of his career.

Some lesser but memorable confrontations on the House floor during Blaine's freshman term have been included in works by his biographers. Several times he went head to head with Samuel S. "Sunset" Cox of Ohio, a seasoned Democrat. On the first occasion, it was to defend Maine's honor against Cox's charge that the Pine Tree State had received an undue percentage of federal largesse. Blaine began, as he often did, with a mild dose of sarcasm. "If the gentleman from Ohio who has given us such a learned lecture on political economy, were as well posted in regard to the industrial pursuits of the people of Maine, he would know that two great leading pursuits are lumber and navigation." Cox was then challenged to name what protection Maine lumber had received from the U.S. since "the gentleman's political associates ten years previously had taken away a subsidy." As to some fishing bounties Maine had been given, Blaine zeroed in on the fact that 6,000 skilled Down East seamen were provided to the Union Navy and no federal bounties paid, as would have happened had they joined the Union Army. "And so long, sir, as I have a seat on this floor, the State of Maine shall not be slandered by the gentleman from Ohio or by gentlemen from any other State." was Blaine's final ringing warning to his antagonist.

But soon he and Cox were again at loggerheads on the slavery question with Blaine badgering the Ohio Democrat to take a clarified position on whether a slave should be returned to his master, even a loyal master, if the black man was a soldier in the Union Army. They went 'round and 'round and Cox admitted, "I opposed putting the Black men in the Army in the first place" and claimed the controversial decision to do so had not "strengthened the Army one jot or tittle." Blaine retorted that "there are more than 150 wounded Negroes in one hospital at Fortress Monroe." Finally, Cox shot back he felt Black soldiers should be sent home to their loyal owners and let "the White men" carry on the war "for the constitutional liberties of White men."

Blaine's reported colloquy with Representative Robert Mallory of Kentucky covered a similar subject: the fighting qualities of the Black soldiers in the Union Army. Mallory had said, "My friend from Maine, Mr. Blaine, lived in Kentucky once, and knows the Negro and his attributes and he knows, if he will tell you what he knows, that they won't fight." Blaine disagreed, countering: "From a residence of five years in Kentucky, I came to the conclusion from what I saw of them that there was a great deal of fight in them." In support of that statement, he told how in Louisiana and Mississippi, "the perfect terror" was a "runaway Negro in the canebrakes" and that—a somewhat far-afield analogy—during the Crimean War, Egypt had furnished fifteen regiments of "pure Negro blood" to help the Turks fight the Russians, English, and French. At this juncture, Cox of Ohio could not restrain himself from entering the fray against Blaine. "They were Abyssinians," he declared to laughter. Blaine corrected him. "These were Nubians," he said, "...naked, black Nubians."[8]

Such spirited sparring with the opposition could only have earned the freshman legislator a lot of brownie points for future leadership from his fellow G.O.P. contingent.

Prior to Blaine's strong speech on the debt issue, he had cast a vote for a resolution introduced by Representative Henry Winter Davis, a Maryland Republican, deploring the French invasion of Mexico and the forced installing of a puppet Austrian prince, Maximilian of Hapsburg, as "Emperor" of the U.S.'s neighbor to the south. Blaine's action is seen in retrospect not simply as a routine bit of party solidarity, but the start of his entry into the world of foreign affairs. His interests, shown by his frequent use of overseas analogies, had always been fairly global. Luther Severance had already influenced him on Hawaii and now he followed Henry Winter Davis's lead on Mexico and how the Monroe Doctrine should be invoked to get the French out. Not until the end of the Civil War did this really happen, leaving the hapless Hapsburg satrap to face a Mexican firing squad, but the imprint on Blaine carried over into his service as secretary of state. Professor Edward Crapol, in a recent book on Blaine's foreign policy, opines he was following "Davis's agenda almost to the letter."[9]

The only difference Blaine had with his Maryland mentor was he believed implicitly in the primacy of the president to conduct foreign policy. He did so in a vote to table—i.e., kill—a Davis resolve to allow Congress to run the nation's diplomacy. For James G. Blaine, his number one *raison d'etre* for being in Congress still was to support Abraham Lincoln.

At the very start of the debt speech, Blaine had well expressed the utter importance for the Union of a united stand behind the president. Cautioning that the war yet had more than another year to run, he stated: "...I have latterly been of those who believe that the leading conspirators of the South intend at all events to prolong the struggle until the approaching contest for the Presidency is ended. They have a hope—baseless enough, it seems to us—that in some way they are to be benefited by the results of that election, and hence they will hold out until it is decided, with a view, indeed, of affecting its decision...."[10]

In truth, many Republicans and Blaine among them did not really feel those fears to be so baseless. The Democratic candidate might be a copperhead. Nor was it altogether certain Lincoln would even be re-nominated. Salmon P. Chase, secretary of the treasury, had been making no secret of his ambition to replace Lincoln at the top of the Republican ticket. Despite victories at Gettysburg and Vicksburg, the war and the hated draft still continued. There *were* grounds for concern. After the Thirty-eighth Congress adjourned on July 4, 1864, Blaine hurried back to Maine to bolster the Republican forces, gearing up for the September state election, which always would be the first in the nation. The press throughout the whole country would focus on how well the G.O.P. did Down East as a bellwether for the November contest.

Beforehand, though, at the Republican convention in Baltimore held on June 7, the president *was* chosen to run again by acclamation. But the G.O.P. delegates, prior to departing, then dealt the Maine Republicans a potentially serious blow. Vice-President Hamlin was dropped from the ticket!

It was a genuinely shocking surprise. On June 4, the usually all-knowing Blaine had written Hamlin from D.C., baldly stating: "My impression is that you will be re-nominated without much opposition. A good many delegates are here today and the feeling *seems* to be confirmed. The only person very prominently mentioned is [Daniel] Dickinson of New York. Andrew Johnson seems to have been dropped all around by a sort of common consent—but may be resurrected at Baltimore.... Cameron [ex-Secretary of War Simon Cameron] was here a week ago "prospecting" but he didn't meet with much encouragement—and now contents himself with neutrality.[11]

As it happened, Cameron did try to pull off a coup and have both Lincoln and Hamlin renamed by acclamation. Loud objections from the floor forced separate selections for the top offices. Following Lincoln's shouted election, a real contest began. Cameron nominated Hamlin, Dickinson's name followed and finally Andrew Johnson's. The first ballot gave Johnson 200, Hamlin 150, and Dickinson 108, but before the gavel came down, a rash of changes favored Johnson, even including Cameron's own 52 from Pennsylvania. Final tally: Johnson 494, Dickinson 27, Hamlin 9.

All three of those men were former Democrats. In Johnson's favor was that he could be seen as more of a War Democrat than the other two, having served as military governor of occupied Tennessee with the rank of brigadier general. Besides, it had been whispered, he was truly the one Lincoln wanted.

Would it hurt the G.O.P. ticket in Maine that their popular native son had been unceremoniously dumped? James G. Blaine did his best to see this didn't happen, enlisting Hamlin to speak in Maine towns for the Lincoln-Johnson campaign and recruiting him, as well, to speak in New York and Pennsylvania.

Meanwhile, he, himself, was continually on the stump, blasting away at Democrat George McClellan whom he characterized as "the only military man who ever ran for president of the U.S. on the explicit and declared basis of a capitulation." He even told an Augusta audience he would resign from Congress if re-elected should that body ever concur with what he called McClellan's intent to "surrender the proud position of the nation."

That September he was returned to office with a thousand vote greater plurality than two years previous. Aided by Sherman's capture of Atlanta, Lincoln and Johnson were easily re-elected. The Republican triumph was complete.

But Andrew Johnson, an unknown quantity, was a heartbeat away from the presidency.

1. Hamilton, p. 138.
2. Charles Eugene Hamlin. *The Life and Times of Hannibal Hamlin by His Own Grandson* (Cambridge, MA: Riverside Press, 1899), p. 462; published by subscription.
3. Ibid.
4. Hamilton, p. 133.
5. Thomas H. Sherman. *Twenty Years With James G. Blaine* (New York: Grafton Press, 1928).
6. Private John W. Haley. *The Rebel Yell and The Yankee Hurrah: The Civil War Journal of a Maine Volunteer*, edited by Ruth L. Silliker (Camden, ME: Down East Books, 1985), p 76.
7. Hamilton, p. 147.
8. The above quotes are from Boyd, pp. 209–20
9. Edward P. Crapol. *James G. Blaine: Architect of Empire* (Wilmington, DE: SR Books, 2000), p. 23.
10. Boyd, p. 200.
11. H. Draper Hunt. *Hannibal Hamlin of Maine: Lincoln's First Vice-President* (Syracuse, NY: Syracuse University Press, 1969), p. 175.

EIGHT

RECONSTRUCTION

THE DRAMA OF RECONSTRUCTION has always been overshadowed by the drama of the actual Civil War, itself, with its epic, gory battles and larger-than-life personalities. That there were some larger-than-life types involved in Reconstruction has been pretty much ignored. As a result, the agonizing conundrum of how to patch our country back together and solve the racial problems growing out of the demise of slavery never receives the attention that hovers constantly over battles like Gettysburg or Antietam or warriors like Grant and Lee and Stonewall Jackson and William Tecumseh Sherman.

For James G. Blaine, the issue of Reconstruction was a paramount consideration throughout his congressional career. The aftermath of the war touched most of the issues in D.C. during those years when he was in the House of Representatives, and if the treatment to be accorded the rebel states wasn't the question of the day, financial matters related to that ultra-expensive conflict would engage his attention.

The Thirty-ninth Congress, in which Blaine served his second term did not assemble until December 1865. For all practical purposes, the Civil War had ended on April 9, 1865, at Appomattox. Five days after that surrender, Abraham Lincoln was fatally shot. Nowhere is Congressman Blaine's immediate reaction to this event recorded, although as horrendous and shocking as the first assassination of an American president had been, the shooting at Ford's Theater could be seen as simply a logical outgrowth of the war. A deadly plot of southern sympathizers had aimed at more than killing the president. Nearly losing his life, too, had been Secretary of State William Seward, attacked in his D.C. home, in a building at Lafayette Square where, eerily enough, Blaine was later to live and eventually to die. No crystal ball could have told Blaine that within a little more than fifteen years, he, himself, as secretary of state, would be personally present at the second shooting of a president, that of his dear friend James Garfield, and one that really made no sense at all.

But sudden, violent deaths of presidents, explicable or otherwise, can produce major political transformations. Had Lincoln not been shot, Reconstruction certainly would have taken a different tack than it did. Father Abraham had signaled his intentions toward the South during his inaugural address in March 1864, using his famous line, "With malice toward none, with charity for all." This tendency had then been resisted in Congress by a group of Republicans dubbed "Radicals," under the leadership of Thaddeus Stevens, Henry Winter Davis, and Senator Benjamin Wade of Ohio. Blaine, classed a "Moderate," is not usually included in this group, which actually took on Lincoln before his death. A clash with the president had erupted in Congress as early as July 1864. Ben Wade and Henry Winter Davis had teamed up to push through a tough Reconstruction bill, one that would make it exceedingly difficult for ex-Confederates to regain office in their states. Lincoln pocket-vetoed the measure and a month later drew a scathing response in the form of a Wade-Davis Manifesto issued by the two Radical Republican leaders. Blaine's pal James Garfield found himself in deep political trouble home in Ohio when he was accused of having written the Wade-Davis Manifesto. Lincoln-loving Midwesterners were furious with him. Summoned to a Republican congressional convention to explain himself, Garfield showed remarkable courage. No, he hadn't written the Wade-Davis letter, he said, but approved of the motives of its authors and, for his forthrightness, was re-nominated by acclamation.

Since a whole year had elapsed until the Thirty-ninth Congress assembled, there is a definite blank page in the Blaine biographers' treatment of this period. With no congressional actions of Blaine's to report or extol, they just skipped on to the opening gun of the Thirty-ninth Congress in December 1865. But glimpses can be had of James G. Blaine's activities while he was awaiting his return to D.C.

In March of 1865 we find him in Augusta announcing the availability of an appointment he can make to West Point. "Any young man who is an actual resident of the Third Congressional District," is the way he advertised in the *Kennebec Journal,* wording which is a bit ironic in view of his untoward request years back to Congressman Washburn to disregard that rule. The following May 4 at Waterville College, interviews would be held and a "surgeon" on hand to conduct physical exams.

Meanwhile, in the third week of April, he took a leading part in "probably the largest" public assemblage in Augusta history, a massive memorial service for Abraham Lincoln in Meonian Hall. Blaine started the ceremonies by introducing a resolution condemning what at first had seemed like the twin assassinations of both Lincoln and Secretary of State William Seward. "The shocking event," that prepared statement ended, "has produced a thrill of consternation and horror throughout the loyal States." But then he did clarify the fact that Seward, although badly hurt, was still alive and "God grant that his life may be spared for many years of usefulness," which eventually happened. U.S. Senator Lot M. Morrill spoke next and finally Blaine took over again with a speech of his own. The most touching section was when he spoke of his visit with Lincoln "precisely one week before" on board the presidential boat anchored in the James River below Richmond, Virginia. "The President," Blaine said, "was in high health and spirits with a bounteous flow of conversation sparkling with that rare type of humor and story which made him in social life so entertaining to his friends." The party broke up at 11 P.M. and Blaine discussed with another attendee how impressed he had been that the president could speak of the impending close of the war "without a particle of *personal* hatred toward any individual rebel in the South." Turning then full face to the packed crowd of grieving Mainers, James G. Blaine eloquently revealed his own feelings about Lincoln: "I thought his kindness of heart, his exalted patriotism, his abounding charity, his lofty magnanimity never shone more conspicuously than in this generous expression made on the heels of a crowning victory over a stubborn foe."[1]

With May, it was back to business. His nominee for West Point, announced eight days after the interviews, was Frank Nye of Waterville, the "best of fifteen applicants." A few eyebrows might have been raised over the revelation that the boy's father was the Treasurer of the Maine Central Railroad.[2]

June brought with it another shocking event, this one personal, involving criminality, yet also a touch of comic relief. The Blaine House, the new home he had begun renovating, was robbed. The theft happened early on a Sunday morning and the total loss was calculated at $350. Not only did the brazen footpad enter through a cellar in an occupied dwelling, but he sneaked right into Blaine's own bedroom while his victim slept and took "his pantaloons and a watch." In the dining room, he helped himself to silver, "nicely discriminating between the old and the plate," and back in the cellar, "he helped himself to cold meats and other refreshments." The illumination of gas lights he'd turned on woke the family while the audacious burglar made his escape down the cellar stairs. As the KJ reported, "The light-fingered gentleman was probably disappointed in finding less than $7 in [Blaine's] wallet." The Congressman promptly offered a $100 reward for help in capturing the assailant.[3]

That September, the KJ reported Blaine sick, and a month later recovering, a set of occurrences that often were to repeat themselves. In this case, he appears to have been stricken by dysentery, followed by typhoid fever. However, even his wife admitted he was a dyed-in-the-wool hypochondriac and his indispositions apt to be labeled bouts of depression, brought on by political tribulations.

Early in November Blaine was seemingly well enough to attend the meeting of a committee to build a new hotel in Augusta. The building would be located on Water Street and possibly was in answer to Portland's claim that the capital should be moved because it lacked facilities for legislators. Chairing the group of local businessmen was former U.S. Senator James Bradbury, that Democrat who thought so much of Blaine.[4]

All this time there was political work the congressman and party leader could carry on from home. Patronage was continually a concern. That his new associate Joe Manley was admitted to practice in several federal courts in 1865, and subsequently appointed commissioner of the U.S. District Court, could have resulted from a congressional nudge. Although Blaine was usually discreet about these matters, a series of his letters during the period has survived to reveal how assiduously he pursued offices for those he deemed worthy—i.e., useful to the Republican Party and/or himself.

A number of these 1864, 1865, and 1866 letters, preserved at the Library of Congress, were to U.S. Senator William Pitt Fessenden, a confidante of Blaine's since his days in the Maine State Legislature.

Even before the Civil War was over, Blaine was working on patronage matters related to Reconstruction. On October 6, 1864, he requested Fessenden's help in finding a job for W. A. Dillingham of Waterville, Maine, who had been a member of the Maine legislature, a stump speaker for the G.O.P. in the campaigns of 1863 and 1864, and a landowner who had lost a lot of property in Mississippi and Louisiana because of the Rebellion. Dillingham was looking for a job in the South, in either a commercial agency or the Freedmen's Bureau. Blaine's suggestion was to send the present holder of a particular office in Natchez—then under Union occupation—to captured Beaufort, South Carolina, and give the Natchez post to his man Dillingham.

Another Republican for whom Blaine stubbornly sought office—this time, in the federal Customs House in Portland—was Charles J. Talbot of Farmington, "long bedridden, but now recovering," a valuable party man in need of money. On June 28, 1865, Blaine was reminding Fessenden, who had already once helped Talbot, why he should help him again, because, "He is a Methodist and the Methodists are very clannish."

The trickiness of juggling posts was well illustrated in an October 1865 communication to Fessenden. A General Cilley from Thomaston had been to see Blaine. He wanted the job of the collector of customs in the town of Waldoboro. Blaine reported he told the general that Thomaston would be a better post for him. The truth, Blaine admitted to Fessenden, was his wish to keep a man named Marble in Waldoboro because he "is the best politician in Lincoln County."

Blaine also sought Fessenden's assistance with a personal patronage problem he, himself, was experiencing. His fellow Republican congressman, John Lynch, was claiming some patronage posts—route agents on the Kennebec Road—that Blaine insisted belonged to him, alone. Declaring it was "rather cheeky of Mr. Lynch," Blaine delicately asked that the U.S. senator reconsider supporting Lynch if he had inadvertently backed him without thinking. "It would be a personal humiliation to me if it should appear that I could not retain the appointments for my district that were accorded to Anson P. Morrill," Blaine stated flat out, sure that Fessenden would recognize this was a matter of no small importance. Besides, the Third District congressman added, Lynch was entitled to three appointments on various Portland railroads, so he should claim those and "not forage and depredate on my domain."

Yet in the summer of 1866, as party chair, Blaine found himself having to devote resources to help Lynch stave off a serious challenge from Democrat ex-Congressman Lorenzo M. Sweat. Blaine had long been wooing former Congressman and ex-Governor Nathaniel Banks of Massachusetts to come to Maine to speak on behalf of G.O.P. candidates. In August 1866, an invitation went out to Banks, asking him to come and assist in the "sharp fight for re-election of the Honorable John Lynch." Sweat, his opponent, was described as a "copperhead of the dirtiest kind...in cordial sympathy and in earnest co-working with rebels as well during the war as now." The object was not only to defeat Sweat but to re-elect Lynch by "an increasing majority."

Blaine, most likely, had won his little patronage skirmish with the First District congressman. Regardless of outcomes, traditionally he was known never to harbor animosities against his opponents. That trait even included the worst antagonist of his entire career—Roscoe Conkling—with whom he was to have a monumental and far-reaching clash in 1866 upon his return to D.C.

However, when the Thirty-ninth Congress did first convene in December 1865, the focus of Republican intra-party antagonism was solely the impending struggle of its congressional wing against

President Andrew Johnson and a plan for the Southern states he had already put in place while the lawmakers were in recess.

Thaddeus Stevens set off the battle on opening day, December 4, when he offered a resolution calling for a joint committee of fifteen members, nine from the House and six from the Senate, to "inquire into the condition of the Southern States and report whether they or any of them were entitled to be represented in this Congress...."[5] Those Southern states had been poised to re-enter Congress on Andrew Johnson's terms. Former rebel and secessionist leaders had seized control of their state governments under the president's lenient eye during the long recess and now, to the utter horror of radical and even moderate Republicans, were planning to link up with northern Democrats and run the fed-

A New Englander, transplanted from Vermont to Pennsylvania, Thaddeus Stevens was the leader of in the post-Civil War Congress of the "radical Republicans," those who were determined to punish the South for its rebellion. Blaine, although sympathetic to these views, clashed on occasion with Stevens. The luxuriant head of hair pictured in this drawing was, by the way, a wig.
RIDPATH, *LIFE AND WORKS OF JAMES G. BLAINE*

eral government, as if the war had never happened. As added salt to the G.O.P. wounds, Alexander Stephens, the vice-president of the Confederacy, was the senator-elect from Georgia. Under "Black Codes," passed by the ex-Confederate-controlled state legislatures, compulsory labor had been re-established in the guise of vagrancy laws. In Louisiana, for example, one law required all freedmen and freed women to have a "comfortable home" within twenty days of its passage or they would be arrested and his or her labor sold to the highest bidder for the rest of the year. To Charles Edward Russell, its obvious intent was "...to return virtually the entire colored population to a state of slavery."[6]

In his resolution for the "Reconstruction Committee," Thaddeus Stevens also included language freezing the admission of purportedly elected members to Congress from any of the secessionist states (like Alexander Stephens). Since the Republicans had an overwhelming majority in the Thirty-ninth Congress and full control over whatever committees they wanted, the resolution passed easily. Nor could Andrew Johnson veto it.

Blaine was not made a member of this special body. But he had been put on the powerful Ways and Means Committee, of which Thaddeus Stevens was still chairman. His position throughout the raging Reconstruction fight has been well summed up by Charles Edward Russell:

> Blaine of Maine stood at Stevens' right hand through it all.... He did not always agree with the leader but on all the vital issues gave him powerful support. In his make-up he had as little of the vindictive as a man may have and get through public life...he would employ all means to conciliate. But the Black Code overwhelmed him, as it overwhelmed many another easygoing man from the North. He felt that the government had to deal, not with a beaten foe to which it could be generous, but with an enemy that sought to win by tricky legislation what it had lost in armed conflict, and on that issue, Stevens himself was hardly more resolved.[7]

Blaine's elevation to the Ways and Means Committee as a second termer was a sign his peers saw him as a "comer." Talk had already begun that he was a good prospect for speaker in the near future, based on the deep knowledge of parliamentary procedure he had exhibited as a freshman. In that Thirty-eighth Congress, he had been deemed the *most promising of the newcomers*, easily eclipsing James Garfield, whom he had originally considered his biggest rival. Henry Winter Davis, destined for a high G.O.P. leadership position and having seniority over Blaine, hadn't been re-elected to the Thirty-ninth and, in fact, by the time of its opening, was dead at the age of forty-eight.

The path to eventual power for the ambitious Maine congressman seemingly lay smoothly open. But with the new Thirty-ninth Congress came an unexpected challenge. New York's Roscoe Conkling was back in the House.

The congressman from Utica had been Blaine's counterpart in the Thirty-seventh Congress—the freshman most likely to succeed. That he hadn't been present in the Thirty-eighth Congress was due to an opposition surge in 1864 preventing his re-election by ninety-eight votes, while his wife's brother Horatio Seymour, a copperhead Democrat, was winning the state's governorship. Now, in the Thirty-ninth Congress, he was eyeing James G. Blaine, sizing him up and seeing him as a serious potential rival. Attention to Conkling, just as certainly, was being paid by Blaine.

The two men were very different, even physically. Conkling was a Nordic type, with a "reddish Venetian beard," blue eyes, fair skin, and a handsome head of carefully coiffured auburn curls. Blaine was of the "Black Celtic" type, dark-bearded, olive-complected, and having deep grey eyes that looked brown. Blaine dressed like a New Englander in a black suit, white shirt, and black string tie. Conkling, a dandy, wore "ice cream trousers" and "moon-on-the-water vests."

"A Hercules in frock coat and white gloves" was the description of Conkling from the pen of José Martí, the great Cuban revolutionary, writing as a journalist-in-exile for the *New York Sun*. In the Cuban's perceptive view, the New Yorker "traversed the Republic with imperial tread," sought not "wealth but pre-eminence," and "was born with his eyes fixed on the White House."

Referring to the inevitable clash between Conkling and Blaine

A striking sketch of Roscoe Conkling, the bully from Utica, New York, an ex-prize fighter who became Blaine's most singular, diehard enemy within the Republican party. After their epic clash in a congressional debate, Conkling refused ever to speak to Blaine again and did everything he could to thwart the Mainer's political career.
BOYD, *LIFE AND PUBLIC SERVICES OF JAMES G. BLAINE*

in his *Selected Writing*,[8] Martí wrote that Blaine, "finding the comparison [of Conkling's style of walking] with a peacock inept because his feet showed the same preening care he gave the rest of his dress," had used the term turkey gobble strut "in a puerile debate in which the smoldering rivalry between these two Republican leaders in the House of Representatives burst into flame"[9]

Some preliminary skirmishes had preceded those ultimate fireworks in the spring of 1866.

Initial verbal sparks flew in a brief debate on January 22, 1866, that Blaine entered unbidden and unwanted. Conkling was presenting a subcommittee report dealing with the tricky problem of how blacks in the South should be counted for voting purposes. Under slavery, each one had been considered three-fifths of a person in determining a state's representation in Congress. New England had a problem with the reapportionment plan proposed by Conkling's group. So when Conkling in his insufferable manner declared that New England would lose no seats and Maine, Massachusetts, and Connecticut would gain, Blaine introduced a set of different figures. Unused to being contradicted, the gentleman from Utica did not try to disguise his disdain in this truncated version of the feisty exchange that followed:

Conkling: "I desire to answer not so much the argument as the witticism of my friend from Maine."

Blaine: "Oh, no, no wit, either perpetrated or intended...."

Conkling: "It is said that New England is the focus of fanaticism."

Blaine: "I thought the gentleman only rose for an explanation."

Conkling: "I am going to make a very brief explanation. New England is the place where the man said the sun riz and sot in his back yard...and...that we cannot do anything here that militates against New England.... I deny that it hits New England and I deny that this proposition benefits New England; in other words, I support this proposition on account of its own merits...."

Blaine: "I am very much obliged to the gentleman for the patronizing care with which he looks after the interests of fanatical New England."

Their minor dust-up was followed by a rather silly but more extensive difference of opinion between these two men, not carried out on the floor of the House, and one that actually came down to a bet. The scene was a dinner party hosted by a Connecticut congressman and attended by both Conkling and Blaine. Somehow during the table talk, the authorship of a literary quote involving the name of Conkling's home town was disputed. Who had written the couplet, "No pent-up Utica contracts our powers. But the whole boundless continent is ours"? Conkling rashly offered to wager a basket of champagne that the answer was Joseph Addison, English essayist, poet, and playwright, and that the lines were from his tragic drama *Cato*. Blaine cautioned Conkling he would lose his bet because he *knew* the correct source. Such assurance only made Conkling all the more stubbornly sure he was correct. But he wasn't. Blaine proved that the lines were by a Jonathan M. Sewall, who had written a work called *Epilogue to Cato* specifically for the Bow Street Theater in Portsmouth, New Hampshire. With ill-concealed poor grace, including an intimation that Blaine had set this whole thing up, Conkling paid off his precipitous bet. When Blaine invited a number of fellow congressmen, including the loser, to share the champagne bounty, Conkling refused to attend the party.

It was on April 24, 1866, that the simmering Blaine-Conkling feud unexpectedly and shockingly reached crescendo proportions. The explosion that day and several succeeding days and its vicious dialogue on the House floor has been remembered ever since as a signal event in the history of the U.S. Congress.

Under discussion was a ponderous piece of legislation entitled: "An Act to reorganize and establish the Army of the United States." It had come from the House Military Affairs Committee, whose chairman, Representative Robert Schenck of Ohio, an ex-general, was trying to shepherd this omnibus measure through the body with a minimum of discussion.

The gentleman from Utica, Mr. Conkling, arose suddenly, received recognition, and offered an amendment to Section 20, which had just been read by the clerk. Section 20 provided that the provost marshal's bureau would hereafter comprise a provost marshal at brigadier general's rank, plus an assistant colonel, and would control all matters relating to recruitment and the arrest of deserters. Conkling's amendment removed Section 20.

Per usual, the gentleman from Utica minced no words concerning his motives. He was, in effect, eliminating the position because "it creates an unnecessary office for an undeserving public servant." And that person was soon identified: General James B. Fry, the present provost marshal, who was to keep his job if the legislation wasn't amended. Conkling was relentless in his attacks on this officer and the work his office had done during the war.

"My constituents remember, and other constituents remember, wrongs done them too great for forgetfulness, and almost for belief, by the creatures of this bureau and of its head... They turned the business of recruiting and drafting into a paradise of coxcombs and thieves.... There has never been in human history a greater mockery and a greater burlesque than the conduct of this bureau...." Conkling also submitted a letter from Ulysses S. Grant, the head of the army, who stated he felt "there is no necessity for a Provost Marshal General."

Stung by the attack, Committee Chair Schenck defended General Fry in particular and, in general, the work of his group, which had been to propose the best organization of the army possible without regard to personalities. Several other congressmen also rose to General Fry's defense.

James G. Blaine came late to the battle. He had been in the diplomatic gallery talking to a friend when Conkling began his harangue. Catching the gist of it, he rushed back to his seat and when he arose to rebut Conkling, he was armed with ammunition his service on the Military Affairs Committee had given him. "I wish to state why the committee reported the section of the bill in which the gentleman from New York shows so much feeling," he commenced. Conkling, himself, it seemed, at the start of the session, had asked the War Department to look into closing the provost marshal's office and Blaine now presented from his files the answer, which was likewise signed by Lieutenant General Ulysses S. Grant. The Maine congressman must have lingered emphatically over one line of Grant's in that document, where the chief of the army stated: "I think the officer best suited for that position [a combined office to deal with desertions and recruiting] is General Fry and would recommend that the whole subject of recruiting be put in his hands and all officers on recruiting duty be directed to report to him."

That put-down of Conkling not being sufficient, Blaine bore in and made a statement calculated to enrage the proud New Yorker beyond endurance. Blaine intimated that the House couldn't care less about "the quarrels of the gentleman from New York with General Fry, in which quarrels it is generally understood the gentleman came out second best at the War Department."

Conkling, the master of withering sarcasm, immediately riposted, "Mr. Speaker, if General Fry is reduced to depending upon the gentleman from Maine for vindication, he is to be commiserated certainly. If I have fallen to the necessity of taking lessons from that gentleman in the rules of propriety, or of right or wrong, God help me...."

So the gloves were off. For the rest of that day, these two highly articulate Republicans went at each other as if they were the most ferocious of partisan enemies, fighting over issues of monumental import. Conkling charged "that the statement made by the gentleman from Maine with regard to myself personally and my quarrels with General Fry and their results, is false." In responding, Blaine counter-charged Conkling had threatened him with a duel by using a phrase that if he had given offense (to Blaine), "I will answer not only here, but elsewhere [on the duelling grounds]." Alleging southerners in Congress before the Civil War had used "and elsewhere" to mean a duel, Blaine called Conkling's remark "cheap swagger."

How much of congressional time was taken up by this unprecedented exchange has not been recorded. But the next day, they were right back into it, with Blaine leading the charge. Holding up the *Globe Report*, which was that era's *Congressional Record*, he accused Conkling of having had his words altered, particularly changing the "cheap swagger when he talked about meeting me 'here and elsewhere' to the very mild phrase 'at all times and places.'"

Striking back, Conkling denied the accusation, calling Blaine's remarks "frivolously impertinent and also incorrect" and his imputation of duel challenging "a cheap way of clawing off."

Did the battle end there—a nasty but hardly immortal display of anger and invective that might or might not be remembered?

Hardly. On the third day, Blaine was back up again and asked to be allowed to have the clerk read aloud a letter from Provost Marshal General Fry.

Unanimous consent of the House was needed for this to be done. Conkling had no objection, but reserved the right to reply.

Before the general's letter was introduced, Blaine confessed that if he had been in error about his remarks concerning Conkling and Fry, "I would, mortifying as it would have been, have apologized to the House." Then, he added meaningfully, "Whether I was in error or not, I leave to those who hear the letter of the Provost Marshal General." The essence of General Fry's communication was that he and Conkling had quarreled over appointments in the congressman's district, that he had removed several of Conkling's favorites as provost marshals and that Conkling's attempts to have the War Department overrule him had failed, so Blaine's contention that Conkling had been worsted was true, not false.

Two other items were then mentioned in the general's letter, one defensive, the other incendiary: 1) in answering Conkling's demand to have the War Department account for Fry" expenditures, a report had been issued and approved by the second controller of the treasury; and 2) that Conkling had violated the letter or spirit, or both, of the U.S. Constitution, Article 1, Section 2, by simultaneously receiving his pay as a congressman and accepting $3,000 for acting as a judge advocate. Furthermore, Fry added about Conkling, "He was as zealous in preventing prosecutions at Utica as he was in making them at Elmira and the main ground of difficulty between Mr. Conkling and myself has been that I wanted exposure at both places while he wanted concealment at one."

Suddenly, the tables were turned. Having attacked Fry when he wasn't able to defend himself, Conkling now found himself accused of improprieties, if not criminal action.

But in the long run, using a congressional commission he controlled, Conkling was able to escape the noose Fry had dangled over his head.

Still, the real impact of this controversy, where it affected Blaine's future, was in what might be termed a final paroxysm of intemperate, albeit witty language he unleashed against his foe. Blaine's ultimate rebuke to Conkling has been long remembered and *de rigueur* for reproduction by his biographers.

Bombastically, Conkling had said, "Mr. Speaker, if the member from Maine had the least idea how profoundly indifferent I am to his opinion upon the subject which he has been discussing, or upon any subject personal to me, I think he would hardly take the trouble to rise here and express his opinion."

However, Blaine did rise and he let go with both barrels. "As to the gentleman's cruel sarcasm, I hope he will not be too severe," the member from Maine began with a mock show of fear. "The contempt of that large-minded gentleman is so wilting, his haughty disdain, his grandiloquent sell, his majestic, supereminent, overpowering, turkey-gobbler strut, has been so crushing to myself and all the members of this House, that I know it was an act of the greatest temerity for me to venture upon a controversy with him...." It remained, however, for a brilliant coda at the end to write *finis* to this episode in a spectacularly brilliant manner. Blaine went on to say that several newspapers had likened Conkling to the late Henry Winter Davis. "The gentleman took it seriously," Blaine said archly, "and it has given his strut additional pomposity. The resemblance is great, it is striking. Hyperion to a Satyr. Thersites to Hercules, mud to marble, dunghill to diamond, a singed cat to a Bengal tiger, a whining puppy to a roaring lion. Shade of the mighty Davis, forgive the almost profanation of that jocose satire."

The House exploded in laughter, in many cases appreciative from members who had been wounded by Conkling's usually unsparing words. The member from Utica never forgave Blaine for this humiliation and never spoke to him again. Charles Edward Russell wrote: "With the country and most of the press, Blaine came forth the victor in one of the most spectacular encounters in Congress.... Some phrases in Blaine's outburst, the 'turkey-gobbler strut' and 'dunghill to diamond, singed cat to a Bengal tiger,' went over the country and clung so long as he was in public life to the Conkling name."[10]

Blaine now had a national reputation, plus greater respect among his peers for having taken on in white knight fashion the bully in their schoolyard. Almost unnoticed in the uproar was that the House approved General Fry's appointment as "Major-General by brevet, for gallantry and meritorious service in the battles of Shiloh, Tennessee, and Perryville, Kentucky" and the Senate quickly followed suit with its approval. This is not the last we will hear of General Fry, in respect to his wartime activities and his relationship to James G. Blaine, and to the State of Maine.

However, in this period of Blaine's career, while diverting as his battle of words with Conkling had been, the overriding issue for the United States and the Republicans still was what to do about the Southern states and Andrew Johnson.

1. Augusta (Maine) *Kennebec Journal*, 21 April 1865.
2. Ibid., 12 May 1865.
3. Ibid., 30 June 1865.
4. Ibid., 3 November 1865.
5. Charles Edward Russell. *Blaine of Maine: His Life and Times* (New York: Cosmopolitan Book Corporation, 1931), p. 149.
6. Ibid., p. 145.
7. Ibid., p. 149.
8. José Martí. *The America of José Martí: Selected Writings of José Martí,* translated by Juan de Onis (New York: Noonday Press, 1953).
9. Ibid., p. 57.
10. Russell, p. 128.

NINE

RECONSTRUCTION
CONTINUES

THE BLAINE-CONKLING AFFAIR was already two months old when the Joint Committee on Reconstruction delivered its all-important report on June 20, 1866. Maine's William Pitt Fessenden was its Senate chairman, having only recently returned to Congress after a short stint as secretary of the treasury at the insistent behest of President Lincoln. This gaunt, craggy-faced Yankee, coupled with another son of New England, the waspish, single-minded, Vermont-born Thaddeus Stevens, brought in the Radical Republicans' recipe for dealing with the South. It was plain and simple. They regarded the secessionist states as defeated foreign enemies, not as fellow misguided Americans who had never left the Union, which was President Andrew Johnson's position.

Their stringent, vengeful view prevailed, since they had ample votes in both House and Senate. The ex-Confederate states were not entitled to automatic representation and Congress, not the president, would run Reconstruction.

Johnson's vetoes against them could not be upheld and one of the major clashes flared when the life of the Freedmen's Bureau, created during Lincoln's time to look after emancipated slaves, was extended despite the president's attempts to kill the agency. At the head of the Freedmen's Bureau was General O. O. Howard, Blaine's old friend from Leeds, Maine.

The author of that key piece of legislation, the venerable abolitionist Senator Lyman Trumbull of Illinois, also had Congress pass another anti-Johnson bill of his by veto-proof margins. No discrimination on the basis of race, color, or previous condition of servitude was to be allowed anywhere in the United States. Charles Edward Russell proclaimed it "the first civil rights bill."

Despite the easy approval, Republican leaders felt they needed something even stronger. The constitutionality of the Civil Rights Act had been questioned and so was born the idea of incorporating the same idea in a constitutional amendment. The Thirteenth Amendment had been adopted already, outlawing de jure slavery. The Fourteenth Amendment was therefore proposed, seeking to do the same to the South's new de facto slavery of the Black Codes.

Other constitutional amendments were being offered. James G. Blaine had one of his own, on an issue that, from the standpoint of a Republican politician as well as a Northerner, he felt to be of the utmost urgency.

He had already locked horns with Conkling over this matter—how to give full representation to blacks in the South as whole human beings, not count each as three-fifths of a person. A mathematical problem with that new formula was an automatic increase of the South's population and subsequent claim to more seats in the U.S. House, and the political problem was that those blacks would never get to vote, but their numbers would add to the power of the unredeemed Southerners, all Democrats. Just as upsetting to Blaine was that the blacks, if they could vote, would vote Republican, for the party that had emancipated them. His suggested amendment essentially would subtract all Blacks not allowed to vote from any state's population, thereby decreasing its congressional and electoral vote.

Quantifying the difference his amendment would make, Blaine made the following points: without it, the South would have 85 Representatives in Congress and the Free States 156; with it, the South would have 58 Reps and the Free States 183. In the Electoral College, the comparable figures would be: South 115, Free States 198 without the amendment; with it, South 88, Free States 225.

Attacked on the House floor by Conkling, among others, Blaine's amendment was defeated. Yet its essential purpose lingered. The Reconstruction Committee included a version in its final recommendations. These easily passed in the House but ran into trouble in the Senate where Massachusetts Senator Charles Sumner, the ardent abolitionist, felt they did not go far enough.

The Blaine-style amendment, run by itself, received a three-vote margin, but needed two-thirds in order to pass.

Ultimately, Blaine's paragraph about representation was included in the Fourteenth Amendment and no rebel state could return to the U.S. unless it ratified the Fourteenth Amendment. At the outset, only Tennessee would ratify. The other stubborn Southern legislatures refused to accept these Northern terms.

Which direction would the nation choose—President Johnson's or that of the Republicans in Congress? This soon became the main question of the impending congressional elections of 1866, and it was really no contest.

The Republicans swept them, winning 143 seats to the Democrats 49, helped also by a wanton massacre in New Orleans of white and black delegates to a state constitutional convention, where it was rumored a plan for Negro enfranchisement would be offered and accepted. Rumor also had it that President Johnson had received advance knowledge of the attack and had ordered the U.S. Army not to intervene. Although such killings on a smaller scale had been going on in the South for some time, this wholesale "murder," as General Philip Sheridan had called it, galvanized the electorate in the North against the reign of terror in Dixie. On speaking tours during the campaign, Johnson was jeered and heckled and in one instance in Cleveland, was so drunk when he addressed a crowd that no one could understand him.

The immediate result of the Republican triumph was a draconian Reconstruction Bill, brought forth by Thaddeus Stevens in February 1867, during a final special session of the Thirty-ninth Congress. The ten states still seen as secessionist were divided into five military districts, to be governed by generals with troops enough to maintain order and suppress terrorism, and the South would remain "occupied" indefinitely. This latter feature bothered Blaine. Still classed as a moderate, he sought to amend Stevens's bill. Like his idol Henry Clay, he had an instinct for compromise, and so he offered a plan by which the Southern states could re-enter the Union. First of all, they would have to accept the civil rights of the Fourteenth Amendment and each individual state constitution needed to provide for "equal suffrage without regard to race, color, or previous condition of servitude" and ratification of these constitutions had to be by all the voters of the state.

Thaddeus Stevens beat Blaine in the House and kept this change out of his Reconstruction Bill. But in the Senate, John Sherman tacked on an amendment incorporating the same proposal. Eventually, with some adjustments, it was passed and also was approved by the House. Johnson's veto did not come until the last day of the session. His backers began a filibuster, hoping to run out the clock. But into the breach stepped James G. Blaine with his superior knowledge of parliamentary procedure. Asking to be recognized, he interrupted the flow of the filibuster and said, "Mr. Speaker, I move that the rules be suspended and the House proceed to a vote on the veto."

He knew his motion took precedence over any further discussion. A vote was ordered. Two-thirds was necessary to suspend the rules and he achieved that easily, 135-48. The Blaine-softened Reconstruction Bill passed the House. A Senate vote of 38-10 made it the law of the land. Congress's battles with Andrew Johnson did not end there. Afraid to adjourn and leave the political field to Andrew Johnson for the next nine months, the Republican leaders changed tactics. The Thirty-ninth Congress expired on March 4, 1867. Moments later, the Fortieth Congress was sworn in, with Schuyler Colfax re-elected speaker and radical Ben Wade made president pro-tem of the Senate, putting him in line to succeed Johnson, since there was no vice-president.

Another nine months would intervene until the climactic battle for power in December 1867, when a full-scale attempt to impeach the president was made.

Meanwhile, there was a lull that May of 1867 and Blaine took advantage of it for a vacation trip, which turned out to last three months. Accompanied by Senator Justin Morrill of Vermont, he went on his first voyage to Europe.

Seen in modern lights, this voyage might appear like a forerunner of those prescriptive travels of American politicians to the homelands of their constituents—the "Italy, Ireland, and Israel" routes, so-called. Blaine was going back to his own family's roots—

Ireland, in particular—where he and Morrill landed from America and afterward, he was to record an impression that was certainly politically charged: "I had no idea of the beauty of Ireland, nor of the fearful effects of absenteeism and the general disaster to the native race caused by the English policy." But the pair were primarily tourists and on a Sunday in Dublin, Blaine and Morrill decided "to go to church on a large scale," so, in keeping with the latter's split religious heritage, they attended "four Catholic and three Episcopal churches." Then, it was off to Wales and, through Chester, into England, itself. The fourteen-mile trip from Wolverhampton to Birmingham, Blaine described as "one continuous Pittsburgh," while other parts of the countryside were more to his liking. Still making comparisons with the U.S., he wrote, "Take the finest finished and ornamental lawn in Brookline, Roxbury, or any of those beautiful towns around Boston and you see there only what you see in all directions in England." Reaching London, these two veteran legislators naturally had to visit Parliament. They were extremely well-received and Blaine, again political, commented: "…a member of the American Congress is a bigger animal in England than he ever was before. Our war has infused a tremendous respect for us into the minds of Englishmen." The Speaker of the House invited them to take seats on the Peers Bench and in the House of Lords, they also had places of honor. When in London, they met with the American ambassador, Charles Francis Adams, and were "very cordially received." (His son, Henry Adams, was to prove not so friendly to Blaine in future years.) Next, they went to the Continent—to Belgium, Germany (where Blaine noted the growing Prussian power), Italy, Switzerland, and France. As with many American tourists, it was always a treat to be reminded of home by meeting fellow Americans. At the baths of Ragatz, near Zurich, they finally caught up with Elihu Washburne (Israel Washburn, Jr.'s, brother and an Illinois Congressman) and a dozen other Yanks and listened to American songs.

In Paris, Blaine encountered an ex-Confederate general in exile, John Cabell Breckinridge of Kentucky, who had once been the vice president of the United States under Buchanan. With some empathy he wrote, "At the *Theatre L'Imperatrice* last night, I saw John

Breckinridge and his wife. They sat but a very few boxes from us, and were very intently gazing on our party the whole evening. They look sad, downcast, and dispirited. He is in Paris *without money*. What situation could be more deplorable?" In Paris, too, Blaine and Morrill were greeted by local politicians as colleagues and invited to attend the Assemblée National. "Saw Jules Favre, Thiers, and all the magnates..." Blaine wrote. "They were discussing the Mexican question, which is now exciting France profoundly. The death of Maximilian is a terrible blow to Napoleon...."[1] By this, he meant Louis Napoleon, the then-emperor of France. His own small legislative role in helping to evict the French from Mexico was, one can be sure, kept under wraps. In like fashion, he had held his tongue about abuses in colonial Ireland during his contacts with British officialdom.

Blaine was back home in Maine before September, helping with the fall election, and then returning to Washington for the fireworks, as the Radical Republicans tried to remove Andrew Johnson from office. Earlier, on March 2, 1867, while still in session, they had, with Blaine's support, passed the Tenure of Office Act, forbidding the president to dismiss any of his cabinet members without congressional approval. Blaine had had doubts about the bill's constitutionality and on December 7, 1867, his doubts were strong enough to allow him to vote against an impeachment motion. Then, in defiance of the lawmakers, Johnson sacked his Radical Republican Secretary of War Edwin Stanton. The uproar led to another impeachment vote in the House on February 24, 1868, and here Blaine reversed himself and voted to oust Johnson. He later said it was the one vote he most regretted in his political career. The Senate vote, however, was the key and Maine Senator William Pitt Fessenden has been credited with a profile in courage by John F. Kennedy for his unexpected supposedly deciding vote not to impeach.

When not having to be in Washington, and with the exception of trips in the U.S., and sometimes to health spas, Blaine most enjoyed being in Augusta, given over to the pleasures of family, Maine life, and his growing status. There were now five children in the Blaine House, which continued to receive renovations, such as the billiard room. Gail Hamilton provides a vivid description of this period, depicting the geography of the neighborhood, with the state house grounds opposite a nearby park that leads down to the Kennebec River and the tomb of young Governor Enoch Lincoln who died in office at age forty-one. "...to this grave led a path bordered by elms; all through these grounds and through the State House woods and Mulliken's farm and up the Betsy Howard hills and by Canada brook, he [Blaine] rambled and roved with his children and friends in ever fresh and keen enjoyment of the common lot of life...."[2]

As the kids grew, they brought their friends home, "and the outside world came in upon him faster and thicker," the enlarged house, particularly in summer when "Father" was home became "radiant and not infrequently rampant with life. The croquet mallet and the tennis racket and the billiard cue kept the balls in leap and no carriage was too fine and no go-cart too shabby for climbing the far-off hills or winding along the river.... Frequent also were excursions along the coast, taking on all the traits of a pleasure party...."[3]

Chronologically, it was at this fairly quiescent period in Maine that a story broke about an ugly local financial scandal, occurring during the Civil War, which might have cut short Blaine's promising future. None of his biographers mention this episode, where large sums of public money were essentially ripped off. In Maine, the whole sorry affair is known as the "Paper Credit Fraud."

Following the end of hostilities, the scam in question, affecting a number of Maine municipalities and some officials, was brought to the attention of the state legislature. After two half-hearted attempts to look into it, the Republican majority lawmakers in 1870 gave in to media and other pressures and began a serious inquiry.

A person recognized as close to Blaine who appeared to have profited substantially from this scheme was Joe Manley. When his name was brought up in one of the early hearings, he left the state, took a job with the U.S. Internal Revenue Service and was somewhere in Pennsylvania, unreachable, when the Maine solons wished to question him. The essence of the Paper Credit Fraud was this: During the Civil War, municipalities throughout the North were each required to provide so many men for the Union Army. It wasn't always easy to fill their quotas and there were penalties if they didn't. Some sharp-eyed individuals in Maine found a way to help them. They had learned in 1864-65, when a call went out to Down East communities for more draftees, that 1,380 men who had joined the U.S. Navy in various cities around the country were somehow credited to Maine. The towns were then offered these names by groups in Maine for a price. Foremost among these sellers of bogus bodies for the military was an operation run, as one antagonist wrote, by "J. H. Manley, Mr. Blaine's lieutenant, and others, Manley having the lion's share."

The accuser in this case, a disgruntled Maine Democrat named Benjamin Bunker from Waterville, offered such judgment in a fiery pamphlet entitled *Political Deviltry, A Record of Maine's Small Bore Politicians and Political Bosses*, published many years after the event, in which the primary devil in Maine politics, in his eyes, had been and still was—in 1889—James G. Blaine. Bunker estimated that Joe Manley's "ring" collected more than $1.1 million from Maine's cities and towns and Manley, himself, pocketed as much as $100,000. He stated that Manley's father-in-law, Governor Daniel Cony, had been terribly frightened and was heard to say of this business, "It will kill me." Bunker even wrote, "Cony became nervous, sickened and died." A. B. Farwell, a Republican state senator allegedly involved, ended his days in an insane asylum, and the only one of the gang to go to prison was a G. M. Delany who, according to Bunker, didn't stay there long, thanks to political influence.

The invisible political fixer, by inference, was—no surprise—none other than James G. Blaine. Bunker never exactly says so directly. But there was a revelation, not suppressed in the 800-page Maine legislature report on the issue, that established another link to Blaine in addition to Joe Manley.

Whose name should surface but that of Provost Marshall General James B. Fry! And in truth, it was Fry who had made Joe Manley's operation possible.

People asked how men who had enlisted in other states could be credited to Maine. The answer was that General Fry had signed a special order. The legislative investigating commission, itself, wrote, "Perhaps it is fairly inferable from what we have of Mr. Manley's testimony that he [Manley] had some agency in procuring this special order...."

But what agency could Joe Manley have had—except through James G. Blaine?

Thus, two years before Blaine was defending Fry against Conkling, (the order was dated December 10, 1864), the two of them seem to have been in cahoots. Replying to the Maine legislature, General Fry vigorously defended himself against any imputations of wrongdoing and his letter was—and this is most unusual—printed in the *Senate Journal*. Although the issue was raised again by a Maine Democrat leader, Eben Pillsbury, in the 1884 national election, Blaine's part in it, if any, never rose to an item worthy of further investigation. The 800-page report was eventually released, no one read it, and the Paper Credit Fraud receded from public attention.

So, too, slowly, did the Civil War. The Reconstruction battles went on and the Republican Party made hay by "waving the bloody shirt," as it was called, hectoring their Democratic rivals over the atrocities committed against Blacks and carpetbaggers in the South. Ex-General Ben Butler of Massachusetts, as a Republican congressman, was credited with having coined the phrase during a speech in which he waved the blood-soaked shirt of a county superintendent from the North who had been mercilessly horsewhipped in Dixie by the KKK.

Andrew Johnson was gone. The G.O.P. took care of that matter at its nominating convention in 1868, choosing Ulysses S. Grant instead of the incumbent. It was a judicious choice. The Democratic nominee, New York Governor Horatio Seymour (Roscoe Conkling's brother-in-law), didn't stand a chance against the Union's super war hero.

So began the reign of President Grant—two terms and an attempt at a third. Any student of American history knows the bad taste he left behind—a sordid tale of corruption, as the press sensationalized it. Possibly an exaggeration. But corrosion certainly was seeping into the body politic in those years and with it, mounting public pressure for disclosure, as witnessed by the Maine Paper Credit Fraud investigation. The Republican Party, once young and pure and idealistic, was slowly, almost imperceptibly, metamorphosing into something else. James G. Blaine was to feel the effects of this transformation, if not to epitomize it, as he moved continually upward through his party's ranks on his climb to the very top.

---

1. This and all other quotes out of his first European trip are from Hamilton and a unidentified document or documents she had at her disposal.
2. Ibid., p. 192.
3. Ibid., p. 193.

TEN

MR. SPEAKER

A WORK CALLED *FACTS ABOUT CONGRESS* had this to say in its section on the 41st Congress, which met from March 4, 1869, to March 3, 1871.[1] "James Gillespie Blaine (Rep., Maine) was elected Speaker on March 4, 1869.... Like Schuyler Colfax (Rep., Indiana) before him, who served as Speaker from the 38th Congress through the 40th Congress, Blaine was able to maintain sufficient control over the House to remain as Speaker from the 41st. Congress through the 43rd Congress."

Like everything in politics, nothing is ever automatic and Blaine's rise to the speakership was no exception.

His putative Republican competition that first time out in 1869 was Henry L. Dawes, a representative from western Massachusetts who had a few years seniority on him. Dawes has been described as "a cunning, experienced, singed-cat kind of man."[2] Almost two decades later, as a U.S. senator, he achieved national notoriety with the Dawes Act, a far-reaching piece of legislation intended to force the assimilation of the Indian tribes in Oklahoma but that essentially dispossessed them of large quantities of their land. His fatuous remark that his bill would push the Indians to "wear civilized clothes, cultivate ground, live in houses, ride in Studebaker wagons, send children to school, drink whiskey, and own property" is still remembered with much bitterness and scorn by present-day Indian activists. Blaine lured him to withdraw his candidacy by promising Dawes the chairmanship of the all-powerful House Ways and Means Committee.

According to Allen Peskin, a James A. Garfield biographer,[3] there was one problem with that maneuver. Garfield, Blaine's closest buddy, had coveted the same chairmanship ever since he'd entered the House.

Peskin does not display a high opinion of Blaine. Under Colfax, Garfield had been appointed chair of the Military Affairs Committee. Apparently, he made it known he wished to keep that chairmanship while also acquiring the Ways and Means chairmanship. These are the kinds of ego problems with which speakers must deal. As Peskin tells it, Blaine deliberately ducked Garfield, who three times tried to see him and was turned away on the pretext the speaker wasn't in. One day, having received his visiting card back with the same excuse, Garfield stood and watched ex-Speaker Colfax walk into Blaine's office with no trouble.

A further illustration of Blaine's deviousness, according to Peskin, was that the man from Maine denied ever making any deals for the speakership, nor even having solicited a vote. Dawes's cynical response supposedly was, "Well, half the House are liars or he is mistaken." On March 12, 1869, Blaine informed Garfield he was to be put on the very powerful Appropriations Committee and likewise chair the Census Committee, the only member of Appropriations to have a chairmanship. In addition, Blaine wrote Garfield: "...as a mark of my special personal regard and interest as a compliment, I place you on the Committee of Rules" [another powerful placement]. To Peskin, all of these extra perks just added insult to injury: "No amount of smooth explanation or expression of 'personal regard' could disguise the fact that Blaine had dealt his friend a crooked hand."[4]

Garfield, himself, confined his thoughts on such matters to the next Congress when re-elected Speaker Blaine had to face the rigmarole of making committee assignments again. The word was soon out in G.O.P. circles that Blaine had promised Garfield the seat he wanted on Ways and Means. However, high-tariff opponents within the Republican Party, like Horace Greeley, the highly influential editor of the *New York Herald Tribune*, did not want Garfield. To appease this faction, Blaine met in a hotel room with a number of them who were threatening to bolt the party. Included was Boston cotton merchant Edward Atkinson who acted as a sort of guru to Blaine on tariff matters. Meanwhile, Garfield was saying publicly, "If Mr. Blaine does not appoint me chairman of Ways and Means, "he is the basest of men."

In the end, Blaine put Dawes back as head of Ways and Means and made Garfield chairman of the Appropriations Committee.

Fully venting his disgust, author Peskin wrote that Garfield "…quickly resumed cordial relations with the Speaker who had now betrayed him two times in a row."[5]

The political body over which James Gillespie Blaine ruled for three concurrent terms had earned its nickname of the "Bear Garden." Blaine did not tame this unruly place all at once, but his imposing presence, wit, knowledge of its Byzantine rules, willingness to enter combat when necessary, fairness and tact, did manage to overawe the membership and he soon gained high marks from both sides for the way he ran its operations. Rarely would he come down from the rostrum and speak—one notable exception occurring when he took on the redoubtable Ben Butler of "Bloody Shirt" fame who had pugnaciously challenged a ruling of his and, claimed witnesses, left the Massachusetts "stormy petrel" speechless and quivering in his seat. Blaine's expressed philosophy was, "The Speaker should, with consistent fidelity to his own party, be the impartial administrator of the rules of the House, and a constant participation in the discussion of members would take from him that appearance of impartiality which it is so important to maintain in the rulings of the Chair."[6] He much preferred prearranging things quietly so the work flowed smoothly.

His wife, Harriet, in her diary-like letters that commenced the year Blaine first became speaker, exposed the long, intense effort he had to expend in making his committee choices. "It's the secret of the power of the Speaker," she stated, aware of the complex difficulties that arose, like his problems with Garfield, and his need to re-arrange and compromise and manipulate his way out of them. "It is a matter in which no one can help him," she affirmed.[7]

This collection of letters, published five years after she died in 1903, has brought into the limelight the one person who throughout Blaine's career helped him the most in just about everything he did. She provided an ever-present stability for the man whose brilliance lent him the air of a chaotic genius. She had no mean intelligence, herself, as the wit and perception in her letters attest. And she ran a household of six children, servants, et. al., with the

Mrs. James G. Blaine, the former Harriet Bailey Stanwood of Augusta, Maine, the Yankee "schoolmarm" Blaine had met in Kentucky, who ran his household with a strong, perceptive hand, played a major role in his political life and suffered the deaths of one toddler, three grown children, and her husband to end her days in a "darkness."
BOYD, *LIFE AND PUBLIC SERVICES OF JAMES G. BLAINE*

same efficiency and flare that her husband displayed in his sovereignty over the U.S. House as speaker. Eventually, she was directing three households every year—one in D.C., one in Augusta, and one in Bar Harbor.

The very first of her letters, datelined simply "Augusta, 1869," was to their oldest son, Walker, then fourteen, a student at Phillips Academy, Andover. Knowing the boy was lonely, she began, "I did you the honor of keeping Father's letters waiting while I read all of yours," and to counter his homesickness, told of her own, when she was sent to boarding school in Ipswich, Massachusetts, at age nine. She wrote that she cried for her "wormwood and molasses," and they gave it to her.

The rest of the letter was merely chatty, naming VIPs who had visited the Blaine home—General Hodsdon, adjutant-general of the Maine National Guard, and Captain Charles A. Boutelle, Bangor editor and future congressman. She wrote that workers "were painting the house, building a portico on the south doors, lowering the chimneys, and re-sodding the north bank..." and "...the Bingham boys and Fred Cony were just going up back of the State House for a walk."

Her next letter, dated April 27, 1869, reflected not only the separation from her son, but her husband's continuous absence in D.C., now as speaker. It's hard to tell, given her dry Yankee sense of humor, if she's complaining or not in the following excerpts from that missive: "To all this large household, I am obliged to be father, mother, aunt, and referral on every subject, spiritual and secular.... Father meets me with the salutation, 'Well, old lady, the separation is over. We have nothing to do now but enjoy each other.'" Blaine, she said, would arrive in Augusta on a Friday and go back on Wednesday, carrying his old traveling bag, "which I could pack asleep, saying goodbye with the best grace I may."

Subsequently, Harriet did write humorously that her husband was home for as long as "it took the Creator to make the world," but that he "rested his six days and on the seventh commenced his labor anew." The letters go on and on with their snatches of insights into Blaine life at this period. Walker had gotten used to Andover, where students are taught to call all adults "Sir." Harriet describes him calling Aunt Caddy "Sir." Also, Emmons didn't want to go to Andover but Mr. Blaine wanted him to do so; Maggie successfully fought having a haircut, despite her Speaker of the House father's threatening and coaxing; James, the baby, was called by his mother *Que J'aime* ("Whom I love," in French)—a bilingual pun. The author of these letters often liked to sprinkle them with French phrases, and she candidly told Walker she was leading two lives "the one when I am with your father, all vanity, wide-awake, gay; the other, all Aunt Susan, sewing machine, children...."

Home at recess, Blaine took sick, but soon was walking two miles out on Augusta's main thoroughfare "by Combs Mills." Tom Sherman, his newly hired secretary, was in the Augusta residence, too, engaged in the never-ending task of getting his boss's papers together. Thirty boxes and bags of mail had been brought up from the Augusta Post Office. The speaker was off to Lewiston for a meeting of the Republican State Committee. There were rumors (this was 1871) of political problems for the Maine G.O.P.. Maggie fell from an apple tree and broke her arm. Cousin Abby (Gail Hamilton) arrived.

Soon Tom Sherman was an integral part of the Blaine household. The position of speaker had come with a few advantages, among them the right to hire an assistant, as well as a "parlor" where he could receive visitors and colleagues in private. Sherman was to hold his job for twenty years, but sometimes precariously. He, himself, didn't tell any stories in his own book of reminiscences, yet the youngest Blaine child, Harriet Blaine Beale, related in an essay how her father was always misplacing papers and blaming Sherman, whom she called "a very member of our family." Young Harriet more than once witnessed a scene she described: "'Mr. Blaine has dismissed me,' he [Sherman] would say to my mother. 'I will go out into the orchard until I can come back.'"[8]

Quite an incident occurred during one of the family's perennial moves from Maine to D.C. Tom Sherman was putting together a box of his boss's papers to ship and having some extra room, asked Mrs. Blaine if she wanted to send anything. She included a pair of curtains. At the same time, she was preparing a box of old clothes to send to some distant cousins in the West. In the mailing, the two boxes got mixed up and the cousins, instead of receiving the expected clothes, found papers that meant nothing to them and a set of useless curtains. Angered, they burnt the papers. Once informed, Mrs. Blaine warned Tom never to say anything about the incident, and Blaine never knew his papers had been lost.

Despite the temporary perils of his position, Tom Sherman maintained in his book that "Mr. Blaine was a saint."[9] Mrs. Blaine, to him, "was a woman of brilliant mind and keen wit, a fitting mate for her husband in mental quality...." We also learn from Sherman that Aunt Susan Stanwood did part of the household duties in Augusta, made the "best apple pie." and "warned" the younger members when they got out of line. Other vignettes of their Augusta life include a depiction of Blaine's library at home as just another playroom for the kids, and of Blaine, a tireless worker who "could write all day," drafting everything in long-hand until the advent of the typewriter, which he used to produce his voluminous *Twenty Years of Congress*. On the rare occasions when Blaine resorted to dictation, Sherman tells of leaning against an apple tree in the garden and using a plank to write on while Blaine paced. His boss's chief exercise, in fact, was walking "over the hills and through the woods in Augusta...."

Trifles bothered Blaine, Sherman acknowledged, but not major happenings like losing a presidential nomination or election, business reverses, or the treachery of a friend. Mrs. Blaine was the "angel who rushed in" when things were missing and found them in places where Sherman "feared to tread."

In 1869 Blaine also bought a house in Washington, D.C. It was in a fashionable part of the city, downtown on 15th Street between H and I Streets, and he accomplished this transaction with the aid of a $30,000 mortgage loan from Jay Cooke and Company, private investment bankers. During winters thereafter the whole family would move to the capital and Harriet Blaine became a Washington hostess of sorts, if a somewhat diffident one. But the hominess of Maine was continued on 15th Street. Professor Muzzey writes, "Other men gave more elaborate dinners, but no other could furnish a more delightful and profitable evening," and he pictures how "distinguished guests" at his "hospitable table...often forgot to finish their courses as they became absorbed in the feast of reason which he set before them from his wonderful store of historical and political knowledge."[10]

The 15th Street house was a mile from the Capitol and Blaine often walked to work, taking his children or guests with him. He was in the speaker's chair by noon. Snacks and even lunches were available in his parlor.

His cousin Ellen Ewing Sherman, married to General Sherman, lived but a short distance away in a home provided by the government. Two of her ex-general brothers, Hugh and Thomas Jr., were in and out of Washington. The former was the American minister to Belgium, and the latter, a D.C. lawyer, later became a Democratic congressman from Ohio. Their venerable father, Thomas Sr., after a brief spurt of new fame when Andrew Johnson wanted to name him vice-president, stayed in the capital city with Ellen in his declining years.

Harriet Blaine's letters didn't shrink from political matters, even when writing to her offspring. In the summer of 1871, after Blaine's successful first term as speaker, she was informing Walker, then sixteen and spending a year in Europe, of Father's acclaimed "Saratoga Serenade Speech" that had the opposition party all upset, and of scurrilous attacks on Father by the *Maine Standard*, an Augusta newspaper. The latter articles may have been in response to the Saratoga declamation where Blaine had gone after the waste and corruption of the Democrats' Tammany Hall "ring" in New York City and contrasted it to the economies of the G.O.P. administration in Washington, D.C. The *Standard*'s slap at the speaker, Harriet wrote her son, cited "his princely style of living, his retinue of servants, and the expensive education he is giving his children—one son now traveling in Europe."

Signifying Blaine's growing prominence in the United States, both of these occurrences made the pages of the *New York Times*. It had become the "Serenade speech" because Blaine was honored at Saratoga's Grand Union Hotel with a serenade from supporters and the headline on page one was: "MR. BLAINE'S SERENADE." Wagner's New York Orchestra played the music for it and a crowd of 10,000 attended and sang, jamming the grand piazza, and "even the ladies indulged in prolonged clapping of hands." Those waves of applause particularly rose "...when reference was made to the honesty of the National Administration as compared with the Tammany role in New York." (Tammany boss, William Marcy Tweed was to be indicted two months later.) But Blaine was also able to tie in the national Democrats by stating: "...the power of Tammany with its money in the North and the power of terrorism in the South are the weapons relied upon by the Democratic leaders to carry the national election next year." He blamed the Northern

Democratic leaders for the unchecked terrorism of the Ku Klux Klan. If they wanted to, they could stop it, he claimed.

Then he went on an odd tangent, but perhaps a brilliant one, given his mixed religious background. He spoke of the municipal government in New York City stopping a Protestant parade that celebrated their seventeenth-century victory over Catholics in Ireland at the battle of the Boyne. It was, no doubt, a pitch to assure Protestant voters of his affiliation with them, as he went on to state, "Protestant myself, I stand for the rights of all…. While I concede the full rights of the Catholic Irish to celebrate St. Patrick's Day, I demand equal rights for the Boyne celebration."[11]

Two-and-a-half weeks later, another long *New York Times* article dealt with Speaker Blaine. Or rather, they reprinted a letter Blaine had sent to the editors of the hostile *Maine Standard* the week before. The *Times'* heading was, "Speaker Blaine: A Personal Explanation Called for by Persistent Slanderers. What He owns and How He acquired it." Here was Blaine at his best, counterpunching, with an air of injured innocence, plus an avalanche of facts. The *Standard* had called him "a millionaire rolling in luxury," who had amassed his wealth through "public affairs."

The only correct fact in their attack, he replied, was that he paid a tax on a valuation of $37,000. No, he did not own any "land and coal property in Virginia," as they had claimed, nor an interest in a Lake Superior copper mine, nor a princely residence in D.C. worth $40,000 or $50,000. Yes, he did own some shares in a land company in West Virginia—which he bought for $2,000 six years ago and would be "glad to sell it to you for that price today." As to the *princely* residence in the nation's capital, he bought it for $28,000, with a mortgage, and it would have cost him $5,000 a year to rent in D.C., but his mortgage payments were only $2,000 a year. Yes, he did own coal and land property in Pennsylvania, near his birthplace. These were bought, he says, in 1857, 1858, 1859, and 1861, "all before my name was even mentioned for Congress." Claiming his income and the increased value of his investments give him "a respectable competency but not great wealth," Blaine ended with a typical flurry of verbal blows. He would have gained much more money if he had been out of public life. "…if you have knowledge that I have ever acquired a dollar improperly, I trust you will publish it.... I cannot afford to have property imputed to me which I do not possess." And finally, he noted how devastating it is to have to reveal one's private affairs.[12]

For the historian, with knowledge of the future awaiting Speaker Blaine, there is something like cosmic irony in the reading of these two *New York Times* entries. Was the germ of the "continental liar" epithet already being laid? A reporter who had dug around then might have uncovered a few juicy tidbits and sensationalized them, for instance, by taking another look at that Washington, D.C., mortgage.

There were several Jay Cooke and Company banking houses. The parent organization was in Philadelphia, where Jay Cooke, himself, presided. Another was in New York City, led by a partner, Harris Fahnestock. And Washington, D.C., had two: the First National Bank of Washington, and Jay Cooke and Company, controlled by Cooke's younger brother, Henry Cooke, which was the investment body from which Blaine had received his home loan.

Most likely, it was Henry Cooke who had arranged this transaction. He was the political arm of the Cooke operation, a lobbyist who concentrated on Congress, since the Cookes had a great deal to do with the government. About Henry Cooke, Harvard Business School's Henrietta Larson, in her biography of Jay Cooke, writes: "Like the Rothschilds, he tried to stay close to men in power. He seems to have known everybody worth knowing; he entertained lavishly at his home; his office was almost like a political club. Needy Congressmen sought loans at his banks...and President Grant enjoyed many a cheering glass at his home...."[13]

The Cookes also had inside contacts within the national press corps and the services of a congressional reporter who used the code name of "Star." Nor were just front-line journalists involved. Pitt Cooke, another younger brother of Jay's has been quoted, "It's only a question of the *price* you will pay whether these Editors will lie for you or against you." This was an era when things were done this way and no one thought much about it. On the Blaine loan, a question could be who had approached whom? Did Henry Cooke first make the suggestion to the new speaker or was Blaine one of those "needy congressmen" seeking a good deal for himself?

With the entrance of Jay Cooke into Blaine's life, there is something of a taint in that fact, alone, although Cooke was something of a hero in the North for his success in selling government bonds to finance the Union victory. He wasn't yet the villain whose financial collapse had ushered in the panic of 1873. His name likewise hadn't yet been overly linked with the railroad building of these post-Civil War years that brought a robber-baron reputation to those who succeeded at it and helped forever sully Blaine's reputation for his actually quite minor forays into its financial vortexes.

Henrietta Larson has unveiled an extraordinary exchange of letters between Blaine and Jay Cooke that showed the new speaker in an aggressive, acquisitive mode vis-à-vis the explosion of railroad building in the U.S. and the financial opportunities it afforded. The year was 1869, not long after Blaine assumed his position of power.

Jay Cooke was involved with the Northern Pacific Railroad and Blaine warned him he should not undertake trying to finance that line without federal aid. This was not exactly disinterested advice, with the obvious message that he, Blaine, could be helpful. The quid pro quo soon became equally as clear. Blaine had some railroad bonds of his own he wanted Cooke to buy.

Through contacts in Boston, the speaker had been given the "opportunity" to make a nice piece of change by selling the stocks and bonds of a small projected railroad in Arkansas—the Little Rock and Fort Smith—that seven years later would become nationally infamous. At this point, in 1869, it was simply a vision of investors, picking up yet another proposed line whose future had been stalled by the intervention of the Civil War. Blaine, who had been given $130,000 worth of paper to sell, for which he would receive a handsome commission, asked Jay Cooke to assume $91,500 of that amount.

The financier's reluctance had nothing to do with the ethics of the situation. In fact, it could be argued, neither man would have seen any conflict of interest under the political mores of that day.

Blaine was absolutely eloquent in making his pitch, using a metaphor taken from early nineteenth-century history that would be totally mystifying today. Knowing that Cooke had an interest in combining his Northern Pacific Railroad with the still unfinished Southern Pacific, Blaine wrote that the Little Rock and Fort Smith Railroad would be "the *Quatre Bras* of the Southern Continental Railroad." The allusion was to a key strategic point—*Quatre Bras*—captured by the Duke of Wellington in his famous victory over Napoleon at Waterloo. "Your House can be and ought to be the leading Railroad power of the world," Blaine cajoled Cooke. By controlling both the Northern and Southern Pacific lines, "you double the profits of each.... And to have control of two Continental lines of Railway is an object, allow me to say, worthy of the highest ambition of any man." No longer was Blaine merely implying he could do favors for Cooke from the speaker's chair. He stated his intention baldly: "I may say without Egotism that my position will enable me to render you service of vital importance and value...." There it was, in writing, with solely the rather weak caveat added—"services for which I cannot desire or accept profit or gain to myself," since he went on to emphasize, "I am willing, however, and ready to do all for you in my power at any time you may desire.... Just how your subscription to the enterprise will aid me, I need not explain—Sufficient that it is so."

But Jay Cooke wasn't biting. He figured he could get Blaine's support in Congress, anyway, and not have to shell out $91,500 for Arkansas railroad bonds and stocks that were probably worthless. Larsen concludes dryly, "One suspects that the heavy loan to Blaine by the Washington house of Jay Cooke was granted to secure the Speaker's good will."[14]

This brazen move by Blaine seems on a par with his 1858 untoward request to Congressman Israel Washburn, Jr., to appoint an unqualified relative to West Point. What is most interesting now is that here, in 1869, Blaine had already engaged himself in what would prove an utter disaster for his future career—his entanglement with the Little Rock and Fort Smith Railroad through a young Boston businessman named Warren Fisher, Jr. The losses from this fiasco initially were merely financial for Blaine, not counted political, as long as carelessly worded letters like Blaine's plea to Jay Cooke could be kept under wraps.

Yet in November 1871, Harriet Blaine was to include this disturbing entry in her letters: "Mrs. Warren Fisher has another daughter.... Mr. Fisher seems to be fast losing in the esteem of all good men. Every new discovery your Father makes only seems to show a baseness still deeper. Will he ever reach the bottom of his treachery toward himself?"

Just around the corner was the presidential election of 1872. Corruption had started to become an issue. It couldn't derail Grant's re-election, but a series of articles in the Democratic *New York Sun* about a major boondoggle in federal railroad assistance stirred up a hornet's nest that soon had the country abuzz, and the subsequent investigation did touch Mr. Speaker Blaine.

1. Stephen G. Christanson. *Facts About Congress* (New York and Dublin: H. W. Wilson Company, 1961), p. 178.

2. Mark Wahlgren Summers. *Rum, Romanism, and Rebellion* (Chapel Hill, NC: University of North Carolina Press, 2000), p. 60.

3. Allen Peskin. *Garfield: A Biography* (Kent, OH: Kent State University Press, 1978).

4. Ibid., pp. 302–03.

5. Ibid., p. 196.

6. Russell, p. 196.

7. Harriet S. Blaine Beale, Ed. *Letters of Mrs. James G. Blaine*, Vol. 1 (New York: Duffield and Company, 1908), pp. 41, 50.

8. Harriet S. Blaine Beale. "James G. Blaine," in *Just Maine Folks*, by the Maine Writers Research Club.

9. Sherman, p. 10.

10. Muzzey, p. 64.

11. *New York Times*, 17 August 1871.

12. Ibid., 3 September 1871.

13. Henrietta M. Larson. *Jay Cooke, Private Banker* (Cambridge, MA: Harvard University Press, 1936), p. 200.

14. Ibid., pp. 274–75.

ELEVEN

STORM, CALM, THEN A BIGGER STORM

CREDIT MOBILIER is an odd name for an American construction company. Habitually printed with an accent ague over the first e, in memory of its French origins, it was founded in the United States, along with its lesser known real estate operation, Credit Foncier, by George Francis Train, a world-traveling American entrepreneur, once called the "Clipper Ship King, who had seen its linked prototype at work in France in the development of Gallic railroads. Such entities were set up to be the recipients of single-source, no-bid contracts from a parent railroad to do the needed work of building rail lines and developing real estate, and they offered innumerable opportunities for kiting bills, pocketing federal aid, and skimming off profits.

In the U.S. George Francis Train chartered his companies under the same French names. In turn, they were bought from him by Dr. Thomas C. Durant, an ex-physician from Massachusetts who had taken over the building of the transcontinental Union Pacific Railroad. This ambitious project had received millions of dollars in construction subsidies and millions of acres of public land from Congress. When a palace coup in 1864 ousted Durant, he was replaced by two Massachusetts siblings who until then had been in the shovel manufacturing business, Oliver Ames and his brother, Congressman Oakes Ames.

Pressure to investigate purported Union Pacific abuses of their federal grants had come from another brother combination—the Maine-born Congressmen, Cadwallader Washburn of Minnesota and Elihu Washburne of Illinois (he'd added an *e* to his surname)— siblings of Israel Washburn, Jr. Frightened his fellow congressmen might listen too favorably to these goody-goody colleagues, Oakes Ames began passing out Union Pacific stock to key members, allegedly selling it, but never collecting any money, although still honoring their dividend payments. Given the complacency and venality of the press of the day, this whole shady business was kept under wraps for a number of years. That the affair erupted in the midst of the 1872 presidential campaign was due to the anger of a Union Pacific trustee, one Henry McComb, who felt he was owed 375 shares of Union Pacific stock Oakes Ames resolutely refused to give him.

Grant's reelection campaign of 1872 had already seen the corruption issue emerge to an extent. Back in 1869, two of the most notorious robber barons in American history, Jay Gould and his partner, "Big Jim" Fisk, had caused the Black Friday crash on Wall Street by trying to corner the U.S. gold market. Although Grant eventually helped stop them by having his treasury secretary sell U.S. government gold, the president's own brother-in-law, Abel Corbin, had been deeply involved in the plot. The start of the presidential year 1872 saw this pair of robber barons in the headlines again—Fisk, because he was murdered in a fight over a woman, and Jay Gould, when he was removed physically as head of the Erie Railroad, from which it was revealed he had purloined millions. Within the Republican Party, there now began a visible reaction against these sorts of financial shenanigans—a bolt of liberal Republicans first to a third party, which chose New York publisher Horace Greeley to challenge President Grant's re-election, then unexpectedly into a merger with the traditional G.O.P. opposition when the Democrats made Greeley their candidate, too.

The Democratic *New York Sun* fulminated against "Congressmen Who Have Robbed The People And Who Now Support The National Robber," referring to a list, released by McComb, of those supposedly bribed by Union Pacific, and Blaine was among them. Stoutly denying the accusation, he hurried to Maine for the traditional September balloting and engineered a smashing Republican victory to help dampen the cries of corruption being hurled at the G.O.P. and the Grant administration.

During this election back home, Blaine argued that Down East voters would resent the "imputations on Grant's character as a personal affront to themselves." His own prediction had been that Republican Governor Sidney Perham would be re-elected by 14,000 votes—a figure scoffed at by opposing editors, but actually exceeded in voting that gave Blaine's party every county, every congressional district, every state senate district, and four-fifths of the house districts. Blaine, himself, running for his seat in Congress again, won all twenty-seven towns he represented, including six Democratic strongholds. November provided a like triumph. Blaine's prediction had been a Grant victory in Maine by 25,000 votes. The ultimate margin was 30,000.

In the interim, Greeley's *New York Tribune* hit Blaine with another sensational charge to add to the Credit Mobilier scandal. On September 28, 1872, they ran a page one story under the headline PROOF OF BLAINE'S FRAUDS. Blaine's denial he had ever owned Credit Mobilier stock was now trumped by the accusation he had been given 32,500 shares—worth more than $1 million—of the Leavenworth, Pawnee, and Western Railroad, organized in Kansas, which had been merged with the Union Pacific. The clinching argument, supplied by the *Tribune,* was that he'd been paid off for pushing a Union Pacific bill through Congress in 1862. The sole difficulty with that argument, Blaine teasingly pointed out, was that he had not been in Congress in 1862. He had not even been nominated for a congressional seat. He was speaker of the house in Maine. "I had no more to do with congressional legislation than the fish wardens and tide waiters on the Kennebec River," he told a partisan crowd in Cleveland, Ohio, while campaigning for the G.O.P. ticket, drawing roars of laughter.

He was equally cavalier in demolishing the argument that he really did own stock in the Kansas railroad but under the name of his brother, John E. Blaine.

Speaker Blaine offered the press some dialogue from an old stage play.

"Does your brother like cheese?"

"I have no brother."

"If you had a brother, would he like cheese?"

But really to belabor the point, he called upon his cousin and boyhood friend, Tom Ewing, Jr., who had worked for the Leavenworth, Pawnee, and Western Railroad. This was done in a public exchange of letters between October 1 and October 7, 1872, while the national election campaign was still raging. Blaine had sent Ewing copies of the *Tribune* articles, which had identified the ex-Civil War general and a Colonel J. C. Stone as the agents of the Kansas railroad who had contracted the alleged stock deal with Blaine. Asking Ewing to clear up this "groundless accusation," the Speaker made sure to emphasize his cousin's Democratic credentials. "The political line that separates us will not, I am sure, prevent your recognizing the claim I have upon your friendly candor."[1] The answer that came back and was given to the press included Ewing's opinion that the factual mistake of the *Tribune* editors had "conclusively disproved" their charge that Blaine had abused his power in Congress, when he hadn't been in Congress. More importantly, on the stock matter, he could affirm James G. Blaine had had no connection with the railroad, but that J. E. Blaine, his brother, a resident of Leavenworth and an early Kansas settler, did have a $10,000 investment. Once General Ewing's letter was released, the *Tribune* withdrew that specific charge, but retained its option of going after the Speaker on the Credit Mobilier affair, where his name had headed the list of congressmen contacted.

The drumbeat went on during the rest of the 1872 campaign. Opponents loudly trumpeted Blaine's ownership of bonds of yet another railroad line—the Iowa Falls and Sioux City Railroad. Nor did Blaine deny the fact. He'd bought them from his friend Abner Coburn and, since this railroad received no federal aid, he declared, "I hold the stock in my own name and the transaction is one which Congress, in my judgment, is no more called on to investigate than it would be to inquire into the weekly expenses of my household."[2] Even after the election, the game of thrust and parry continued. Accused of having spent $100,000 to win the Maine September elections, Blaine opened his Republican State Committee records, showing an expenditure of only $12,000.

What effect this muckraking in 1872 was to have on American politics did not essentially reveal itself at the time. Grant easily defeated Horace Greeley, who died shortly afterward. The Liberal Republicans ceased to exist as a separate political entity. The voters, it seemed, were still not too stirred up about corruption, as such. The Gilded Age of growth and high living was kicking into gear, and an extremely clever and agile politician like Blaine found no difficulty in treading carefully through the minefields that all these financial opportunities presented to those in public life.

In fact, where the threat of Credit Mobilier remained over his party, he made a preemptive strike as soon as a new Congress had been seated and he, himself, chosen Speaker again.

On opening day, his first act was to summon "Sunset" Cox, the Ohio Democrat, and make him Speaker pro-tem. From the floor, Speaker Blaine then offered an order, carefully drawn up beforehand. It created a special Credit Mobilier investigating committee, whose members he had already chosen. For its leader, Blaine had picked an ideal figurehead, Vermont's Luke P. Poland, white-bearded, venerable, of stern Yankee-visage, the very image of squeaky-clean probity, albeit a veteran G.O.P. operative. Blaine's original idea had been to have this ad hoc group meet behind closed doors but such a howl went up that he quickly retreated. To no one's surprise, the first witness before the Poland committee turned out to be James G. Blaine. It was now common knowledge that Oakes Ames's list contained only potential prospects, so at once Blaine was able to testify how he'd been offered Union Pacific stock and declined it. Turning to a powerfully built, obese, bullet-headed man in the committee room, he asked: "Is that not so, Mr. Ames?" Representative Oakes Ames answered simply: "It is so, Mr. Blaine." Their terse exchange completed, the Speaker stepped down and later received total exoneration in the committee's written report.

In fact, the only two congressionals really burned by the Credit Mobilier scandal ended up being Oakes Ames and James Brooks, also of Massachusetts, the sole Democrat caught in the web of corruption. There was talk of expelling both from the House. This idea, in the end, was commuted to mere resolutions of censure, which soon were blamed for the deaths of these two men—from natural causes—shortly after the close of the session.

Vice President Schuyler Colfax, named in the scandal, suffered, too. Early on, he had lost his place on Grant's 1872 ticket, then had had to endure the opprobrium of having been caught lying about his Union Pacific holdings and realizing any future political career for him (he'd entertained presidential hopes) was finished. But from Blaine's point of view, the worst threat had been to his friend James A. Garfield. Like Colfax, Garfield had told the Poland committee, "I never owned, received, or agreed to receive any stock of the Credit Mobilier or of the Union Pacific Railroad, nor any dividend or profit arising from any of them." Yet this wasn't quite true and, as with Colfax, it seemed Garfield would be put down as a liar and any future for him in politics essentially ruined. The problem was a mere $329—the dividend, according to Ames, from $1,000 in stocks (ten shares) that Garfield *had* accepted, despite his sworn statement. Although the final committee report gave no hint Garfield had lied, it did print Ames's version and the Ohioan's future remained imperiled.

Charles Edward Russell has written, "From this state of ignominious defeat he was rescued by one man. Blaine had been triumphantly and with great eclat re-elected speaker. He went out of his way, far out and many times, to show esteem, regard and consideration for Garfield."[3] Gone for good now, assuredly, was any lingering bitterness Garfield may have felt over being denied the chairmanship of the Ways and Means Committee. Blaine let him keep his almost as prestigious Appropriations Committee chair. The Speaker also allowed himself to be seen, to quote Russell, "often with Garfield on terms of cordiality.[4]

Once more, Blaine, because of the Credit Mobilier scandal's outcome, not despite it, was viewed in a "white knight" mode publicly. And he could even afford to use his speaker's prerogative and win some gratitude from affected party members by opposing expulsion and substituting censure for the worst miscreants. Russell tells how Blaine had kept the vote open on the resolution calling for censure instead of expulsion, until he could maneuver a switch of eleven votes.[5] Also reported is the fact that after Oakes Ames's death, his hometown of Easton, Massachusetts, built a public hall it named for him and Blaine contributed a testimonial when the building was dedicated.[6] Gail Hamilton later documented Blaine's efforts to ameliorate Ames's plight in painting a picture she had witnessed with her own eyes: "I have seldom seen a more pathetic sight than that of Oakes Ames [whom she called: "a man of honored ancestry and stainless name"]...sitting silent, stunned into immobility before Mr. Blaine's library fire with his head bowed on his breast while the younger man, alert and intent, applied himself indefatigably in and out of the house, arranging for his defense...."[7]

It has been postulated that the period in which he was speaker constituted the happiest years of James G. Blaine's life. He was doing a job he loved, which he did with exceptional skill, earning plaudits on all sides. He now had two comfortable homes and by 1872, six lovely children who, except for some worrisome bouts of illness, were thriving. He was on a fast track to even greater honors and power, getting by quite well financially, and had survived his first big political crisis—Credit Mobilier—with complete success, so much so that his stature had soared along with his name recognition nationally.

Mrs. Blaine has left us many word pictures of the family aspect of that new and heady life, especially for 1872. On January 8 of that year, she was writing from Washington, D.C., to her oldest daughter Alice, who had stayed home in Augusta to attend St. Catherine's, the Catholic school she enjoyed so much. The Blaine entourage had arrived in the nation's capital the late afternoon before, "very tired, very dirty, and very anxious to get rest, a bath, and something to eat. It seemed good to see Robert at the carriage door, and have someone carry our bundles even into the house. And here let me give you a little piece of advice,—to pack everything away before starting on a journey so as to go arm free. We were thoroughly loaded down with shawls, bags, muffs, overcoat, basket, and baby...."[8] Besides Robert, who seemed to be a combined handyman/butler, and other servants named Martha, Mary Wilson, and James, there was a Miss Sanborn, a nanny, helping out with Maggie, J'aime (young James), and the newly born baby, named Harriet for her mother, but usually referred to by Mrs. Blaine as Little Sister. "We found the [D.C.] house in beautiful order and at six precisely were called down to dinner. It was served, of course, in beautiful order, Robert taking his stand at the back of Mr. Blaine's chair in his old style. Soup, macaroni, then a splendid roast of beef, slaw, cranberry, celery, etc., apple sago pudding, oranges and apples, and as good a cup of tea as I ever tasted. It seemed to me I had never seen the house look so well...."[9]

There they were, a comfy, well-off family of the Gilded Age— upper middle class, one would say. Blaine was no tycoon on the order of Jay Cooke, from whom he'd borrowed money, or Jay Gould, with whom he was to have a political connection, or Andrew Carnegie, with whom he became good friends. But they were solid folk, living much better than most in that nineteenth-century American society

Father was a celebrity, to be sure, and so their social rounds were with celebrities of the political and business worlds. The trunks shipped from Augusta had barely arrived when Harriet Blaine had to hurry off to a luncheon, barely having time to un- pack a black silk dress, red shawl, and brown hat for her to wear. She was going to Mrs. Creswell's—John A. J. Creswell, a U.S. sena- tor from Maryland had become postmaster general under Grant— and it was "a most elegant affair," she wrote Alice. All the ladies of the cabinet were present.

Invitations were pouring in, she wrote. She had two from Fer- nando Wood, who was a neighbor and a member of Congress. Wood and his wife are mentioned a number of times and appear to have become friends, although Wood was a dyed-in-the-wool Dem- ocrat. He had been mayor of New York City, had first entered Con- gress, like Blaine, during the Civil War, but as a Peace Democrat, the most outspoken of "copperheads," aligned with Clement Val- andigham. Perhaps his redeeming political feature in James G. Blaine's eyes was that he had broken with Tammany Hall under whose auspices he had begun his political career.

Nevertheless, one of the first persons Harriet Blaine went to see shortly after arriving in Washington in January 1872 was Mrs. Wood. Starting that day, she had visited the nearby White House to pay her respects to Mrs. Grant but on her way back, stopped at the Woods' home, wishing to inquire about a school for "M." (Maggie). The Woods had a daughter who appeared to be about the same age as Maggie. We also learn that concurrently, "J'aime," (young James) was "very, very sick," struck down by remittent fever, which had gone to his brain. In a letter to oldest son Walker at Madame Hedler's School in Paris, France, she described J'aime's progress, which, following a middle-of-the-night crisis, appeared to be improving. In the course of this trauma, we hear more of Mrs. Wood. "We have depended mostly on milk for J'aime's nourishment and most of it has come from Mrs. Fernando Wood." She also wrote she had persuaded her husband to go to a soirée at the Woods, while she stayed home with the invalid, "as this was our second invitation." Blaine went, escorting Cousin Abby and both had "an agreeable time."

Their own entertaining at home had to be curtailed because of J'aime's illness, from which he eventually recovered fully. She described a scene after breakfast one day where "he is dressed though he does not sit alone," where Maggie "is playing about the room with Alice Wood, too happy for anything because she has a play-fellow" and "Cousin Abby is reading the newspapers." She informed Walker she, herself, had three dinners to give—one for "Mr. Hale" (Eugene Hale, a Congressman from Maine, and close political ally of Blaine's), one for the president and one for the Ewing family. "A number of Ohio Ewings are spending the winter with Mrs. Sherman, all in black [still mourning the recent death of the patriarch Thomas Ewing, Sr.]—so they do not visit in public."[10] Then followed a report on the presidential dinner held in the Blaine home. "Oh, how glad I am to have it over," Harriet confessed to Walker. Her feelings toward Grant appear to have been mixed, for she wrote, "The President is so heavy in everything but feeding—there he's very light. He talked incessantly about himself. I have a certain sympathy with him, for I think him an honest man, and indeed he feels dreadfully assailed."[11]

Back in Maine after the political season, the social whirl was not quite so heady or cosmopolitan, but there *were* visits to Augusta from dignitaries—President Grant included. Grant had been Down East before, two years previously, when he had gone to Vanceboro on the Canadian border to cut a ribbon for the European and North American Railway project, which was slated to extend its line from Bangor to Nova Scotia. The president, on that occasion, was only to stop in Augusta for twenty minutes, but Blaine had to accompany him to Vanceboro, a task he accepted with great reluctance, since he was then in the throes of making his committee assignments for the House.

The August 1873 presidential trip was more leisurely for both men, although requiring an even greater time commitment for Blaine. Grant remained at the Blaines' five days, accompanied by his daughter Nellie and two sons Jesse and Ulysses S. Jr., Mrs. Grant having been kept from coming due to the terminal illness of her father. The *Kennebec Journal* characterized the visit as a "private and special one to Mr. Blaine's family and no public demonstrations are anticipated." Traveling from Boston by train with his party, the president reached Augusta at 4:15 P.M. Yet notwithstanding the *KJ's* admonition, a crowd of several hundred at the depot, with the aid of Berry's Band, serenaded Grant. Speaker Blaine, as master of ceremonies, said he knew the demonstration wasn't for himself, "but for the President of the United States, a man who had shown great valor in time of peace as in time of war and a man of 'deeds not words'"[12]—an introduction that allowed Grant not to speak.

The highlight of this extended stay was an elaborate ball held in the Blaine House, itself. "The ladies were very elegant," the *Kennebec Journal* reported. Seventeen-year-old Miss Nellie Grant wore white silk, with an embroidered overdress and a blue sash that was "very attractive," and the president "was very agreeable to all." Additional gas jets had been installed in the Blaine home and a carpeted pavilion tent stretched along its ell facing the statehouse. Flowers and rare plants were everywhere, and the festivities for the 150 guests—including dancing and a midnight supper—continued until the wee hours of the morning.

The next day, Grant departed for Rockland, where he was to take the revenue cutter *McCulloch* (named for Hugh McCulloch, a Maine-born secretary of the treasury) to Bar Harbor. Blaine and Maine's two U.S. senators, Hannibal Hamlin and Lot M. Morrill, accompanied his party. Unfortunately, a thick Down East fog kept the *McCulloch* from reaching Mount Desert, and an unscheduled stop was made at North Haven Island, where they were entertained by a local character named Mr. Mullen. Then, returning to Augusta, the guests overnighted. On Sunday morning, Blaine took Grant to the Granite Church to worship and after services, these distinguished visitors left to finish the rest of their journey.

Summing up, the *KJ* said of the president, "He has seen us as we are at our homes and we have seen him acting himself as a private individual, so that the visit has been mutually profitable...." No other president, except James K. Polk, had ever come to Augusta. And an obvious reason for this latest recognition was voiced, "Primarily the honor of the visit is due to the official and friendly relations which have existed between the President and Mr. Blaine."[13]

While on the whole, that relationship had been free of friction, the two had, however, disagreed on one of Grant's top priorities— the annexation of Santo Domingo, or what is now the Dominican Republic, by the United States. This may seem a bit out of character for Blaine who, in his stints as secretary of state, was considered the "Father of American Expansionism." Most likely in this instance, he was following the lead of Massachusetts Senator Charles Sumner, who saw a host of future problems, including the acquiring of a whole new black population, and their fears of re-enslavement. Once a Treaty of Annexation had been defeated in the Senate, Blaine was invited to meet with Grant. "We had a frank chat on Santo Domingo," Blaine wrote Gail Hamilton, and the upshot was a very Blainean compromise. Blaine would support a House committee effort to reconsider the matter, "but am against the final acquisition," should that committee recommend it. In the end, Grant let the whole effort die, after assurances he and his agents would be absolved from all charges of corruption made against them during the Senate debate.

At this point in Blaine's career, he seemed well in sync with his fellow Republicans. Some undercurrents existed, but he was assured in a letter from New York Congressman William A. Wheeler that they meant nothing. Urged by a few in the New York delegation to run against Blaine for speaker, Wheeler had declined and he had spurned similar pleas from "a number of Western men." Reasons behind the restiveness were given as opposition to New England domination of the G.O.P. leadership and fear that Blaine might give "the best places on committees" to those implicated in the Credit Mobilier scandal. Wheeler, who within three years would be the vice president of the United States, steadfastly had maintained, "I will not suffer myself to be pitted against Mr. Blaine in any contingency." While he was at it, the upstate New Yorker took the opportunity to ask for the chairmanship of the Foreign Relations Committee, declaring he didn't want "to have any further connection with railroads."[14] Other letters exhibited by Gail Hamilton show a similar rapport at the same time between the Speaker and prominent members of the Democratic opposition.

"Sunset" Cox wrote him, "...We have lived an eventful life together under trying circumstances [Credit Mobilier?] and to miss your face in the House; and as its head, would be to miss the House, itself." Then, he sought membership on Ways and Means and ended: "...with the assurance that you will be Speaker beyond a peradventure and with the wishes for a happy winter—a happier than last..." the scrappy Ohio Democrat signed the letter as "your friend."[15] Philadelphian Samuel J. Randall, another leading Democrat, also destined to be speaker, wrote Blaine, as well, in the fall of 1873. "Do you expect to be south soon, say as far as New York or Philadelphia? I would like to see you and confer as to some legislation during the next session, principally upon a subject which has caused much public expression during the recess." This may have been a contentious measure they had previously passed, popularly nicknamed the "salary grab," that had provoked more constituent anger than any of their other bills. In it, the lawmakers had given themselves a raise and made it retroactive. Randall, in his letter, did speak of the "back pay" bill and how his district was "quiet" about it and that he was sure to be renominated and reelected. He also gave Blaine a heads-up on problems he might have among Pennsylvania Republicans because of committee assignments.

His smooth handling of another—and very difficult—rank-and-file Democrat is shown in a rather touching incident related by Gail Hamilton, one she claimed had never been revealed by Blaine.

That Democrat was William S. Holman of Indiana, who was called "the Great Objector" because he would question every spending bill before the House—setting it aside by objecting when unanimous consent was sought to push it through. Although this was a period when the Democrats were the party of fiscal austerity and the Republicans were known and castigated as spenders, in Holman's case, his penny-pinching was never a matter of party politics. He applied it to Democrats and Republicans alike.

The money bill that Blaine needed immediately involved the daughter of the late President Zachary Taylor. She was Ann Mackall Taylor Wood, by then the elderly destitute widow of a former surgeon-general of the U.S. Army, and she desperately had to get to Europe where her daughter lay gravely ill in Austria. Blaine, who had been alerted to her plight by General Sherman, had devised the clever solution of providing her with a private pension bill, for which she was eligible, dated back four years to her husband's death, that would give her more than twice as much as the $1,000 necessary for the overseas trip, plus a yearly stipend for the rest of her life. Any obstruction by Holman would have ruined these plans.

Speaker Blaine sought out the Indiana Democrat. "I have a little matter of great interest which I want to rush through. Please don't object," he began; he explained the problem, and added: "Every American should blush to find a President's daughter in such a penniless state." Holman at once replied, "Go ahead, Mr. Speaker. I will be out of the way in the cloakroom."

The salary grab furor produced uncomfortable moments for all of the congressional lawmakers. Blaine was smart enough to write himself out of the bill as speaker with an amendment while still producing the pay increase for his colleagues. He did so highhandedly, jotting the word "hereafter" next to the mention of the speaker in the bill and gaveling the change through without a vote. Any salary rise, he could argue, would be for a future speaker. To illustrate the hostility that piece of legislation had stirred up Down East, Maine Congressman Eugene Hale used some typical dry, Down East wit. "I swear," he said, "if I traveled by the railroad as far as it would take me and then had to take the stage coach, and then go by horseback and at the end of that came on a man chopping a log—whatever he did not know, he would know all about the salary-grab and be the maddest of all!"

That storm blew over. Blaine, in his *Twenty Years of Congress*, never mentioned it, as he might have, had it affected the political scene during the 1874 congressional elections.

Instead, an utterly unexpected event happened, totally beyond Congress's reach. On September 20, 1873, the various banking houses of Jay Cooke's empire—in Philadelphia, New York, and Washington, D.C.—closed their doors. Without warning, the Panic of 1873 commenced.

For James G. Blaine, the only immediate fallout from the collapse of his bankers was a correction he received from the bankrupt Jay Cooke and Company about his indebtedness to them, concerning figures that had been printed in the *New York Times*. Their publication soon brought forth a tongue-in-cheek letter from Blaine's Democrat neighbor, Fernando Wood, pledging financial help. Wood wrote, "Supposing that in your position a favor from a political opponent would be more desirable than from one who might have favors to ask in return, I offer myself as a personal friend."[16] And Blaine's reply had a similar joshing tone: " I thank you none the less heartily because I am not under the necessity of availing myself of your generous tender of aid. The stringency in the money market pinches me somewhat, but not beyond my power of control."[17]

That "stringency in the money market" and the failure of the federal treasury to take action was blamed for what next ensued. As Blaine wrote in *Twenty Years of Congress*: "The financial panic which swept over New York in the preceding September (1873) [closing the Stock Market for ten days] was followed by a deep depression throughout the country. Wrecks of business enterprises were everywhere visible, the financial markets of the world were disturbed and alarmed, doubt and hesitation filled the minds of senators and representatives. A black flag seemed to overhang the finances of the Government as well as of individuals...."[18] Some specific statistics included that 266 of the nation's 666 iron blast furnaces were idled; 50 percent of the rail mills shut down; in New York City, 25 percent of the workforce was without jobs, amounting to 100,000 by the winter of 1873-74. Unemployment soared nationwide. Throughout November and December, the jobless marched in Boston, Cincinnati, Chicago, Detroit, Indianapolis, Louisville, Newark, New York City, Paterson, Pittsburgh, and Philadelphia, calling for public aid and public employment. The answer from the authorities, as in New York's celebrated Tompkins Square riot, was police action, casualties, mass arrests and media condemnation of "communists."

Since the Republicans were in charge, the voters at the midterm congressional elections of 1874 took out their frustrations on them. Here was that peradventure "Sunset" Cox had predicted never would happen. When James G. Blaine, reelected by his own folks in Maine without any problem, went back to Washington, he was no longer speaker. The Democrats controlled. The best his fellow Republicans could do was choose him for their minority leader.

1. Hamilton, p. 279.
2. Ibid., p. 284.
3. Russell, p. 250.
4. Ibid.
5. Ibid., p. 252.
6. Ibid., p. 256.
7. Hamilton, p. 286.
8. Beale, p. 75.
9. Ibid., p. 79.
10. Ibid., pp. 81–86.
11. Ibid., pp 90.
12. *Kennebec Journal*, 13 August 1873.
13. Ibid., 18 August 1873.
14. Hamilton, p. 306.
15. Ibid., p. 307.
16. Ibid., p. 306.
17. Ibid., p. 307.
18. James G. Blaine. *Twenty Years of Congress*, Vol. 2 (Norwich, CT: Henry Bill Publishing Company, 1886), p. 561.

TWELVE

IN THE MINORITY, BUT...

THE LAME DUCK SESSION of the Forty-third Congress, in which Blaine was still speaker, ended on March 3, 1875, not with a whimper but with a decided bang. Several "force bills" were pushed through by the Republicans before they surrendered their majority—bills given a pejorative nickname by the Democrats as civil rights bills *forced* upon the South. One that kept the House in session—and turmoil—for twenty straight hours, drafted by Ben Butler, would have "prohibited the exclusion of Negroes from juries and granted them equal enjoyment of accommodations, advantages, facilities, and privileges of inns, public conveyances on land and water, theaters and other places of amusement...." His fellow Republicans criticized Blaine for not using his speaker's power arbitrarily to prevent the Democratic delay tactic of refusing to recognize the opposition's members. He couldn't do that, he argued; he remained fair in his rulings and still won the day for the contentious legislation.

In the final hour, a resolution was presented and adopted unanimously, thanking Speaker Blaine for "the impartiality, efficiency, and distinguished ability with which he has discharged the trying and arduous duties of his office during the Forty-third Congress." Speaker Blaine followed with a short, graceful speech. To the Democrats, he expressed his thanks for their "generous courtesy" toward him. He also acknowledged they would be taking control of the House the next day "by one of those sudden and decisive changes which distinguish popular institutions, and which conspicuously mark a free people...." The scene right after he stepped down from the rostrum has been described as one nearly of bedlam—a roar erupting from a standing crowd on the floor and in the galleries, "repeated salvos of applause, running in waves from side to side, with almost delirious cheering, clapping of hands, and waving of handkerchiefs...."[1] For fully five minutes, the noisy tribute continued and for another half hour, members and visitors came up to shake his hand.

Once Blaine was in a minority position, however, the gloves soon came off. Even before he formally had the title of minority leader, he waded right into a bruising battle at the opening of the Forty-fourth Congress. At issue was a disputed congressional election in Louisiana.

Post-Civil War America had begun to produce its own new political issues—massive railroad construction and the concomitant corruption that seemed forever attached to it, and the boom and bust nature of the unfettered capitalism then rampant, to name the two most important—but the war, although a decade past, still packed an emotional wallop. Federal troops continued to police some of the Southern states, combating Ku Klux Klan and White League terrorism in an increasingly losing effort to ensure free elections, and nowhere was the Reconstruction combat fiercer than in Louisiana.

Blaine sought to maintain his party's ever-dwindling base in the South. Thus, when it was a question of admitting disputed congressmen from Louisiana to the Forty-fourth Congress, Blaine had to fight, even from a disadvantageous minority position. The sticking point became the admission of a Republican named Frank Morey. Five out of six voted-in Louisianans had already been seated. Their certificates of election had all been signed by the recognized Republican Governor William P. Kellogg, and four of these had also been signed by a Democratic gubernatorial pretender, John McEnery. The battle, therefore, arose over Morey, bearing a Republican certification, alone, versus his Democratic challenger, whose certificate had been signed only by the unrecognized Democrat, McEnery. Fernando Wood tried to keep Morey from being admitted and wanted the matter sent to the Democrat-controlled House Elections Committee. On his feet instantly, Blaine protested, "McEnery has no more right to call himself the Governor of Louisiana than Mr. Wood has to say he is the Governor of the Empire State." The ruckus Blaine raised was so intense and skillful that Democratic Speaker Michael Kerr sent word to have Fernando Wood's motion withdrawn.

Elated by their victory, the Republican members hastened to thrust "the whole conduct of their affairs" into Blaine's hands and apotheosized him as a man who could "achieve the unprecedented parliamentary triumph of defeating and demoralizing the majority on the first day of the session" and who would be "sure to shape the action of any caucus or conference...," neither fearing "his foes of the other party nor rivals in his own."[2]

Mark that last phrase "rivals in his own." Already, G.O.P. thoughts were turning to the presidential campaign of 1876, and Blaine's name was being favorably mentioned. Tom Sherman has described how "for a year preceding the presidential campaign of 1876," letters were pouring in to his employer from "all parts of the country" beseeching him to run for the top spot, promising support and seeking assurance that he would.

For example, from Ohio: "I want to vote the Republican ticket this year and therefore I want to see you the candidate.... I have talked with four or five leading men and they all prefer you to Governor Hayes...." From Illinois: "We write you as 'native Pennsylvanians coming here from the locality where you were born...and it is a great pleasure to us to see the attention of people turned to you as their candidate for President...." From Massachusetts: "If you should get the nomination for the presidency next year...you may depend upon my lifting up my voice like a pelican in the wilderness, or a sparrow on the housetops...."

"We were literally swamped with them," Sherman wrote. "They were briefly jacketed for ready reference if he would ever take them up...." Convinced these correspondents wanted a reply from their hero, himself, Sherman would occasionally put some of the most important in front of Blaine for a response. His boss's reply to him was, "I will not touch them. Get such help as you want and answer them yourself." But ever the smart politician, he also offered some experienced advice. "Now I would do the later ones first," Blaine said. "If you keep on that other way, you will be eating sour apples all the time." In spite of this interest, Sherman genuinely felt, "He [Blaine] did not think he would be nominated and made no effort looking to that end."[3]

The political mores of the age dictated that office seekers at least seem indifferent to their chances of election. Most campaigned by sitting at home on porches and receiving well-wishers. Blaine did that, too, but he also kept a sharp eye out for opportunities. Why else, one might ask, would James G. Blaine of Maine in 1875 take such an interest in a gubernatorial campaign in Ohio?

Rutherford B. Hayes had just won the G.O.P. nomination in Ohio to seek a third term as the state's chief executive. Blaine seemed particularly witty in his congratulations. "And so our friends in Ohio thought wise and well to take a ready-made Governor—having gone through fire twice, the presumption is in favor of your salamander qualities." But there was another line in the communication that gave the ex-Speaker away. "Pray advise me of 'the situation' in Ohio as you see it."[4]

By situation, Blaine meant an issue, as Hayes had to know, that was red-hot in Ohio and could well figure in the national election a year hence. It was nothing less than a vicious Protestant-Catholic clash over Bible-reading in the schools. Unlike today, it was not a question of whether or not the "Good Book" should be read; it was which Bible, the Protestant King James Bible, the standard text used then in the schools, or a Catholic version. Hayes's opponent in the Ohio Republican primary had been Judge Alphonso Taft, founder of the famed Cincinnati political dynasty, and Taft had supported the highly unpopular Catholic position that their kids shouldn't have to be subjected to readings from the King James Bible. At the same time, Catholics were also demanding public funds for their parochial schools. Hayes trounced Taft two to one because of his stance, particularly after inflammatory remarks said to have been made by Archbishop John B. Purcell of Cincinnati were publicized including that "Instruction must be given in the Catholic faith or the public schools will be denounced as Godless and…destroyed if the Roman Catholics can destroy them."

Blaine clearly saw the danger—especially to him—of being taken for a Catholic sympathizer. A characteristically shrewd move of his was to make public a letter he wrote on October 29, 1875, to A. T. Wilkoff, the chairman of the Ohio Republican State Committee. In it, he spelled out a Constitutional amendment he planned to present as soon as Congress reconvened that would prohibit the expenditure of public school funds on religious schools. "Those who would abolish the non-sectarian public schools necessarily breed ignorance," he told Wilkoff, "and ignorance is the parent of intolerance and bigotry."

Therefore, the first public bill presented to the Forty-Fourth Congress was a joint resolution sponsored by the minority leader from Maine calling for a constitutional amendment whose essential thrust would be that "no money raised by taxation in any state for the support of public schools or derived from any public fund thereof, nor any public lands devoted thereto, shall ever be under the control of any private sect." Aware that states were not covered by the separation of church and state ordained in the U.S. Constitution, Blaine also added to his would-be Sixteenth Amendment language that states could not make any law "respecting an establishment of religion or prohibiting the free exercise thereof."

Trying to arouse publicity for his amendment, Blaine contacted his friend Whitelaw Reid, who had taken over the *New York Tribune* from the late Horace Greeley. With the argument that only a constitutional amendment could solve the problem exhibited in Ohio, he asked Reid to print his letter to Wilkoff in full and editorialize in support of the proposal.

This was only one side of the equation. Another request from Blaine to Whitelaw Reid was to reprint a copy of a Carlisle, Pennsylvania, newspaper which detailed a visit of his to relatives still in that city where his great-grandfather had lived, how he had attended services in the old Stone Presbyterian Church built by his ancestors, and also how he and his son Walker, who had accompanied him, were fifth and sixth generations of Scotch and Scots-Irish Protestant stock. In urging Reid to run the piece, Blaine argued, "Because my excellent mother was a Catholic and because I am a cousin of Mrs. General Sherman, certain people are determined to force me—*nolens volens*—into the Catholic Church for a reason which I need not recall to you."

Reid, however, didn't think the story would help Blaine politically and declined to reproduce it, despite the rather frantic accusation that the Blaine-is-a-Catholic canard was "connived at, if not originated, by men who sat with me in a Presbyterian Bible Class. The charge is part and parcel of the tactics of the Cameron gang to rob me of the Pennsylvania delegates...."[5]

So much for the idea that Blaine was indifferent to his presidential prospects in 1876. The Blaine Amendment on public schools passed the House with only seven nays, but ninety-eight absentees. Oddly, it died in the Republican Senate. Senator Lewis Bogy of Missouri claimed the amendment was nothing more than a "substitute for the bloody shirt," that tried and true harping on Civil War emotions to arouse feelings against Democrats and the South, and Senator William Wallace Eaton of Connecticut called it a "dodge" by Blaine to obtain the Republican nomination.

On this issue, Blaine heard from "Mrs. General Sherman," as well. Ellen Ewing Sherman was disgruntled with her relative, but for a different reason than his stance on parochial schools. "My Dear Cousin," she began. "Here I am fighting Catholic editors and going forth daily armed 'cap-a-pie' in your defense...*and you have not condescended to answer my letter....* I am for you always...and as a family we all are—the general included, for we know that you would fill the position of President with honor and dignity, and add, by your administration, a luster and glory to the country."[6] Then, she questioned his strategy. "But shall we have that satisfaction?..." She thought his amendment would "play sad havoc with your interests among our Irish friends and Catholics..." but hoped the passage of time would change their minds.

Another risky blockbuster tactic Blaine used to achieve frontrunner status for the 1876 election was a sophisticated variation on the tried-and-true Bloody Shirt stump speech. Some supporters were to doubt his wisdom in attacking Jefferson Davis, since the electorate was tired of Civil War rhetoric, but his opportunistic verve in doing so did seem to pay huge political dividends.

On December 15, 1875, the Democratic floor leader in the House, Samuel Randall, introduced an amnesty bill, the intent of which was to pardon all remaining Confederates still incurring civil disabilities of any kind. During the previous Congress, such a bill had passed the Republican House (where Blaine was speaker), only to have it killed by the Republican Senate. Consequently, Randall expressed surprise after Blaine arose and said some Republicans wished to speak against the new measure. Randall rejoined that the same exact bill had been passed by the Republicans before and he wanted it passed prior to the holidays so "every man in this country may feel he is relieved from past disabilities." To which argument, Blaine rather sardonically replied he wished Randall "the most joyous of holidays, but I think you have had several pleasant holidays since I have known you with these same gentlemen under disabilities."

As it turned out, the holidays came and went before the amnesty bill was debated. On January 10, 1876, Minority Leader Blaine offered an amendment to the Randall bill. It essentially did only one thing: of the 750 Confederates still unpardoned in the country, all would be amnestied, with a single notable exception—and that was "Jefferson Davis, late President of the so-called Confederate States." Blaine, seconded by Garfield, requested that the bill and proffered amendment be sent to an appropriate committee, considered and reported back, a request Randall adamantly refused.

The parliamentary jousting between Blaine and Randall on this issue made national headlines and brought the Civil War back front and center into the consciousness of American voters. James G. Blaine was speaking for the millions of Union veterans who had suffered throughout those four deadly years, and doing it in the white-knight sort of fashion that was soon to be attached to his name. Besides, he was being fair, not vindictive, he claimed. All ex-Confederates now would be pardoned, except the one dastardly leader, "Jeff Davis," whom they all had once sung they would hang from a "sour apple tree." But why exempt Davis? Blaine made his point crystal clear: "I except him on this ground, that he was the author, knowingly, deliberately, guiltily and willfully of the gigantic murders and crimes at Andersonville."

There was no need for Blaine to explain Andersonville, the notorious hell-hole of a Confederate prison camp, to his audience. For Northerners, it was the Auschwitz of its day.

He was immediately greeted by a cry of "And Libby!" from an unidentified ex-Confederate member of the House, trying to equate a Northern prison with the Southern camp where so many captured Yankees had died. Blaine pooh-poohed Libby, before launching into the most quoted and provocative section of his peroration. "I have read over the details of those atrocious murders of the Duke of Alva in the Low Countries.... I have read the details of the Massacre of St. Bartholomew.... I have read anew the horrors untold and unimaginable of the Spanish Inquisition...." But none of these well-known war crimes, he declared, "begin to compare with the hideous crime of Andersonville."

Wild applause burst out on the floor and in the galleries and Speaker Michael Kerr rapped his gavel vigorously and threatened to clear out all visitors. Congressman Robbins of North Carolina cried that Blaine had uttered "an infamous slander." And that outburst promptly led Blaine into a powerful speech, describing in chilling, disgusting, all-too-vivid details conditions at Andersonville recorded by a bi-partisan committee of inquiry formed by a previous Congress. He finished this extraordinary performance by saying he had opposed the indictment and trial of Jefferson Davis after the war, that Davis was now as free as any other man in the U.S. But if this amnesty bill passed, Jefferson Davis would be eligible "to fill any office up to the Presidency of the United States." For his part, he would not countenance that possibility and so, "I here protest and shall with my vote protest against calling and crowning with the honors of full American citizenship the man that organized that murder."

Charles Edward Russell wrote, "When that day was done, discerning men everywhere said that James G. Blaine had made inevitable his nomination by the next Republican Convention."[7]

Initially, though, there was criticism of him, even from Republican newspapers like the *New York Tribune,* and a noted Republican colleague, William "Pig Iron" Kelley of Pennsylvania, actually chided Blaine, saying the centennial year of 1876 should be "a year of jubilee," not contention. But Southerners, anxious to present a rebuttal, overplayed their hand. They could not let Blaine's "slander" go unanswered. To speak for them, they chose Congressman

Benjamin H. Hill of Georgia who, in Russell's words, "was a brilliant debater and one of the ablest men that ever sat in the House of Representatives."[8]

Thus did the fiery Blaine-Hill debate enter the annals of Congress. It was a no-holds-barred contest and the consensus in the North, needless to say, was that Blaine had triumphed. Hill was described as having stayed up until late at night in the Library of Congress with two stenographers in preparing his speech, which lasted two hours. The House and galleries were packed the next day to hear him. Blaine was accused of "an act of showmanship" by taking his seat late to listen, as "the shrill voice of the Southerner shrieked out charge after charge."[9] The themes Hill hammered away at were that, contrary to Blaine's assertions, the Republican-controlled post-war U.S. government had NOT treated the South with magnanimity and that lack of medicine and food due to the Northern blockade had caused the deaths at Andersonville and, besides, the mortality had been just as great at the Elmira prison in New York as at the so-called "death camp" in Georgia.

Such rhetoric, perhaps, was exactly what Blaine had been waiting to hear. He had researched his opponent's record during the war when Hill had been a member of the Confederate Senate. Suddenly, he interrupted the Georgian, charging that in 1863, after Lincoln's Emancipation Proclamation, Hill had, himself, introduced a resolution that all captured Union soldiers and officers be put to death until the proclamation was rescinded. Stopped in his oratorical tracks, a flustered Hill muttered he couldn't remember ever having done such a thing, and he finished with a mild appeal that presently "there are no Confederates anywhere." James Garfield, as a former Union general, now joined in, alluding to Jefferson Davis's proclamation that all of Ben Butler's officers deserved death and so did any "slaves captured in arms," and he said it was common knowledge Black Union prisoners had been summarily executed.

Strong suspicion of a collusion between Blaine and his friend Garfield could be deduced from this debate. Moreover, Charles Edward Russell, who probably covered the marathon four-day event as a journalist, has asserted that Garfield's performance enabled him to rehabilitate himself from the political shame he had suffered because of the Credit Mobilier affair. To Hill's argument that Yankee prisons had been as bad as Andersonville, Garfield came back with, as Russell wrote, "letters and telegrams from Democrats, soldiers, and citizens, utterly refuting the charge."[10] Blaine finished the assault. He harped again and again on Hill's "resolution" and finally induced him to admit he had submitted it and next quoted a recent speech by the Georgian saying the South should once more go to war if the Republicans tried to steal the next election.

The hullabaloo raged on and James G. Blaine was at the heart of it, pro and con. His "old friend" Sunset Cox, aroused as all Democrats, North and South were, cried at him on the floor, "Well, howl away. You are a hyena!" Congressman John Tarbox of Massachusetts joined in the condemnation, referring to "the gaunt and gory specters which the gentleman from Maine, like some magician of the black art, with devilish incantation, had called up from the political inferno to mar the fair form of the festal cheer of the Republic...."[11] The upshot was the total defeat of Randall's amnesty bill. Without Blaine's amendment, all 750 Confederates, including Davis, never had their disabilities removed. The former Confederate president, himself, entered the fray, supporting Blaine's amendment on the grounds that he didn't want a Damn Yankee pardon.

Utterly excoriated in the South, Blaine was just as big a hero in the North. "Allow me to congratulate you on your triumph," wrote Wendell Phillips, the grand old veteran abolitionist. "Such a protest was needed just now to stun this drunken people into a sober estimate of their position and danger. You were most emphatically *the* man to make it." Writing from Albany was the Honorable Charles Emory Smith: "I must congratulate you upon your brilliant fight and splendid success in the House. It was magnificent. Its effects are being felt everywhere. Republicans are stirred and enkindled, the opposition confounded and overwhelmed...." And the Honorable J. W. Webb, seventy-four years old, a long-time party worker, wanted to say it was his judgment that Blaine's chances for president had "been increased an hundred fold by your course on the amnesty bill. Men and women who only respected you before absolutely admire and love you now. You have struck the chord to which all the better feelings of their nature respond, and be assured that thousands everywhere who cared little one week ago who received the nomination from the Republican convention, now offer up prayers for your success...." Other professional Republicans concurred. A letter reached Blaine from Chicago written by an attendee at a meeting of "about fifty of the captains, lieutenants, and sergeants of the party...from all parts of the State..." and that "the presidential expression was quite generally in your favor."

In Washington, D.C., there was an immediate sense of elation. Here was the scene at a reception given shortly afterward by Mrs. Hamilton Fish, wife of the secretary of state: "Mr. Blaine received another 'perfect ovation.' Everybody was congratulating him and Mrs. Blaine. General Garfield could not contain himself. He nearly hugged Mrs. Blaine. 'Oh, your glorious old Jim.' It was the first time I ever heard anyone call him Jim, but I forgave Mr. Garfield on the spot. General Garfield says that in the whole thirteen years he has been in the House of Representatives, he never saw so brilliant a victory as that of Mr. Blaine's yesterday."[12]

The man from Augusta was on a roll. By his own efforts, Blaine had made himself the frontrunner for the Republican nomination. Right after the Jefferson Davis bombshell, the G.O.P. in Maine had made him their "Favorite Son." Most importantly, his only real worrisome rival, President Grant, had renounced seeking a third term, except under unusual circumstances, like a national emergency.

How much had luck to do with it—not just his own skill—in coming so far so fast? Certainly, in reviewing his recent past, he would have shuddered, remembering something that had happened just outside of New York City in the spring of 1875. His highly promising career had nearly come to a screeching, shocking end because of a railroad accident, and his description of the incident begins starkly, "The car I was in was thrown down headlong from the track and rolled clear over and there we were, an undistinguishable mass of men, women, chairs, sofas, carpet-bags, umbrellas, and so forth."[13] Blaine's ultimate judgment was, "Had this car taken fire, I don't see how anyone of us could have ever gotten out, but fortunately there was no kerosene."[14]

At first he thought he'd broken some ribs on his right side—a pain that proved to be from mere contusions once he was examined by a doctor at the Fifth Avenue Hotel. So, in the end, the trauma he'd suffered would have had to reinforce a belief that he had been saved for a greater destiny—nothing less than the top position in the government of the United States.

For a family man like Blaine, there also had to be those twinges of guilt of any politically ambitious father. One expression of it did come after a really scary moment in Boston, when little Jamie wandered off by himself in the city at dusk. A frantic search was instituted. Blaine went up Tremont Street and son Emmons went down it and, suddenly, as he wrote, "up near the Park Street Church I met the little toad, as quietly looking at the sights as anybody. I never let him know I had been uneasy...." But Blaine had been touched enough to confess, "I feel very badly about going away. I am pursued here by telegrams and I can be ill spared. But I am doing my duty and that always squares matters."[15]

He was still speaker then. Losing that job, paradoxically, had only put him in a better position to become the Republican champion in 1876. An amusing story is told of a scene in the Blaine household the day after he had to give up the speakership. Young Jamie was teasing his younger sister Harriet, saying to her: "...do you know your papa isn't going to be speaker anymore? He's going to stop being speaker. Aren't you sorry?" Little Sister sweetly and logically replied, "Well, he isn't going to stop being papa."

Thus we see Papa Blaine on track more than quite possibly to be the next President of the United States. Yet his luck, despite all his talent for positioning himself, was about to take a decisive turn.

---

1.   H. J. Ramsdell, Esq. *Life and Service of Honorable James G. Blaine* (Philadelphia: Hubbard Brothers Publishers, 1884), p. 112.

2.   Hamilton, p. 322.

3.   Sherman, pp. 61, 62.

4.   H. J. Eckenrode. *Rutherford B. Hayes: Statesman of Reunion* (New York: Dodd, Mead, and Company, 1930), p. 102,

5. Sister Mary Carolyn Klinkhamer. "The Blaine Amendment of 1875: Private Motives for Political Action," *Catholic Historical Review,* Vol. XLII, No. 1, April 1956.

6. Hamilton, p. 382.

7. Russell, p. 271.

8. Ibid., p. 271.

9. E. Merton Coulter. "Amnesty For All Except Jeff Davis: The Hill-Blaine Debate of 1876," *The Georgia Historical Quarterly,* Vol. LVI, No. 4, Winter 1972, p. 464.

10. Russell, pp. 271–72.

11. Coulter, pp. 479.

12. All the above quotations are from Hamilton, pp. 378–82. The scene at Mrs. Fish's reception is described in a letter only identified cryptically as "From V." Who "V" is never is explained—it could be Gail Hamilton, herself, or Harriet Blaine; certainly someone very intimate with the Blaine family.

13. Hamilton, p. 372.

14. Ibid., p. 373.

15. Ibid., p. 368.

THIRTEEN

1876

A S THE CENTENNIAL YEAR, celebrating a hundred years of the existence of the United States, the year 1876 should have stood out no matter what was happening. That it was also to be the year of an extraordinary election, challenging the Constitution almost as seriously as the Civil War, added another significance to that date. No American writer has shown this distinction better than novelist Gore Vidal, in a work of fiction entitled simply *1876,* the third part of a trilogy he published with deliberate timing in the bicentennial year of 1976.

The Gilded Age glitter of this period in American history is viewed by Vidal through the eyes of his leading character, Charles Schermerhorn Schuyler. The author has made him an illegitimate son of Aaron Burr, who starts the novel off by returning from an extended stay in Europe on December 4, 1875, with his thirty-five-year-old daughter Emma, the widow of a French prince, and therefore, a princess, herself.

These fictional beings easily mix with real-life historical figures like James G. Blaine and also Charles Nordhoff, the German-born Washington correspondent for the *New York Herald*, who is present at the Maine man's first appearance in the book. The scene is a D.C. restaurant. Entering it, Blaine spies Nordhoff, who is with Schuyler and Emma, and comes over to join the trio.

Vidal describes the newcomer as follows: "Blaine was already full of drink but not drunk. I don't suppose he is fifty yet. The face is ruddy; the small eyes are like polished onyxes—they look out at you so brightly that you cannot look into them. The ears are elephantine, and often paler or rosier than the rest of the face—do they respond to his moods first or last? The nose is somewhat potato-shaped but, all in all, the face (what one can see of it above the clipped General Grant beard) is pleasing enough, as is the voice, prime requisite for a national politician nowadays...."[1]

Once Blaine leaves, Nordhoff tells the others he knew Blaine would be there that night and he wanted them to meet him. Then, this dialogue takes place:

"'You like him?' I [Schuyler] asked."

"'It is quite impossible not to,' said Nordhoff."

"'And is he also corrupt?' I inquired."

"'Oh, Papa! Don't you know the answer by now?'" [said Emma, who had previous to his entrance described herself as "enchanted" by Blaine].

"Nordhoff first barked, very sharply; then said: 'Yes, but with considerable style. I think he's the most interesting man here.'" [i.e., in Washington, D.C.]

In real life, Blaine was no lady's man, exactly, although Vidal gives him some gallant remarks addressed to the beauteous Emma. He seemed utterly devoted to his wife and family and was nationally known for his impeccable behavior in this regard. On the other hand, Vidal's novel plays up Roscoe Conkling's historic enough sexual peccadilloes, since he was seen, in the book as in actuality, to be Blaine's principal competitor in 1876 for the Republican nomination. All of Washington knew of Conkling's infidelity to his wife and his affair with Kate Chase Sprague, daughter of Salmon P. Chase, who was married to a rich but alcoholic Rhode Island U.S. Senator, William Sprague. All Washington, too, had chuckled and cackled over the farce-like story of Conkling's being driven off one night at shotgun point from the grounds of the Sprague estate in Newport by Kate's "drunken mad husband," as Vidal describes him. The same mixture of fiction and fact has the narrator call Harriet Blaine "the charming Mrs. Blaine," when Vidal works her into an imaginary dialogue at a White House reception where Schuyler and Lucretia Garfield discuss the forthcoming 1876 election.

Says Schuyler, indicating their present hostess Mrs. Grant, "Then come next January, Mrs. Conkling will be in this room doing the honors." Mrs. Garfield does not agree, but replies: "I should say that Mrs. Blaine will be at the head of this table, poor woman. She has such a good mind. But *six* children! I mean she has no peace."

All of this is pure fiction, needless to say, underscored by the conscious irony Gore Vidal, aware of the future, gave to the scene. Blaine would not win the 1876 G.O.P. nomination. Garfield, then a barely known congressman, would become president four years later. Conkling would go nowhere in 1876, and the dark horse who prevailed that year would be the third-term Ohio governor whose support James G. Blaine had tried to cultivate, Rutherford Burchard Hayes.

To read H. J. Eckenrode, one of Hayes's biographers,[2] you might believe all of Blaine's political troubles in 1876 stemmed from his spectacular verbal assault on Jefferson Davis. A Virginia academic who taught history and economics at Richmond College, Eckenrode labeled Blaine's "Andersonville" attack in the House "perhaps the most offensive speech ever uttered in that body." This Confederate apologist, writing sixty-five years after Appamattox, was probably even more inflammatory in his language about slavery than Davis, himself, would have been, with statements like, "As a matter of fact, the slave owners and poor whites were the victims of slavery rather than the slaves, who absorbed nearly all the profits of the system" or condemning the Radical Republican oligarchy, with "insisting on the equality of African savages with Anglo-Saxons…" and saying a civil rights bill was "designed to render the Anglo-Saxons of the South still more prostrate under the feet of their ex-slaves."

But Eckenrode's analysis of the effect of Blaine's Jeff Davis ploy on his chances for president were generally perceptive. "Seldom is a wicked act followed by such prompt retribution as Blaine's bloody-shirt speech. He won vast applause from the veterans, his objective, but at the same time he gained the hatred of the Democrats in the House of Representatives, many of whom had been his admirers and some of them his friends. The Southerners, accustomed to being called rebels and traitors, were electrified as murderers. In fact, Blaine had violated the ethics of politics, and he soon paid the price."[3]

We are now on the cusp of one of the signal if overlooked dramas in American political history. What ifs abound. Had Blaine become president, would the woeful civil rights problem in the South have turned out differently? Had Blaine not made such an enemy of Conkling, could he have been the nominee? Had he not so alienated the South, would the Democrats not have zeroed in on him so hard? Why was it that a Republican appointee blew a whistle on him, setting in motion the year-long political turmoil that dominated headlines and literally shook the nation to its roots?

The Hayes-Tilden election of 1876, like the Bush-Gore contest of the year 2000, presented the U.S. with challenges unforeseen by our Constitution. Had it been a Blaine-Tilden contest, it can be claimed we might have been spared that earlier crisis, which, while it was happening, brought on dire predictions of another civil war erupting. Therefore, the unraveling of Blaine's 1876 quest for the Republican nomination becomes a matter of some import "for the record," as the expression goes in politics.

The initial still-faint inkling of trouble appeared on February 28, 1876, slightly more than a month after Blaine's Jefferson Davis outburst. On that date, John S. C. Harrison of Indianapolis, in his capacity as one of the U.S. government's representatives named to the Union Pacific Railroad's board of directors, revealed he had found some worthless bonds among the assets of the company and they had come from Congressman Blaine, who had received Union Pacific money for them.

There was no immediate outcry. But on April 11, an anti-Blaine newspaper in Indianapolis broke the story, adding gratuitously but with some accuracy that it would "forever blast the prospects of a certain candidate for office." The most damning item in Harrison's account was that these seventy-five bonds had been issued by the Little Rock and Fort Smith Railroad in Arkansas, and because Blaine had done a favor for the Union Pacific, that company had loaned him $64,000 and taken this junk paper as collateral. The order to pay Blaine had come through Thomas A. Scott, president of Union Pacific, and the funds were issued by Morton and Bliss Company, New York bankers. Incidentally, this "loan" had never been repaid.

Not until almost two weeks later did James G. Blaine reply. Pressure was put on him, in the press and elsewhere, to call for an investigation as he had done in the Credit Mobilier affair. However, with the House in Democratic hands—including a heavy infusion of southern Democrats—Blaine had to be aware any investigating committee would be hostile to him. Instead, cannily, he elected to address the question directly in a speech on the floor of the House.

Having taken his own good time to respond, he had—as usual—done his homework. Not only did he have an exculpating speech, but also a series of letters to back up his protestations of innocence. "I never had any transaction of any kind with Thomas A. Scott, concerning bonds of the Little Rock and Fort Smith Railroad, or the bonds of any other railroad...," he declared categorically, and added to his denial, any "officers or agents or representatives" of the Union Pacific or the reception of even "a single dollar from the company."[4]

The letters he proceeded to read aloud to his colleagues included ones signed by E. H. Rollins, the Union Pacific treasurer, asserting no Union Pacific money had been disbursed to Blaine; then from Morton Bliss and Company, making the same statement; from Sidney Dillon, current president of the Union Pacific, who said, "There were never any facts to warrant..." the newspaper accounts; and a deposition from Thomas A. Scott, who maintained, "All statements to the effect that Mr. Blaine ever had any transactions with me, directly or indirectly, involving money or valuables of any kind, are absolutely without foundation in fact."[5] The rest of Blaine's speech dealt with two main factors: 1) why he didn't call for an investigation, as he had for the Credit Mobilier charges; and 2) his relationship to the Little Rock and Fort Smith Railroad.

In the former response, skirting the issue of Democratic control and political bias, he merely stated he didn't want to wait two months for exoneration, as he had in the Credit Mobilier situation, before he could present his side of the story. And on the latter subject, he gave a complicated explanation about buying Little Rock and Fort Smith bonds from a group of Boston investors, losing more than $20,000 on the transaction, trying to raise money for the Arkansas venture, and since the State of Arkansas, alone, had backed the railroad, there was no federal involvement, so he had a perfect right as a U.S. citizen to buy its stock without a conflict of interest.

Gore Vidal handles this real-life episode in his historic fiction. He has the narrator of *1876*, Charles Schermerhorn Schuyler declare, "But today—April 24—the beleaguered colossus of the Republican party rose to his feet in the House of Representatives and, on a point of personal privilege, proceeded to make one of the most eloquent speeches in the history of that body, or so everyone says...."[6] His daughter Emma had provided an eyewitness account with exclamations like, "He was adorable, Papa!...You've never seen so many enthusiastic people.... His voice shook. He sobbed at one point...." And she had finished her encomiums by confessing, "He convinced me.... Well, perhaps he did not convince but he overwhelmed us all. There were even cheers from the people in the press gallery while in the ladies' gallery where I was, well, you've never seen so many handkerchiefs waved, so many hurrays!"

Vidal includes Charles Nordhoff, the cynical journalist, in the scene. "'He [Blaine] read a letter,' stated the veteran reporter.

"'From whom?'

"'From the treasurer of the Union Pacific Railroad.' Nordhoff looked down at his notebook. 'Dated March 31st, saying that the railroad never paid any money to Blaine.'

"'As if the treasurer would have written anything else to Blaine.' I must say the man is bold, the public gullible." Schuyler states this and then thinks to himself that whatever Blaine said, he said it so well he had at least saved himself this one day.

Nordhoff's version is even more direct. "'Blaine's got away with it.'"

But, in the real world, not for long, not with the Democrats in control of the House. On May 2, a northern adversary, Congressman John Tarbox of Massachusetts, introduced a resolution calling for a special investigating committee to look into the charges against Blaine. Gail Hamilton was later to comment tartly that only one of its eventual members was not a former "rebel." Under the chairmanship of Representative Proctor Knott of Kentucky, the committee commenced its operations on May 15, with the Republican convention only several weeks away. Such timing did not seem coincidental. Blaine's strength among the G.O.P. delegates slated to vote in Cincinnati was considered very strong. It had even reached into Conkling's own backyard in New York State, where Blaine was reported to be ahead two to one. New Hampshire was solidly for Blaine; so were Illinois, Missouri, Iowa—and these last-minute hearings brought forth nothing damaging, just a rehash from the big wigs who'd corroborated Blaine's protestations of innocence. Yet just before the curtain was about to come down, a sensational surprise was sprung. Three spectacular witnesses arrived from Boston—"Mr. Elisha Atkins, Mr. Warren Fisher, Jr., and Mr. James Mulligan."

"The Mulligan Letters" has been a name forever attached to this extraordinary episode in American political history. It was not because of any letters James Mulligan wrote, but due to the batch of Blaine's letters, which, in some mysterious fashion, had come into his possession and which he had brought with him to Washington. They should, in all honesty, have been called "The Fisher Letters." They had been written to Warren Fisher, Jr., from whom Blaine had obtained the Arkansas railroad stock he was to sell on commission. Mulligan, once a clerk for Blaine's brother-in-law Jacob Stanwood, had had a fight with his employer over money. Brought in to referee, Blaine, as the story goes, ruled against Mulligan, who supposedly was heard to mutter, "Blaine went back on me." Now, Mulligan worked for Fisher, also estranged from Blaine.

How Congressman Knott's investigating committee had heard of these two potential enemies remains a murky question. One rumor has it that Ben Butler had tipped them off, still furious after the tongue-lashing he'd received from Speaker Blaine. Just as likely, Fisher and Mulligan could have contacted the hostile committee, themselves.

The third man, Elisha Atkins, had no particular bone to pick with Blaine. He was simply a director of the Union Pacific Railroad who lived in Boston and his testimony did not help the anti-Blaine cause. All he knew about Blaine's worthless Arkansas bonds ending up at the Union Pacific he'd heard from Mulligan, and he was aware Mulligan had a grudge against Blaine. Mulligan muddied the waters further by saying Atkins had told him about Blaine's bonds. Nor was Fisher any more effective. But that was before the letters were produced.

Knowing they were coming, the Blaine forces were able to secure an adjournment of the committee the day prior to their scheduled appearance.

Gail Hamilton has left a vivid portrait of James G. Blaine during all of these proceedings, "Mr. Blaine sat in the committee-room, lost in thought, communicating with no one, every feature drooping.... Often when thinking, his soul seemed drawn away, leaving his face inert, vacant.... In a committee-room crowded with alert foes and newsgatherers, this change from his usual intent attention was almost embarrassing to his friends...." But then she reveals where his mind really lay, where this self-directed pondering was centered: "In truth, Mr. Blaine was not so much interested in the testimony or in the committee, as in his own letters so treacherously manipulated."[7]

The letters! All eyes were on those letters! Blaine's naïve habit of including incriminating remarks in his letters and instructing the recipients to keep silent about them was coming back to haunt him in the most hurtful way. "Burn this letter," he had admonished Warren Fisher in one of these missives. The enemy press, he knew, would have a field day with such embarrassing disclosures. Vehement protesting that his private correspondence should not be made public had fallen on completely deaf ears in the committee.

The man's bravado was breathtaking. On the day of the adjournment, Blaine went to the Riggs Hotel where Fisher and Mulligan were staying, demanded to see the letters, examined them, put them in his pocket, and walked out of their room. Or this was Blaine's version. Mulligan reported the incident differently, claimed Blaine had offered him money, had wept when the bribe was refused, threatened suicide, and had touched the possessor of the letters so deeply that he'd handed them over.

Whatever happened, Blaine had the fifteen letters. He next did two things with them. They were submitted to a respected bi-partisan duo, a Democratic congressman from Pennsylvania and a Republican senator from Wisconsin, who declared them irrelevant to the committee's inquiry, and he then read them aloud to a full session of the House of Representatives! That is to say, he read sections of them. "Burn this letter" was not included.

Called the "most dramatic incident in the life of Mr. Blaine," the Man from Maine holds up the Mulligan Letters before the U.S. House of Representatives and then proceeds to read selected portions from them to Congress.
RIDPATH, *LIFE AND WORKS OF JAMES G. BLAINE*

But in the uproar over his audacious bit of theater, his picking and choosing wasn't noticed, and to add a delicious finale to his superb performance, he made a public fool of Committee Chairman Knott.

In his summing up, Blaine pointed out: "They sent to Arkansas to get some hearsay about bonds. They sent to Boston to get some hearsay. Mulligan was contradicted by Fisher and Atkins, and Scott swore directly against him, etc., etc.... Now, gentlemen, those letters I have read were picked out of correspondence extending over fifteen years. The man did his worst, the very worst he could, out of the most intimate business correspondence of my life. I ask, gentlemen, if any of you—and I ask it with some feeling—can stand a severer scrutiny or more rigid investigation into your private correspondence?"

Having set the stage, and paused for effect, Blaine continued, "There is one piece of testimony wanting…" and he explained it was a cable dispatch of signal importance to his case. Turning to Proctor Knott, he said, "I ask the gentleman from Kentucky if that dispatch was sent to him."

The sender was identified as Josiah Caldwell of the Little Rock and Fort Smith Railroad, who was then on a business trip in Europe.

Knott replied he had tried unsuccessfully to obtain Caldwell's address.

Blaine pressed him. Did he not receive a cable dispatch from Caldwell?

Knott equivocated.

"I want a categorical answer," Blaine demanded.

"I have received a dispatch purporting to be from Mr. Caldwell," Knott admitted.

"When did you get it?"

Knott dodged the question.

Then, holding up a copy of the cablegram, Blaine declared, "You got a dispatch last Thursday morning at eight o'clock from Josiah Caldwell completely and absolutely exonerating me from this charge—*and you have suppressed it!*"

Gail Hamilton's description of the aftermath aptly conveys the emotion of the scene. "There was one instant of silence. Then went up from the great congregation such a sound as never those halls had heard before. It was not a shout, not a cheer, but rather a cry, the primal inarticulate voice of all souls fused in one, a victorious voice of horror, anger, exultation, triumph; rising, swelling, sinking, renewing in an ecstasy that could not end. The House simply went to pieces…."

A quick resolution put in by Blaine ordered the Judiciary Committee to investigate its own sub-committee about the suppression of evidence and then that morning session adjourned to more "wild long-continued applause from floor and gallery."[8]

On June 4, 1876, a day before this tumultuous coda to the Mulligan letters episode, Harriet Blaine wrote to Joe Manley. Her opening sentence well expressed the crisis of nerves she had been experiencing throughout the Mulligan episode, "My dear friend—

The only tears I have shed in all this bitter time have been over your letter. I have always said that those who know him best, love him best...."[9] After a few remarks about "the great Republic playing into the hands of the Confederates," she concerned herself with the forthcoming convention, about to open on June 14, and stated, "I have never been enthusiastic for the nomination. The intensest feeling I had was that it should not go to Bristow. But now I want Mr. Blaine to have it."

Her worry was not only Benjamin Helm Bristow, a Kentuckian who had been Grant's secretary of the treasury and now was the darling of the reform-minded Liberal Republicans for exposing the "Whisky Ring" of Grant's cronies; that same June 4, Harriet had also been concerned enough to write to Emmons, then a student at Harvard, and confess, "I have been afraid you might go into Boston and do something to Mulligan, but you have sense to know that nothing could be worse for your Father than notoriety of that kind."

Anything can happen at a national convention—more so in those days than in our TV world today—and to no one's surprise, conceivably, there was, indeed, a big surprise in Cincinnati. A veteran politico like ex-Vice President Hannibal Hamlin could easily, glibly account for the fact that early favorite James G. Blaine didn't win the nomination. "There never was so *gallant* a struggle for any man as was made for Mr. Blaine," said Hamlin, who had been a Blaine delegate. "We were defeated by means that were *dishonorable* and *dishonest*—means that I would resort to for no one."[10] Those means weren't specified, but Hamlin also did let it be known that if he'd been in charge at the convention, his fellow Mainer would have won.

To an extent, this was standard sour grapes on the part of a losing effort. All of the other candidates ganged up against Blaine—also standard practice when no one candidate had the strength to win on the first ballot. Blaine took an early lead. In the opening round, it was Blaine 285, Governor Oliver P. Morton of Indiana 124, and Bristow third with 113. But there were another 200 votes scattered for favorite sons and others like Conkling, Governor Hayes, and the Camerons' choice, Governor Hartranft of Pennsylvania.

If any merit existed in Hannibal Hamlin's complaint of "dishonorable and dishonest" tactics, it could be directed at an adroit maneuver Blaine's opponents pulled off on June 15. That day, the nominating speeches had been given and the one for Blaine was a masterpiece. Schoolchildren afterward memorized it for their declamations as an example of American political oratory at its best. The deliverer of that speech was Robert Green Ingersoll, the former attorney general of Illinois and one of the most interesting figures ever to grace the American public scene. Ingersoll was nationally known for his speaking ability, as well as his maverick views on religion. He was called an atheist (although agnostic would have been more correct), a man ferociously attacked by establishment clerics, and a strange choice for a Blaine supporter and close friend. The climax of his stirring plea for Blaine has been quoted ad infinitum ever since, particularly the lines immediately picked up as a theme for all of Blaine's future campaigning. "Like an armed warrior, like a plumed knight, James G. Blaine marched down the halls of the American Congress and threw his shining lance full and fair against the brazen forehead of every traitor to his country and every maligner of his fair reputation. For the Republican Party to desert that gallant man now is as though an army should desert their general upon the field of battle...."

The momentum those words gave Blaine's candidacy could have propelled him to victory had the vote been taken then and there that evening. But once the roaring applause had died away, his opponents took advantage of another standard trick. They moved for adjournment, and the convention chairman, Edward McPherson, clerk of the U.S. House, although a good friend of Blaine's, allowed it to go through on the grounds that darkness was upon them and appropriate lighting was not available.

Ingersoll's metaphor had alluded to Blaine's triumph over the Democrats' attempt to crucify him through the Mulligan Letters. Yet that victory had not been without its wounds and the failure of the man from Maine to dominate the Cincinnati gathering from the outset showed that doubts had developed about his viability in the fall. The knight image had caught imaginations, but chinks in his glistening armor had also been revealed.

James G. Blaine had not always been held in such low esteem by the reforming wing of the party that was supporting Bristow. Henry Adams, who became Blaine's indefatigable enemy, originally had turned against him after Blaine in 1875 allegedly had tricked the Liberal Republicans, "pretending interest in civil service and revenue reform."[11] One of the charges Adams later made against Blaine was that he had twice blocked the writer's father, Charles Francis Adams, Sr., from receiving the G.O.P. nomination for president. Personal gripes aside, Adams also greeted Blaine's theatrics in the Mulligan case with utter scorn. "Poor Blaine squeals louder than the other pigs," he wrote, and referring to another recent sensational national exposé, that of famed preacher Henry Ward Beecher, entangled in a messy adultery affair, he added, "I think Blaine's [speech] of Monday matches for impudence and far exceeds in insolence anything that Beecher ever did."[12]

Adams was writing to his close friend, Henry Cabot Lodge, Sr., future U.S. senator from Massachusetts, who was then a delegate to the Cincinnati convention. "Go for Bristow with all your energy," Adams told Lodge. "The game is not unlike that with Blaine last winter [the ex-speaker's brief dalliance with the Liberal Republicans] except that Bristow is a more honorable man and will not deceive us."

Another blow to Blaine's chances had occurred unexpectedly and unbelievably on June 11, three days before the G.O.P. convention. It was a Sunday. Blaine and his family were going to services in Washington, D.C. Feeling exceptionally good, Blaine had walked down to breakfast with a child on each shoulder and, instead of taking his carriage, decided they would all go on foot. It was a hot, sultry day, as only D.C. can be during June. Mounting the church's stone steps, the congressman began daubing his handkerchief at his eyes. Little Harriet asked several times, "Have you got something in your eyes, Father?" and he finally answered, "No. My head! My head!" then sank down, collapsing into unconsciousness. Taken home by omnibus, he lay in a coma and even the sharp voice of General Sherman crying, "Blaine! Blaine! Don't you know me!?" could not arouse him.

"BLAINE FEIGNS A FAINT" was a headline over the startling incident in 1876 when he was felled by sunstroke at the time of the GOP nominating convention that year. The electrifying news of his collapse on the steps of his church in Washington, D.C., reached the Republicans in Cincinnati and his rivals there used the event to their advantage in thwarting Blaine's first attempt to win his party's nod.
MAINE HISTORIC PRESERVATION COMMISSION

Rumors he was dead filled Cincinnati, as did other false sentiments following his later indisputable recovery, i.e., that he was too gravely ill to be president or—Henry Adams must have liked this—that he was faking to gain sympathy, as in the alliterative headline of a hostile newspaper: BLAINE FEIGNS A FAINT. Either way, what was obviously an attack of sunstroke at the most inconvenient time had the effect of siphoning off more doubtful delegates.

Blaine's highest total was 351 votes. To win, Hayes ultimately garnered 384 votes. By the sixth ballot, this dark horse Ohio governor was in second place. On the seventh ballot, most of New York's votes went to him and the nomination was his. William A. Wheeler, an anti-Conkling New Yorker, was made the G.O.P. choice for vice-president.

Party loyalist to the end, Blaine immediately wired Hayes his congratulations and pledge of active support, drawing the future president's comment, "My deepest emotions were on receiving Blaine's dispatch of congratulations."

Although that cable of Blaine's had promised he would return to Augusta as soon as his health permitted and devote himself to "securing you as large a vote in Maine as she would have given for myself," he also later went on the road for Hayes in the Midwest. Walker went with him to Indiana, where they teamed up with General Logan and both spoke at Fort Wayne. Several distant relatives were encountered, the oldest son wrote home—a Mrs. Colerich, whose mother was a Gillespie, and Johnny Ewing, son of Philemon from Lancaster, Ohio, now a student at Notre Dame who'd come to see Blaine—"a nice looking boy. Sent my love by him to Mother Angela" [a Catholic cousin, mother superior of a convent in South Bend]. Down in southern Indiana, Blaine addressed "eight to ten thousand people, all Hoosiers" and "spoke an hour and spoke well." An incident from that part of the trip stuck in Walker's mind: "While we were at the depot in Mitchell, a fellow came by; his face was streaming with blood and a crowd of about twenty were hooting and chasing at his heels. He was drunk and had shouted 'Hurrah for Tilden!' Of course he was not badly hurt, but it was not a pleasant sight at best."[13]

Walker's letter had been sent to his mother and by the end of October, she, herself, was in the Midwest. From Wisconsin, she wrote about a trip to Peoria, Illinois, where she stayed at the home of Robert G. Ingersoll, which she called the "Ingersoll Mansion." Met by Mrs. Ingersoll "in a beautiful brown silk costume," three carriages and "a dozen gentlemen" at 6:00 A.M., Harriet Blaine confessed, "Perhaps I never felt so welcome anywhere in my life." At a mammoth breakfast held after Ingersoll and Blaine returned from campaigning, the latter was asked to carve. He demurred, saying he never did it at home and, besides, he was so hungry he could only fill three or four plates. Consequently, a Miss Susan Sharkey was brought in from the kitchen to do the honors, "a most wholesome, respectable-looking woman." That evening a great crowd serenaded Blaine and there were even three cheers for Mrs. Blaine.

Such efforts eventually paid off. Hayes did become president and the consequences of this disputed electoral result still remain a subject of controversy. In 2004, the chief justice of the United States, the late William H. Rehnquist, wrote a book about the election of 1876 called *Centennial Crisis* and some reviewers saw it as an apologia for his role in 2000 when the U.S. Supreme Court cut off a recount in Florida and gave the electoral decision to Republican George W. Bush. The 1876 event was settled in a more complicated fashion, and the problem was not one state but three—Florida again, Louisiana, and South Carolina, plus the fight over a single elector in Oregon. For the Republicans to win, they needed every one of these votes and they eventually obtained them.

How this happened has been told as a sordid tale of alleged bribery and deal-making and the partisan votes of an electoral commission, set up by Congress, which had five House members, five senators and five Supreme Court justices. Rehnquist reports all of this maneuvering dispassionately enough, including the so-called "Devil's Bargain," negotiated by agents for Hayes and Democrat Samuel Tilden, by which the Republicans agreed to pull out all remaining federal troops from the South in return for their opponents' political compliance. James G. Blaine was never a party to these machinations. He was openly opposed to the electoral commission, fearing it would be pro-Democrat (it wasn't, after a Democratic-leaning justice resigned when made a U.S. senator), and he later publicly deplored the results of the G.O.P.'s abandonment of the Blacks and its other supporters in the South.

Once Hayes was installed in the White House, the president did remove those federal troops. The age of Jim Crow commenced in earnest.

1. Gore Vidal. *1876* (New York: Ballantine Books, 1976), pp. 185, 186.
2. H. J. Eckenrode. *Rutherford B. Hayes: Statesman of Reunion* (New York: Dodd, Mead and Company, 1930).
3. Eckenrode, p. 117.
4. Hamilton, p. 338.
5. Ibid., p. 340.
6. Vidal, p. 2.

7. Hamilton, pp. 349–50.

8. Ibid., pp. 362, 363.

9. Beale, p. 136.

10. Mark Scoggins. *Hannibal Hamlin: The Life of Abraham Lincoln's First Vice President* (Lanham, MD: Union Press of America, Inc., 1994), p. 240.

11. Ernest Samuels. *Henry Adams: The Middle Years* (Cambridge, MA: Belknap Press of Harvard University Press, 1958), p. 89.

12. Worthington Chauncey Ford. *Letters of Henry Adams, 1859–1891* (Boston: Houghton Mifflin Company, 1930), p. 286.

13. Hamilton, p. 423.

FOURTEEN

THE GREAT STATE STEAL

CYNICS MIGHT HAVE SAID that James G. Blaine's complacency in losing the Republican presidential nomination in 1876 was basically attributable to his knowledge that a U.S. senator's slot awaited him. All along, it was known that President Grant was forcing Secretary of the Treasury Benjamin Bristow to resign, and that U.S. Senator Lot M. Morrill of Maine was to replace Bristow, leaving a vacancy Down East. This actual switch did not come off until after the Cincinnati convention, but Blaine assuredly knew that Governor Selden Connor, a protégé of his, was set to name him and that the G.O.P.-dominated legislature would rubber stamp the selection.

Thus, on July 7, 1876, Morrill became secretary of the treasury and on July 10, Congressman Blaine resigned from the House and entered upon his career in the U.S. Senate.

Those Maine Republican bigwigs who thought they should have had the seat kept their silence. Israel Washburn, Jr., would have been one of those who gnashed his teeth privately. He'd already shown his ambition in 1869, after William Pitt Fessenden died, and Blaine "begged" Hannibal Hamlin to try to discourage Washburn from running against Lot Morrill, saying, "Washburn will beat his brains against a stone wall unless you can prevent it."[1] Washburn later ran against Senator Hamlin, himself, and came in last with only 18 votes out of 135 cast. Another grumbler could well have been Joshua Chamberlain. In addition to having been Maine's single greatest Civil War hero, he had served four terms as governor and by his fourth term, his eyes *were* on a future Senate seat. In 1870 he took the job of president of Bowdoin College, while still nursing his aspirations for the Senate. All hope had to have vanished when Blaine took the seat himself.

Eight months later, in March 1877, when the original term expired, Blaine was sent back to serve out a full term and the vote in the Augusta state house was unanimous, Republicans and Democrats alike. Blaine's new term started on March 4 of that year— the same day Rutherford B. Hayes was sworn in as the president of the United States.

The next day, Blaine received a letter from his friend, the venerable abolitionist Wendell Phillips, and it was full of grim prognostications. "If Hayes withdraws the troops from the South," Phillips wrote, "murder and intimidation will rule there. The South...," he continued, would be "substantially victorious in spite of Appomattox" and "there will be no Republican state south of Pennsylvania." A much longer and similarly alarmed letter then reached Blaine from the pen of the really "Grand Old Man" of abolition, William Lloyd Garrison. He praised Blaine for his defense of Republicans in the South, condemned "pseudo-Democratic organs" that "writhed and howled at the delivery of your nobly patriotic speech on the amnesty bill," and expressed the hope that Hayes— regardless of rumors of a deal with the ex-Confederates—would remain true to his inaugural address promises and "be a shield of defense to the oppressed against their lawless oppressors."

Thanks in part to Blaine, there was a Republican in the White House. Ordinarily, that might have meant opportunities for a faithful, powerful party leader like Blaine. The picking of Hayes's cabinet became the first "sticking point," so to speak. Blaine's close associate Congressman Eugene Hale was offered a post, but declined. The suggestion to substitute another Blaine crony, William Frye, was rejected because Hayes didn't know him. Later, accusations were made that "a Radical Republican Oligarchy" of Blaine, Conkling, and Cameron (an unlikely trio) had "opened a fierce attack" on Hayes's choices, notably David Key, postmaster general, because he was an ex-Confederate, and Republicans Carl Schurz and William Evarts, because they were "reformers."[2] However, a letter [most likely from Harriet Blaine] dated Augusta, March 26, 1877, asserts that some of the president's nominees were men

Blaine would have appointed himself, like Evarts, John Sherman, and McCreary. "So you can see how wild are all the stories about Mr. Blaine opposing the Cabinet."[3]

At this early stage, the president was no doubt counting on some thoughts he'd penned in his diary during the campaign that Blaine was "hopeful and friendly" and had "almost my hopes and views as to the South." That soon turned out to be wishful thinking, for shortly after Hayes's inauguration, Blaine made a major speech in the Senate on what was happening in the South, which was really an oblique attack on the Faustian agreement that had put the Ohioan in the White House. One can guess whether this was heartfelt anguish on Blaine's part or the opening gun of a new assault on the White House four years hence.

Blaine zeroed in on Louisiana where the electoral *returning board* had counted Hayes in and Stephen B. Packard, the Republicans' gubernatorial candidate, out. Packard, by the way, was a Union veteran from Maine, but Blaine wasn't just being parochial in his speech. The junior senator from Maine was going after the whole Republican swap. "Discredit Packard and you discredit Hayes. Hold that Packard is not the legal governor of Louisiana and President Hayes has no title, and the honored vice-president who presides over our deliberations has no title to his chair..." and on the question of the "arrangement" [pulling out the troops], Blaine said: "I deny it for him [President Hayes] and I shall find myself grievously disappointed, wounded and humiliated if my denial is not vindicated in the policy of the administration."

Although Blaine worked in that state election year of 1877 to keep Maine's Republican convention from condemning the president and did support him on currency matters when he'd vetoed the Silver Dollar Bill, the two were often at more or less constant loggerheads. H. J. Eckenrode, hostile as always, wrote that "Blaine subsided into sullen opposition...and lost no opportunity to assert that Hayes was in corrupt collusion with the Democrats." The Hayes biographer also belittled Blaine as a senator, saying he'd been a "great bully" in the House but his "stentorian voice and kimboed arms had no terrors"[4] in the upper body. It was obvious that Blaine never felt as at home in the Senate as he had in the

House. But his new position let him indulge an interest in foreign affairs that he hadn't had time for previously. Coincidentally, this could be useful tack for a presidential race and he could even zing the president on these issues, as he did in charging Hayes with a possible conspiracy in collusion with the Democrats to invade and conquer Mexico.

The admixture of politics and international outlook in this case was not absent from other overseas matters that Blaine handled. Brazil was an example. Blaine had met its emperor, Dom Pedro, in Washington when he was speaker and the two of them cooked up a plan to build "a great line of steamships from New York to Rio de Janeiro," with the help of John Roach, a New York shipbuilder of Irish ancestry. It was not an accident that the British held a monopoly of shipping to Brazil and would be supplanted. Being anti-British made a strong play for the Irish-American vote. Similarly, a fisheries dispute with Canada that Blaine entered pulled the British lion's tail, too, as well as standing him in good stead with his own Maine fishermen. Blaine vigorously protested the composition of an arbitration panel that had decided against the U.S. in this case. Pushing also, as he did, for a stronger U.S. merchant marine and navy didn't hurt him, either, in his home state, with its strong shipbuilding industry.

Nevertheless, this was a slack period for James G. Blaine between presidential elections, and so glimpses of his family life predominate in this brief lull during 1877–78 when he was essentially marking time.

Father Blaine could show a domestic side. "See that Fred sows more grass and inquire of George W. what good fertilizers can be used to eliminate the bare places…" appears in his correspondence. The Blaine children were growing up: Walker graduated from Yale, Emmons at Harvard, Alice was seventeen, and a host of young ones. Walker joked he couldn't keep their birthdays straight.

Early in January 1878, Maggie, age thirteen, began a diary. The family was mostly all together in Washington, D.C., and she noted that her two big brothers Walker and Emmons made a listing of the people they should call on—fifty in all. After fifteen calls, the two young men came back home, as Maggie wrote, "just to smoke cigarettes." An important visitor was the real-life Charles Nordhoff, the reporter, and she mentions a story he told about two missionaries who were twins sent to the Sandwich Islands (Hawaii) and then the Philippines.

Her brothers' smoking provided a series of entries in her girl-hood notebook. Maggie had decided to dangle a cash bribe before Walker to make him stop. Shortly before New Year's Day, a letter came from Papa who was away at Hot Springs, Arkansas, regarding a request she had made for $100. After stating he didn't like being in the "wilds of Arkansas without a single one of the family," he asked her why she wanted the money. If the reason were good enough, he would give it without requiring her "to give up Sylvia" (presumably her horse or pony). The reason was sent forthwith—to pay Walker if he gave up smoking. On January 7, 1878, Blaine, still in Hot Springs, mailed her the $100, adding, "in full payment for Sylvia and I am her owner hereafter." He hoped Walker "will appreciate the sacrifice you are making for his good" and advised her to let "Cousin Abby show you how to endorse the check."

The story doesn't end there. On January 11 she forwarded the check to her brother. She had finished eating lunch and described hearing cries in the Washington house of Hurrah! Hurrah! "We all rushed into the entry and there were Mama and Jamie and H. (young Harriet) rushing upstairs and Betty and Mary (nurses) and after I had kissed Mama, Betty nabbed me and opening a basket she had in her hand, there was the black kitten Liffie, which then got away out the back yard." The next day, there was still no sign of the kitten, which may have been intended to ease her "loss" of Sylvia. Papa Blaine, home from Arkansas finally, compensated Maggie with "a lovely little trinket for my watch chain."

Soon, she heard from Walker, who refused her challenge. The check was returned on January 21 and Maggie wrote, "I forgot to say that I have not yet returned the check to Papa, trying to get my courage up to that point tomorrow."

This young teenager was also a U.S. senator's daughter. A day later, she went up to the Capitol building as a spectator of the unveiling of a statue inside of William King, the first governor of Maine and the man most responsible for Maine's breaking away from

Massachusetts. It turned out to be an extraordinary political happening and her eyewitness account and commentary makes for piquant reading:

"First Mr. Hamlin made a speech about William King, then Papa got up and made one about him and he in it said some things about Massachusetts, up jumps Mr. Dawes and defends Massachusetts by saying among other things something about her railroads which traversed her from end to end and about her paying for them with money which all comes from Massachusetts and some more such trash…. Then up jumped George Hoar and then they had tit for tat, first Papa then Hoar, then Dawes or vice versa. Papa was so much victor that (again quoting Cousin Abby) it was so much of a victory and they were so completely put down that it was no victory at all. Hoar was infamous, even said the reason papa was against Massachusetts was not because of the War of 1812 but because of later things that happened within two years, meaning because Massachusetts did not go for Papa at the time of the nomination at Cincinnati…it was infamous of G. Hoar…" and she ends back in her own world with…."I have not yet got my courage up to tell Papa about the check."

Then, "a lovely letter" arrived from Walker, saying he was sorry if he hurt her feelings and promised to stop smoking for a month. Maggie swears to herself she'll try to "*induce* him to stop forever and then I shall make him take the check." Half grownup, half little girl, she portrays important figures of the time with a delightful freshness. William Walter Phelps, a wealthy congressman from New Jersey and a close political ally of Blaine's, came to stay with them. So did Whitelaw Reid, owner and editor of the *New York Tribune*, and a strong Blaine supporter. Maggie writes, "First saw Mr. Reid at breakfast this morning. I like him very much; as for Mr. Phelps, well, I hate him." What was the reason for this animus? She has a section where she writes of Phelps, entering her home and saying to her, "Won't you walk over to the mantelpiece and let me see how tall you are" or "Do you play on the sidewalk?" or "Let me see what sleeve buttons you have on"—just the sort of condescending adult nonsense that's totally icky to a budding young lady. On May 11, we read: "Liffie is back, but gets away again."

In June the Blaine family returned to Augusta. "The aunts are all the same," Maggie reported. The Blaines and the Manleys and the latter's relatives, next door neighbors to the Blaines, the Homans, became reunited. "Hattie," Maggie's younger sister, Harriet, was bitten by a horse. Toward the end of July, Father Blaine went to spend a week at York Beach, boarding with a Mrs. Bigelow Lawrence. Shortly afterward, Maggie noted, he was on the campaign trail to Belfast "going to speak about greenbacks, I think."

An unusual interlude that summer was the visit of a group of Russian sailors, invited by Senator Blaine to attend a reunion of the First Maine Cavalry. Eleven showed up, and Maggie wrote they "looked very funny with their hair standing on end." On August 12 Maggie made her last entry in this, her first but not last attempt at a diary, recording the overnight visit of Robert Gardiner, from nearby Gardiner, Maine, of a most distinguished Maine family, and his friend, "Mr. Lowell," conceivably James Russell Lowell, the poet, aesthete, and diplomat. "They are going to a party at the [Augusta] Insane Asylum." Her final lines were: "Diary, I close this book and will soon begin another, which will be written better, dear old Di."[5]

It is interesting that Maggie should mention "greenbacks" to her "dear old Di." Whether she knew the meaning of that political connection is perhaps unlikely. At least, the full import of the Greenback movement, both nationally and in Maine, would surely have escaped her. But for Papa Blaine, the Greenbackers were going to be a huge problem right in his own backyard, beginning with the state elections in 1878!

This political phenomenon had started in the Midwest—among the farmers in Illinois, Indiana, Iowa, Kansas, and Michigan, among others, debtors primarily, who saw their financial salvation in the continuation of U.S. government paper money (which used green ink) rather than a fixed gold standard. By 1876 they had fielded a third-party slate for president and two years later, they made their strongest showing, electing fourteen congressmen nationwide!

Two of those Greenbacker congressmen won in Maine!

It might well be asked if Blaine saw this astounding change coming in September 1878. Newspaper warnings were not lacking.

One from the Androscoggin County town of Turner stated, "The political pot is steaming here as it never steamed before. Street corners are occupied by knots discussing the all absorbing topic of national finances.... The mass of country voters are ready to adopt the Greenbackers' platform," and the story ends by saying how "astonishing" it was how many Republicans were becoming Greenbackers.[6] But Blaine could discount most of a report like this in that its source was the *Eastern Argus*, a highly propagandistic Democratic newspaper that was wont to exaggerate any Republican difficulties. Besides, he knew that Turner was a hotbed of Greenbacker agitation. The state leader of this "famers' revolt" was from Turner, an engaging and picturesque old codger, "Uncle" Solon B. Chase, who toured Maine with a yoke of oxen he called "them steers," comparing the price he'd paid for them with what they would fetch in the current depressed market. He was also a candidate for Congress in Maine's Second District (Lewiston-Auburn and Androscoggin County), challenging Blaine's political lieutenant William P. Frye, and no one was going to beat Bill Frye.

Blaine was right about that prediction. Frye won, but only by a whisker, and the other one of the senator's close associates in Congress, Eugene Hale, "Blaine's little bub," unbelievably, lost his seat to a Greenbacker in the Hancock County District and so did another veteran Republican, Llewellyn Powers, running out of Bangor. If these two astounding losses weren't enough, there was the further shocking news that a Republican no longer would fill the governor's chair. Their candidate, Selden Connor, trying for his fourth term, failed to achieve a majority. The legislature would have to decide the winner and the Republicans no longer dominated. At least, the house wasn't theirs and since the house made the nominations, a "Fusion" of Democrats and Greenbackers thus were able to send two names to the G.O.P. senate to pick from and they forwarded only a Greenbacker and a Democrat. As the lesser of two evils, the senators chose the Democrat, a businessman and medical doctor from Lewiston named Alonzo Garcelon.

The *Eastern Argus* was beside itself with glee. Its headlines told the whole story the day after the voting.

All Hail To The Fourth District
Ladd Elected
And Powers Given Indefinite Leave of Absence
Large Democratic Gains
Hale Undoubtedly Defeated
House Anti-Republican

Those two Greenbacker congressmen—each of whom was to serve two terms in D.C.—were George Washington Ladd, a Bangor lumberman, druggist and grocer, and Thompson Henry Murch, a union official, and secretary of the Granite Cutters International, whom the Democratic *Argus* slightingly referred to as a "Greenback Labor Agitator," while agreeing he was better than a Republican. Their editors, admittedly, were much happier with the eventual choice for governor, Democrat Garcelon, and the "Fusionists" were also able to choose a governor's council, to serve alongside the unexpected new chief executive.

But the Maine Democratic newspaper's biggest crowing had to be over the crushing defeat handed Blaine and his ambitions by this amazing turn of events. One *Argus* editorial opined, "And if anything were needed to forever destroy Blaine's prospects of securing the Presidential nomination in 1880, this election would supply it. A man who upon a sharply drawn issue and after a thorough canvas cannot carry his own state is not a man to lead a great party to victory.... The Blaine-Hamlin ring have long considered themselves invincible, but at one blow they are laid low. They are routed, horse, foot and dragoons."[7]

Such sentiments were soon echoed in other parts of the country. The *Philadelphia Record* declared, "The name of Blaine is sponged off the slate for 1880. The Greenbackers have their use." And in the *New York World*, there was this judgment, "The Republicans of Maine were caught by Monday's cataclysm much as the antediluvians were surprised by the flood."

Blaine, for his part, remained mute about these setbacks. His only memoir, *Twenty Years of Congress,* simply notes blandly that in organizing the Forty-sixth Congress on March 18, 1879, Mr. Randall was reelected speaker, receiving 143 votes to James A. Garfield's 125, "while 13 members elected as Greenbackers cast their vote for Hendrick B. Wright of Pennsylvania."[8]

Never one to show panic in the face of adversity, Blaine bided his time and planned his strategy for the following state election a year later. Assuredly, the Republicans would be better prepared, better financed, more energetic. Its results would confront him with possibly the greatest challenge of his career—and, if rumors can be believed—nearly cost him his life!

That campaign of 1879 has been etched into Maine history as the most extraordinary ever held. It quite literally brought the state to the brink of civil war. I have chosen to call it "The Great State Steal"—mixing two of its nicknames, "The Great Count-Out" and "The State Steal" into a single double pun, in which an election was almost stolen by "counting out," i.e., rejecting bonafide winners, and the physical state seal, the legal embossing emblem of Maine, was briefly purloined by one of two contending secretaries of state.

Prior to all this turmoil, we find James G. Blaine's Herculean efforts to reverse his political fortunes in Maine reflected in the following excerpt from the *Portland Transcript*, dated August 30, 1879. "Emmons Blaine, second son of Senator Blaine, who graduated at Harvard last year, is showing much aptitude for political work and is assisting his father in the labors of the State Committee. He goes this week to the Canadian settlements and will speak to the Frenchmen in their own language." Omitted was the fact that Emmons' journey represented the first attempt—certainly by Republicans—to approach the Acadian French populations in the uppermost northern reaches of Maine along the Canadian border. Here was an enclave of Catholic families displaced from Nova Scotia in the eighteenth century, only part of Maine since 1842, who clung to their culture and language and generally voted Democratic (as they still do today). One can picture young Emmons' attempts to use his Harvard French (the local *patois* has been described as sixteenth-century French with an English accent), but these friendly people would have appreciated his effort and he might well have picked up a few votes the G.O.P. otherwise wouldn't have had.

The Republicans certainly were scrambling. They had replaced their previous candidate for governor, Selden Connor, with a fresh face, Daniel Davis, a relatively young state legislator from Corinth in Penobscot County. The party bosses, led by Blaine and Hamlin, settled on him primarily because he was a Civil War veteran. They did so at a backroom dinner meeting during the G.O.P.'s state convention, where Blaine reportedly was so absorbed in the discussion that he kept eating from a plate of food set out for the whole group and finally Hamlin had to have the plate moved away.[9]

Democrats lost no time in attacking Davis's war record, claiming he'd never seen a day of battle and had spent most of his service either in a hospital because of a stomach ailment or back home in Maine recuperating. He became known as "Diarrhea Davis." The Republicans, in turn, took aim at the Greenback candidate, Joseph Smith, whom they deemed their strongest rival. Smith, dubbed by them "the Shylock of Old Town," had become a rich moneylender, they claimed, through usury and was a "bondholder," precisely the kind of plutocrat the Greenbackers said they loathed. Out-of-state speakers were brought in by the G.O.P.. Ohio Congressman James A. Garfield eagerly came. So did ex-Michigan Senator and Secretary of the Interior Zachariah Chandler, a multimillionaire, whose son-in-law was Eugene Hale. U.S. Senator William B. Allison of Iowa, a financial expert, was another G.O.P. superstar from "Away." These men were referred to as the "Big guns that Blaine relied on to wallop the Republican kickers back into the traces whenever they had balked or kicked over the lines."[10] And at first it seemed the Republicans had scored a smashing victory, increasing their previous vote by 12,000, while the Democrats saw theirs trimmed by 7,000. The G.O.P. apparently had won back the Maine House of Representatives in Augusta, taking ninety seats, while holding on to a seven-vote margin in the Maine Senate. This was all important to their political control because, once again, the Republican gubernatorial candidate had failed to win an absolute majority in the popular vote. Although "Diarrhea Davis" had merely missed a majority by 840 votes, the election of the state's chief executive would still have to be decided by the legislature.

That term "Count-Out" had been around in Maine for some years. The Republicans earlier, using technicalities, once had denied election to a Democratic state senator named Madigan from that same French-speaking area in the St. John Valley where Emmons Blaine had gone to campaign and also the Democrats could point to the "stolen" presidential election of 1876. So it didn't take long after the September 1879 election for rumors to surface that the Democrats and Greenbackers were thinking of a massive "count-out" of their own to upset the results in Augusta and once more obtain the governorship.

By November, those rumors were strong enough to achieve front page coverage in the *New York Times*, then an openly partisan Republican newspaper. A month later, such rumors became fact. Governor Garcelon and his seven-man Fusionist executive council issued certificates of election that disenfranchised thirty-seven Republicans, turning the G.O.P.'s ninety seats into fifty-eight and elevating the Democratic total to seventy-eight from sixty-one, a clear Fusionist margin. In the state senate, too, the same nit-picky tactics had been employed: twenty Democrats had been seated for a nine-vote margin, erasing a seven-vote Republican edge.

This news was first reported by the *Times* on December 18, 1879. A list of subsequent headings in the *Times Index* aptly illustrates the chronology of a brewing crisis:

> December 20: Augusta Indignation Meeting—
> Senator Blaine Speech
> December 21: Bangor Indignation Meeting—Senator Hamlin's
> Speech, Counseling an Uprising
> December 23: Senator Blaine's Letter to Gardiner Indignation
> Meeting—General Garfield Denies Advising Violence
> December 25: Mr. Morrill's [ex-Governor and U.S. Senator
> Lot M. Morrill] Letter—Suggesting Reference to Supreme
> Court [of Maine]
> December 26: Bangor Citizens Opposition to Removal of Arms
> December 29: Mr. Morrill's Reply to Governor Garcelon, Suggesting Questions for Supreme Court
> December 30: Augusta Mayor's Letters as to Danger of Disorder at Meeting of Legislature

Filling in the outline was a series of articles about mounting tension in the northeasternmost corner of the nation. Blaine had rushed back from Washington to take charge of the Republican forces. He was still being mentioned for the 1880 G.O.P. nomination, but his flag was drooping, as shown by a poll of 100 Republicans in Ohio—taken on December 19, 1879—that had his boyhood acquaintance U.S. Senator John Sherman with 63, ex-President Grant, more and more looking like a third-term candidate, with 25 and the "magnetic" Mainer with a paltry 8.

Hardly surprising, then, was that the first "indignation" meeting in Maine should be held in Augusta at Granite Hall to a turn-away crowd. After an introductory address by Blaine's neighbor, old Joseph Homan, ex-Governor Selden Connor was elected to preside. The immense throng began loudly calling for Blaine and his appearance was a signal for the "wildest demonstrations and applause." Somewhat surprisingly, Blaine chose not to dema-gogue. His tone seemed almost scholarly, although his indignation had to be apparent as he described the Fusionists' "conspiracy" to discover "fatal defects, as Governor Garcelon and his council termed them," in the election returns. "Here and there, an 'I' was not dotted or a 'T' not crossed or a man had 'Jr.' left off his name or the initial letter of the middle name was wrong…." Thus did Blaine introduce his audience to what he called "pitiful and wicked pettifogging." Not one Democrat or Greenbacker had a defect, he pointed out. If this action were allowed to stand, he argued, quite logically it would happen again—in 1880, a presidential and con-gressional year at the polls, and in 1883, when reapportionment would be done. His conclusion, which must have brought back those lusty cheers that had met his entrance, was, "A great popular uprising will avert these evils and restore honest government to Maine…."

Senator Hannibal Hamlin was even more explicit the following night at another monster gathering of protestors in Bangor. "Make everyone an outcast and a wandering Jew" who supported the Fusionist action, he cried. There was little doubt that Blaine—with the help of Hamlin and other Republican leaders—was behind these meetings popping up all over Maine. But keeping a presidential profile in the midst of this whirlwind, Blaine deliberately pulled in his sails. At the next big meeting, which was in his neighboring city of Gardiner, he didn't attend. As he explained in a letter he had read aloud, he wanted to leave all initiative to local people, alone. He had spoken out in his own city of Augusta. "I shall say nothing elsewhere." However, his epistle to the Gardinerites stated that Garcelon and his council had gone "far beyond George III" in their tyranny and that Jefferson had included vote tampering among the grievances he'd cited in the Declaration of Independence as justification for the American Revolution.

Possible violence in this volatile climate soon became another theme. A *Washington Star* article reported that in telegrams to Blaine and Hamlin, "General Garfield advises resistance, even to the extent of force." But it was a statement Garfield speedily denied having made. While part of the Blaine strategy—the indignation meetings—did stir up emotions, a second prong of the attack was to seek a peaceful resolution through the law. Thus Lot M. Morrill's proposal to submit the matter to the Maine Supreme Court did put enough pressure on Governor Garcelon so he considered the matter, although that judicial entity consisted almost entirely of Republican appointees.

The first overt violent act occurred when a Republican mob stopped two wagons in Bangor, one loaded with 120 rifles, the other with 34,000 rounds of ammunition, underway from the state armory to the capital. The adjutant general's clerk, a young man named French, said he had received a verbal order from Governor Garcelon to move the weaponry. Faced by an angry mob at Kenduskeag Bridge, French wisely turned back. But it was only a temporary retreat. Rumors were rife that Blaine was arming his followers. One national Democratic newspaper editorialized, "...if Mr. Blaine resists Governor Garcelon openly and with arms and takes life with those arms, it will be right and proper to shoot Mr. Blaine." The *Boston Dispatch* wrote, "Republicans are forming secret military associations and threats have been made that they would seize the arms in Bangor." Somehow, though, Governor Garcelon got those Bangor weapons and ammo shipped to Augusta, but not trusting the local state militia officers, equipped his own

Fusionist paramilitary force—seventy-five riflemen—who guarded each window and door in the state house. Snipers were set up in the building's dome. As the story goes, one of them took a bead on Blaine, whose house was at close range across Capital Street. About to squeeze the trigger, he had his rifle knocked away by a more level-headed companion.

An argument for not shooting might have been that there were women and children in the Blaine House. Harriet and her household hadn't fled. Her home had become the battle station for the G.O.P., a magnet for politicians and armed volunteers a stone's throw from the state house, now derisively nicknamed Fort Garcelon. Teenager Maggie has left us a diary entry, dated January 13, 1880, of what those tempestuous days were like: "Papa, Mr. Hale, and others had a fiery argument after dinner today about what was now to be done. What is the use of my trying to be kind.... Mr. Hale took offense and was very rude...to Father. There was a caucus this afternoon and after it—the right Representatives and Senators that went over to the State House were qualified by Mr. Stratton, clerk of the courts. They had sessions all the evening and organized everything.... They have referred to the Supreme Court how to decide which is the rightful Legislature." One day later, she was writing about an alarm that "Fusionists were going to attack the State House [which had been surreptitiously occupied by the Republican legislators].... Today, men have been arriving by all the trains...50 men from Winthrop.... General Chamberlain has been telegraphed to come back immediately.... I do not know when I shall return to the quiet of Farmington [in Connecticut, where she was going to boarding school]." The youngest Blaine child, Harriet, likewise later wrote in her memoirs, "I remember my Mother lifting me out of bed one night and saying, 'Look, do you see those men?'" When she did peer out, the little girl saw a line of silhouettes against a snowy background, patrolling pickets, guarding her family's residence.[11]

What was the role of Governor Alonzo Garcelon in this fracas? It was later claimed that the seventy-year-old doctor had been "swept along by younger and less scrupulous men."[12] The real ring-leader of the "Count-Out" was said to be Democrat Eben S.

Pillsbury, who on three occasions had lost a governor's race to Joshua Chamberlain. Yet Garcelon was front and center throughout the turmoil. To a raucous, loudly applauding audience of 3,000 Democrats and Greenbackers in Lewiston, Garcelon on December 28 resolutely declared, "If there has been an act of my life of which I am proud, it is of the performance of my duty in tabulating and counting those returns." On the other hand, one other act of his may have been the key to solving the dispute without bloodshed—that is, his bringing "General Chamberlain" into the picture.

The war hero, president of Bowdoin College then, was also the overall commander of the Maine Militia. Garcelon liked and trusted Chamberlain, as opposed to other officers of what today would be the National Guard, and he knew that his prestige and Republican credentials would inspire respect. Could the soldier who had held the line at Gettysburg hold the line against a budding civil war within his native state?

Coming to Augusta, Chamberlain declined to mobilize the militia, convinced Garcelon to dismiss his own armed band, and sent back the Bangor military supplies. For protection, Chamberlain arranged a squad of 150 municipal police from Augusta Mayor Charles E. Nash.

As if in a western movie, the moment of greatest drama occurred when, alone and unarmed, Chamberlain faced an infuriated, gun-toting crowd of Fusionists outside the state house. The day before, the Republicans had sneaked into the now unguarded capitol and secured physical possession of the house and senate chambers. Warned before he went out to confront the mob that they might kill him, Chamberlain calmly replied, "Killing is no new thing to me," adding he would enforce the laws of the state. When guns were pointed at him, he opened his coat and invited the Fusionists to shoot. But as luck would have it, one of his veterans from the Twentieth Maine was among the crowd. The man raised his own weapon and swore, "By God, General, the first man who dares to lay a hand on you, I will kill him on the spot." The crowd, cowed and ashamed, melted away.

Both sides were causing Chamberlain trouble. One of his own subordinates at Gettysburg, now General Thomas Hyde, owner of the Bath Iron Works shipbuilding company, arrived in the capital with 300 men—"sent for by Republicans," Chamberlain wrote his wife "...and greatly annoying to me and embarrassing, too.... I wish Mr. Blaine and others would have more confidence in my military ability." A letter to Blaine, dated January 16, 1880, 3 P.M., which Chamberlain said he'd had to "write in snatches for the last 2 hours," turned down the senator's request to have the state house seized by force to keep the Fusionists from doing the same. "Neither force nor treachery nor trick shall get the mastery of the situation out of my hands," Chamberlain assured Blaine, adding, "Whoever first says 'take arms!' has a fearful responsibility on him and I don't mean it shall be me who does that."

Allegedly, offers already had been made to Chamberlain of political favors—specifically an election to the U.S. Senate by whichever party would control the legislature. The Fusionists, arguing "Look, Blaine and his gang are the worst enemies you have,"[13] made their pitch and were rejected, and Lot Morrill, sent with the message, "Mr. Blaine said he will give way and leave the way clear for you to go to the Senate if you will recognize the Republican organization of the two Houses" was equally rebuffed.

All along, Chamberlain had been opting for Morrill's solution to submit the dispute to the Maine Supreme Court, On January 17, 1880, the justices handed down their decision that Daniel Davis was the legal governor. Davis and entourage immediately went to the statehouse, had the lock on the governor's office jimmied open, and did the same at the secretary of state's office where it was discovered that Fusionist Secretary of State Prince A. Sawyer had made off with the official state seal. After sending Chamberlain home, Davis also called out the militia. Troops arrived and set up a Gatling gun at the state house entrance. Photographs have shown this primitive form of machine gun in place and also we have Governor Garcelon's bitter statement in a booklet he subsequently published that, "The revolutionary and irregular legislature, fearing the wrath of the people, filled the State House with armed soldiery for the first time in the history of the State. A deadly Gatling gun frowned upon all who were allowed to enter the Capitol."

Meanwhile, we have a jubilant Maggie Blaine telling "Dear Di," "The decision of the Supreme Court was received late last evening. It is glorious. The Legislature met—elected Daniel F. Davis. This evening 200 or 300 men came to call on Papa. They gave three cheers for our next President."

1. Scroggins, p. 232.
2. Vann Woodward. *Reunion and Reaction: The Compromise of 1877 and the End of Reconstruction* (Boston: Little, Brown and Company, 1951), p. 216.
3. Hamilton, pp. 429, 430.
4. Eckenrode, p. 245.
5. All of Margaret Blaine's diary excerpts are from the James G. Blaine Collection, Madison Building, Library of Congress, Washington, D.C.
6. *Eastern Argus*, 29 July 1878.
7. *Eastern Argus*, 11 September 1878.
8. James G. Blaine. *Twenty Years of Congress*, Vol. 2 (Norwich, CT: Henry Bill Publishing Company, 1886), p. 638.
9. From a collection of articles, "Governors of Maine and the Times," printed in the *Portland Sunday Telegram,* 16 October 1910–10 December 1911, issue of 17 September 1911
10. Ibid.
11. John J. Pullen. *Joshua Chamberlain: A Hero's Life and Legacy* (Mechanicsburg, PA: Stackpole Books, 1999), p. 100.
12. "Governors of Maine" series, 3 September 1911.
13. Pullen, p. 95.

FIFTEEN

ONCE AGAIN, A BRIDESMAID

T HERE ARE HINTS THAT James G. Blaine, except during his first try for the presidency, really didn't have his heart in running for the top post. With her husband deeply embroiled in Maine politics early in November 1879, Harriet Blaine wrote, "Grant is booming along, and welcome, if I were the only one to be consulted." The successful conclusion of the "Great State Steal" may have changed the dynamic—for both Blaines—but reports of a laggard candidacy on Blaine's part continued to spread throughout 1880, leading his campaign manager, New Hampshire's William E. Chandler, to voice aloud his concern, "I think he [Blaine] owes it to himself and to his friends all over the country who are ready to sacrifice everything for his success to do all that is in his power to win at Chicago."[1]

The counter-argument has been posited that Blaine was simply trying to preserve his own physical strength for the grueling effort ahead if he gained the nomination. His fainting in Washington, D.C., was still remembered. Fear of a stress-induced repeat may have led him to turn down Chandler's plea that he appear in Chicago personally and dazzle the delegates. "Such things just aren't done," he told Chandler, in all likelihood hiding behind an age-old tradition.

Had Blaine gone to Chicago, would he have carried the day? The boldness of the move, in keeping with his reputation for flair, might have struck a note and his charm done the rest. So how badly did James G. Blaine want to be president in 1880? He apparently had told Garfield he did not expect to win and had only run to stop Grant. But why would that be important? Did he see the third-term issue leading to a Republican disaster? Was there a per-

Another famous anti-Blaine cartoon, this time by Thomas Nast, arguably the most noted cartoonist of his time. The incident on which this drawing is based was the contentious "Count Out" or "Great State Steal" protracted event that almost led to a civil war in Maine, when Democrats and Greenbackers tried to count out a Republican majority elected to control Maine government and were defeated by Blaine. Although usually impervious to editorial attacks, Blaine was so angered by the insinuation he wanted to resort to violence, he wrote Nast a blistering letter of protest.
MAINE HISTORIC PRESERVATION COMMISSION

sonal animus against Grant? Or was it against Conkling, who was orchestrating the plan to bring the ex-president back? Or was just plain old ego simply the motive?

It was rare that Blaine ever showed a prickly side of his nature. During the "Count-Out" strife in Maine, a cartoon by Thomas Nast of *Harper's Weekly* did get under his skin, and he took the unusual step of complaining to its author in a carping letter. He had been depicted as Indian Chief Powhatan brandishing a huge club, about to brain a supine figure, and only being halted by Joshua Chamberlain as Pocahontas, telling him, "No, don't Jim, you'll only make a mess of it"[2]—in other words, accusing him of fomenting violence to solve his political problems at home. If Blaine sought an apology from Nast, he never got it; in fact, more and more anti-Blaine ink came from that pen over the years.

As far as is known, Blaine remained his equable self toward those with whom he had clashed, including Conkling. Indeed, he could even point to a message, sent on July 16, 1879, to Conkling in Utica, and signed by himself, seeking the New Yorker's help in the crucial Maine election that year. "I am directed by a unanimous vote of the Republican State Committee to invite you to address a meeting at Portland or one at Bangor.... Hamlin joins in making the request." Apparently, Conkling never responded, despite a second message sent him, nor was he ever known to have spoken another word to Blaine since their celebrated run-in in 1866.

Roscoe Conkling was gearing up to be a kingmaker at the Chicago convention. President Rutherford B. Hayes—"Rutherfraud"—had announced he would only serve one term, saying he favored a single six-year term and no reelection. Unlike Blaine, Conkling was the showiest of egotists and power, not money, was his ultimate lust. In 1880, aware of his own poor showing at Cincinnati four years earlier, he latched onto Grant. As one of his biographers, Donald Barr Chidsey, wrote, in Conkling's eyes, "There must be no more accidents like Rutherford B. Hayes. What the country needed was another term of General Grant, and the Senator [Conkling] meant to see that it got this. Nor would he take any chances with a blundering, vacillating New York delegation. This time he would go *in person* to the national convention. He would supervise the job *himself*."[3]

No wonder Blaine's campaign manager William Chandler was so anxious to have his candidate appear in Chicago. Blaine's stock had risen considerably, but always there was an undercurrent against him. James Garfield expressed it well in his journal, "...I like Blaine, always have, and yet there is an element in him which I mistrust." That was it—the lurking discomfort with this charismatic man from Maine expressed by his best political friend. Donald Barr Chidsey picked up on the same quirk: "...yet so many of the men who liked to spend time in his [Blaine's] company felt, for some reason they could not quite explain, that it would not be proper to put such a man in the White House. There was something vaguely disgusting about his fondness for money and for millionaires. And while nobody ever was to prove any dishonesty against him, always there were hints, there were whispers...."[4]

At the same time, Grant's comeback was gathering force. The ex-president had gone around the world, been feted in foreign countries, and, upon landing in San Francisco, had been mobbed by well-wishers before conducting a triumphal cross-country railroad trip to the East, cheered at every stop along the way. Organizationally, Grant looked strong, too. Three of the toughest political operatives from three key states—Black Jack Logan of Illinois, Don Cameron of Pennsylvania, and Roscoe Conkling of New York—had lined up solidly behind him. The key to their effort was the unit rule—a majority-takes-all situation—locking up whole delegations. On this score, the three big state "bosses" delivered their own fiefs handsomely; despite split votes at their state conventions, Pennsylvania, New York, and Illinois had given Grant an edge and the winners enforced discipline with majorities for the unit rule.

The press was lining up the G.O.P. race as a contest between two opposing forces—the "Stalwarts," those for Grant, and the "Half-Breeds," whose acknowledged leader was James G. Blaine. Yet other contenders were also at Chicago. The strongest among these more minor players appeared to be John Sherman. The leader of his campaign, in fact, was Blaine's good friend James Garfield, who had felt he had to go with a fellow Ohioan. The Bristow "reformers" of 1876, were now backing a U.S. senator from Vermont, George F. Edmunds, sometimes called "Moses" because of his long, white beard. Two others who had thrown their hats into the ring were Elihu Washburne, the Maine-born ex-congressman and diplomat from Illinois, and William Windom, a U.S senator from Minnesota. All of the non-Grant candidates proceeded to gang up on the unit rule. If it could be denied to the Grant forces, the convention would be wide open for any of them. And that is essentially what happened. The tactical fight was over the selection of a permanent chair. The temporary chair, Don Cameron of Pennsylvania, son of the venerable G.O.P. boss Simon Cameron, tried hard to keep Massachusetts Senator George Frisbee Hoar from attaining this full-time post and, failing that, he sought to sabotage a vote by the entire body on whether or not to kill the unit rule. Threatened with the loss of his position as chairman of the Republican National Committee, Cameron backed down, allowed the vote, and saw the unit rule defeated 449-306. This was followed by a resolution allowing roll call votes of delegations. The squabbling was so intense that Garfield, in a letter to his wife, wrote about there being "more passion than there was at [the battle of] Chicamauga."

Before the balloting actually began, Garfield, who had distinguished himself fighting against the unit rule, also shone when he countered an ill-advised move by Roscoe Conkling. The New Yorker had started out all right, proposing a motherhood-and-apple-pie resolution that pledged all delegates to support the eventual Republican candidate, whoever he might be. The vote was 716 to 3, and all three of those naysayers were stubborn mountaineers from West Virginia. The imperious Conkling then overstepped his bounds. His motion to have the trio expelled—they were all Blaine delegates—met with a howl of protest, eloquently led by Garfield, and Conkling was forced to retreat from his mean-spirited stance.

What looked like a Conkling-Garfield feud soon developed. The former gave a spectacular nominating speech for Grant. It was followed by Garfield, nominating John Sherman, and in praising his candidate, the latter used a nautical metaphor, saying that "this assemblage seems to me a human ocean tossed in tempest...but I remember that it's not the billows but calm level of the sea from which all heights and depths are measured...." Conkling rudely exclaimed in a loud voice: "This man is making me seasick!" and stormed out of the hall.

However, Sherman, a cold, aloof but capable man, did not do well in the early voting—running a distant third behind Grant and Blaine, who were only twenty votes apart on the first ballot. To win, 378 votes were necessary. Grant never went higher than 313 and Blaine was always a little below him. The three dark horses, Edmunds, Washburne, and Windom, merely represented a scattering. Vote after vote was taken, more than thirty of them, and nothing substantial changed.

On the thirty-fourth ballot, Wisconsin unexpectedly put in sixteen votes for James Abram Garfield. The Sherman campaign man-

John Sherman, U.S. senator from Ohio and secretary of the treasury, the brother of William Tecumseh Sherman, a man who had known "Jim" Blaine since they met as boys together in Sherman's hometown of Lancaster, Ohio. In later life, they became rivals for the Republican presidential nomination.
BOYD, *LIFE AND PUBLIC SERVICES OF JAMES G. BLAINE*

ager rose and protested that he was not a candidate, only to be gaveled down by Chairman Hoar who ruled him out of order. On the thirty-fifth ballot, Grant reached his highwater mark of 313 votes and Garfield had risen to 50. Before the thirty-sixth ballot, Blaine, who had had a telegraph installed in his Augusta home, made a decision. It was clear to him *he* could not gain the nomination. If he gave his help to Garfield at the crucial moment, he could turn the tide. Grant would be blocked and he would be a king-maker—and, besides, Garfield was at least a close political ally and personal friend. The wired word went out from Maine to his troops: support Garfield. Of the 257 votes Blaine had on the thirty-

A hatless James A. Garfield, showing his near baldness. He and Blaine, despite some rough spots in their relationship, became enduring political and personal friends. Blaine was by Garfield's side when he was shot and was also the unanimous choice to deliver his funeral oration.
BOYD, *LIFE AND PUBLIC SERVICES OF JAMES G. BLAINE*

fifth ballot, 215 went to Garfield. Grant dropped to 306, and the rest of the delegates gave Garfield 399 and the nomination. A call from Chairman Hoar to make the decision unanimous saw Roscoe Conkling, no doubt gritting his teeth, rising to make the motion.

His true feelings were shown almost immediately. The Garfield forces offered General Stewart L. Woodford, a Cronkling crony, the vice-presidential spot. Asked for his advice, Conkling told Woodford, "I hope no sincere friend of mine will accept." The same thing happened when Levi P. Morton, a New York City banker and Conkling pal was approached. But Garfield's people still wanted a "Stalwart" for balance on the ticket, preferably one of the 306 Grant

"Old Guard." This is where Chester A. Arthur came into the picture. No one was more of a Conkling errand boy than this paunchy, mustachioed dandy. But he had lost his cushy job at the New York Customs House and said yes to the vice-presidential proposition without consulting Conkling, who was furious but unable to prevent a Garfield-Arthur pairing once the convention endorsed it.

Back in Augusta, Harriet Blaine was the chronicler of her family's roller-coaster emotions. Even before the Chicago convention opened, she told Maggie, "I am almost sure a combination will be made against your Father...." There was no hint now she had once written it would be all right if Grant won. Word came of the tremendous reception given the mere mention of Blaine's name—the frenzied cheering and the vain attempts of the Grant men to drown the roar by shouting and waving flags. "Conkling, himself, condescending to wave...," Mrs. Blaine tartly commented. Included by the Blaine contingent was a stunt in which Eugene Hale, that dignified Maine politico, poised atop the shoulders of four of the tallest Blaineites standing on settees and waved an American flag furiously. "Think of the position for a man who is not an acrobat," was another of Harriet's deadpan Yankee comments. "Meanwhile, Mr. Blaine," she revealed, "went off to bed dead sleepy, and is this morning reading the papers with provoking indifference. He is not indifferent, of course, but self-possessed...." William Chandler had telegraphed that he considered Blaine's chances of victory 4-1, "but not to be counted on until it comes." Seeing her husband's victory in the offing, Harriet contrarily wondered in print whether "it was a pity to take him away from the Senate after all."

A hiatus exists in her correspondence from that moment of euphoria until, without her husband on the ballot, the Republican campaign had begun. At the end of June, she wrote Emmons, who was attending Harvard Law School, "The Hancock nomination [the Democrats had put up Winfield Scott Hancock, a popular Civil War general as their champion] makes Garfield's prospects problematical in the extreme." But by the end of October, she reported her husband home from campaigning in the West, "full of enthusiasm for Garfield and the Republican triumph." Once Garfield and Arthur had won, Harriet Blaine immediately expressed relief, "For now there is no danger that any of the tomfoolery of the Hayes policy will be tried," and followed with some personal exultation, "Oh, how good it is to win and to be on the strong side!" It was all the more heartfelt, too, because it looked like James G. Blaine would be the new secretary of state and the leading member of Garfield's cabinet and administration.

The stage for this eventuality had already been set right after the Chicago convention ended. Recognizing he would have to play a strong role in Garfield's campaign, Blaine had gone for a rest cure at White Sulphur Springs, West Virginia, rooming with U.S. Senator Newton Booth of California and describing the "very agreeable routine" he and Senator Booth were pursuing—hot springs baths, leisurely meals, horseback rides, early to bed—"My gout is rapidly disappearing and I think I shall come out all bright and new."[5]

Garfield, at home in Mentor, Ohio, gave him a week to himself and then the nominee's letter arrived, beginning: "MY DEAR BLAINE: I was greatly disappointed at not seeing you again before I left Washington, for there were many things I wanted to say to you, and still more which I wanted you to say to me...." So commenced a series of MY DEAR BLAINE, MY DEAR GARFIELD communications that went on throughout the campaign and afterwards. That first one came right out and acknowledged Garfield's debt to Blaine: "Your friends, partaking of your own spirit, are generous and helpful, because they love a common cause, and because you and they are responsible for my nomination." Then, right down to work. Garfield needed help on his letter of acceptance, which would be his initial revelation to the American people of what he stood for and how he presented himself. Specifically, he wanted Blaine's input on several issues that he listed: the Chinese (immigration) question, the civil service question, the Southern question, the silver question..."and finally anything else that is in your heart," the nominee requested.[6]

Five days later, Blaine's answer went back from the spa to the nominee. The bulk of his response was about handling the thorny matter of the coolies on the West Coast who drew such hostility, or the "Yellow Peril," as some of the media had demagogically characterized it. On the floor of the Senate a year before, Blaine

Harper's Weekly, *another anti-Blaine publication, illustrating the hypocrisy of a politician who favored kindly and equable treatment for Negroes yet railed against the Chinese and a so-called "Yellow Peril" faced by the nation if Asian immigration wasn't stopped.*
MAINE HISTORIC PRESERVATION COMMISSION

hadn't been far behind in the implied racism of his remarks, supporting a bill to exclude all Asian immigration, despite a U.S. treaty with the Chinese Empire. "The Asiatic cannot live with our population and make an homogenous element" was among his milder comments. Hannibal Hamlin openly disagreed with him, but Blaine was playing for western votes, arguing that the three Pacific states would be overrun by Chinese hordes if they weren't stopped. In softer language, in his letter to Garfield, he equated his stance to the Republican crusade against black slavery and the saving of "free labor." But he also told the candidate he "should clothe the proposition" in his own language.[7]

By the time Garfield wrote him again, Blaine was back in Maine. Nitty-gritty politics had to be discussed—meaning Conkling and his demands. "I want to know how large a force C. has behind him and what the trouble is," Garfield, still in Ohio, wrote on the eve of a trip he was taking to New York City. He said he "would go over the ground" with Blaine when he reached New York "and I want you to find out the exact situation if possible before I arrive."

The scene was being set for a top-level G.O.P. showdown. "In the annals of political backroom deals, the Fifth Avenue Summit of August, 1880 deserves its own special pedestal,"[8] wrote Kenneth Ackerman in his biography of James A. Garfield. The site was the Fifth Avenue Hotel, that quasi-headquarters for nineteenth-century Republicans in Manhattan, where Broadway and Fifth Avenue nearly converge near 23rd Street. All of the party's senior brass were on hand—Blaine, John Sherman, "Black Jack" Logan, the new party chair Stephen Dorsey, New York Governor Alonzo Cornell, Tom Platt, a rising star in the New York State Republican contingent—everyone, except the one man Garfield had come to see— Roscoe Conkling!

It wasn't exactly a snub. Conkling was letting his emissaries, Platt, Levi Morton, Chet Arthur, and a Richard Crowley do some negotiating for him. Did they extract a quid-pro-quo from Garfield? Without Stalwart support, the Democrats would win New York and the election. Conkling's price was total patronage in New York. There are varying versions as to the exact promises Garfield made to this clique. A mammoth torchlight reception, held in nearby Madison Square Park, where 50,000 people cheered the Republican standard-bearer, must have buoyed Garfield's spirits. Yet when he left for Ohio, he carried the chilling knowledge that Conkling—quite possibly the key to his election—was still not firmly on board. As it turned out, only toward the middle of September did Conkling agree even to make a speech for Garfield. In all, he made around twenty. Frequently, Grant would also appear with the man from Utica.

On the other hand, Blaine made so many speeches for Garfield throughout the East, West, and Midwest that his voice gave out in late October. And this touring did not start until after the usual September vote in Maine, which—shockingly—failed to produce a Republican victory for governor. Maine had switched to a plurality system and a Democrat, General Harris Plaisted, running as a Fusionist, sneaked into office by a few hundred votes. Blaine, who had told Garfield he expected a 5,000-vote margin, was definitely embarrassed. Nor did the Republicans regain their two lost congressional seats. But Garfield consoled his friend by writing, "The Democracy of Maine has again enabled you to fight a great battle in the presence of the nation for the purity of the ballot box...." And in the next breath, "I will have your Ohio meetings announced tomorrow morning...."

Still, this new sign of slippage in Blaine's Maine allowed his enemies within the national party to put their own "spin" on the ultimate Republican victory in November. The argument was that only by having Senator Conkling and President Grant come to the rescue in October had the G.O.P. avoided the loss that Blaine's September defeat in Maine had seemed to make inevitable. Stalwarts boasted, "If Mr. Garfield is indebted to Mr. Blaine for his nomination, he will have to thank Mr. Conkling for his election."[9]

James Abram Garfield could see what was coming and he was no fool. Some Republicans found him affable enough but vacillating and even a tad slippery, thanks to the Credit Mobilier business. He was not just a soldier like Grant, whom he resembled in stature somewhat mainly because of his beard (when he had his hat on— he was partially bald). A well-educated graduate of Williams College, he had been a professor and college president (at Eclectic University, now Hiram College in Ohio) before joining the Union Army as colonel of the Forty-second Ohio Regiment, quickly rising to brigadier general through his exploits in Kentucky and his bravery at the otherwise disastrous battle of Chickamauga. In absentia, in 1863, his home folks chose him to represent them in Washington, D.C., and he agreed to leave the military only after a talk with Lincoln, who said he needed him on the political front more than in battle. Garfield was generally considered the best-read man in the U.S. Congress—that is, next to James G. Blaine. And it was certainly plain to this astute Ohioan of New England ancestry that he was going to have to choose between Blaine and Conkling in the operation of his administration. Following the election, Blaine, at the president-elect's request, had presented him with a thorough analysis of the three main forces within the Republican Party: the Blaine section, "all yours, with some additional strength that Blaine could not get"; the Grant section, mostly all of the South, which would never vote Republican again; plus the machines in New York, Pennsylvania, and Illinois—"having the aid of rule or ruin leaders..."; and the Reformers, "the 'unco good'...upstarts, conccitcd, foolish, vain...." Earlier, Garfield had visited Blaine at his 15th Street home in Washington and broached the subject of an unspecified cabinet position. "Before you answer," the nominee said to his friend, "please tell me whether you are or will be a candidate for President in 1884."[10]

Blaine's answer was that he would not run in '84 and would consider giving up his Senate seat for a cabinet post.

The deal was struck on December 20, 1880. Secretary of state, it would be, the acme of political plums, first among equals in the Cabinet! As Kenneth Ackerman writes, "By this one action, Garfield had managed to shift the axis of power in American government. Instead of the New York stalwarts who had won him his election and demanded tribute, Garfield would now anchor his line to James G. Blaine...."[11]

1. Kenneth D. Ackerman. *Dark Horse: The Surprise Election and Political Murder of President James A. Garfield* (New York: Carroll and Graf Publishers, 2003), p. 75.
2. Pullen, p. 101.
3. Donald Barr Chidsey. *The Gentleman From New York: A Life of Roscoe Conkling* (New Haven, CT: Yale University Press, 1935), p. 273.

4. Ibid., p. 275.
5. Hamilton, p. 485.
6. Ibid., p. 486.
7. Ibid., p. 488.
8. Ackerman, p. 168.
9. Ibid., p. 224.
10. Ibid., p. 225.
11. Ibid., p. 226.

~⟨⟨⟨⟨⟨⟨≪

SIXTEEN

AN INEXPRESSIBLE
HORROR

To BORROW FROM DICKENS, it was the "best of times," soon to turn into the "worst of times"—for the Blaines.

While the immediate post-election machinations within the G.O.P. were being ironed out, Harriet Blaine was feeling sorry for herself. Writing "Miss Dodge" from Augusta, she told Cousin Abby what it was like to be left "absolutely alone with my servants, every want anticipated, not a room in the house not at summer heat [on December 3], four horses and a pony in the stable, sleighs and robes in abundance and the beautiful snow...." Finally, explaining her melancholy, she penned one of her most felicitous insights into her life with that "Magnetic Man" who now stood to reach yet new heights in American political life.

"First of all, I miss Mr. Blaine. I cannot bear the orderly array of my life. I miss the envelopes in the gravy, the bespattered table linen, the uncertainty of the meals, for you know he always starts out on his constitutional when he hears them taking in dinner. I miss his unvarying attention and as constant neglect..."[1]

No man can be a king in the eyes of his wife, and James G. Blaine was no exception. Her letters paint a picture of a far different figure than the bearded superstar who could hold an audience of thousands spellbound and set them to roaring his name in a paroxysm of adulation.

Here is an almost comic interlude from Harriet's pen, featuring the august U.S. secretary of state-to-be in an episode described to Walker: "...after being driven to Etna from East Corinth [he] procured a ride for himself on a handcar to Newport, that he might see Mr. Dexter about the old wagon. The night was dark, and first he lost his hat, for which they retraced their steps some half mile, and then his bag was found missing, and for this they went back two miles, but found it not; but the next morning at ten, the express delivered it, much the worse for its travels, the Pullman having gone over it. The contents were found spilled along the side of the track. One shirt was cut all to pieces, the toilet apparatus was never found, and the bag was ruined. But it never seemed to enter his dear head that the escapade was a risky and foolish one and not to be expected from a man of his habits. And although he saw Mr. D., he forgot to ask the price at which it was sold, so we are in as much uncertainty as ever...."[2] It seems she could have been writing about some fuddy-duddy, twang-talking old Yankee farmer, working it into a routine that today would be called "Maine humor."

Yet the new year of 1881 was but sixteen days old when she was writing Walker again (he was in St. Paul, Minnesota), "All the world is paying court to the coming or expected Secretary of State."

Harriet by then was in Washington, at the Blaines' relatively modest home at 821 15th Street. She'd been bracing herself "with a half bottle of champagne," to feel better after taking sick. The dinner party she'd gone to the night before, where the meal hadn't agreed with her, had been a glittering affair. Its guest composition had included the chief justice of the United States, General of the Armies Sherman, the existing secretaries of state and interior, and the German, French, and English ministers (today we would call them ambassadors). The hostess was Mrs. George Bancroft, wife of the famed historian and diplomat. Back home afterward, thoughts of the inadequacy of their current quarters for such "grand dinner parties" may have struck Harriet, since before long the Blaines were contemplating building a new—and very grand—house for themselves in D.C. This particular letter to Walker ended with how attentive his father had been during her bout of food poisoning. "He would not go to the Senate...broke all his engagements and excused himself to everybody on the ground that he could not leave me. In my room he sat on the bed or creaked across the floor from corner to corner, making me feel a guilty wretch to cause him so much misery. He is a dear, dear old fellow." He was fifty-one years old at the time.

That January, Blaine still held his Senate seat. Garfield would not be inaugurated until March. The Republican Maine legislature would fill the vacancy but neither Blaine nor Garfield wanted to give Maine's Democratic governor any kind of an interim appointment. Meanwhile, the two of them had kept up a steady correspondence between Washington and Mentor, Ohio, in which Blaine offered numerous suggestions about prospective cabinet members. "Your Secretary of the Treasury should be taken from the West," he wrote on December 24, 1880, four days after he, himself, had agreed to join the cabinet. His first choice was Senator William Allison of Iowa. Left unspoken was that Blaine did not want Garfield to reappoint John Sherman, the present incumbent, who'd been appointed by Grant. But as these pen-pal discussions continued, it became obvious that the most aggravating question they had to face was still what to do about Conkling. Blaine didn't pull any punches.

"It would be personally unpleasant and politically disastrous to have him in Cabinet association.... No Cabinet could get along with him, nor could the President, himself.... He would insult everybody having business with his department whom he did not happen to like, and he really happens to dislike about ninety-nine in every hundred of his acquaintances...."[3] On another occasion, Blaine was even more caustic—brilliantly so—in his denunciation of his rival. Putting Conkling in the cabinet, he told Garfield, "would act like strychnine upon your Administration—first bring convulsions and then be followed by death."

At the end of January, Garfield was writing Blaine: "The Conkling men want me *to go to them*." Blaine's appointment to head the State Department was still a secret and would remain so until February. But the word was already out, "You are to dominate the administration to the exclusion of other elements," Garfield wrote his friend. Blaine's retort was, "I shall never urge a man upon you for the Cabinet, but I will not hesitate to protest vigorously against *wrong* men." Garfield also spoke of his difficulty in finding a cabinet member from the South. "Do you know of a magnolia blossom that will stand our Northern climate?" he coyly asked his secretary of state designee.

On March 4, 1881, James A. Garfield was inaugurated as the twentieth president of the United States. A message quickly went that same day to 15th Street. "DEAR BLAINE.... Come to me at the White House the first moment I am free. With the love of comradeship of eighteen years with faith in the next four...I am ever yours...J. A. Garfield."[4]

In due time, the cabinet appointments were settled, mostly to Blaine's satisfaction. A southerner had been found—Judge William H. Hunt of Louisiana—and made secretary of the navy. John Sherman had been removed as secretary of the treasury, the post with the most patronage, and it had been given to Senator William Windom from Minnesota. Robert T. Lincoln, the slain president's son, seemed a particularly happy choice at the War Department. The stickiest problem, satisfying Conkling, had been finessed. The New Yorker had demanded the treasury for his crony Levi Morton and nothing else would do. Garfield's offers of other positions were haughtily turned down, so to avoid the charge of "insulting New York," Blaine and Garfield included Thomas A. James, New York's postmaster, a Stalwart and a Conkling man, who accepted the postmaster general's job, although without clearing it first with the man from Utica.

Temporarily, anyway, a Blaine-Conkling showdown within the Garfield administration was averted. Conkling, however, wasn't the only one unhappy about the eventual selection. Back in Maine, Israel Washburn, Jr., who had been nursing his anger in silence against Blaine for numerous years, was so upset to see his former errand boy in such a position of power that he sat down and wrote nine pages in his journal, full of scathing criticism. While admitting he had always thought highly of General Garfield—"a man of great scope and power," he added this caveat, "Yet I fear he lacks...the nerve and insistence..." to stand for his "ideas and instincts," i.e., he would knuckle under to Blaine, as it seemed he already had. Washburn called these appointments "the weakest cabinet, on the whole, ever seen in this country" and "not only weak, but bad." Next, he went after Blaine, whom he appeared to deem responsible, with lines such as, "Mr. Blaine is not and cannot be a statesman" or "Mr. Blaine has been a Republican from policy, never from principle," and there followed a litany of Blaine's flip-flops, switches, betrayals, evasions, zigzags, and opportunistic poses, in particular, his virulent attack on those Chinese coolies in order to win Pacific states' support. One really sore point was how Blaine "moved heaven and earth" to defeat Samuel Spring's G.O.P. nomination for governor in 1866 but had Spring on his side a decade later—that as soon as Blaine made an enemy, he tried to conquer him, but he had never conquered Conkling. Nor would he ever win over Israel Washburn, Jr., was the implication. Curiously enough, none of this diatribe ever saw print during Washburn's lifetime and only recently has come to light.

Another diehard infuriated by Blaine's influence on Garfield, was the famed Brooklyn, New York, minister Henry Ward Beecher. The root of the antagonism, according to a Beecher biographer, Paxton Hibben, went back to the 1880 campaign. Blaine had summoned the preacher, a Garfield supporter, to the Fifth Avenue Hotel and tongue-lashed him for spreading false rumors that he, Blaine, had accepted bribes. Afterward, Beecher stormed out "with a bitter hatred of Blaine that was in no wise lessened when Garfield's Cabinet was announced.... Henry Ward Beecher was not even mentioned for an ambassadorship."[5] Noted for the power of his sermons and an adultery scandal since died down, the clergyman struck back at Blaine four years later. Ironically, his sister, famed novelist Harriet Beecher Stowe, who lived in Maine, was a close friend of the Blaines and her husband, Bowdoin professor Calvin Stowe, always a loyal Blaine voter.

In 1881 the United States had been a going concern for almost a century, far outlasting the predictions of continental intelligentsia who argued that a republic could only endure in a small country. The Civil War, which had almost proved them right, was now a decade-and-a-half in the past and the country was ready for a "robust" foreign policy—of the kind that James G. Blaine was prepared to give them, once he was ensconced in the odd-looking, many-columned, many-porticoed building off Pennsylvania Avenue that housed the State, Navy, and War Departments. But before he could settle into his new job with any comfort, Blaine had one more political task to perform—overcoming Conkling and other obstreperous Stalwarts. Telling Garfield how they should be routed, his striking phrase was: "Cut their throats with a feather."

In effect, that's what was done, although it could be argued Conkling, himself, did his cause the most damage. His adamant position on patronage became his undoing, his ego his Achilles heel, his open contempt for the president a challenge as deadly as any General Garfield had faced on the battlefield. On March 23, 1881, the White House announced certain appointments guaranteed to turn Senator Conkling apoplectic. The choicest political plum in all of New York, collector (of customs) of the port of New York, was going to his number one political enemy, William H. Robertson, a backer of Blaine who now led the state's Half-Breeds. The man he replaced, Edwin Merritt, had been bought off with the cushy consul general's post in London, displacing Grant's former private secretary, and Blaine's campaign manager was going to be made solicitor-general. This, indeed, was cutting throats with a feather.

Using his utmost force and influence, Conkling fought these appointments, most especially that of William Robertson. He raged that he'd been betrayed, threatened to tie up the U.S. Senate and turned Garfield into a hero who held his ground against this boorish bully. On top of that, a brilliant stroke, probably conceived by Blaine, led to Conkling's ultimate political downfall. Garfield withdrew all his appointments of any New Yorkers—except for Robertson. No Robertson, no New York Stalwarts in the government.

On the brink of defeat, Conkling, at the suggestion of his fellow New York Senator Tom Platt, followed what proved to be a suicide course. The idea was that they would both resign from the U.S. Senate to show their disapproval of Garfield's latest maneuver. The country would be shocked. The New York legislature would overwhelmingly and instantaneously reinstate them and they would return to D.C. as conquering heroes, to whom the president would have to bow.

Today, we might ask, *What were those guys smoking?* The scene in Albany became a slapstick comedy. Platt was caught in a seedy hotel room with a lady of the evening by Peeping Tom legislators, who seemed in no hurry to vote Conkling and Platt back into office. Blaine and Robertson worked behind the scenes to stimulate this opposition, and to add insult to injury, the two G.O.P. senators were eventually replaced by two Democrats. Prominent New York Republican John Hay, holding Conkling responsible, called this bizarre episode, "a freak of insanity on the part of a man who has lost sight of his true relations with the rest of the world."

In addition, forty-eight hours after the Platt-Conkling resignations, William Robertson was confirmed unanimously, and President Garfield came out of the confrontation, as they say in politics, "smelling like a rose."

Settling in at the State Department, James G. Blaine could now proceed with full faith that his political flanks were covered. His confidence was such that one of his very first acts smacked of hubris—he put his own son Walker on the payroll as his private secretary, en route to becoming, through presidential appointment, third assistant secretary of state. Tom Sherman also came on board to continue his services.

The home on 15th Street was deemed too small for the receptions the secretary would have to hold, so plans were speeded up for a much grander residence. The Blaines saw eight years ahead of them for this type of living and so Harriet wrote, "We intend to put up a very nice and expensive house,"[6] They bought a lot on 16th Street, but soon soured on the location because of some odoriferous stables nearby. Their attention moved to another site when Blaine ended up "fastening his affections on a lot of Massachusetts Avenue, P and 20th Streets." Amazingly, the owner was discovered to be their good friend Congressman William Walter Phelps and an amicable deal was arranged: the Blaines bought the Phelps property and sold their 16th Street purchase to Senator George H. Pendleton, an Ohio Democrat.

Near Dupont Circle, that palatial home, built in 1881–82, still stands, an imposing, massive red brick structure, now housing office space. The land cost Blaine $60,000 and the two-and-a-half-story dwelling, $48,000. It contained sixty-four windows, a "baronial" main hall," a "great fireplace," "large parlors and drawing room," a library, piazza, and dining room paneled in oak or mahogany and "decorated with carvings." This Blaine Mansion was "one of the earliest great houses on Dupont Circle," according to

Etching of Blaine's mansion-like home that he built near Dupont Circle in downtown Washington, D.C., but where he spent relatively little time. It was really too grand for a frugal Yankee like Harriet Blaine and was eventually rented out and then sold. The marriage of the Blaines' oldest daughter Alice was the only major event held there. This imposing red-brick building still stands fronting Massachusetts Avenue and is used today for offices.
MAINE HISTORIC PRESERVATION COMMISSION

the D.C. Commission of Fine Arts, an edifice of "brooding strength," incorporating "obvious elements of Romanesque, Gothic, and Renaissance details which provide character."[7]

These new quarters were still in the planning stage during the spring of 1881. "The Secretaryship grows more and more agreeable," Harriet wrote Maggie on Friday, March 18, 1881. On Tuesday, she and Secretary Blaine had attended a requiem mass for Czar Alexander II of Russia, who had been assassinated five days before. On Wednesday, they had dined at the English legation and she proudly announced she had sat between their host (the English ambassador) and Lord George Campbell, who was the brother of the Marquis of Lorne (not bad for a wool merchant's daughter from Augusta, Maine, was left unstated). "Jacky gets along beautifully," she added, using her pet name for Walker. Indeed, he was getting letters addressed to "the Honorable Walker Blaine," and he had already made a speech at a tony dinner party. "The house is filled with flowers all the time, an immense horse shoe, surmounted by a ship of state, fills our parlor table."

Luck, as proposed by the floral horseshoe, was holding out for everyone, except the poor Czar of Russia. Yet that shocking event even prompted a touch of levity from the Yankee lady who teasingly started one missive to Maggie with, "What are you doing in peaceful Farmington while Czars are dying and Czarowitches [sic] mounting the throne?" On March 24 Harriet was writing Maggie again, highlighting the president's anti-Conkling nominations sent in to Congress the day before. "They mean business and strength," she commented. There was a news bit that Robert Hitt of Illinois, an experienced diplomat, would be first assistant secretary of state and Walker would stay where he was—and an item about the intended new house—i.e., that their plans were "so huge and so expensive" that they were "now engaged in striking out every pretty thing to reduce the expenditures to the limits of your Father's purse...." A great crowd had come to her second reception at the present home, she reported, and they took a visiting Maine couple to the White House where they "saw the Garfields and the Hayes' china." Plus a cheerful letter had been received from Aunt Caddy. March 28th: "I am writing in my room; present, your Father,

Alice, Walker, Tom Sherman, and a messenger from the State Department; subject, shall we send message, recognizing Charles as King of Roumania?... Flowers have just come from Mrs. Garfield, and yesterday, she and the President were both here...." She skipped to May 17, 1881 and started with a touch of wry humor. "Your Father [she is writing to Maggie again] has lost one pair of glasses and I have stepped on his spectacles. I need not say who enjoys those still extant, so I write blindly, unable to discern one letter...." The day before had produced the "sensational resignations of Conkling and Platt" and she added, "I have yet to hear one criticism complimentary of Conkling, though I have seen all sorts of people and of every shade of cowardice,"[8] presaging caustically the political downfall of her husband's inveterate enemy.

Meanwhile, the secretary of state was not idle in what he was supposed to be doing—managing the nation's foreign affairs. At this point in time, the agency was relatively puny, despite its importance in the cabinet. The U.S. had only twenty-four ambassadors, a handful of charge d'affaires and 300 consuls to cover the entire known world. Its small D.C. staff was located in the south wing of its still uncompleted French Empire-style quarters. One hundred years later, President Bill Clinton was to write, "It was here in the old State, War, and Navy Building that America's role as a superpower was born."

The idea that the United States could play a prominent role on the world stage had been formulating in James G. Blaine's mind ever since his *Kennebec Journal* days. Luther Severance had opened his eyes to the possibility of our someday acquiring Hawaii. In the intervening years, he had had time to think about the U.S. as a Pacific as well as an Atlantic power and apply the Monroe Doctrine to the two oceans. He boldly pronounced that "Hawaii, although much farther from the Californian coast than Cuba is from the Floridian peninsula, holds in the western sea much the same position as Cuba in the Atlantic. It is the key to the maritime dominion of the Pacific States as Cuba is to the Gulf trade." While neither Cuba nor Hawaii were to be annexed, they were essential components of his "American Commercial System." His predecessors, he felt, had been flaccid and less than zealous in

The ornate D.C. building—then known as the State, War, and Navy Building—in which Blaine did his work as secretary of state. Today, it is the Dwight D. Eisenhower Office Building and no less ornate.
MAINE HISTORIC PRESERVATION COMMISSION

resisting European—particularly British—incursions, and this was all the more evident in the realm of business. Hadn't he tried hard to break the English monopoly of shipping to Brazil?

One of the first items on his desk in this regard was a ban by European countries on exports of American pork. The source of the problem had been the report by a British vice-consul in Philadelphia, a man named Crump, alleging trichinosis in U.S. hogs with graphic descriptions of the horrid effects of eating such unsafe meat. France and Germany had followed the U.K. in this discrimination. So Blaine set to work debunking Crump's story as a total fabrication. He threatened retaliation against French wines. Although he wasn't in office long enough to see these efforts come to fruition, the Europeans finally relented and, all along, Blaine gained gratitude for himself and the Garfield administration from the nation's farmers and agricultural interests.

In the scale of international events, this pork fight was a fairly picayune matter. Far more serious, with important ramifications, was the Chile-Peru War that had broken out two years earlier. The *casus belli* was control of valuable guano deposits, rich in nitrates for fertilizer, that both countries claimed. By the time Blaine arrived, Chile had clearly won. Bolivia, Peru's former ally, had given up the struggle, Peruvian forces had been routed at the battle of Tacna, Lima had been captured and the country's president had fled to the mountains. But Blaine was determined that Chile would not set a precedent by keeping captured territory. He sent instructions for the U.S. to recognize a new Peruvian government and told his diplomat on the scene, "...in no case would Chile extract territory save where Chilean enterprise and Chilean capital had developed the desert and where today nine-tenths of the people were Chilean."[9] The Chileans were furious and resisted. Blaine was forced to send a seasoned negotiator, William Trescott, along with Walker, as a special team to deal with them, which was delicate, since at that period the Chilean Navy was actually stronger than the U.S. Navy. Nevertheless, Blaine kept right on pursuing his policy of tamping down inter-American conflicts and preventing stronger powers from conquering territories by backing Guatemala in a dispute with its much bigger neighbor Mexico.

This new direction in American foreign policy was not universally admired. It was "reckless," some pundits insisted. An accusation even surfaced that Blaine had a financial interest in Peruvian guano. Not intimidated, however, Blaine went even farther, launching a truly breath-taking initiative, establishing in effect a peace process for all of the Americas, with the U.S. playing an arbiter's role in hemispheric relations. He was summoning every one of the South American and Central American nations to a Pan-American conference in Washington, D.C.—the first of its kind ever to be held—scheduled for the early part of 1882. In this awesome endeavor, he had the full support of President Garfield, as he did in all of his foreign policy efforts.

These included protests to the imperial Russian government over anti-Semitic outbreaks following the Czar's assassination and, especially, mistreatment of American Jews visiting or living in the Empire; similar complaints about British abuse of Irish-Americans in Ireland, with a protest against the arbitrary arrest of a Pennsylvanian named Joseph B. Walsh; and warnings to Great Britain and several continental countries not to meddle with the Monroe Doctrine after hearing rumors that "the great powers of Europe may be considering the subject of jointly guaranteeing the neutrality of the inter-oceanic canal now projected across the Isthmus of Panama." Blaine also served notice on the Brits that he wanted to revise the Clayton-Bulwer Treaty of 1850, which would allow Her Majesty's government a hand in regulating a Panama Canal.

Indisputably, Blaine could see himself and his career in a new light. The idea of being president was receding and not solely because Garfield would have a lock on the 1884 nomination. What Blaine saw for himself was a step up to statesman from the grubbier role of mere politician. It must have been a comforting thought to Blaine, after all the wounds he'd suffered, that he would now be pictured on a higher intellectual plain, out of the trenches of patronage and partisanship, and heading for the history books in a whole new dimension.

The first cloud on this happy horizon was a serious bout of illness in May 1881 that struck First Lady Lucretia Garfield. For a while, she was not expected to live, although Harriet Blaine hoped if she recovered (and she did) that "Crete" would come to Maine in the summer and recuperate. More of an annoyance than a cloud at this juncture was the publication anonymously of the novel *Democracy,* which had official Washington all a-buzz over who might have written it and how James G. Blaine obviously was the model for its villain.

The story is centered on a wealthy, glamorous socialite, Mrs. Madeleine Lightfoot Lee, widowed at an early age, who moves from New York to Washington, D.C., with her equally beauteous younger sister, Sybil. Bored with the social scene in Manhattan, she was now bent, as the author put it, "...upon getting to the heart of the great American mystery of democracy and government." Her guide in this pursuit became a U.S. senator, the Honorable Silas P. Ratcliffe, from Illinois, a presidential aspirant who as the curtain unfolds in this fiction, is being mentioned for secretary of state. The parallels to Blaine are unmistakable, and the lessons Mrs. Lightfoot Lee learns in the course of the novel are those that an unprincipled, powerful senator would be able to teach. In turn, the plot has Ratcliffe smitten by the lady's good looks and intelligence, asking to marry her and being rejected.

Five years after the book's 1880 publication, its author was revealed to be Henry Adams, who had left his teaching post at Harvard and moved to D.C. Others earlier suspected of having written it included the diplomat John Hay, Adams's closest friend; Clarence King, the geologist, another Adams intimate; Mrs. Henry Adams; and, paradoxically, James G. Blaine, himself, with the help of Gail Hamilton.

In actuality, Blaine was furious, personally aggrieved enough to take his anger out on Clarence King, whom, as speaker, he'd assisted in setting up the U.S. Geological Survey that King headed. Another aspect, not noticed except for Blaine's own discomfort, was that life other than in politics may have been imitated in art on the pages of *Democracy*. The model for Mrs. Lightfoot Lee was a real glamorous socialite widow with New York, D.C., and even Maine ties—Mrs. Elizabeth Bigelow Lawrence. Her late husband had been Timothy Bigelow Lawrence, heir to the textile fortune of his father, mill owner Abbott Lawrence, the founder of Lawrence, Massachusetts. Readers will remember the mention in Maggie Blaine's diary that her father was to spend a week in York Beach and "take his meals with Mrs. Bigelow Lawrence." The actual site was York Harbor, where Mrs. Lawrence's summer residence still stands as a glitzy bed and breakfast, Chapman Cottage. Chapman was her maiden name, as well as that of her younger half-sister Fanny, who was the model for Sybil in Henry Adams's novel. This relationship of James G. Blaine and Mrs. Bigelow Lawrence was— for Washington society—epitomized by the catty remark of Marian Adams, Henry's wife, that "If Blaine were a widower, she would not long be a widow."[10]

How platonic were these two? In a biography of Elizabeth Chapman Lawrence,[11] subtitled "The high life of a dazzling Victorian lady," the introduction by well-known author-historian James Michener states specifically that "Blaine...had more than a passing interest in her." Harriet Blaine, who kept any anxieties on this score to herself, did include a mention in one of her 1881 letters that her husband had planned to spend Christmas Day with Mrs.

Mrs. Elizabeth Bigelow Lawrence, née Chapman, the "dazzling Victorian Lady," whose close friendship with James G. Blaine was deemed to be platonic, but cynically suspected of being otherwise. The widow of the son of Abbott Lawrence, textile magnate and founder of Lawrence, Massachusetts, she was the model for the heroine of Henry Adams's novel, Democracy, *just as Blaine was the model for the story's villain.*
MERCER MUSEUM, BUCKS COUNTY HISTORICAL SOCIETY

Lawrence at her Doylestown, Pennsylvania, home until young Harriet made such a fuss that he stayed with his family instead. Elizabeth's biographer, Helen Hartman Gemmill, writes that "James G. Blaine quickly became one of her closest friends,[12] that "EL liked him 'better and better' as she saw 'from year to year how firm his friendship continues'" and that this *liaison* "could not fail to cause Harriet an occasional pang."[13] There is evidence that Blaine tried to buy property in York Harbor near Elizabeth's, but that the owners, the Barrell sisters, sold it to Colonel Alexander Bliss because, as a Kennebunk newspaper reported, they were Democrats and didn't want to sell to a Republican. Colonel Bliss was the son-in-law of historian George Bancroft and part of the set with whom the Blaines socialized in D.C.

Another member of that in-group was a young American woman, born Lillie Greenough in Cambridge, Massachusetts, then living in Washington as the wife of the Danish ambassador. Under her mouthful of a married name, Lillie L. de Hegemann-Lindencrone, she published a charming memoir, *The Sunnyside of Diplomatic Life*, the first section of which depicted her experiences in the U.S. capital. Particularly close to Elizabeth and Fanny, she was often at parties where Blaine was present.

Here we get glimpses of James G. Blaine, the raconteur, something of a wit, relaxed and charming. Lillie's tale of an evening at the Capitol, at a reception Blaine hosted, leads off the anecdotes. She wrote, "As I can't talk politics and would not if I could..." she amused herself by observing the numerous spittoons placed around the premises. Those "that tried to be pretty were the most hideous," she felt, and when she made this observation to Blaine, he responded with the tale of a new congressman from the West, not used to such decorated objects and not knowing what they were, saying, "If you don't take that darn thing away, I'll spit in it." Then, at a party of her own at the Danish embassy, Blaine arrived late. Clapping her husband Johan on the shoulder, he exclaimed, "My kingdom for a glass of whiskey! I have just dined at the White House," where Rutherford B. Hayes's wife was dubbed "Lemonade Lucy," since she forbade the serving of any alcoholic drinks. Lillie had observed both Blaine and Conkling at first hand and contrasted them, "Mr. Blaine is an excellent talker, very popular with the ladies. In a drawing room, he is generally found in a corner, quoting poetry (a specialty of his) to some handsome lady. He knows all the poetry in the world! They say he is the best Speaker the House has ever known; it is quite wonderful to see the rapidity with which he counts the Ayes and Noes, pointing at each voter with the handle of his club.... Roscoe Conkling is quite a different type. He is very dignified and pompous—perhaps a little theatrical, not at all a society man, and although he may be less vain than Mr. Blaine, he has the appearance of being more so."[14] She also revealed Blaine's addiction to poker—that "Mr. Blaine and Mr. Robeson (secretary of the navy) supplemented by General Schenck (a congressman) are great poker players." Their continued talk of poker mystified the foreign diplomats, she noted.

In 1880, Lillie's husband was transferred and she had to leave Washington to go to Rome and abandon "The National Rational International Dining Club" she had formed with Elizabeth Bigelow Lawrence and Fanny Chapman.

On June 28, 1881, Blaine had been secretary of state, following his hectic if pleasurable schedule for four months already, when he took some time to write his old college pal Tom Searight. It was a thank-you note for a special western Pennsylvania type of candy his boyhood chum had sent him, but much more than that, it was a chance to reminisce and savor how far he'd come in life. "MY DEAR FRIEND: The 'maple molasses' came to hand and revived memories of boyhood days.... The flavor recalled the Fulton House and 'Joe' and George Driver and the 'Squires' most vividly. Every time I get a line from you I am quickened in my desire to visit the familiar scenes long gone by...." His ending was maudlin: "But to me the country is still the land of forty years ago with stage-coaches and wayside inns...and the college full of good fellows and the seminary crowded with pretty good girls and the dances at Caldwell's Tavern and the sleigh rides...and the sweethearts that we loved so freshly and gushingly—and who are now mothers and some of them, alas, grandmothers, while you and I, separated by chains of mountains and a generation of years, still have hearts that beat warmly for each other."[15]

Four days later, July 2, 1881, Secretary of State Blaine was accompanying President Garfield to the Baltimore and Potomac Railroad station at 6th Street and (what is now) Constitution Avenue, approximately the site of today's National Gallery of Art. It was a short carriage ride from the White House and in those pre-Secret Service days, Blaine, himself, was handling the horse's reins. The president was on a nostalgic trip of his own, en route to his twenty-fifth reunion at Williams College, and his thoughts had to contain much of those same rosy memories Blaine had just shared with Tom Searight—a welcome relief from his burdensome new position and especially the clamor of the incessant job-seekers who constantly bugged him at the White House. Undoubtedly, too, he and Blaine discussed politics, since he deliberately had asked his secretary of state to drive him to the train so they could talk.

A day earlier, Garfield had strolled from the White House to Blaine's home on 15th Street and arrived unannounced. Blaine wasn't there and while Mrs. Blaine entertained their distinguished guest, Tom Sherman was asked to locate Blaine by telephone, which he was unable to do. Consequently, the president dictated some notes to leave for the secretary of state. As he did, Garfield suddenly stopped, laughed, and told his friend's wife the following story, as recorded by Tom Sherman:

"Harriet, you know that all through my adult life, I have taken a more or less active part in public affairs. Here I am shut up in the White House spending more than half my time on trivial matters, listening to applicants for office, etc., etc. The other day I was notified by the State Department that on a certain day and hour I was to receive the British Minister, Sir Edward Thornton, and the little speech I was to make on that occasion was sent to me from the State Department. At the appointed hour, surrounded by department officials, I, who have been accustomed all my life, in Congress and out, to speak impromptu, took from my pocket and read off like a schoolboy a speech written for me by Walker Blaine, a lad whom I dandled on my knee when he was a baby! And then Sir Edward recited like a man his reply learnt by heart."[16]

When Blaine soon returned, the two men left and, arm in arm, strolled down 15th Street together. But the next day, on July 2, they were not arm-in-arm but slightly separated, walking into the women's waiting room entrance of the red brick railroad station, taking a short cut to the main waiting room.

A pistol shot rang out. It had been fired from behind Garfield and the bullet hit him on his right side. "My God! What is this!?" Garfield cried, partly turning. Another shot hit him in the back on the same side. His knees buckled and he went down hard. On the floor, the president of the United States lay bleeding, vomiting, but still conscious. Blaine rushed to him, wanting to protect his friend in case there was yet another shot. And he also saw the would-be assassin running away—and recognized him! A man named Guiteau—an office seeker—a pest. At the exit on 6th Street, a policeman stopped the fugitive. People were yelling, "He shot the president!" Others began shouting: "Lynch him!" The first policeman, joined by others, hustled him off, now disarmed. Guiteau said to them, "I did it. I will go to jail for it. I am a Stalwart and Arthur will be President."

Blaine, who had nearly been shot by Garfield's assassin, stands by his fallen friend, who is cradled by a Susan White, a ladies room attendant in the women's waiting room of the Baltimore and Ohio Railroad's Washington, D.C., station.
MAINE HISTORIC PRESERVATION COMMISSION

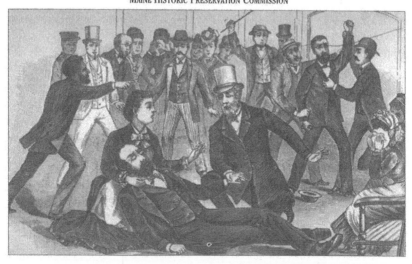

Still, Garfield wasn't dead. He lay cradled in the lap of the ladies room attendant, Sarah White, both soaked in his blood. The president's two oldest sons, Harry and James, who had been at the station to take another train, stood helpless by his side in tears. Incredibly, cabinet member Robert Todd Lincoln, the son of the first U.S. president to be assassinated, had come to see Garfield off and now was witness to a second terrible, unbelievable scene.

On a mattress taken from a Pullman car, the president was transported to a private room upstairs in the station where a doctor examined him. He said Garfield would recover. The ex-combat veteran said he didn't think so.

So, in some respects, the real unimaginable horror these insane few minutes had wrought was just about to begin.

---

1. Beale, Vol. 1, p. 185.
2. Ibid., p. 162.
3. Hamilton, pp. 497–98.
4. Ibid., p. 503.
5. Payton Hibben. *Henry Ward Beecher: An American Portrait* (New York: George H. Doran Company, 1927), p. 335.
6. Beale, Vol. I, p. 191.
7. J. L. Sibley Jennings, Jr., Sue A. Kohler, Jeffrey R. Carson, eds. *Massachusetts Avenue Architecture,* Vol. 2, 1975, page 128.
8. Beale, Vol. I, p. 199, and other letters quoted start on p. 191.
9. John Clark Ridpath. *Life and Works of James G. Blaine* (Philadelphia: Historical Publishing Company, 1893), p. 339.
10. Ernest Samuels. *Henry Adams: The Middle Years* (Cambridge, MA: Harvard University Press, 1958), p. 93.
11. Helen Hartman Gemmill. *EL: The Breadbox Papers: The High Life of a Dazzling Victorian Lady* (Doylestown, PA: Tower Press, 1983).
12. Ibid., p. 205.
13. Ibid., p. 211.
14. Lillie L. de Hegermann-Lindencrone. *The Sunny Side of Diplomatic Life* (New York: Harper and Brothers, 1914).
15. Hamilton, p. 538.
16. Sherman, pp. 77–78.

SEVENTEEN

THE AFTERMATH

CHARLES GUITEAU HAS BEEN described as a "little man." He was also loquacious and nervy, and, once the 1880 election had ended, was observed buttonholing Republican officials whenever possible, incessantly reminding them of his great service to the party and the need for them to reward him with this or that important, well-paying post. Of Huguenot heritage—thus the French surname—he had come east from his native Illinois, living in New York and Boston, until Garfield was nominated. Jobless per usual, he at once returned to New York City to offer his services to the G.O.P. and soon was hanging around the Fifth Avenue Hotel, the center of the party's activities. The big wigs he mingled with included vice-presidential candidate Chester A. Arthur, who was runnimg the New York State effort and gave the importuning Guiteau a few minor speeches to make. To add to Guiteau's overblown sense of his own importance was the fact that on his way from Boston to New York City, he had miraculously survived a shipwreck that had taken eighty lives. Divine intervention was Guiteau's perhaps bipolar-tinged verdict: the Lord had intended him to do great things.

After Garfield was inaugurated, Guiteau hastened to Washington to seek his fortune in the new administration. The Foreign Service was his first choice—initially to be U.S. consul in Vienna, but then he thought Paris more suitable. With hundreds of others, he thronged the White House to beseech the president personally. Ultimately, he obtained a brief appointment, handed Garfield a printed copy of a speech he'd given during the campaign, with "Paris consulship" written in pen under his name, and later was told his application had been sent to the proper channels.

James G. Blaine's contact with Guiteau began with a letter in which the job seeker said he had spoken to the president about a consular post and enclosed the "Garfield Against Hancock" speech he'd been peddling. Next was an impromptu meeting when Guiteau cornered the secretary of state near the private entrance to his office, reminded him of the "Garfield Against Hancock" speech and drew a polite "Oh, yes," from Blaine. In time, he became a regular at Blaine's public audiences.

Once it finally dawned on Guiteau he was not going to receive any kind of job, never mind a political plum like a consulship in Europe, his murderous anger turned against Blaine and Garfield. With a certain mad logic, it then devolved into the notion of killing only Garfield, so Vice-President Arthur would succeed him and with the Stalwarts in the seat of power, there might still be a chance for Charles Guiteau. He procured a pistol and began stalking the president.

On that afternoon of July 1 when Garfield had visited Blaine's home unexpectedly and later the two men strode arm-in-arm back to the White House, Guiteau was walking behind them. He had planned to shoot Garfield but desisted, afraid he would hit Blaine, which wasn't in his plans. The next morning, having been alerted by the press to the president's itinerary, he struck.

An eyewitness account of events, the moment the terrible news reached the Blaine household, was set down in a letter from Harriet to Maggie: "July 3. Your father got up quite early yesterday morning in order to drive the President to the station, and at 9:30 Tom, the boys, Alice, and I had breakfast. In the midst of it, the doorbell rang and Tom was called out. Then he called Walker...we paid no attention to the prolonged absence of the absentees; but shall I ever forget the moment when Maggie, nurse, came running into the room crying: 'They have telephoned over to you, Mrs. Blaine, that the President is assassinated.' Emmons flew, for we all remembered, with one accord, that his Father was with him. By the time I reached the door, I saw that it must be true—everybody on the street, and wild. Mrs. Sherman [Ellen Sherman, the General's wife] got a carriage and we drove over to the White House. Found the streets in front jammed and the doors closed, but they let us through and in. The President still at the station, so drove thitherward. Met the mounted police clearing the avenue, then the ambulance; turned and followed into that very gateway where, on the fourth of March, we had watched him enter. I stood with Mrs. MacVeagh [wife of cabinet member Attorney General Wayne MacVeagh] in the hall, when a dozen men bore him above their heads, stretched on a mattress, and as he saw us and held us with his eye, he kissed his hand to us—I thought I should die; and when they brought him into his chamber and had laid him on the bed, he turned his eye to me, beckoned, and when I went to him, pulled me down, kissed me again and again, and said, 'Whatever happens I want you to promise to look out for Crete' the name he always gives his wife. 'Don't leave me until Crete comes.' I took my old bonnet off and just stayed. I never left him a moment. Whatever happened in the room, I never blenched, and the day will never pass from my memory. At six or thereabouts, Mrs. Garfield came, frail, (just recovered from her near fatal illness), fatigued, desperate, but firm and quiet and full of purpose to save, and I now think there is a possibility of succeeding."[1]

A full account of Harriet's experiences included her reflections that day earlier, how she was sitting in the bay window of her 15th Street home, pondering the president's trip to Williamstown. He was to stay the night first at Cyrus Field's mansion on the Hudson, having met up with Lucretia at Philadelphia, and Harriet knew "Mr. Blaine would insist on the whole party's coming to Augusta." She was pondering how to entertain them when the president appeared. He was "a handsome and happy-looking man...dressed in a summer suit of grey, a flower in his hat, his face beaming..." and after Blaine came, the two of them going off together in the "fast-fading" afternoon light...and behind them "followed the assassin who had dogged Garfield from the Executive Mansion..." and "had watched the [Blaine] house from the alley opposite, looking to his pistol that all was right for a fatal shot, which was held back only by the unforeseen company of Mr. Blaine...."

So in the days that followed, there were untold opportunities to dwell on the what-ifs. What if Garfield and Blaine had gone into the station arm-in-arm? What if they had glanced around in back of them on July 1 and seen Guiteau stalking them and suspected something? What if Guiteau had died when his ship had sunk in that collision? What if someone had given him a job?. Yet there was still hope that the president would survive.

On July 6, Harriet wrote Maggie, "It looks as though Gaffy (her own nickname for the president) will live. He is now, six o'clock, still comfortable and has asked for beef steak." She didn't think they'd let the president have it and if they did, it shouldn't come from the White House kitchen. "Such tough leather as they had there for breakfast the other morning is a disgrace to the cattle on a thousand hills." Another relative of theirs, Father Thomas Sherman, a Jesuit priest, son of Ellen and the General, had come to tell the Garfields that his entire order was praying for a full recovery. Harriet's letter sounded optimistic, although she added, "but if they will only put the President's room into the hands of professionals, I shall live content and have greater hope that he will not die."

It has been claimed that the incompetence of his doctors killed Garfield, not the two bullets Guiteau shot into his body. One of those lead balls had lodged deeply in his back and the doctors kept probing for it without success, despite the warning of a doctor from Kansas, "Do not allow probing the wound…. Saturate everything with carbolic acid, one part to 20 parts water…. Use quite freely of this about the wound. Probing generally does more harm than the balls…."[2] But the medical team, dominated by military surgeon Dr. Willard Bliss, Garfield's boyhood friend from Ohio, persisted. Fears expressed in several newspapers—"I am afraid Bliss will probe the wound and if he does inflammation will set in"[3]—were eventually to come true.

It took almost two-and-a-half months, a roller coaster ride in which at first it seemed Garfield was almost himself again, only to be struck down by a fever, from which he rallied, but then progressively wasted away, having left D.C.'s killer summer heat for the Jersey seashore, slowly dying, as Kenneth Ackerman wrote, "of infection, blood poisoning, and starvation."[4] On September 19, 1881, after a courageous struggle that won the hearts of all Americans, James Abram Garfield expired, coincidentally on the eigh-

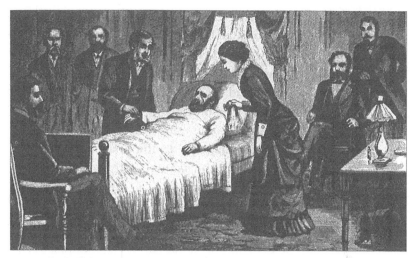

Garfield during the three months he lingered before expiring from his deeply infected wound. Under modern medical conditions, the president would easily have been saved.
CONWELL'S *LIFE AND PUBLIC SERVICE OF JAMES G. BLAINE*

teenth anniversary of the Battle of Chickamauga in which he had first won public notice.

Blaine's role began as soon as the shooting ended. He stayed at the station while the doctors examined the president upstairs, but rode back separately to the White House, stopping off at his home to send two telegrams—one to Vice-President Arthur in New York City, the other to London, to Ambassador James Russell Lowell, who was to alert our diplomats in Europe as to the president's condition—"very serious, though not necessarily fateful." In the White House, he had difficulty getting in to see Garfield and had to agree to take his turn at nursing, since only medical personnel and Mrs. Garfield were allowed inside. When Garfield recognized Blaine, he pulled him close and said, "You know how well I love you, even though people have sought to prejudice me against you." Asking Blaine who had shot him, he learned it was that nuisance Charles Guiteau, the office seeker. Garfield exclaimed: "Why did he shoot me!? I have done him no wrong!"

Outside in the hallway, after his visit, Blaine was met by reporters. They wanted to know if he thought Guiteau had been part of a conspiracy, the way John Wilkes Booth had been. Blaine shook his head. It didn't seem so. Most likely, at that moment, Blaine knew nothing about Guiteau's political remarks—remarks that brought such angry popular repercussions against Conkling and Arthur they both had to be provided with bodyguards. Instead, a shaken Blaine, after his chat with the newsmen, walked wearily to the executive mansion telegraph room and sent another wire to the vice-president who hadn't responded to the first one. "There are strong grounds for hope and at the same time the gravest anxiety as to the final result" was included in the message. Since most of the cabinet had now reached the White House, Blaine convened a meeting, which was his prerogative and duty as secretary of state. The business of the government had to go on. That evening, a third telegram reached the vice-president from Secretary of State Blaine. The cabinet had decided by unanimous vote he should come to the capital immediately. Postmaster General Tom James, the one Stalwart in the cabinet, wired Arthur, too. "The President is no better and, we fear, sinking." Accompanied by U.S. Senator John P. Jones, a Republican from Nevada, Arthur took an overnight train he caught in Jersey City and arrived in D.C. the next morning. One of his reasons for traveling with Jones was he could stay at his apartment in Washington and not in the one he shared with Conkling at the city's Wormley's Hotel.

That was possibly the first sign of a crack in the Conkling-Arthur alliance and much deeper ones were to appear after the dapper Stalwart politico from New York finally became president. Arthur was not able to see Garfield and had to go back to Jones's quarters and just wait, while some newspapers like Democrat Henry Watterson's *Louisville Courier* were already speculating in print that Conkling and Arthur were behind Guiteau's crime. This ugly situation only tempered off when the president's situation bettered after the Fourth of July. Hopeful news began issuing from the White House and Blaine wired Lowell in London on July 11 that "Arthur can go back to New York and we soon to Augusta." However, because Blaine still ran the cabinet, Harriet determined that although she could leave for Maine, her husband had to stay and "he cannot be left alone," as she wrote Maggie.

Later, as the crisis continued its frustrating course, Harriet would write: "Your Father says an administration with a sick bed for its center is not a pleasant thought...."[5] Midway through this agony, Blaine suggested to the cabinet that Arthur should become president before Garfield's demise. His colleagues shouted him down and even uncharitably accused him of trying to secure a place in Arthur's cabinet. The vice-president, himself, refused to hear of the idea. That unhappy summer dragged to a close, the federal government functioning (without a lot to do) until the tragedy's denouement in September when Garfield finally suffered a fatal aneurysm at Elberon, New Jersey, in the wee hours of the morning. The moment Chester A. Arthur was sworn in at 2:15 A.M. on September 20, the only immediate change for Secretary Blaine was that he no longer had to conduct the cabinet meetings. The new president asked all members to stay on prior to the return of Congress in December 1881, and while Blaine tried to resign in October, Arthur refused to let him. He kept at the job until the December deadline.

By way of an epilogue into Blaine's first venture directing U.S. foreign policy, there is this commentary from Gail Hamilton: "So long as Mr. Blaine remained in the State Department, its foreign policy was wide in scope, high in motive, positive, progressive, imposing"—a statement one would expect from a hero-worshipper such as "Cousin Abby." Then, her bitterness showed. "When he [Blaine] retired, it was broken in pieces. To its integrity, to its destruction, the President [Chester A. Arthur] maintained an attitude of equal acquiescence."[6]

Joined to her condemnation of Arthur's indifference was the outright hostility from Blaine's replacement—Frederick Frelinghuysen. Their paths had briefly crossed when Frelinghuysen was a U.S. senator from New Jersey and Blaine would have known him, anyway, from Republican circles, where he was associated with the Stalwarts. Freylinghuysen's Uncle Theodore had run for vice-president on the same ticket with Henry Clay in 1844, and Blaine would also have remembered singing the Whigs' famous rhyming campaign jingle, "Hurrah! Hurrah! The Country's Rising; Henry Clay and Frelinghuysen."

Blaine, Garfield's closest political friend, delivers his funeral oration
before a packed joint session of Congress, February 27, 1882.
MAINE HISTORIC PRESERVATION COMMISSION

Relations between the two men soon became more than frosty. Less than three weeks after taking office, on January 9, 1882, Frelinghuysen cancelled Blaine's ground-breaking Pan-American peace conference. More than half the invited Latin American nations had already accepted. Just as galling was the fact President Arthur had given the event his blessing, even though it was a Garfield-Blaine initiative, and now he had reneged in a most public and humiliating manner.

Deemed a political hack and a stooge for Roscoe Conkling, Chester "Chet" Arthur was put on the G.O.P. ticket as a party unity compromise. He proved to be a better president than most people expected—but not good enough to be given the chance for a second term by his party. Blaine easily beat him for the nomination. Not known to the public was that Arthur suffered from a fatal illness—Bright's disease—the same kidney ailment that a decade later was to kill Blaine, himself.
BOYD, *LIFE AND PUBLIC SERVICES OF JAMES G. BLAINE*

Never one to suffer in silence, Blaine fired off an open letter to the new president on February 3, 1882. He pointed out that:

1. The idea of a "Congress of all American nations" had been "warmly approved" by "your predecessor."
2. That Arthur had approved sending out invitations.
3. That Frelinghuysen's communiqué to Special Envoy Trescott in Peru and Chile (with Walker) canceling the conference had

After Garfield's death, Blaine saw that his role as secretary of state under Chester A. Arthur had become untenable and he presently resigned. Succeeding him was Frederick T. Frelinghuysen, a U.S. senator from New Jersey, whose uncle, Theodore Frelinghuysen, had run for vice president in 1844 on a Whig ticket with Blaine's boyhood hero Henry Clay. The new secretary of state promptly undid much of what Blaine had tried to accomplish, particularly in Latin America.
RIDPATH, *LIFE AND WORKS OF JAMES G. BLAINE*

implied the reason was the fear of offending some European powers (the implication was Blaine's).

4. European Powers didn't consult the U.S. if they held conferences in Europe.

5. What an insult to our "American neighbors" and what a loss of prestige for the U.S., even in Europe.

Finally, Blaine couldn't resist a last red, white, and blue wallop, with this pithy statement: "To revoke that invitation for any cause would be embarrassing; to revoke it for avowed fear of 'jealousy or ill will' on the part of European Powers would appeal as little to American pride as to American hospitality...."[7]

His broadside was first published in the *New York Tribune* and then circulated nationally. If to some Republicans it seemed like an open declaration of war by Blaine on the Arthur administration, its author ignored such criticism. He followed right up with a lengthy essay in the *Chicago Weekly Magazine* defending his policies under Garfield. Moreover, the Monroe Doctrine badly needed to be enforced, he argued. It wasn't enough just to warn Europeans to stay out of the U.S.'s spheres of influence; active diplomatic interventions were called for, especially to keep the peace among feuding Latin American nations.

Even before assuming office in December, Frelinghuysen had told Blaine he wished Walker to stay on as third assistant secretary of state. Whether he wanted him or not, it was a gesture to lessen the friction he knew would occur with Blaine. But it didn't work. Walker was already in Peru, on his mission with Trescott, and had to stay at his post in any case, but on April 9, 1882, he wrote his mother from Lima, "I cannot tell you how disgusted, mortified, and humiliated I feel by the action of our government in Washington..., For the love of Heaven and my own self-respect, get me ordered home and let me resign."[8] Not until the beginning of June did Walker get back to his parents' house in D.C.

Shortly afterward, his companion in Chile and Peru, William Trescott, a South Carolina Democrat, came with him to Augusta and they all had a rollicking good time. Harriet revealed (but not until many years later) the Blaines' attitude toward the prohibition ordinance that had existed in Maine since the 1850s. Somehow, "nine cases of anti-Maine law," as she wrote, "put in their timely appearance...." Mr. Trescott and others partook, and so did Judge Libby of the Maine Supreme Court, "the claret and the whiskey proving incomparably good." That summer of 1882 the Blaines had resumed their habit of spending summers in Maine. There was now no reason to stay in the sweltering capital. Since the new house on Massachusetts Avenue still wasn't ready, Blaine had held onto their old house on 15th Street, despite offers from General George McClellan to buy it. Even in November, he wouldn't let Harriet move out. She complained to Maggie, "All day I have been arguing with him to give up the house now, and let me go on and get a few rooms ready in the new domain for immediate occupancy."[9] The final transfer happened only in December.

It was never a house that became a real home to them. Built for a secretary of state who would have to entertain lavishly, that huge showplace was too big, too fancy, for these Maine folks as an everyday residence. The Blaines did throw one major party there—the wedding of oldest daughter Alice to Colonel John J. Coppinger, a career military man. But they hadn't really settled into the Dupont Circle mansion by the time this happy event took place. The ex-secretary and his wife were at the Fifth Avenue Hotel in New York when Alice came in from the opera and told them Coppinger had proposed. Back in Washington, trying to get settled, Harriet wrote Maggie, who was in Paris, the exciting news, describing Coppinger as "an Irishman by birth, a Catholic, and a very popular officer," and she added, "Don't you think this is an astounding event to drop into the midst of my curtains and carpets and paper hanging, with which I thought my whole soul was filled?"

Maggie was the only family member not present for the wedding, which after Father Blaine gave his blessing, was scheduled for February 8, 1883. Meanwhile, Harriet's fairly rueful word picture of the new house went out to the missing daughter in France. "We are living…in Bohemian fashion, no gas on the first floor…one little sitting room, hastily pulled together, beds put up in six rooms…the most primitive dining room in the billiard room…."[10] There was other news, some of it sad, like the death of Harriet's sister, "Aunt Emily," in Augusta. The story of the ceremony, told in elaborate detail, soon followed in the mail to the absent sibling. Included was the hair-dressing of the females at breakfast, Blaine able to don a "full morning dress" by himself, an army of attendants swarming around Alice, the second hall used as dressing rooms for guests, Emmons in charge of the "Reception," assisted by brother Jamie, Tom Sherman, and William Walter Phelps. A Father Chappelle performed the nuptuals. "Alice looked and appeared beautifully, her dress was a marvelous success...." Among the guests were "Mr. Bancroft and the President" (presumably Chester A. Arthur). "The service was all in English [no Latin]," and "Everybody said it was the prettiest wedding Washington has ever seen."[11]

Earlier, Mother Blaine had vented some frustration at the Massachusetts Avenue edifice, with lines like, "This dreadful house still makes its incessant demands.... When I look at Colonel Coppinger's quarters, a photograph of which he has sent Alice, containing only four rooms, I am absolutely envious.... It seems to me I never want to hear again of a large house...." But, in the same paragraph, she also surmised she would get over her fit of pique and "like it so well that I shall wish to live [there] forever."[12]

That latter emotion apparently never jelled. Before long, the Blaines leased their mansion to a Chicago millionaire, Levi Leiter, and afterward they led a somewhat nomadic existence in D.C, renting first the Windom House at Scott Circle, then the old Marcy House on the west side of Lafayette Square, and finally settling in at Seward House, alongside that famous park across the street from the White House entrance.

Prior to Alice's wedding, despite the disruptions, Blaine had begun a new and fairly monumental project for himself—writing a book. For the first time in two decades, he held no governmental job and he had also ended his reign as chairman of the Maine Republican State Committee. Therefore, what was probably a long contemplated intention in his mind became a reality—*Twenty Years of Congress*—a work of history, would be his contribution to Americana. In the end, the work would run to more than 1,000 pages in two volumes and also make him a good deal of money.

Cynics saw it as merely another gambit in his still unrequited quest for the presidency. No matter what James G. Blaine seemed to do, he was always a standing target for political controversy, ungenerous interpretations, and outright charges of malfeasance. His record as secretary of state, brief as it was, drew a particularly scathing attack and even a congressional investigation. It was suspected the same vague forces in the Arthur administration who had killed his policies were behind this vendetta, although ostensibly it was carried out by Democrats, led by a young New York Congressman, Perry Belmont. The accusation against Blaine was that he had been in cahoots with a firm called Credit Industriel, which had a relationship with Republican kingpin Levi P. Morton's investment firm and was seeking to gain control of the Peruvian nitrate beds. Those beds, claimed also by Chile, were now under Chilean occupation, and Blaine's moves to prevent their annexation were stated to be in his self-interest. However, this was a supposition that didn't stick, once the former secretary of state testified before the investigating committee. One of its members, a Massachusetts Republican, Congressman William Whitney Rice, who introduced a resolution to end the investigation, wrote Blaine, "...the more they investigate your action as to Chile and Peru, the better you will stand with the people of the country."

Rice's resolution passed, as it turned out unanimously, Republicans and Democrats, alike, "sick and tired of it," Walker in D.C. informed his father who had gone home to Maine. As for Perry Belmont, Harriet Blaine saw him as "the cat's paw of others"— including his father, the multimillionaire socialite August Belmont, the American representative of the Rothschilds, who for a number of years had been the Democratic National Committee Chairman. Here, the normally decorous if tart-tongued Mrs. Blaine forgot herself by adding, "But I thank thee, Jew, even for all your baseness, since through..." the failed investigation, her husband had been able to get his South American policy "before the world...."[13] Unbeknownst to her, her seemingly anti-Semitic remark was technically misplaced. Perry Belmont had been born of a non-Jewish mother (making him non-Jewish under Jewish religious law). She was the daughter of Commodore Matthew Perry, and Perry Belmont's parents had been married in an Episcopalian church and he, himself, raised in that faith. August Belmont, although born Jewish and never baptized, attended the same church.

After the quashing of this alleged witch hunt, a triumphant moment in the public spotlight soon followed for Blaine. It took place on February 27, 1882, in the hall of the U.S. House of Representatives. He had been called upon to eulogize the late President Garfield and—reluctantly, it was claimed—had allowed himself to be coaxed into doing this by Ohio Congressman William McKinley. It was certainly an emotional task for him. Harriet has described how he insisted she sit in the same room with him as he composed his speech, not allowing her to talk, and when he grappled with the most difficult part of the memory, "the long sickness with its fatal termination," she saw him "taking from the drawer a fresh pocket handkerchief with which he vainly tries to dry his tears, and this time wholly overcome, he has beaten a retreat to the blue room...." So preoccupied was Blaine that one day he inadvertently snubbed his own son, young Jamie, who proclaimed that he had been "crushed by a eulogist."[14]

As the day of the speech approached, public excitement mounted. "The pressure for seats and tickets is enormous," Harriet wrote Maggie. The Blaines had thirty tickets and hundreds of people after them. Among those favored few who did come with them were Mrs. Bigelow Lawrence, Fanny Chapman, and Colonel Alexander Bliss. Lucretia Garfield, unable to be present and sent an advanced copy, wrote back, "I have tried to collect my thoughts and gratitude into some fit expression to tell Mr. Blaine how satisfied I am with all he said. It was such a true, unvarnished tale of his life...if the spirit of General Garfield is in the great Universe, he must have been in that old hall, smiling upon his old friend a grateful recognition...."[15] Another advance copy went to their neighbor "Uncle" Homan, back in Augusta and he read it to a group of local Maine friends at the very same hour Blaine delivered the actual eulogy on Capitol Hill.

The result was a triumph for Blaine, if temporary. It was too lengthy to be remembered like a Gettysburg Address, but its closing lines were moving, and have been repeated often: "Gently, silently, the love of a great people bore the pale sufferer to the longed-for healing of the sea, to live or to die, as God should will, within sight of its heaving billows, within sound of its manifold voices. With wan, fevered face tenderly lifted to the cooling breeze, he looked out wistfully upon the ocean's changing wonders; on its far sails, whitening in the morning light; on its restless waves, rolling shoreward to break and die beneath the noonday sun; on the red clouds of evening, arching low to the horizon; on the serene and shining pathway of the stars. Let us think that his dying eyes read a mystic meaning which only the rapt and parting soul may know. Let us believe that in the silence of the receding world he heard the great waves breaking on the farther shore, and felt already upon his wasted brow the breath of the eternal morning."

The entire assassination drama reached finality with the hanging on June 29, 1882, of Charles Guiteau. Harriet Blaine received the news in Augusta by telephone: "He was hung at 12:35; he died instantly..." and then she commented, "Every servant stopped his work to say, 'I'm glad he's gone,' and even Mr. Homan could almost desire to give up his anti-capital punishment principle in favor of Guiteau. Oh, if he only could have died one little year earlier, the difference to me!" Her sentiment was underscored for the whole family in a letter of Walker's sent a day later. They would learn he was now "out of office and a private citizen" and, he noted, "A little coincidence that I should have gone in as almost the last act of Garfield before he was shot and out the day Guiteau was hanged."[16]

Seemingly, for James G. Blaine and his family, the limelight was about to dim, their place at the forefront of the American political stage about to end.

Nothing could have been further from the truth.

1. Beale, Vol. 1, pp. 210–11.
2. Ackerman, p. 411.
3. Ibid., p. 403.
4. Ibid., p. 420.
5. Ibid., p. 421.
6. Hamilton, p. 517.
7. Ibid., p. 522.
8. Ibid., p. 562.
9. Ibid., p. 617.
10. Beale, Vol. 2, p. 69.
11. Ibid., p. 85.
12. Ibid., p. 76.
13. Ibid., p. 11.
14. Hamilton, p. 557.
15. Ibid., p. 559.
16. Ibid., p. 566.

EIGHTEEN

THE ELECTION OF 1884

T THE CONCLUSION of our first chapter, James G. Blaine was left on his lawn in Augusta, Maine—stretched out in his hammock—pondering the extraordinary play of events that had brought him a real chance at the presidency. That sentimental journey—and we have seen how extensive and drama-laden it was—had to climax with a realistic analysis of what his chances reasonably were. He was a hard-nosed pol beneath his amiable exterior. And the auguries for the G.O.P. ticket in 1884 were far from entirely favorable.

For starters, there was the possibility of voter fatigue with one party domination of the White House. The Republicans had held the executive office for almost a quarter of a century. Then, too, the G.O.P. had to face a Democratic "Solid South." In 1876, Hayes had needed the support of South Carolina, Florida, and Louisiana in order to win by a single electoral vote. Four years later, Garfield did win without any Dixie states in his column, but primarily because he held onto New York State. Whoever the Democrats ran in 1884 would start with the advantage of a huge block of support below the Mason-Dixon line.

The odds-on money was betting that Blaine's opponent would be Grover Cleveland, the extremely popular governor of New York. To make the Empire State even tougher to win was the Stalwart-Half Breed split. Conkling was still a force to be reckoned with, although not as powerful as he once had been. He'd lost his U.S. Senate seat and had alienated President Arthur, his former flunky, yet Arthur had no love, either, for Blaine, who had deprived him of a second term. Finally, there was the problem of the "Mugwumps."

The derivation of this strange nickname for the former "Liberal Republicans" remains a bit murky. Supposedly, it was an Algonquian word for "big chiefs." To them, Blaine was already the "Continental Liar From the State of Maine." In their eyes, he was dishonest and devious, uncouth despite his obvious charm and intelligence, and taking the Republican Party in the wrong direction. A number of the Mugwump elite were journalists like E. L. Godkin, editor of *The Nation,* and George William Curtis, editor of *Harper's Weekly,* or Henry Adams, who had briefly edited the *North American Review,* and among the active politicians, Carl Schurz, the German-born U.S. senator from Missouri and secretary of the interior under Hayes, was the most prominent. Civil service reform was their special passion and, in the past, they had drawn especially biting scorn from Roscoe Conkling, who invented a Gilded Age synonym for "sissy" or "girly-boy" with which to tar them, saying they were "man-milliners." Similar if not as pungent disdain was reserved for Schurz from Blaine, a most unusual posture for him to take publicly; this German-American was the only figure he really spoke ill of in his entire 1,000-page *Twenty Years of Congress* book, in which he'd even complimented Conkling. Blaine's beef about Schurz was his inconstancy in politics, his willy-nilly changing of party allegiances, and that "He has taken no pride in appearing under the title of a citizen of the United States."[1]

While this uncharacteristic bitterness on Blaine's part was not published until after the election, it did seem to indicate how much he resented Carl Schurz's indefatigable attacks on him and vociferous support for Grover Cleveland. Blaine's monumental work, which he'd started right after leaving the State Department, came out in two volumes—Volume I before the 1884 election and Volume II (containing the remarks about Schurz) in 1886. Per usual, Blaine was accused of political cleverness because Volume I made its debut in the spring of 1884, just before the Republicans' nominating convention in Chicago. Writing to Maggie about Father's literary effort, Harriet Blaine gave no hint about motives, merely saying candidly, "It will not probably be interesting to you and to me..." then added: "but think of the many, many, who will want to read and own it."[2]

General William Tecumseh Sherman, a longtime friend and relative of Blaine. When Blaine wrote to Sherman in secret suggesting that Sherman might be nominated for president, Sherman replied with a firm no.
SHERMAN'S MEMOIRS, COURTESY OF TED LAITALA

Whether or not *Twenty Years of Congress* was a Machiavellian ploy, a curious incident that occurred as the G.O.P. prepared to meet in the Windy City spoke of a reluctance by Blaine to be the G.O.P. candidate. There was an extraordinary exchange between the man from Maine and his longtime friend and relative by marriage, General William Tecumseh Sherman. Blaine had been telling a few people he wanted Sherman to be the Republican Party's candidate. Among them was Murat Halsted, editor of the *Cincinnati Commercial Gazette*, whose help Blaine tried to enlist in persuading the general. His reasoning was, "With the South against us, we cannot succeed without New York and I cannot carry that State."[3]

Furthermore, the G.O.P. should put Robert Lincoln on as "Cump's" running mate and they would have a "dream" patriotic ticket.

On May 25, 1884, Blaine sent a letter to Sherman marked "(*Confidential*) strictly and absolutely so," and continuing, "MY DEAR GENERAL: This letter requires no answer. After reading it carefully, file it away in your most secret drawer or give it to the flames." Thus, he began and the next two sentences spelled out his meaning in no uncertain terms: "At the approaching convention in Chicago, it is more than possible—it is indeed not improbable—that you may be nominated for the presidency. If so you must stand your hand, accept the responsibility and assume the duties of the place to which you will surely be chosen...." In the body of the letter, Blaine includes the stricture that Sherman could no more refuse the popular demand of a draft than he could have disobeyed an order when a lieutenant in the army. "Do not answer this" was his final injunction.

But three days later, Sherman wrote back from his home in St. Louis, Missouri. He first assured Blaine, whom he addressed as "MY DEAR FRIEND," that he would keep the letter absolutely confidential, "not intimating even to any member of my family that I have heard from you" (he did not have to remind Blaine that his own brother, Senator John Sherman, was also vying for the same nomination), and then offered his resolute refusal. It was not exactly put in the terse, unequivocal statement that has come down to us through history—*If nominated, I will not run; if elected, I will not serve*—but he left no wiggle room in his declination. "I will not, in any event, entertain or accept a nomination as a candidate for President by the Chicago Republican convention or any other convention for reasons personal to myself." Additionally, he let his inner feelings about politics magnificently run on: "I owe no man a cent, have no expensive habits or tastes, envy no man his wealth or power, no complications or indirect liabilities, and would account myself a fool, a madman, an ass, to embark anew, at sixty-five years of age, in a career that may, at any moment, become tempest-tossed by the perfidy, the defalcation, the dishonesty or neglect of any one of a hundred thousand subordinates utterly unknown to the President of the United States, not to say the eternal worriment by a vast host of impecunious friends and old military subordinates...." Sherman's letter ends, "No—count me out. The civilians of the United States should—and must, buffet with the thankless office and leave us old soldiers to enjoy the peace we fought for and think we earned."

Once Blaine did secure the nomination, another letter came to him from "Cump" Sherman. Tongue-in-cheek, the general told Blaine that he really had all along been his rival at Chicago, but was now "nevertheless willing to congratulate you on your brilliant success before the august body and I honestly wish you success at the election next November." He also wished the same success to Senator Logan, the vice-presidential candidate who had been "an ardent, brave, enthusiastic general under me...." But bluntly, Sherman had to confess that post-war, Logan had been "a bitter enemy of mine." The reason was that as a member of Congress, Logan had cut Sherman's military pay and caused him financial hardship, notwithstanding which, he would still have Sherman's support at the polls. One other thing, though, the crusty general cautioned Blaine that Logan had not been on the famous March to the Sea, as was stated at the convention and included in a campaign biography. "I would advise him to correct it himself before it is tortured to his prejudice by a political enemy."[4]

Blaine's winning the nomination had not occurred without some determined resistance. His forces in Chicago were put in the hands of a rising star in the Republican Party, Stephen B. Elkins, who had been the territorial delegate from New Mexico to the U.S. Congress in the 1870s and then had moved to West Virginia, in both of which areas he had amassed fortunes in land, coal, and railroads. Yet that ineffable word momentum seems to have had as much to do with Blaine's Chicago victory as Elkins's energy, money and organizing skills. Blaine's "time had come," as the political saying goes. Among Republicans in states they could carry (not the South), he was a runaway favorite, not the least because of his ties to the martyred Garfield. He was the heir-apparent and his strongest opponent, the incumbent president, still suffered from the stigma of the assassin's boast that "Arthur will be President."

This fact was clearly shown at the New York Republican state

The arrival of a trainload of Blaine supporters at Chicago in 1884. On his third try, the Man from Maine finally became the Republican standard bearer.
MAINE HISTORIC PRESERVATION COMMISSION

convention in late April, 1884. Held in Utica, Roscoe Conkling's hometown, the headlines that emerged from it helped sink Arthur's hopes. "THE PRESIDENT'S CANDIDACY KILLED IN HIS OWN STATE," the *Philadelphia Inquirer* proclaimed. Blaine had taken the votes of 240 New Yorker delegates and Arthur only 176. At this Utica gathering, the Mugwump candidate, Vermont Senator George F. Edmunds made a decent showing of 75 votes, largely thanks to young Theodore Roosevelt who, a year out of Harvard, had been elected to the New York Assembly. The *New York Tribune* reported, "Mr. Roosevelt was the active man in the so-called Edmunds campaign…" and then expressed sarcastic surprise that certain of the party bosses close to Arthur, who'd had nothing but contempt for him in Albany, were now showing Teddy "sudden affection."

In Chicago, Roosevelt also made a name for himself, promoting Edmunds. He engineered the one tactical loss the Blaine forces incurred when their man for temporary chairman, Powell Clayton,

Scene outside the convention building in Chicago in 1884, where jubilant supporters of Blaine celebrated of his nomination.
MAINE HISTORIC PRESERVATION COMMISSION

an ex-carpetbagger, was defeated by John Lynch, a black congressman from Mississippi who'd been born a slave. But that glitch proved evanescent. Every time Blaine's name was mentioned, the hall filled with roaring cheers. Just before the fourth ballot, with the Mainer's total mounting, Blaine's opponents tried to push through a motion to adjourn as a delaying tactic. When

Photo of Stephen B. Elkins, an important Republican politician from West Virginia, who served as Blaine's campaign chair during the election of 1884. A multi-millionaire U.S. senator, Elkins was always controversial and Blaine frequently found himself attacked for their association.
RIDPATH, *LIFE AND WORKS OF JAMES G. BLAINE*

Teddy Roosevelt tried to speak for the move, Blaineites shouted, "Get down, you young fool!" and the attempt was quashed by an overwhelming voice vote. The roll of delegates was then called. Once Illinois was reached, favorite son John A. Logan provided Blaine 36 votes and won himself a place on the ticket.

Given that outcome, Theodore Roosevelt faced the first real daunting political decision of his career. Should he desert the Republicans along with so many of his friends and supporters? He decided, no, he would stick with Blaine, despite the grief it would cause him, and so did his bosom buddy Henry Cabot Lodge of Massachusetts, who found himself ostracized by his Brahmin neighbors. Regular Republican newspapers like the *Cincinnati Enquirer*

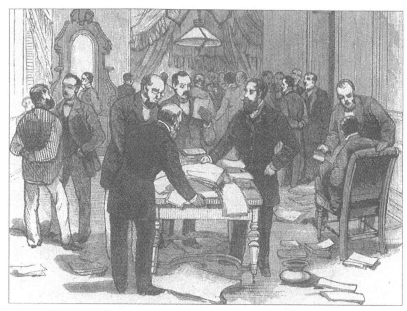

*The 1884 G.O.P. convention. A scene inside Blaine headquarters at
Chicago's Grand Pacific Hotel.*
MAINE HISTORIC PRESERVATION COMMISSION

*Sketch of the scene at the 1884 Chicago Republican Conven-
tion where Blaine was nominated.*
RIDPATH, *LIFE AND WORKS OF JAMES G. BLAINE*

An advertisement in 1884 for the G.O.P. presidential team of Blaine and Logan. Note how it has been joined by pleas for over-the-counter patent medicines.
MAINE HISTORIC PRESERVATION COMMISSION

exulted with headlines such as, "THE PLUMED KNIGHT ONCE MORE HURLS HIS SHINING LANCE," playing on Robert Ingersoll's 1876 figure of speech of a white-feathered medieval helmet (attributed to the gallant Henri IV of France), which image was soon displayed over and over again in 1884 Republican rallies, despite Blaine's distaste for it. To him, a white feather denoted cowardice. But there it was, flaunted in bad poetry, too, in the partisan press, as exemplified by the following from the *Evening Critic* of Washington, D.C.

> The Plumed Knight
> See his white plumes waving high
> Hark! The glorious battle cry;
> Our cause still lives, it cannot die –
> Our leader—Blaine of Maine.
> Once again, we'll face the foe;
> Once again, we'll lay him low;
> Once again, our prowess show –
> We're led by Blaine of Maine.[5]

The *Cincinnati Enquirer* also printed a number of humorous one-liners on the election from its columnist John R. McLean, such as "Two Many Shermans Spoil The Broth," "Blaine Went Through With Yells," and, most pointedly, "The handful of Independents should lose no time in bolting the ticket," with reference to "George William Curtis dudes and namby-pambys." Indeed, the Chicago convention had barely ended when in Boston the Massachusetts Reform Club met at the Parker House on June 7. Mark Wahlgren Summers in his recent account of the 1884 election wrote, "The list of names read like a reunion of the *Mayflower's* descendants."[6] An anti-Blaine committee of a hundred that was formed had Charles R. Codman as president, and Moorfield Story, George V. Leverett, Stephen M. Weld, William H. Forbes, and others on its board. Charles Francis Adams sent his blessings to these G.O.P. blueblood insurgents and his son Henry, in Washington, D.C., was heartily in agreement. In New York, Carl Schurz became a leader immediately; with him were E. L. Godkin of *The Nation*, R. R. Bowker, Everett Wheeler, and—no surprise to Blaine—the Reverend Henry Ward Beecher in Brooklyn, who declared: "Put me down against Blaine one hundred times in letters two feet long."[7] The Honorable Matthew Hale, a New York Republican office holder, publicly stated his "conviction that this so-called 'Plumed Knight' is a false knight... unfit to hold the office first filled by one 'who could not tell a lie' and in more recent times by one whom the people respected as 'Honest Abe.'" The hostile *Harper's Weekly*, probably through the pen of George William Curtis, likewise employed a comparison with Lincoln. The choice of Blaine and Logan showed, the magazine editorialized: "...how dangerously far the Republican standard has fallen.... The sad and kindly face of LINCOLN whose portrait hung in the hall, seemed to watch the proceedings of the Convention with an air of earnest solicitude and apprehension and it had disappeared from its place before the nomination was made."[8]

Thus, even before the Democrats selected their candidate, who did turn out to be New York Governor Grover Cleveland, small cadres of people of the better sort were abandoning their Republican roots. By themselves, they could not swing the election. But their loud voices were heard and generally in a chorus that emphasized Blaine's biggest weakness—his character could be made to seem that of a scheming, ambitious conniver and con artist who was none too honest. During the run-up to the G.O.P. convention, a political cartoon, perhaps instigated by these internal foes, struck Blaine a harsh and lasting blow. It was popularly referred to as "the Tattooed Man," but its actual title was "Phryne Before The Chicago Tribunal"—a take-off on a classical painting. Depicted was James G. Blaine in his underwear being displayed to a crowd of Republican dignitaries and all over his body were tattooed letterings full of pejorative meanings, such as LITTLE ROCK RR, MULLIGAN LETTERS, N. PACIFIC, BONDS, CORRUPTION, LOBBY, and so forth. Drawn by Bernhard Gillam for *Puck* magazine, this powerful satire appeared June 4, 1884, just as the Chicago event was to start. Masterfully crafted, it haunted the Blaine campaign forever afterward. The Republicans tried to counter it seventeen days later in a publication called *The Hatchet* under the heading, "The Hatchet Sees Puck's Tattooed Man and Goes Two Tattooed Men Better." On Blaine, those new tattoos now read, "STATESMANSHIP, THE MANTLE OF GARFIELD, WISDOM, COURAGE, MAGNETISM," and on Logan, "A SOLDIER AND THE SOL-

*The most famous of all the anti-Blaine cartoons and one that had a
major impact on the 1884 election, known popularly as "The Tattooed
Man." Paradoxically, the artist who drew it, Bernhard Gillam, later
stated that he voted for Blaine.*
MAINE HISTORIC PRESERVATION COMMISSION

DIER'S FRIEND, FROM PRIVATE TO MAJOR-GENERAL, the names of battles he
was in, and despite General Sherman's admonition, "I MARCHED
THROUGH GEORGIA." Ironically, when the general election came,
Gillam, the creator of the original devastating portrait, announced
he was voting for Blaine.

Not so Thomas Nast, with whom Blaine had clashed back in
1878 during the "great state steal" crisis in Maine. In 1884, Nast
was no less stinging, among other things pillorying Blaine for hypocrisy in wooing the Irish vote in view of his past editorial support for anti-Catholic Know-Nothings. In fact, once Cleveland's
victory had been ascertained, a delirious crowd gathered outside
Nast's home to celebrate and congratulate him for his contribution to Blaine's defeat. One of the placards held up by the throng
spelled out in layman's shorthand an analysis of the entire campaign, why Blaine lost and why the Democrats now had a president for the first time in almost a quarter of a century.

THE WORLD SAYS THE INDEPENDENTS DID IT
THE TRIBUNE SAYS THE STALWARTS DID IT

THE SUN SAYS BURCHARD DID IT
BLAINE SAYS SAINT JOHN DID IT
THEODORE ROOSEVELT SAYS IT WAS THE SOFT SOAP DINNER
WE SAY BLAINE'S CHARACTER DID IT
BUT WE DON'T CARE WHAT DID IT
IT'S DONE[9]

The Harper Brothers publishers who employed Nast had been among the "Independents" who "did it" to Blaine, and Blaine's rejoinder had been that they were unhappy he hadn't let them publish his *Twenty Years of Congress*. Nast had used that "20 years" theme in several of his most biting anti-Blaine cartoons, where he had the G.O.P. candidate identified with a carpetbag labeled, in one case, "20 Years A Canvasser for Votes for Blaine," and in another, "20 Years of Masquerading By Blaine." The latter cartoon charged Blaine with being in secret cahoots with Ben Butler, the Massachusetts maverick, then running as a third-party "Anti-Monopoly" Greenbacker-style candidate who, Republicans hoped, would take votes from the Democrats. Also in the 1884 race was a fourth-party candidate, the Saint John of the placard, who was John P. St. John, the Radical Republican ex-governor of Kansas, running as a Prohibitionist. In a contest as close as that of 1884, these additional candidates had an effect, as illustrated by the placard writer's allusion that Blaine, himself, blamed St. John's attraction of Republican voters as the reason for his loss. In New York State, the key to the election by just over 1,000 votes, more than 20,000 votes went to the Prohibition Party.

Blaine's strategy had been to run his campaign entirely on the tariff issue. The Republicans were for protection, high duties to keep out cheap foreign goods, and that the continuation of this policy offered insurance of sustained prosperity in the U.S. But as happens in the three-ring circuses by which Americans choose their highest leaders, events spin "messages" out of control.

It was not Blaine's wish to institute a vicious attack upon Grover Cleveland's private life. That impulse came unbidden from G.O.P. partisans in Buffalo, the Democratic candidate's hometown, where he had been mayor before becoming governor of New York

Benjamin Butler of Massachusetts ran on just about everybody's ticket at one time or another. A Democrat before the Civil War, he was a Union general during the fighting—the notorious "Beast Butler" (so-called because of his harshness as the war governor of Louisiana)—and then a congressional Republican after Appamattox. In 1884 he was an independent candidate, representing the Anti-Monopoly and Labor-Greenback party, but encouraged by the G.O.P., which thought he would be taking votes away from Grover Cleveland.
RIDPATH, *LIFE AND WORKS OF JAMES G. BLAINE*

State. On July 21, 1884, the *Buffalo Evening Telegraph*, in a story headlined A TERRIBLE TALE, broke the electrifying news that Grover Cleveland, who had also once served as sheriff of Erie County, had fathered an illegitimate child!

Accompanying this bombshell announcement were lurid details of Cleveland's double life—a law enforcement officer and a respected official in the daylight, and in the darkness of night, a drunkard, regularly consorting with prostitutes and fallen women—in the words of a local minister repeated by the Republican newspaper, a "whoremonger" and a "barroom roisterer." A cartoon in another G.O.P. publication called *Judge* soon became as famous as the "Tattooed Man." Pictured was a woman gripping an agitated baby reaching out to Grover Cleveland who held his hands to his ears while the child screamed, "I want my pa!" This image soon generated a Republican war cry, as marching ranks of the G.O.P. at rallies chanted, "Ma, Ma, where's my Pa?"

Blaine was appalled. "Dirty politics" like these were a diversion from his tariff message and he saw them as not amounting to anything in terms of votes. What he didn't see, most likely, was how the same tactics might be used against him by exposing his personal life.

At first, to the Mugwump opposition, this moral issue seemed to present a genuine crisis. They were holier-than-thou in their attacks on Blaine's honesty; how could they defend Cleveland's sexual sins? But, by and large, they swallowed hard and not only stuck with the Democrat but helped him, too. For example, the Boston Committee of One Hundred financed a "truth squad" to investigate the charges against Cleveland and found many of them—particularly the drinking and whoring—entirely spurious.

Cleveland helped his own cause by manfully accepting responsibility for the son he allegedly had fathered by Maria Halpin, a woman of doubtful virtue who was known to have had affairs with various local men. One of these males, the story was eventually put out, the true father, had been Cleveland's law partner, a married man, and that he, as a bachelor, gallantly covered for him.

Momentum changed then, and Blaine soon found himself on the defensive in a way he could never possibly have imagined. He was accused of having married Harriet back in 1851 "at the muzzle of a shotgun." The Democratic *Indianapolis Sentinel*, in as lurid and sensational a manner as the Republican press had used, pointed out that the Blaines' marriage had been recorded in Pittsburgh on March 29, 1851, and their first child, Stanwood, the boy they had lost, had been born only three months later on June 18, 1851. One can imagine how upsetting this accusation was to the Blaines by dredging up memories of their dead son. His gravestone in Augusta was actually tampered with, the date of his birth being chiseled away. Blaine, himself, rushed out a defense that told of an earlier secret marriage with Harriet in Kentucky on June 30, 1850, which had never been recorded, while simultaneously he instructed Indiana Senator Benjamin Harrison's law firm to file a libel action against the *Sentinel*. This response, however, did seem a bit belabored and did nothing to lessen James G. Blaine's reputation for trickiness, which his foes continually exploited.

In the long run, Blaine was right—the sex stuff had no lasting effect on either candidate. It was the muckraking, when it touched on public life, that hurt him far, far more than Grover Cleveland.

In the Portland (Maine) Public Library, on the shelves of a room dedicated to books about the Pine Tree State, there is a volume entitled *The Charges Against Mr. Blaine Examined*. It is not a book by a single author but a carefully put together compilation of materials from the 1884 campaign. Pros and cons vis-à-vis Blaine are both included, some as photocopies and transcripts of speeches and newspaper articles and some as pamphlets actually distributed during the election. Familiar names emerge: Carl Schurz and Henry Ward Beecher on the anti-Blaine side; William Walter Phelps as a defender of the "Magnetic Man." There are names, even of celebrities, which hadn't surfaced in other accounts. One was author Edward Eggleston, also a Methodist clergyman, famed for his novel, *The Hoosier Schoolmaster*, who excoriated Blaine by saying, "His is a magnetism that draws the filth and rubbish of the opposite party..." while the Republicans who desert Blaine are "...men of very high order. I do not find the pot hunters of the party among them."

Lesser known attackers of Blaine were people like John J. D. Trenor, creator of a pamphlet entitled *BLAINEISM, A Short Catechism for Honest Voters*, and John O. Sargent, writing as *A Berkshire Farmer* in another pamphlet, this one printed by the *Valley Gleaner* of Lee, Massachusetts. The latter piece, done to an extent in the old-fashioned rural caricature style once traditional in American politics, also focused on a parochial issue for residents of the Bay State—Blaine's quixotic bad-mouthing of Massachusetts six years earlier when that statue of William King, Maine's George Washington, was unveiled in the Capitol. "Here Mr. Blaine comes in with a venomous attack not on the leaders of the Federal Party…[whom William King fought to win independence for Maine]…but on the PEOPLE OF MASSACHUSETTS." Included by Sargent, too, was a fawning letter of his to Warren Fisher, Jr., Blaine's nemesis in 1876, who was resurrected ad nauseum in 1884. Unsung defenders of Blaine in the collection were, among others, Edwin D. Mead of Boston, who described himself as "a very devoted Republican during my brief voting life," and George Bliss Sawyer, whose preface stated, "I have never been a follower of Mr. Blaine. I was at the National Convention at Cincinnati in 1876 as a supporter of Mr. Conkling…and active in pushing for Mr. Hayes…" and in 1884, as a President Arthur supporter, "was heartsick when Blaine was nominated." But since then, he had sat down and studied "the Mulligan Papers…."

So was it repeatedly in these documents that the 1876 case, the whole business with Fisher and Mulligan and the Little Rock and Fort Smith Railroad bonds, was diced and rediced and hashed and rehashed down to the smallest bits of information by both sides. Carl Schurz, speaking at Cincinnati on September 25, 1884, on behalf of the National Committee of Republicans and Independents, told his audience, "See Mr. Blaine's letters to Warren Fisher, Jr., of May 26, 1864, August 9, 1872, August 31, 1872, November 18, 1869, December 9, 1870…." Highly damaging to the Blaine interests, without question, had been the re-release of the Mulligan letters in 1884, including ones he had not read aloud in his dramatic performance before the House of Representatives. The most devastating of these latter epistles was to Warren Fisher, Jr., and it not only contained a statement drawn up by Blaine—exonerating him from any misbehavior—that he wanted Fisher to make public under his own signature. But even worse than this revelation of sleaze, it displayed a line in capital letters printed below Blaine's own signature: BURN THIS LETTER. Thereafter, Democratic rallies bore posters proclaiming BURN THIS LETTER and a cry of the same words burst repeatedly from thousands of throats as their partisans marched.

As the campaign progressed, the general impression of Blaine was that of a candidate continually on the defensive, no matter how skilled those who tried to plead his cause, including himself, might be. Nor did his opponents lack previously unmentioned scandals to throw at him, adding "Slippery Jim," "Continental Liar," "Scoundrel," "Manipulator," "Dishonest" to the adjectives continually aimed in his direction.

Out of the past, there even came the "Paper Credit Fraud" of the Civil War, with which Blaine had never openly been connected when the Maine legislature had investigated this expensive scam. Now, the *New York World,* recently bought by Joseph Pulitzer and strongly Democratic, ran some sensational headlines in September 1884, such as: "THE GREAT 'PAPER CREDIT FRAUD' OF MAINE THOROUGHLY ANALYZED, THE TATTOOED MAN'S NEXT DOOR NEIGHBOR GROWS SUDDENLY RICH, BAD AS MULLIGAN LETTERS." Quoted in the news story was the Republicans' foremost foe in Maine, Eben F. Pillsbury. In effect, what was being re-cycled here was a nine-year-old "open letter" in the Maine press from Pillsbury to Blaine, with innuendo added that Blaine and General James B. Fry had been intimately linked with "the infernal fraud."

Yet another scandal unearthed was "Blaine's Hocking Valley Venture." The charge here was that Blaine and Stephen B. Elkins had tried to corner a monopoly of certain coal-mining lands in Ohio. Blaine's credibility once more took a blow. No sooner had he denied owning coal lands in the Hocking Valley than Elkins, who was still running his campaign, contradicted him. Pegged as one of the mine bosses, Blaine was then castigated as "part owner of the Ohio Mines, where wages were cut down and honest toilers turned out to starve"—there had been strikes there—in an effort to lessen what had been considerable labor support for the Republican candidate because of the protective tariff issue.

Attempts were also made to whittle away Blaine's attractiveness to normally Democratic Irish Catholic voters. His openly anti-British positions in the Congress and as secretary of state had won him support in certain Irish-American quarters among those who sought independence or at least home rule for the Emerald Isle. Gaelic nationalist publications like Patrick Ford's *Irish World,* John Boyle O'Reilly's *The Pilot,* and John Devoy's *The Irish Nation,* began touting Blaine and there is even an indication that E. L. Godkin, the English-born editor of *The Nation* and *The Evening Post,* encouraged Blaine's position on Ireland before turning against him as a leading Mugwump and assailing him for not having helped Irish-Americans enough when arrested by the British.[10]

But the ultimate death knell for Blaine's Irish support was struck, quite unconsciously, by the ill-considered remarks of an obscure Presbyterian minister from a parish in Manhattan's fashionable Murray Hill section. He was the Reverend Samuel D. Burchard, whose surname also figured on that placard waved outside of Thomas Nast's home, the implication being that he, alone, had torpedoed Blaine. While Burchard is now no longer a household word, his one small bit of seemingly clever alliteration has remained a fixture in American history—"Rum, Romanism, and Rebellion"—the smarmy tag he put on the Democratic Party. Blaine called Burchard "the preacher in the shape of an ass" who, along with a heavy rainstorm on election day, had killed his chances in New York State.

Despite all of the nasty ammunition fired against him, Blaine still had had an opportunity to win as the campaign was drawing to a close. Against his better judgment, he had answered the pleas of Elkins and other of his handlers to leave Augusta and stump in person in the Midwest. His magic hold on voters had seemed to revive in the fantastic G.O.P. enthusiasm his magnetic presence aroused, and during these waning hours, as he headed east, he was also persuaded to stop and speak in upstate New York. Then, they wanted him in New York City—and he made a fatal decision to go, although advised to return straight to Maine.

Consequently, on October 29, 1884, "the day of ill omen," to quote biographer Professor David Muzzey,[11] Blaine found himself descending a staircase in the Fifth Avenue Hotel to face a crowd of Protestant clergymen especially assembled for him to address. The idea had been to contrast his support from this God-fearing group with the moral laxity the Republicans were trying to pin on Grover Cleveland. Not a bad strategy, but in politics, there is always the unexpected. A certain Baptist minister had been designated as the spokesperson to greet Blaine, but unfortunately he had been detained in Philadelphia and Burchard was the last-

Puck, attacking Blaine again, for his anti-British positions as a cynical, pandering play for the Irish vote—"to Please Pat"—the cartoon's title asserts.
MAINE HISTORIC PRESERVATION COMMISSION

minute replacement. His brief welcome ended with these words, which also took a slap at the "Independents" who had abandoned the G.O.P. candidate. "We are Republicans and don't propose to leave our party and identify ourselves with the party whose antecedents have been rum, Romanism, and rebellion. We are loyal to our flag. We are loyal to you."

Poor Blaine was exhausted. It has been said he didn't really hear Burchard's statement. If he did, then it didn't register. In any event, the remark slipped out, was picked up by a Democratic "spy" present, released in the hostile press with a "spin" that Blaine, himself, had uttered it and the quote put into handbills passed out at Catholic church doors the Sunday prior to election.

That wasn't the only disaster the campaign incurred in Manhattan. The next night, the infamous "soft soap dinner" was held at Delmonico's Restaurant, New York's fanciest and most expensive eatery. The slang term "soft soap," then in use, meant money in politics, and assembled in a lush private dining room were all of the "heavy hitters" backing Blaine, the fat cats of American industry—unpopular millionaires like Cyrus Field and Jay Gould corralling their rich friends to cough up dough for Blaine. The truth was that the campaign needed last-minute funds—Blaine had already sunk in about $100,000 of his own money—and thus a second public relations fiasco occurred.

Again, a cartoon expressed the damage the Blaine campaign had inflicted upon itself. Entitled "Belshazzar Blaine and the Money Kings," drawn by Walt McDougall, it appeared in the *New York World* on October 30, 1884. Pictured passing by the table at which that glittering assemblage sat—caricatured faces of recognizable tycoons—was a poor family—father, mother, little girl—with the father's hand held out for needed alms. This was another powerful visual, and one guaranteed to knock down Blaine's final vote.

That tally in the electoral college, with New York in the Democratic column, ended up Cleveland 219, Blaine 182. There were G.O.P. mutterings about "stolen votes" and in New York State, talk of a recount. When this idea was bruited about, Roscoe Conkling came forward and offered his legal services to the Democrats at no cost. His disservice to Blaine had been camouflaged to an extent earlier—carping articles in the *New York World* under the pseudonym of "A Stalwart Republican" and a witticism, often requoted, that when asked to give a speech for Blaine, he replied, "Gentlemen, I have given up criminal practice." His native Utica, needless to say, did not deliver its usual Republican votes.

It was all over. Blaine lost no time in conceding. And the delighted Democrats had a new marching bit of doggerel. The mocking chant of "Ma, Ma, where's my Pa?" could now be topped with an addition of "Gone to the White House, ha, ha, ha."

An editorial comment, pro-Blaine, on how he had been denied victory in 1884.
MAINE HISTORIC PRESERVATION COMMISSION

Harriet Blaine's post-mortem, in her only printed letter of 1884, explained how she felt about their defeat to daughter Alice, who, away out west with her army officer husband, had missed the entire campaign. "It is all a horror to me. I was absolutely certain of the election as I had a right to be from Mr. Elkins' assertions. Then the fluctuations were so trying to the nerves. It is easy to bear now, but the click-click of the telegraph, the shouting through the telephone in response to its never-to-be satisfied demand, and the unceasing murmur of men's voices, coming up through the night to my room, will never go out of my memory—while over and above all, the perspiration and chills, into which the conflicting reports constantly threw the physical part of one, body and soul alike rebelling against the restraints of nature, made an experience not to be voluntarily recalled."[12]

The unmistakable inference was that there would be no more presidential runs for James G. Blaine in the future.

By way of consolation, if that were the case, there was this thought expressed in a letter sent to Blaine from St. Joseph's Asylum, Washington, D.C. "My beloved cousin," wrote Angela Gillespie, saintly nun, Civil War nurse, and retired mother superior, "with deepest and tenderest love, I come to you this morning—my heart goes out in prayer for you. Be strong and cheerful..." and she ended with an other-worldly piece of advice: "Let the past go—many truly happy great years are before you. If four years at the White House were worth six months of labor, will not ever lasting happiness be worth *much, much* more...?"

But could James Gillespie Blaine give up his dreams of worldly greatness entirely?

1. Blaine, *Twenty Years of Congress*, pp. 439–40.
2. Beale, Vol. 2, p. 92.
3. Summers, p. 124.
4. This, and all other Blaine-Sherman correspondence quotes, are from Hamilton, pp. 624, 625, 626.
5. *Washington Evening Critic*, 6 June 1884.
6. Summers, p. 198.
7. Ibid.
8. *Harper's Weekly*, 14 June 1884.
9. Summers, p. 297, as quoted from Albert Bigelow Paine, *Thomas Nast, His Period and His Pictures* (New York: Harper and Brothers, 1904).
10. Trowbridge H. Ford, article in *Mid-America, An Historical Review*, Vol. 57, No. 1, January 1975 (Loyola University, Institute of Jesuit History).
11. Muzzey, p. 316.
12. Beale, pp. 120–21.

NINETEEN

CIVILIAN LIFE

O UT OF PUBLIC OFFICE for the next four years and eight months, from November 1884 to March 1889, James G. Blaine was ostensibly just a private citizen, a *"civilian,"* as some folks in governmental positions jocularly refer to those in the general public. On the surface, then, the ex-Republican leader was simply a writer, completing his second volume of *Twenty Years of Congress* and, after that, a traveler, taking Harriet and Maggie to Europe for a gilt-edged tour of the British Isles and the Continent, and all the while, watching his children grow up, being a grandfather, and seemingly finished with national politics.

The grandchild in question, their first, was James Gillespie Blaine Coppinger, better known as "Blainey." Because his father and mother were at a garrison in Indian country out west, the little boy spent three years under his grandparents' care. He was most certainly a welcome, lively addition to the bustling Blaine household, which, in Harriet's use of language, was always making "hegiras," gypsy-like pilgrimages from one site to another—Augusta, Washington, D.C., and from the summer of 1884 on, Bar Harbor, Maine, on beautiful Mount Desert Island.

Apparently, Blaine had given up the notion of a place in York Harbor after his rebuff there and turned his affections more Down East to that breathtakingly lovely sea-girt corner of Maine where rock-faced mountains dramatically come right down to the ocean's edge. His campaign had been launched there in the summer of 1884 from rented quarters and a year later, he pronounced himself serious about building a "cottage"—using the euphemistic name the locals gave to the grandiose summer homes springing up all over this glorious location. Harriet wrote Walker on August 19, 1885, "Your Father came at four yesterday...full of a delightful enthusiasm for Bar Harbor and a house there, which he thinks would build up his health…. There are two lots with a bay front of 175 feet…. The situation would please me, but the price knocks my little castle into pieces…."[1]

Somehow, though, the money materialized. Less than a month later, Harriet wrote they were being visited by a "Mr. Camac"—he was William Masters Camac of the Philadelphia architectural firm of Furness, Evans, and Company—and he was about to include "Stanwood," the thirteen-bedroom cottage of the Blaines', among the five structures he was to design at Bar Harbor. The *Mount Desert Herald* had already reported on August 28, 1885, that J. G. Blaine had purchased the land and intended to build. Harriet, herself, visited Bar Harbor in late September and stayed with Walker to sign the contract. However, following an afternoon of laying out stakes at a particular site, another more scenic one was chosen once Father Blaine returned from a visit to the Lewiston Fair. It was on a "higher part of their land," where the real estate developer they employed, Charles How, had built an overlook. Having climbed some rickety steps and seen the fabulous panorama, Blaine, "without the slightest preface," said to his architect, "Camac, I shall put my house here."

Stanwood, the Blaines' thirteen-bedroom cottage at Bar Harbor.
MAINE HISTORIC PRESERVATION COMMISSION

By October 23, 1885, the *Mount Desert Herald* could report that "Work on the cottage of Mr. James G. Blaine is now well underway."

That Blaine had run off to the Lewiston Fair in the midst of this house building effort was a sign that politics, at least in Maine, still had his attention. To this day, candidates continue to show themselves at county fairs in the Pine Tree State. Two years later, we find Blaine, after settling in at Bar Harbor, becoming involved in this municipality's affairs, and using his clout with the Maine legislature in lobbyist fashion.

At the time, the actual name of the town from which Bar Harbor sprang was Eden, Maine. Blaine's real estate man, Charles How, had formed the Eden Water Company in response to complaints that the existing utility, the Bar Harbor Water Company, owned by the Roddick family, wasn't doing its job. Mr. How enlisted (or most likely hired) Blaine to push a bill in Augusta that would allow the new company to supplant the old one.

A glance at the *House Journal* for March 16, 1887, demonstrates the effect of Blaine's mere presence in the Augusta statehouse. A Bangor representative named Barker, upon spying him, immediately sought recognition from the chair. "Mr. Speaker—I see upon the floor of this House a gentleman whom Maine has always d-lighted to honor, one of the greatest statesmen our country has ever produced. I move you, sir, that the House take a recess of ten minutes in order that the members may have the opportunity of shaking hands with the Honorable James G. Blaine."

One can imagine the scene as the lawmakers, Republicans and Democrats alike, rose from their seats and swarmed around the white-bearded visitor. He still knew how to get votes. Nor did it hurt that the judiciary committee to which the water company bill had been assigned included his trusty sidekick Joe Manley. Motions to kill his bill were beaten by margins of almost 3-1 in both bodies. It should be noted that this maneuver was used simply as a threat to the Roddicks so that they got their act together and gave better service to the fast-growing Bar Harbor community.

Indeed, with the help of people like Blaine who, himself, brought celebrities including presidents of the United States to the town, Bar Harbor, in the words of one of its chroniclers, soon "stood in the top rank in America in fashion...and linked in popular estimation with Newport."[2]

How *did* Blaine support himself during this period when he was without a salaried job, yet erecting another mansion? Odd political tasks for which he might have received a stipend would hardly have filled the void. But he had his investments and coal properties in Pennsylvania, if not Ohio, had he been telling the truth about the Hocking Valley. The bulk of his earnings at this point were from his books and they were significant. He once told Andrew Carnegie that the subscriptions for his volumes were in the 200,000 copy range, could go as high as 400,000, and he expected to make $300,000 from the project, a staggering sum. Obviously, these long hours of writing weren't solely a labor of love.

An eager audience was already anticipating Volume II. General Sherman wrote Gail Hamilton, "Tell Blaine that as a matter of course I have read his first volume with greedy interest and that I await still more for his second volume..." hoping, as he explained, that it would cover "Reconstruction," which he saw as the root of Blaine's failure to become president because of its creation of a Democrat "Solid South." In including an appraisal of Blaine in the same letter, Sherman repeated his remembrance of him in Lancaster, Ohio, as a "bright and handsome thoroughbred colt," but now, after having seen Jim Blaine in action as a politician for at least twenty years, could say, "His qualities are literary, not administrative. His oration on Garfield was worthy of a Pitt. But to be honest, I would not choose Blaine to command a regiment or frigate in battle. Many an inferior man would do better than he. He was at his best as Speaker of the House and his true arena is the Senate of the United States...."[3]

An advance copy of the first seventeen pages of Volume II was sent to Sherman, who was pleased by them, reading every word "with thrilling interest and wonderment that in the great mass of events you have been able to keep a straight course...."[4] There was also an assurance that "these sheets shall see no human eyes" except for his "trustworthy" clerk and a few paragraphs shown to R.—presumably his daughter Rachel, a contemporary and close friend of her cousins, the younger Blaine girls. Sherman's own thoughts on the Reconstruction period, which he expressed frankly, were surprisingly pro-South. The Republicans had made a big mistake in alienating the young Confederates who "went off like a herd of buffaloes into the opposition" because of G.O.P. efforts (abetted by Blaine) to enfranchise and give political powers to the ex-slaves.

Harriet once had made noises about getting her husband out of his "hot library," but she also expressed pride over the progress he was making on his monumental writing feat. One particular night at the end of December 1885, he read the family his finished chapter on the fisheries dispute that had pitted the United States—and Maine fishermen—against England and Canada, following which, according to Harriet, he sat down and wrote a "witty and brilliant" letter to two women in Washington, D.C., identified as *Mrs. H.* and *Mrs. H.*, who had jointly written to him.

That cryptic reference might have remained totally obscure to posterity had not Gail Hamilton obtained a copy of Blaine's frivolous answer and rather mischievously included it in her biography of him. It is not a matter of any real importance, except to show Blaine in a remarkably relaxed condition in the throes of his literary labors and further exhibiting a flirtatious and bantering side of himself in respect to ladies, such as we have seen when he was at parties reading poetry and acting gallantly as he did with Mrs. Bigelow Lawrence and her set. The "wit" in this letter that Harriet deemed "brilliant" consisted of plays on the fact that the two women's surnames began with same letter. They were, in fact, a Mrs. Hazen and a Mrs. Hitt, the latter the wife of Robert Hitt, who was Blaine's assistant secretary of state and a family friend. "Mrs. H., for instance, has not the slightest idea how profoundly I admire Mrs. H., nor would I for the world let Mrs. H. know the things I have said of Mrs. H." Having set this theme, Blaine then urges, "Write me singly…. If each of you will write me and swear in advance that neither will show the answer she receives to the other—then, why then, I will be profoundly sure to distrust both of you." Next, he employed a belabored poker image, saying this bit of flirting "differed" from the card game because a *pair* would beat "three of a kind" and he ended, in almost Lewis Carroll non-

Robert Walker Blaine, Blaine's oldest son. (Actually, he had been preceded by a first-born brother, Stanwood, who died at the age of three.) Walker, in later years, was very close to his father, filling important positions in the State Department on the two occasions when the elder Blaine was secretary of state.
HAMILTON, *BIOGRAPHY OF JAMES G. BLAINE*

sense, with, "…if you ask me how I will constitute the pair and get rid of the third, my simple and direct answer is, that I will drop Mrs. H. and cling to Mrs. H."

That Harriet was made privy to such carryings-on indicates that, if there had ever been any tension in their marriage about his attentions to other females—e.g., Elizabeth Bigelow Lawrence—that all seemed in the past. We do not hear anymore about E. L. and Blaine at this juncture and wonder if she even supported him when he ran for president. She had always been a Democrat, anti-Lincoln, anti-abolitionist, and her father had been a Democratic congressman.

Walker, who was job hunting in this period, took time to write his father about what he saw as the future for James G. Blaine. His first point was that the book was a centerpiece of the Blaine legacy. "I can really look back in many ways upon the outcome of the election in '84 with pleasure," Walker stated, "for I feel that with the responsibilities of the presidency, added to the necessity of finishing your book, the work would have been too great. As it was, the book took more than a year of hard work in the quiet of the country and of Washington and will prove as valuable a memorial of your fame as a successful administration. But for the future I have great hopes and great ambitions, centered not upon the presidency, but upon your going back into public life...." And Walker added, "I am glad you think of having a home once more in Washington."[5]

Meanwhile, at home in Maine, Blaine also briefly left off writing and involved himself in the planning of a "Reunion" of the legislature and state government, perhaps the original forerunner of a tradition now celebrated annually in the Augusta state house and known as "Welcome Back Day." Harriet, who was enlisted to help in organizing this three-day gathering, January 5-8, 1886, shared her husband's skepticism that it should not have been held in the winter. "The Reunion will turn out badly. All my Congressional invitees have written me they must stay in Washington," she informed Walker.[6] Yet these festivities were a smash success. Despite a pouring rainstorm the first night, a large, elegantly dressed crowd attended Governor Frederic Robie's reception in the capitol building. "Mr. Blaine came in to pay his respects to the Governor about 8 o'clock, but preferred the small groups of the Governor's rooms to the 200 or more in the large hall," the *Portland Daily Advertiser* reported, and that Mrs. Blaine and members of her family were sitting quietly, generally unrecognized, among those resting on the benches in the big rotunda. The next day, Harriet Blaine was seated up front in the house chamber, where 400–500 persons had assembled for ceremonies and nostalgic talks from ex-members like eighty-seven-year-old Seth O'Brien of Warren, the oldest present, and the venerable Democrat, William Dickey of Fort Kent, who spoke of his dear colleague, the late Jonathan Cilley of Thomaston, who as a Maine congressman, was the last elected official to die in a duel in D.C. James G. Blaine was a featured speaker that evening at the concluding banquet, where among other things, he "deplored the change from annual to biennial sessions." He also brought Uncle Solon Chase up on the stage and invited him to entertain the audience, which the old Greenbacker did presumably with a bunch of "snappy" rural Maine humor stories.

Later that same year of 1886, Blaine took a more extensive sentimental journey, but one that political pundits could classify as having an eye toward a presidential horizon. He went back to his home region of Pennsylvania and toured the area with all the fanfare and flourish of a candidate.

Although Blaine wasn't running for anything, he *was* accumulating favors by promoting G.O.P. hopefuls in this southwestern section of Pennsylvania. He'd brought along his two younger sons, Emmons and Jamie, as well as his former campaign manager, Stephen B. Elkins. The *Pittsburgh Commercial Gazette* of October 22, 1886, chronicled every step of the journey, which proceeded from Pittsburgh and traveled south down the Monongahela to the town of Elizabeth, Pennsylvania, where Blaine's late mother had lived with his sister, Elizabeth Blaine Walker, who a year and a half previously had also passed away. They were met in West Elizabeth by a Dr. J. E. Shaffer, described as an old friend of the Blaine family, and he guided them up the river to Lock 3, from which "Mr. Blaine's farm of over 1,000 acres of coal land" on the river's right bank could be observed. Also in sight was the shattered wreck of a coal barge, which drew the not unexpected wisecrack, "That's all that's left of the Democratic Party." Climbing to the highest point of land at Lock 3, Blaine stated he had first been to this spot as a boy of twelve. It had retained a special place in his heart and he revealed that in Maine, he had often thought of building "a neat little cottage there to end his days." Pointing to the coal lands, he also referred to them as his "savings account." His knowledge of regional history next came into play. Lock 3, he told the assembled crowd, had been the site of an encampment of U.S. soldiers sent by President Washington to put down the Whisky Rebellion in 1793. He noted, too, that across the river had been the northernmost boundary of

Williams Emmons Blaine, named after a friend of his mother's family, Emmons. Like his older brother Walker, he attended the prestigious prep school Phillips Academy, Andover (at least for a time), and then went on to Harvard while Walker went to Yale. He married an heiress, Anita McCormick, daughter of the creator of the famous McCormick Reaper. Like Walker, he died young, while his parents were still alive.
HAMILTON, *BIOGRAPHY OF JAMES G. BLAINE*

the Province of Virginia's claim to Pennsylvania territory prior to the Revolution and the establishment of the Mason-Dixon line.

Then, the Blaine party returned to Elizabeth—to East Elizabeth—pausing at Dr. Shaffer's home for a reception and visiting the house in which Blaine's mother and sister had lived. In West Elizabeth, they had meetings with "Judge Ewing and Colonel Searight [his aged uncle, John Hoge Ewing, and his college classmate, Tom Searight]". The town of Belle Vernon, also on the river, was the next stop, where Blaine was presented with two glass canes from the R. C. Schmertz glassworks. As he was accepting them, a voice from the crowd called out, "Protect the glass workers!" and

Blaine, quick as a wink, reflecting his record on protective tariffs, shot back, "Is not that what I have been doing for twenty years?" Blaine's famously prodigious memory was continually called into play during this trip. The Honorable George V. Lawrence tried to test it and Blaine responded by remembering how he'd heard Lawrence speak in 1840 when running for Congress (at the time Blaine was ten years old). Likewise, Blaine reminisced about a certain Dr. Louis Marchand who, during his boyhood, lived in a particular house people pointed out and that he was called "Mad Dog Marchand," because he had a sure cure for rabies.

West Brownsville, Blaine's birthplace, was reached around dusk and he showed his sons where he'd been born. Afterward, they all went across the Monongahela into Brownsville, where a crowd of 3,000 was waiting. It was estimated that Blaine shook 3,000 to 4,000 hands at a subsequent reception in the Monongahela House. Here, another memory test took place and was recorded in full by the *Gazette* reporter. A man named Van Hook approached Blaine and asked, "When did you last see me?" Blaine replied, "Thirty-nine years ago." Van Hook shook his head. "No, thirty years." Blaine countered, "No, you and I were at the theater in Pittsburgh in 1847." Van Hook, after a long, thoughtful pause, conceded, "Right."

Before leaving Brownsville, Blaine took his boys to see their grandparents' graves in St. Peter's Cemetery, following which the party moved on over the National Road to Washington, Pennsylvania, and his alma mater, Washington and Jefferson College, where, he addressed the Young Republicans. On the sour grapes side, the Pennsylvania Democrats were quoted as saying that the poor condition of Republicans in the state had prompted Blaine's "rescue mission."

Yet he did, as well, receive a note several weeks later sent from overseas by a prominent Democrat, ex-U.S. Senator George H. Pendleton of Ohio, currently the U.S. ambassador to Germany, saying "...I am pleased to see you have had such a gratifying tour through Pennsylvania...." Pendleton, it may be remembered, had bought Blaine's 16th Street lot in Washington and built a house on it and he is also remembered for the Pendleton Bill, the first real civil service reform after Garfield's assassination.

Some eight months later, the Honorable and Mrs. James G. Blaine left on an extended trip to the British Isles and Europe, accompanied by their two unmarried daughters, Maggie and Harriet. This version of the classic grand tour abroad may well be viewed as a reward for the completion of *Twenty Years of Congress* and a well-earned respite for Blaine from his herculean labors.

Their sailing date was June 7, 1887. Two days before, Harriet recorded this piquant if scary episode taking place: "Augusta, June 5, 1887: Blainey ran away yesterday noon just as his dear grandpa was about sitting down to his last [before the trip] dinner. I galloped. H. galloped, we galloped all three, and the dear little culprit was found hunting his home in the Sturgis' yard. 'I didn't run away, grandpa; I didn't go near the track.'"[7] With that high-pitched plaintive cry in mind, we then have grandma's testimony of the following day when the Blaines set out on the first leg of their journey, taking that same railroad track, which runs at the end of what is now Capital Park across the street from their home. Blainey came to wave goodbye, seated on the river bank with four maids and José, the mastiff dog, and catching sight of him, the normally phlegmatic Mrs. B. admitted her "heart broke…. *That* little figure in a Hitt hat [a present from the Hitt family?] with its red streamers, waving to his grandma, I shall never see again [meaning he was going back to his parents]." They were en route to New York City, where they boarded the German steamer SS *Ems,* bound for Southampton, England. All of this intelligence was included in a letter from shipboard sent to "Miss Dodge" and her postscript to Cousin Abby was, "I received your good-bye at the Fifth Avenue [Hotel] on that last day of unutterable confusion. You must come out to us…" which "Miss Dodge" eventually did, joining the Blaines midway during their trip.

London was the first stop—for theater-going, fancy dress dinners, the Queen's Garden Party, etc., and Queen Victoria's arrival was described, coming through a line of visitors, using "a little cane"—coaxing a bit of Yankee tut-tutting from Harriet regarding

English females going ga-ga over royalty. "It was not an impressive sight to see all the ladies falling backward before this little and old woman, like waves dying on the seashore. That they should be willing to do it, I found it hard to understand, for the curtseying amounted to obeisance...." And Harriet finished her assessment of British ways with, "Nothing here has surprised me more than the gloomy character of English enjoyment, as compared with the gaiety at home."[8]

From London, the Blaines went to Scotland and a highlight of the entire overseas adventure—the first of two visits to Andrew Carnegie's castles. Harriet wrote how they were pampered: "...a gillie in tartans to wake us every morning with his pipes, a coach and four to take us daily whithersoever we will, two cooks to spread a table before us in this garden of the Lord, and twenty servants to wait upon us at bed and board. Andrew Carnegie may be little, but his hoard and heart are great and he is a happy bridegroom [he had married Louise Whitefield about three months earlier] and rejoiceth as a bridegroom to have his happiness sure...."[9] The friendship between James G. Blaine and Andrew Carnegie seemed a solid one. How it began is not exactly clear. In March of 1882, Harriet mentioned Carnegie's name for the first time in her correspondence, with Blaine off to western Pennsylvania to inspect his coalfields and scheduled to meet Carnegie at Harrisburg. But there was apparently more to their connection than merely a shared interest in coal and steel and the greater Pittsburgh region. One of Carnegie's biographers, Burton J. Hendrick, in *The Life of Andrew Carnegie*, explained, "Blaine's nomination [in 1884] had been received joyfully by Carnegie, for the men were friends, had many outlooks in common, and Blaine's intellectual brilliancy in Carnegie's eyes set him far ahead of the ruck of contemporary American politicians...."[10]

Also, an appellation applied to Carnegie—"the star-spangled Scotsman"—could in a sense be applied to Blaine, too. They certainly shared a "Scottishness" and when, in the summer of 1884, sailing off the West Country coast of southwest England, Carnegie heard of Blaine's G.O.P. victory at Chicago, he fired off a telegram of congratulations, very Scottish in its borrowing from *MacBeth*:

The anti-Blaine humor magazine Puck, *commenting on Blaine's position in 1888, watching the fight for the G.O.P. presidential nomination from one of Andrew Carnegie's estates in Scotland. (That's Carnegie behind Blaine, in a kilt and with a fishing rod.) Blaine didn't run that year.*
MAINE HISTORIC PRESERVATION COMMISSION

"Glamis thou art and Cawdor, and shall be what thou art promis'd."—an unfortunate choice of role model, perhaps, given the Scotch usurper's gory end in Shakespeare's drama. Yet with Carnegie entertaining his political friend in Scotland and a Republican National Convention of 1888 less than a year and a half away, speculation on Blaine's intentions had to be in people's thoughts. Who else did the G.O.P. have to run against Grover Cleveland?

Nothing made it seem more certain that Blaine was running than some actions he took after their party exited Scotland, vis-

*The Blaines and the Carnegies at one of the multi-millionaire's castles in
Scotland in 1888. Carnegie, himself, holding his bowler hat, stands
behind an imperious-looking Harriet Blaine. James G. Blaine is seated to
the right, and between them is Carnegie's bride, Louise Whitefield, whom
he had married three months earlier.*
HARRISON, *A TIMELESS AFFAIR*

ited Germany, and settled temporarily in Paris. The tariff was still
a major issue in the U.S., and back home, President Cleveland sent
a message to Congress on December 6, 1887, proposing reductions
in its high rates. On December 8, Blaine fired back a rebuttal, using
an exclusive interview he'd sought from the Paris correspondent
of the *New York Tribune*, G. W. Smalley. Billed as setting forth the
protectionist's point of view with "clearness, force, subtlety, and
cunning,"[11] his message received instant national attention. A Grover Cleveland biographer, Alyn Brodsky, characterized this note-
worthy intervention as follows: "Its gist: if *he* were President [and
the interview suggested he was entering the lists once again] he
would maintain the high tariff, repeal the internal revenue tax on
tobacco [giving millions of Americans a Christmas present of
cheaper cigars] and earmark the whiskey taxes...to fortify [with
shore batteries] all major Atlantic cities."[12]

However, once having established himself as the odds-on favorite for the 1888 G.O.P. nomination, Blaine proceeded to send out

more news from overseas. Florence, Italy, became the site for his shocking announcement, contained first in a letter sent from that Renaissance city to B. J. Jones, the Republican National Committee chair and aired subsequently in a *New York World* interview, that he would not be a candidate again, believing a candidate who had run and been defeated, should not reenter the lists. A heads-up on what he was planning had been sent by Harriet to his faithful sidekick Joe Manley shortly before he released the Jones letter. "Mr. Blaine wishes me to write you a confidential letter to prepare you for his letter of declination which is now nearly ready to be mailed...." A point she emphasized was that other candidates wanted the job and "he thinks the only nomination which would be mandatory on him would be a unanimous one."[13]

One explanation at the time for this quixotic decision was illness, that he had caught a chill on their way to Italy and been bedridden in Milan before moving on to Florence. A lively fear attacked Blaine, a noted hypochondriac, that he had suffered paralysis, but in Florence, a Doctor Baldwin told him it was "not paralysis at all, but uric acid, which is the acid of gout."[14]

Consternation and disbelief on the other side of the Atlantic was widespread. Letters poured into Maine, and the "Plumed Knight's" old supporters tried to rally around John L. Stevens, Blaine's former partner at the *Kennebec Journal*, who had come back to live in Augusta after fifteen years in the diplomatic corps. During that spring of 1888, there was no lack of dismay, hope, armchair quarterbacking, and speculating. An Ohio lawyer, W. H. West, was among the disheartened. "The Florence letter of Mr. Blaine has greatly depressed his numerous and enthusiastic following." On the other hand, the chief justice of the Kansas Supreme Court, Albert H. Horton, insisted that the entire Kansas delegation, all for Blaine, might go for him, anyway. Back in West Virginia, Stephen B. Elkins saw a ray of light that if a majority of the New York State delegates "should insist upon Blaine's nomination," it could lead to his receiving the G.O.P. nod unanimously and he also noted how Patrick Ford of the *Irish World* was "insisting no other Republican could be elected." The chair of the Republican State Committee in Pennsylvania, Thomas Cooper, was afraid "the Blaine men will drift." One letter spoke of "thousands in the West who will wade 20 miles through mud to vote for Blaine." A Democrat named H. B. McGregor even wrote from Illinois, "Stevens—keep up the fight. Double shot your guns. Any patriot is your friend...." This man liked Blaine's foreign policy—enforcing the Monroe Doctrine—"ready to show a whiff of gunpowder...."

But as the date of the convention neared, the signs from Europe were not encouraging. In early May, Whitelaw Reid, the ardent Blaine supporter and editor-publisher of the *New York Tribune,* let Stevens know he'd heard from Andrew Carnegie who wrote that Mrs. Blaine had written to Mrs. Carnegie from Italy that the Blaine family would "certainly not sail [for the U.S.] until after the [Republican] convention."

As it happened, the Blaines had returned to Scotland and were staying with the Carnegies in Scotland at another of their castles during the Chicago events. It has been said that the "the convention marked time" for three days, waiting for word from Scotland. Carnegie pleaded with Blaine to change his mind, but to no avail.

Stephen Elkins was in Chicago, in touch with Carnegie and Blaine at Cluny Castle and able to receive messages. Finally, this bit of cipher reached him: "Too late the victor immovable take trump and star whip." So just as Blaine, eight years earlier, had been able to play kingmaker by throwing his support to Garfield, here, too, he was dictating the outcome, or a part of it. The cryptic communication translated as, "Tell the boys to go for Indiana's Benjamin Harrison for President and New Jersey's William Walter Phelps for Vice-President." Only the fact that Phelps declined the honor spoiled a perfect gambit. That place on the ticket went to Levi P. Morton of New York.

Was all of this maneuvering Blaine's clever game of poker? His gamble, if such it had been, did pay off. Harrison took the presidency, with further help from him, and offered him his old job back of secretary of state. There was no hesitation in his accepting the post, as if that had been his real goal all along.

Certainly, he showed no chagrin about not running. Harriet stated, "Not for worlds would he have had the campaign on his hands." Still with Carnegie in Scotland when this "final scene in

In his later career, Blaine became extremely friendly with Whitelaw Reid, who bought the previously unfriendly New York Tribune and made it into a pro-Blaine organ. Reid, in 1892, was the Republican nominee for vice president with President Benjamin Harrison, but they were defeated by Grover Cleveland and Adlai Ewing Stevenson.
RIDPATH, *LIFE AND WORKS OF JAMES G. BLAINE*

Blaine's life-long aspirations for the Presidency,"[15] was being played out, Blaine was having too good a time to feel sorry for himself, learning how to fish and dancing the Virginia reel on the castle lawn. Only many years later, after Charles Edward Russell published his book in 1931, was another dimension added to the motives for James G. Blaine's mystifying failure to seek the presidency in 1888. Fear of illness aside and any secret conniving to be secretary of state aside, Russell claims a highly personal reason

The media's view of Blaine's respective weight in President Benjamin Harrison's cabinet—equaling if not surpassing all the other members put together.
MAINE HISTORIC PRESERVATION COMMISSION

underlay the Plumed Knight's withdrawal from the battlefield. His sources, Russell swore, were Walker and Emmons Blaine. Covering the Chicago convention in 1888, he encountered both Blaine boys and was astonished to discover they were there to work AGAINST any boom for their father's nomination. The off-the-record secret, Russell says he learned, was that Harriet had put her foot down. She had been deeply mortified and hurt by the "scandal" over Stanwood's birth raised during the 1884 campaign. She saw such "dirt" being slung anew if Blaine ran again. So this imperious lady, sometimes dubbed "the Queen of Sheba," had intervened. Russell stated it this way, "She conceived that campaign scandals threatened or were likely to threaten her social welfare and she insisted to her husband that he should never again be a candidate."[16]

In any event, the inevitability of his second chance in that all-important post was the talk of D.C. and the nation. *Puck* published a cartoon in its German-language edition that showed Blaine posed next to the president's empty chair, saying to bring on the rest of the Harrison administration to him. A letter to a notable Maine Democrat from a bureaucrat in the lame-duck Cleveland government, dated January 8, 1889, stated positively: "It looks like Blaine for Secretary of State.... Blaine is demanded from all quarters, although he has bitter opposition [and this is interesting in light of subsequent events], especially from the wives of all the leading Republicans, and Mrs. Harrison is in the movement to keep Mrs. Blaine out...." Added, too, is the prediction that if Blaine is named, "there will soon be trouble, as Blaine will attempt to run the Administration."[17]

Blaine's becoming secretary of state once more could therefore be considered a win-win outcome of possibly a whole set of machinations.

1. Beale, Vol. 2, p. 121.
2. Richard Walden Hale. *The Story of Bar Harbor* (New York: Ives Washburn, Inc., 1949), p. 168.
3. Hamilton, p. 633.
4. Ibid., p. 634.
5. Ibid., p. 640.
6. Beale, Vol. 2, p. 128.
7. Ibid., p. 149.
8. Ibid., p. 154.
9. Ibid., p. 156.
10. Burton J. Hendrick. *The Life of Andrew Carnegie* (Garden City, New York: Doubleday, Doran and Company, Inc., 1932), p. 250.
11. Russell, p. 404.
12. Alyn Brodsky. *Grover Cleveland: A Study In Character* (New York: St. Martin's Press, 2000), p. 210.
13. Beale, Vol. 2, p. 171.
14. Ibid., p. 174.
15. Hendrick, p. 327.
16. Russell, p. 408.
17. Letter to shipbuilder Arthur Sewall of Bath (a future Democratic vice-presidential candidate) from a C. B. Morton at the Bureau of Navigation, Department of the Treasury, January 8, 1889.

—◄──

TWENTY

MR. SECRETARY
REDUX

*R*EDUX, SINCE IT MEANS "restored" in Latin, seems an apt qual-
ifying adjective for James G. Blaine's second term as U.S.
secretary of state. To a certain degree, his service in that
all-important post had a seamless quality, those first nine months
in 1881 merging into the three plus years from 1889–92 to be looked
upon in retrospect as a whole. A student of Blaine's foreign policy,
Professor Edward P. Crapol of William and Mary College, even
allowed himself this ringing statement about the choked-off start
under Garfield: "In less than a year, Secretary of State Blaine had
launched a series of diplomatic initiatives that, when fully imple-
mented by his successors, would establish the United States as
one of the major world powers."[1]

The outlines of that new direction initiated by Blaine have already been seen, particularly treating the United States as a Pacific nation and stretching the boundaries of the Monroe Doctrine
concept to fit in Hawaii and other locations in the world's biggest
ocean. One site, well beyond Hawaii, where Blaine had gone to
work in 1882, was Korea, when he gave a green light to an American naval officer, Commodore Robert W. Shufeldt, to open up what
was then called the Hermit Kingdom to American influence.

Closer to the U.S.'s own sphere of influence in the Pacific were
the Polynesian islands of Samoa, lying between Hawaii and New
Zealand. They were a target of the burgeoning European imperialism of the period with—in this case—the Germans and British
looking to displace the native rulers as the French had done in Ta-
hiti. The U.S. Navy also had its eyes on the Samoan island of Tutu-
ila and its harbor of Pago Pago, the finest in that part of the Pacific,
wanting it for a key coaling station between San Francisco and

Australia. In July 1881 Blaine had set in motion the steps by which American Samoa exists today as a U.S. territory. When Blaine arrived at his desk in the State Department in 1889, the Samoan question, German intentions, and civil war in the islands was the first major mess he had to confront.

It proved to be Blaine's initial triumph, as well. With the instincts of a politician, he set the conflict up as a contest between himself and Germany's redoubtable "Iron Chancellor," Otto Von Bismarck, forcing the Germans to reenthrone a Samoan king, Malietoa, who had been exiled. Told that Bismarck was furious, Blaine was said to have responded grandly, "The Chancellor's irritability is no measure of American rights," a remark that has been debunked by Professor David Muzzey as "pure myth" contending the chancellor was not even at the conference in Berlin that settled the matter.[2] It was his son, Count Bismarck, who headed the German delegation, negotiating with Blaine's good friend William Walter Phelps and fellow Mainer, Harold M. Sewall of Bath, the ex-U.S. consul in Apia, Samoa's capital. On October 15, 1889, Phelps wired Blaine from Berlin that he had met young Count Bismarck at a party the night before and been told the "good news" that an agreement had been reached. "I knew your Mr. Blaine would find some way to fix it right," Count Bismarck concluded.[3] In the end, the Germans kept control of Western Samoa, which they relinquished to New Zealand after World War I, while the Americans have hung onto the easternmost islands. Today, Western Samoa is an independent country.

In 1889, also, Blaine would devote a lot more of his attention to Hawaii and U.S. relations with the Sandwich Islands, as they were also known then—an independent native Polynesian kingdom, but one more and more influenced by a growing *haole* (nonnative) population. One of Blaine's first acts was to appoint his old *Kennebec Journal* partner, John L. Stevens, as the U.S. ambassador to the Kingdom of Hawaii. Stevens previously had been our ambassador to Uruguay, Paraguay, and Sweden. It was on June 22, 1889, that the one-time clergyman, in Augusta, received a packet from the State Department in D.C. containing a blank form he could bring to any notary public for taking his oath of office as "Minister," the official title, plus the word that he would receive instructions within thirty days before proceeding to his post and he could spend his waiting time in Maine. The enclosed letter was signed by Walker Blaine and included a postscript sentiment, which one suspects, had been dictated by his father, "I am very glad to offer this recognition of your lifelong services to our party."

Patronage and blatant partisanship were still a lot more acceptable in those days and yet we see a bit of care on Blaine's part, in hiding behind his son's signature the acknowledgment that the Hawaii post was a G.O.P. plum.

However, Blaine made no attempt to conceal his strong effort to have Walker appointed *first* assistant secretary of state. Harrison balked. Blaine contemplated resigning, reconsidered, swallowed his pride and accepted a lesser job for his highly qualified son. But it was an opening rift between the two men.

Another applicant for that same post was Theodore Roosevelt. Here, *Blaine* said no. When Anna Davis Lodge, the wife of Henry Cabot Lodge, was dispatched to plead with him, presumably on the theory that Blaine had a soft spot for charming ladies, he still said no. The reason he gave was Theodore Roosevelt's impulsive and unpredictable temperament and his closing line was, "I do somehow fear that my sleep at Augusta or Bar Harbor would not be quite so easy and refreshing if so brilliant and aggressive a man had hold of the helm."[4]

Blaine's intuitive caution, it should be noted, was later born out by young Roosevelt's subsequent behavior in 1898 as assistant secretary of the navy, in unilaterally launching Admiral George Dewey's attack on Manila on a day his boss was absent from the office. Neither Roosevelt nor Lodge had been fans of Blaine, but had stayed on his good side by voting for him in 1884 and could be deemed his "philosophical descendants" by later pushing an expansionist course for the U.S., arguably beyond Blaine's wildest dreams. Another cohort of theirs in this endeavor, the naval captain Alfred T. Mahan, whose books on sea power inspired them, initially had not liked Blaine, either. In command of a U.S. Navy vessel stationed in Peru at the time of the Pacific War, Mahan ironically had seen Blaine as too reckless, too aggressive, and once declared in 1884, "Luckily, Mr. Blaine is not yet President…. If that magnetic statesman were in office, I fancy the American diplomats would be running around in the magazine [ammunition supply room] with lighted candles."[5]

Although Blaine never set forth a coherent U.S. policy for annexation of territory beyond our continental limits, he once did famously endorse the idea that three places merited consideration "to be taken." All were islands or groups of them—Hawaii, Cuba and Puerto Rico. The context of his remark was in answer to an inquiry from President Harrison about the possibility of the U.S.'s buying the "Danish Islands [now the U.S. Virgin Islands]." At the time, Blaine did not consider that purchase (which was not accomplished until 1917) a worthy project and he so informed the White House in a communication sent from Bar Harbor. However, by implication, Secretary of State Blaine did seem to keep the U.S. among the contenders of the new imperialism sweeping the world in the latter decades of the nineteenth century. That message of Blaine's to President Harrison in 1891 actually included a sort of timetable. Opportunities for "taking" Cuba and Puerto Rico were "not now imminent and will not be for a generation," he wrote, with amazing foresight. On the other hand, he claimed, "Hawaii may come up for decision at any unexpected hour…and I hope we shall be prepared to decide it in the affirmative."

While Blaine and his surrogate in the Sandwich Islands, John L. Stevens, awaited that ripening of events, the secretary of state still faced a full plate of crises and opportunities that thrust themselves into the forefront of American foreign policy. Resurrecting his suspended "Pan American Congress" was a prime order of business for Blaine, and its opening in the fall of 1889 could be termed an opportunity, as well as a personal vindication. Delegates from eighteen nations crowded into the diplomatic room of the State Department quarters to hear an opening speech of welcome from Blaine. Professor Crapol has pointed out that one enduring legacy of Blaine's "tenacity in launching the modern Pan-American movement" was the erection in Washington, D.C., of a "splendid and imposing headquarters of the Organization of American States."[6] Blaine had been clever enough to appoint his

Blaine's crowning achievement as secretary of state was the convening of the first meeting of the U.S. and Latin American nations and the formation of a permanent organization to help maintain peace in the Western Hemisphere.
MAINE HISTORIC PRESERVATION COMMISSION

friend Andrew Carnegie a U.S. delegate, and seed money for the later building came from that notable philanthropist.

This "International American Conference" began on October 2, 1889, and in his remarks, Blaine said he was speaking on behalf of "the people of the United States" and his welcome extended "to every section and to every State of the Union." Thus, at the close of his speech, he announced the convened meeting would be recessed for a trip of all delegates around the United States, financed by the U.S. government, "with the double view of showing to our friends from abroad the condition of the United States and of giving to our people in their homes the privilege and pleasure of extending the warm welcome of Americans to Americans."[7]

Other rhetoric in Blaine's speech that day had contained some of the factual, even statistical touches he liked to slip into his political talks. "The aggregate territorial extent of the nations here represented falls but little short of 12 million square miles—more than three times the area of all Europe..." and "These great possessions today have an aggregate population approaching 120 million, but if peopled densely as the average of Europe, the total number would exceed 1 billion..." and the nations represented had "borders on both the great oceans whose northern limits are touched by the Arctic waters for a thousand miles beyond the Straits of Behring [*sic*], and whose southern extension furnishes human habitations farther below the equator than is elsewhere possible on the globe."[8]

This sense of vastness of the Americas and, in particular, its contrast with Europe, was a deliberate bit of chauvinism. Blaine's unexpressed agenda—exemplified to an extent by the tour of the U.S., which had been arranged in concert with many chambers of commerce—was to wean our neighbors from their heavy commerce with Europe, especially England, and get them thinking American in their trade policies. The "American states" and the "American nations" were expressions Blaine used again and again in spelling out a program on which they could all agree, such as, no "standing armies beyond those which are needed for public order..." or that "friendship and not force, the spirit of just law and not the violence of the mob" should rule relations within and between American nations, and that the Americas should be drawn together more closely by the "highways of the seas" and work toward the connections made possible by an Isthmian canal, as well as "land routes."

On November 18, after its jaunt around the United States, the group was back in Washington and ready to go to work. Their accomplishments can probably best be expressed by the simple fact that these ultra-individualistic countries, many with a history of distrust not only of their big neighbor to the north but of each other, were even brought together. Some small steps did result; for example, that the U.S. State Department installed a permanent Bureau of American Republics to provide information on Latin America, that some regular steamship routes between North and South America were initiated, and partial reciprocity treaties and arbitration measures were discussed, albeit not totally instituted. A general agreement to oppose any territorial acquisitions by aggression or conquest was unanimously accepted—a plus for the previous U.S. position of opposing Chile's land grab of Peruvian soil and halting (in Blaine's earlier term) a Mexican plan to invade Guatemala. On the negative side, the very pro-English Argentines vetoed a customs union proposal because it might affect their meat and grain exports to the British Isles, nor would they go on the Chamber of Commerce tour, and a Mexican delegate, Mattias Romero, writing in the *North American Review*, expressed his suspicion that the whole thing was a veiled effort to foster a *Yanqui* takeover. The belated addition of Hawaii to the invitees may have lent his bluntness some credibility. Still, the Pan-American idea had legs. The delegates did prepare for similar future events by establishing the International Union of American Republics that later morphed into the Pan American Union and finally became the Organization of American States, which continues active to this day.

On April 19, 1890, at the closing session, Secretary of State James G. Blaine once more addressed his fellow Americans. In his opinion, their greatest accomplishment was in dedicating "two great continents to Peace," speaking of a "new Magna Carta, which abolished war and substituted Arbitration between the American Republics...." And this was not just his opinion. He read them a special statement sent to him from the poet and abolitionist John Greenleaf Whittier, who declared, "If in the spirit of peace the American Conference agrees upon a rule of Arbitration which shall make war in this hemisphere well-nigh impossible, its sessions will prove one of the most important events in the history of the world."[9] As compared to other regions of the globe, the track record in the Americas ever since of keeping armed aggression between countries to a minimum does have to be counted a score to chalk up for Blaine's vision. Furthermore, between October 1889, when the Congress opened, and April 1890 when it ended, James G. Blaine had suffered an unthinkable personal tragedy that would have been enough to crush any man.

In mid-January, 1890, Walker Blaine, living with the family in D.C, came down with a bad cold and within a few days, died of pneumonia or flu at the age of thirty-four. This incredible shock had still not worn off when, beyond all belief, less than three weeks later, another Blaine child was dead. Alice Blaine Coppinger had come east to attend her brother's funeral, caught perhaps the same deadly bug, and expired in the same Blaine home at age thirty, leaving behind two young children. Two funerals of two beloved offspring inside of a month—it could almost appear as if the trials and tribulations of Job had been visited upon the "Magnetic Man" and the remainder of his family.

We can only guess how Harriet felt. Her letters end in the autumn of 1889. Her literary executor, her daughter Harriet, admitted that she, herself, had lacked the courage to look beyond that year for more letters and how her mother went "from sorrow to sorrow, into a darkness that was never lifted in this life."[10]

Blaine did express the obvious thought—"I can find relief only in earnest and constant work"—that one might expect of someone who has suffered such a grievous loss. This sentiment came in a letter he sent from Bar Harbor in September 1890 to his faithful Irish Catholic supporter, Patrick Ford. Included with an apology for not having written earlier, particularly on Irish matters in his role of secretary of state, was a truly pathetic baring of his parental soul—"the afflictions of the past winter"—being his excuse for the delay. "My oldest son and my oldest daughter were taken from before my eyes as it were in a moment, and I was left to the soreness of deep grief. Walker was to me as my right hand. He was as affectionate and as dutiful as a young child—and able enough and wise enough to be my most trusted adviser. He was my constant companion, and besides being a son he was my most intimate and my most treasured friend. My daughter's loss rent my heart; she was a dear child—child always to me though she had two children herself. She had with great devotion and piety connected herself with the Catholic Church, and left behind two interesting boys who, according to her wishes, shall be brought up in their mother's faith...."[11]

Also in existence was a letter sent to Blaine from William Tecumseh Sherman written the same morning the news had reached him in New York City that Alice had died. Whether his words had any effect in bucking Blaine up for the official tasks he had to continue can never be determined, but they had to have touched the stunned, mourning father deeply. The general told the secretary of state, "Now is the time for you to stand by your post of duty.

Walker and Alice are lost to you, but a large family and troops of friends remain." And Sherman reminded Blaine that during the Civil War, his own oldest son, William Ewing Sherman, "Willie," age nine, a redhead like his father and beloved by everyone, including all of his troops, had perished almost overnight from malaria. Rhetorically, Sherman asked in his condolence letter, "What would you have thought of me in 1863, when my Willie died at Memphis, had I faltered in the great movement then begun which resulted in the end of the war in America?" The crusty career military man with the redhead's temperament finished by admitting, "...I know you will construe me aright as one of your oldest friends, who is as proud of James G. Blaine as his warmest panegyrists...."[12]

Life went on, as it always does. Emmons had been married the previous September to Anita Eugenie McCormick, daughter of the Chicago magnate Cyrus McCormick, owner of the huge McCormick Reaping Machine Works. Following the deaths of Walker and Alice, the young couple learned they were about to have their first child, so the Blaines could at least savor the news of another grandchild on the way and have a flood of pleasant memories accompany these rosier thoughts. At Anita and Emmons's pre-nuptial reception, given in honor of the secretary of state by the bride's father (although a lifelong Democrat), another happy tryst had been announced—the engagement of Maggie to the soon-to-be famous musician Walter Damrosch. The two had met in Scotland during the Blaine visit to Andrew Carnegie's Cluny Castle, where Damrosch had played Wagner on the piano every evening by candlelight. Maggie and Walter's wedding on May 27, 1890, at the Blaines' rented home in Washington, an event graced by the presence of President and Mrs. Harrison, provided a bit of cheer after the loss of Walker and Alice, as did the birth of Emmons Blaine, Jr., on August 29, 1890.

When the Blaines returned to D.C. after book-writing, travels, and the 1888 election, they did not seek to take over their grandiose mansion on Massachusetts Avenue, even though Father was going to be secretary of state again. Instead, they found adequate quarters in the Seward House, which faced Lafayette Square, practically abutting the White House, and so-called because another

*Walter Damrosch, the famed German-American musician—composer
and conductor—who married the Blaines' daughter Maggie after
meeting her at one of Andrew Carnegie's Scotland estates.*
BOYD, *LIFE AND PUBLIC SERVICES OF JAMES G. BLAINE*

secretary of state, William Seward had lived there. He had almost
died there, too, narrowly escaping being stabbed to death at the
hands of one of the plotters involved in the Lincoln assassination.
Some superstitious folks considered the place "cursed." Even earlier, on its very doorstep, a sensational murder had occurred. Daniel Sickles, a pre-Civil War congressman and later a Union general,
shot and killed Phillip Barton Key, son of Francis Scott Key of "Star-
Spangled-Banner" fame, and successfully defended himself on the
grounds that the victim had been carrying on an affair with Sickles's wife. The tragic demise of the Blaine children within those
walls simply added to the uncanny history of that dwelling.

James G. Blaine, at least, could throw himself into his work at
the State Department. There was no lack of drama and confrontation on which to focus his political skills. A trio of major ones during the rest of his term of office were: a particularly nasty clash
with Great Britain, fronting for Canadian seal poachers, who were
violating laws to conserve the fur seal populations on Alaska's Pri-

bilof Islands in the Bering Sea; a lynch mob outrage in New Orleans where Mafia members acquitted by a local court, some of them Italian citizens, were shot to death, prompting unacceptable demands from Italy; and a flare-up of anti-Americanism in Chile leading to a street fight in which two American sailors were killed and sixteen others injured.

The Alaska troubles were nothing new. Once every year, northern Pacific fur seals come ashore in great numbers on the two main Pribilof Islands, St. Paul and St. George, to mate and bear their pups on the beaches. A controlled hunt had been allowed there since Russian days, and the U.S. government leased the 100,000 annual kill out to a company that transported the skins to London in what was a $12 million-a-year industry. But in 1886, Canadian poachers first disrupted this restricted practice, aimed at conserving the resource, by hunting the seals, including pregnant females, out in the open ocean. A crisis brewing for almost half a decade reached its head when in August 1889 several Canadian vessels were seized by the U.S. revenue cutter *Rush*. Pages upon pages of diplomatic notes, histories, and legal arguments were exchanged between the U.S. and Her Majesty's government in London, with Blaine to all extents and purposes taking the high road, as Edward Crapol has written, "by expounding the environmentally sensitive position that...pelagic sealing placed the entire Bering Sea seal population in jeopardy and violated international morality or, in the diplomatic terminology of the time, was *contra bonos mores*...."[13] Well after Blaine left office, an arbitration award upheld his principle of banning seal hunting on the open seas. Yet, as happened with James G. Blaine in the Chile–Peru guano business, a revisionist view of his motives appeared alleging that here, too, he was being false, the "continental liar" again, protecting a pecuniary interest of his or at least of some of his close friends.

The *Alaska Journal* in its winter issue of 1973 carried an article by James T. Gay, who charged that in March 1890, a new lease for Pribilof land sealing was given to the North American Commercial Company whose leaders included several persons with ties to Blaine. The closest was Stephen B. Elkins and another the equally rich Darius Mills, whose daughter was married to Whitelaw Reid.

The author here attacks Blaine for wanting to keep the land seal-ing open while closing the open sea sealing to the Canadians and ignoring the recommendations of a government naturalist named Henry W. Elliott to stop all sealing. Gay's indictment is reminiscent of 1884 and the Mugwumps: "Mr. Blaine tried to suppress the truth as to the abuse on the islands and lay all the blame on the poach-ers...the whole business was one of systematic duplicity, pettifog-ging and secrecy in the State and Treasury Departments...and Blaine and C. Foster, dominated by Steve Elkins, a silent partner in the present Seal Company." The *London Times* was not shy, after Elliott made his views public, to equate Blaine's action, which in-cluded stonewalling the British offer to cease all seal hunting, to the "Little Rock Railway Affair" and claim that Blaine was deter-mined "to allow the North American Commercial Company to have the benefits of its contract with the U.S. government."

War With Italy were headlines in the next crisis Blaine faced—that is, in the more yellow-journalism newspapers of the era. It was an overblown reaction to a stinging telegram Blaine had received on March 24, 1891, from the Italian foreign minister, the Marquis Rudini. In peremptory terms, Rudini demanded the punishment of the New Orleans lynch mob members who had slaughtered those Italian prisoners, plus an indemnity, or face the threat of the recall of the Italian ambassador "from a country where he is unable to obtain justice." With infinite patience, Blaine tried to explain the complicated system of justice in the United States, its different jurisdictions, and how the punishment of the perpetrators in this instance fell into the bailiwicks of New Orleans or the State of Lou-isiana, or both—and only after a good bit of no doubt uncompre-hended verbiage did he throw in his politician's deal—that under a certain treaty with Italy, the U.S. government would be able to pay "relief of the families of the Italian subjects who had lost their lives by lawless violence." The Marquis Rudini apparently felt he had a good enough out for his government and the war talk, far fetched as it might have been, faded from the newspapers.

There was nothing farfetched about a possible war with Chile. The USS *Baltimore* docked in Valparaiso right after the elected pres-ident of the country had been driven into exile and an anti-American chief of state put in his place. On shore leave, a number of sailors off the *Baltimore* were accosted and a Chilean who spat in an American's face was floored by a punch. In the melee that followed, two Americans, a bo's'n named Riggins and a coal heaver named Turnbill, were killed, and sixteen others injured, and the Americans blamed the local police and Chilean soldiers who took the side of the mob. On top of this outrage, a demand was issued from Santiago for the removal of the American ambassador, Patrick Egan, who at home the Democrat press called a "Blaine Irish-

An artist's rendering of the "New Orleans massacre," a lynching of arrested Mafia members by a rifle-toting mob of local citizens. Blaine was again U.S. secretary of state at the time and his deft handling of the anger of the Italian government prevented an international incident with more serious consequences.
RIDPATH, *LIFE AND WORKS OF JAMES G. BLAINE*

man." Chile's demand was ignored by Blaine, but at the same time, he sought to restrain President Harrison who'd ordered other American warships to the area, from taking precipitous action. Nevertheless, Blaine's opponents accused him of fomenting war while the more jingoistic Republican press accused him of being a coward. In his own mind, assuredly, he hung onto the principle he'd proudly promoted at the Pan-American Congress of settling disputes in the Americas by negotiations, not force. These were tense moments. Riggins's body was brought back and provocatively laid out in state in Independence Hall, Philadelphia. Eventually, as Blaine had hoped would happen, the Chilean government reorganized itself and wiser heads in Santiago prevailed. On January 30, 1892, Blaine expressed his pleasure to Egan that the Chilean hotheads had been rebuked and reparations were to be paid the American victims and their families.

Of continuing interest to Blaine throughout these stormy days, if not always of front page import, was Hawaii. He had sent John L. Stevens to the islands and whether or not he had told him privately to work for the kingdom's annexation is something that can never be determined. Even someone as careless as Blaine in leaving written proofs of his indiscretions would not have been that obtuse. But the two of them were residents of a region, the Kennebec Valley of Maine, which amazingly had a remarkable connection with that far-off tropical archipelago in the Pacific. The connection was so pronounced that Hawaiian historian, Tom Coffman, in his book *Nation Within: The Story of America's Annexation of Hawaii*, includes a two-page centerfold labeled "Life on the Kennebec River" with inset pictures of Luther Severance, missionary Daniel Dole, James G. Blaine, and John L. Stevens superimposed over a drawing of the Augusta waterfront, plus a photocopy of the masthead of the *Kennebec Journal* in 1855, focused on the names of Stevens and Blaine.[14]

Daniel Dole is a name new to us among these Maine personalities connected to Hawaii, but Dole and those islands have an intimate tie. The progenitor of this Hawaiian–American dynasty hailed from the town of Skowhegan upriver from Augusta on the Kennebec, and it was said that Daniel Dole was inspired to do his missionary labors in Hawaii after reading Luther Severance's editorials in the *Kennebec Journal*. In order to be accepted for that work, he needed a wife and he found Emily Ballard, downriver on the Kennebec at Hallowell, willing to accept his marriage proposal. Together they went first to Honolulu and then to Koloa on the island of Kauai, where Dole established several schools. Other Hallowell folks were in Koloa, the Goodale sisters who had married William Ladd and Peter Brimstad, both, themselves from Hallowell and the men who had started Hawaii's first-ever sugar plantation in that small southern Kauai community. The name Ballard, too, was preserved in the Doles' son Sanford Ballard Dole who, as president of the republic that replaced the native kingdom, was one of the most important players in the incorporation of Hawaii into the United States.

What we have here is a snapshot from this one Kauai village of the forces working to make Hawaii American—missionaries, sugar planters, and second-generation politicians—and also, since Dole, to most Americans, means *pineapple,* it was cousins of these Doles who brought that crop to the islands.

Oddly enough, possibly the first concrete act by James G. Blaine in fastening America's permanent hold on Hawaii occurred in 1887 at a time when he was completely out of office. It had to do with U.S. control of Pearl Harbor as a navy base. It also had to do with trade reciprocity, a strong Blaine interest, for when the Hawaiian-U.S. Reciprocity Treaty of 1875 was being renewed, the "Magnetic Man" from Maine used his contacts in Congress, particularly his successor in the Senate and protégé William P. Frye, to slip in an amendment giving the U.S. exclusive rights to Pearl Harbor. Until then, the king of Hawaii, David Kalakaua, had resisted doing so and Kalakaua was someone Blaine never trusted, suspecting him of wanting to sell his kingdom to a foreign power, especially Great Britain. As secretary of state under Garfield, Blaine had worked hard to thwart a British plan to import a large number of workers from India to toil as cheap labor on the sugar plantations, claiming such an influx would "subvert the independence of Hawaii by joining it to an 'Asiatic system.'"[15]

It was in 1887, in addition, that Sanford Dole, then an elected member of the Hawaiian legislature, led a coup that forced a new constitution upon King Kalakaua. Backed by an armed group of *haoles* who called themselves the Honolulu Rifles, Dole and his fellow Americans within the government severely restricted the monarch's remaining powers under a document ever after known as the "Bayonet Constitution." Dole was heard to say that the king would have been attacked if he hadn't signed. "Subverting Hawaii's independence," it seemed was already underway, but from within.

When John L. Stevens was sent in 1889 by Secretary Blaine, David Kalakaua was still king, but on a trip to the U.S. in 1891, he died unexpectedly in San Francisco and was succeeded by his sister, who became Queen Lili'uokalani.

Today in Hawaii, a newly arisen native nationalism—often called the "Sovereignty Movement"—has made of Lili'uokalani a revered heroine and martyr. She was the last of the Hawaiian royalty, forcibly removed from her throne in a "revolution" carried out when it was thought she would try to revoke the Bayonet Constitution and not just remain a puppet. John L. Stevens is seen as the villain of the piece because as the American ambassador he called in U.S. marines and sailors to protect the American insurgents who overthrew the queen, established a republic, and named Sanford Dole its president.

The date was January 17, 1893. At the time, James G. Blaine lay gravely ill in Washington and ten days later, he died. He had not been secretary of state for the past eight months, but assuredly had some sense of the turmoil occurring in the Hawaiian Islands. Whether news ever reached him of the actual revolution and downfall of Queen Lili'uokalani is unknown, and the immense political complications that unfolded before Hawaii was accepted by the U.S. all took place after his death.

It seems certain that he would have approved, not exactly as to how the takeover and annexation were accomplished, but that it was done. In Blaine's expansionist ideas, the uppermost thought always expressed was fear of outside powers intruding upon perceived American interests. Except for his uncharacteristic racist railing against Chinese immigration, his outward look seemed low-key, avoiding Kiplingesque expressions of "White Man's burden" and the Anglo-Saxon chauvinism then becoming fashionable in the United States—perhaps because he was more Celtic than Anglo-Saxon, himself.

The Reverend John L. Stevens who, like Blaine, wrote books, had no compunction about dosing his photo-illustrated volume entitled *Picturesque Hawaii* with professions of Anglo-Saxon superiority in regard to the Polynesian inhabitants of the islands. That this work was co-authored with a Professor W. B. Oleson of Honolulu, and the photo captions provided by his daughter, Miss Nellie Stevens, makes it a bit hard to charge all of the prejudice to Stevens, but beyond any doubt these views so strongly expressed are his beliefs.

Describing Honolulu, the text states that the visitor to that city knows he is in the tropics, seeing palm trees, smelling magnolia and plumeria, but adds: "And yet it is impossible for him to be ashore five minutes without realizing that, after all, the enginery [*sic*] and propelling power in this wonderful land is not tropical but Anglo-Saxon...the Anglo-Saxon is the moving spirit.... He wears a summer suit 12 months in a year but rarely looks tropical in any particular.... Such is the Anglo-Saxon whose home is in this land of sunshine...he retains to the full his race characteristics... seeming indeed to be a foreigner in the presence of this unique vegetation, he is yet its author, having made Honolulu what it is by his enterprise in introducing foreign plants and in encouraging their growth. Most people do not realize this. They do not know that when the white man came, Honolulu was a treeless sandy plain, with a fringe of cocoanut trees along the shore."[16]

The implicit meaning was that without the white man (read Anglo-Saxon), Hawaii would be a desert and that the same raison d'etre used on the American continent to absorb Indian land was applicable in the islands. The *Kanakas* (a pejorative term for Hawaiians) didn't work it, so they should lose it. It was argued that "*Poi* [the basic Hawaiian food made from taro root] has proved the greatest obstacle to the advancement of Hawaiians" because the ease of growing taro relieves the natives "from any genuine struggle for life...." Taro grew so well, according to Stevens and Oleson, that Hawaiians had no incentive to acquire more land, so they were left with much time on their hands. "...he [the Hawaiian] passes away the balmy hours in innocuous desuetude, lying prone on the grass for hours in some convenient shade....Today's comfort fills his horizon and there is only one date in his almanac."[17] Clearly, that shameful perpetual indolence had to end and who better to uproot it than those doughty Yankee missionaries from rock-bound Maine and other "hard-scrabble" U.S. locations. The authors could boast, "Christianity saved the Hawaiian race from complete collapse and disappearance from the earth...." And they could also predict, with total inaccuracy, one might add, that "the wicked, sensual *hula* dance has gradually died away as civilization advanced" and would disappear entirely before long.

The book in many respects is one continuous effort to excuse and justify that "Revolution of January 1893," led by the secret Annexation Club, with Stevens's overt help. At the time of its publication, Sanford B. Dole's "Republic" was in power, but there was resistance in D. C. to annexation and Stevens was out of the State Department and being strongly criticized for his go-it-alone actions in bringing American troops ashore to help the local "Committee of Safety" accomplish its aims.

James G. Blaine is mentioned only once. The authors quote from a dispatch sent by him, dated December 1, 1881, while he was still secretary of state in the Arthur administration, to the then U.S. ambassador at Honolulu. It began, "The decline of the native Hawaiian element in the presence of newer and sturdier growths must be accepted as an inevitable fact, in view of the teachings of ethnological history...." This vacuum created, Blaine went on, must be filled "in an American sense, not in an Asiatic or a British sense," and he added, "There is little doubt that, were the Hawaiian Islands, by annexation or district protection, a part of the territory of the Union, their fertile resources for growth of rice and sugar would not only be controlled by American capital, but so profitable a field of labor would attract intelligent workers thither from the United States."[18]

Clearly discernible in these words was that sense of Blaine's attitude toward expansion previously mentioned. There was no talk of Anglo-Saxon domination; indeed, a fear of the most Anglo-Saxon of nations, Great Britain, stepping in, and also the strong link to American commerce, a hallmark of his own career in the Republican Party, which he helped make an instrument of American capitalism and big business.

Tom Coffman, in his book a century or more later, plumbs the question of what role Blaine, while still secretary of state under Harrison, did play in producing the eventual results. He depicts Stevens writing Blaine in early 1892 and stating, "...the time is not distant when the U.S. must say yes or no to the question of annexation," and then later asking that question point-blank: "...are you for annexation?" From Secretary Blaine there was only discreet silence. No paper trail, anyway. But as Coffman writes, "Had he disapproved, he should have sent a strong caution. By not doing so, Blaine...incurred a clear responsibility for Stevens's actions...."[19]

Also, "Slippery Jim" was accused of another of his diabolical acts of cleverness in failing to help American sugar planters in Hawaii keep their advantage when a new Republican tariff schedule authored by future President William McKinley went through Congress. Blaine had fought manfully and successfully, although he was not in Congress at the time, to implant the idea of reciprocity in the McKinley Bill. But this particular reciprocity—the maintenance of a price advantage for Hawaiian sugar—was not restored. Therefore, the argument was, those American agriculturists in the Hawaiian Islands were given an added motive for wanting to join the United States. It is well known that Blaine, as secretary of state, met with Lorrin Thurston, a leader of the Annexation Club, who arrived in D.C. with a letter of introduction from Stevens. Thurston was frustrated that Blaine had not been well enough to spend more time with him, according to Coffman,[20] and on his way back to Hawaii, he sent Blaine a long list of reasons for annexation, beginning with the McKinley Tariff and ending with a prediction (mostly erroneous) that native Hawaiians would welcome the move.

Not long afterward, in the spring of 1892, Blaine resigned as secretary of state. It was true he had been ill a good deal. But health wasn't the reason for his curt note to President Harrison, giving up his job. The president's curt note back, accepting his decision, demonstrated, as well, the estrangement between them. Harrison had been worrying for some time that Blaine would run against him. Various elements within the Republican Party, like New York State boss Tom Platt, were opposed to another term for Harrison. The West supposedly wanted Blaine to combat the growing strength of Populism in that region. He was said to be more popular in Indiana, Harrison's home state, than the president.

The astounding fact was that Blaine *had* decided to run. Thus, his resignation. Why hadn't Harriet protested? The simple answer: she had changed her mind. The objections of 1888 no longer carried any weight with her; verily, she was openly eager for her husband to win—and in a letter printed by Gail Hamilton, there was this discussion of Blaine's health that encompassed the rationalizations of his wife: "Understand, if we get the nomination, I don't think your father any more likely to lose his health than if we don't. Likewise with the presidency. He may be ill but there will in no wise be cause and effect, judging from the past. His worst illness was his first when he was in the prime of life. His best work has all been done since then. He has too much life in him to lay himself on the shelf for its lack...."[21]

The Republican nominating convention of 1892 was held in Minneapolis. Walker was dead but Emmons, now living in Chicago, attended and this time his mission was not to block a nomination but once more help to defeat an incumbent president and have his father go forth a second time to be the Republican Party's plumed champion.

---

1. Crapol, p. 61
2. Muzzey, p. 401.
3. Hamilton, p. 713.
4. Warren Zimmerman. *First Great Triumph* (New York: Farrar, Straus and Giroux, 2002), p. 211.
5. Ibid., p. 86.
6. Crapol, p. 121.
7. Hamilton, p. 680.

8. Ibid., p. 678.

9. Ibid., p. 681.

10. Beale, Vol. 2, p. 257.

11. Hamilton, p. 714.

12. Ibid., p. 715.

13. Crapol, p. 132.

14 Tom Coffman. *Nation Within: The Story of America's Annexation of Hawaii* (Kame'ohe, HI: Epicenter, n.d.).

15. Crapol, p. 78.

16. John L. Stevens and W. B. Oleson. *Picturesque Hawaii* (New York: Union Publishing House, 1894), pp. 49–50.

17. Ibid., p. 16–17.

18. Ibid., p. 10.

19. Coffman, p. 111.

20. Ibid., p. 117.

21. Hamilton, p. 719.

TWENTY-ONE

LAST BLOWS
AND LAST ACTS

EVER THE JOURNALIST, in an eyewitness account of an event that he covered, Charles Edward Russell paints a stunning picture of James G. Blaine toward the close of his life. It happened near the end of May 1892. Rumors Blaine would resign as secretary of state and oppose President Harrison had been rife. Russell, who alone among biographers raised the story of Mrs. Blaine's reluctance for him to run in 1888, now told another story about why she'd changed her mind. She didn't like Harrison. Not only had he refused to appoint her son as assistant secretary of state, but he had also blocked a promotion for her widower son-in-law Colonel Coppinger—"deliberate hostility," she'd deemed it, and besides she'd been assured that the dirt-slinging of 1884 could not be repeated. The word was out, as early as 1891, that she had told her husband to go for the prize.

The scene Russell described in May 1892 happened a few weeks before Blaine's actual resignation and the start of the Republican National Convention. Russell, then a political reporter for the *New York Herald*, was at Jersey City where Blaine arrived by train, preparatory to boarding a ferry to Manhattan. "I saw him descend from the parlor car. With astonishment I watched him move down the platform toward the ferry. If ever there was a man whose appearance proclaimed physical wreckage it was his. The hand of death seemed upon him. He had always been pale, but now his face was overspread with an ashen grey and more heavily lined than I had ever seen it...."[1] About half a dozen reporters were there. The time was about 3:00 P.M. Blaine told them to come to the Fifth Avenue Hotel where he'd be staying for an interview at 6 P.M., and did so, Russell commented, "in a manner all different from his old-time self-possessed geniality."

When Blaine met the press in a little private dining room, he looked "inexpressibly tired and unhappy." His greeting was, "Well, gentlemen, what can I do for you?" and his "hollow and weak" voice was "Full of poignant weariness." The hard-boiled reporters seemed touched, Russell felt. They questioned him about any plans of his to run for president. At this point, all he would answer was, "I have come to New York only to see my oculist, and for no other reason," a response he repeated several times, emphasizing that his visit had "no political significance." As the reporters exited, Russell recorded that George Spinney of the *New York Times*, in a "strange, awe-stricken" whisper, asked him, "Did you ever before interview a dead man?"

Yet once again, Blaine, Russell learned, was being "Slippery Jim." That same day, a colleague on the Blaine-friendly *Chicago Tribune* tipped him off that the Plumed Knight really *was* a candidate for the presidential nomination, a story he was able to break the next morning for publication.

The result in Minneapolis, however, was a fiasco. There was a good deal of enthusiasm in the hall for Blaine, the shouts of "Blaine, Blaine, James G. Blaine" ringing to the rafters, but the votes went to Harrison overwhelmingly on the first ballot.

While the convention was still in progress, the Blaines were traveling from Washington to Bar Harbor. Harriet has left a record of that trip and their seemingly equable reaction to Blaine's fourth defeated attempt for the presidency. She pictures herself facetiously as "the watchman," attending to what is happening in Minneapolis and also keeper of "the eye-glasses—he has broken his." At Portsmouth, New Hampshire, a voice—that of James G. Blaine—calls "Mother" from the other side of the compartment. "I reply, 'Reid is nominated,' that is all"—meaning their good friend Whitelaw Reid has been named the vice-presidential nominee. "From Brunswick to Bangor, I know nothing, nor does he." In Bangor, they have coffee and crackers. They reach Ellsworth after an overnight trip, and Blaine only awakens in time to take the ferry to Mount Desert Island. At 10:00 A.M., they are at Bar Harbor and stop to send telegrams, including one to Whitelaw Reid. "At the house is home. José [the mastiff] on the lawn and a sea and sky triumphant.... How can one be petty when he sits beneath a canopy not of the creation's making and looks on the sea which has outlasted all that we have of knowledge, communing with one's own heart, not head?" Presently, they had a response from Whitelaw Reid and Harriet expressed her opinion that Blaine's congratulatory words to him had relieved "an anxiety" Reid might have had that his longtime friend and hero might be jealous the younger man had won a nomination while he had not.

A famous photograph taken at "Stanwood," the Bar Harbor home of the Blaines, in 1889. The secretary of state has brought the president to his summer retreat. From left to right, front row: Mrs. Henry Cabot Lodge, President Benjamin Harrison, Mrs. Harriet Blaine, James G. Blaine, and (allegedly) Margaret (Maggie) Blaine. On the stairs are: Henry Cabot Lodge, Walker Blaine and Harrison's secretary, E. W. Halford. During the visit, a boat trip was taken on Somes Sound, and the rough water left both Blaine and the president "rather white" and the Turkish minister crying out (in French), "My God, why did I come?"
MAINE HISTORIC PRESERVATION COMMISSION

If there were any lingering chagrin of Blaine's or Harriet's about the loss at Minneapolis, soon, all too soon, they were to know a far greater calamity than just losing another election. All that lovely calm and scenic beauty at Bar Harbor was not to be a heavenly balm for long.

The convention was over by June 12, the date of Harriet's account. Emmons arrived back home in Chicago, "dispirited and worn out," as Gilbert A. Harrison reported in his biography of Anita McCormick Blaine.[2] On June 16, Emmons, who'd been suffering from an undiagnosed intestinal ailment for several months, took sick again. While in bed for the next three days, his temperature rose to 105 degrees. And then, with unbelievable swiftness, like his two other siblings, he was dead, "of ptomaine intoxication with uraemia as a fatal complication," the medical report attested. Some indications were of acute appendicitis. Anita tried without success to get the press to hold back the story until her in-laws in Maine could be informed, but since there were telegraphic problems in Bar Harbor, the Blaines learned from the newspapers that their third child in two years had died. They made it to Chicago for the funeral with daughter Harriet and their only surviving son, James G. Blaine, Jr.

On top of everything else, Jamie, then twenty-four years old, had been a source of aggravation, if not heartbreak, to his parents for the past six years. The trouble had started in the summer of 1886. With the rest of the family in Bar Harbor, the eighteen year old had stayed home by himself in Augusta while being tutored in preparation for applying to college in the fall. On August 16, an attractive young woman from New York City about the same age, Marie Nevins, came to the Maine capital with members of her family on a visit. Eighteen days later, on September 3, Miss Nevins went back to Manhattan. With her—secretly—went Jamie, and the next day they were married!

In such shocking, thoughtless, inconceivable fashion did the nightmare begin for Mother and Father Blaine. Although in 1886 he no longer held office, James G. Blaine was still a towering figure in American public life, a power, and yet he found himself helpless in this situation. A Catholic priest, Father Thomas I. Ducey, rector of

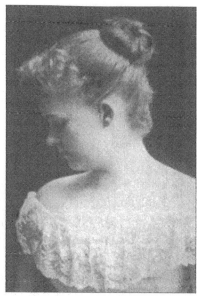

Left: Young "Que J'aime," as his mother punned his name in French, James G. Blaine, Jr., the youngest male in the family. He shocked and horrified his parents by marrying suddenly at age eighteen without their knowledge or permission.
BOYD, *LIFE AND PUBLIC SERVICES OF JAMES G. BLAINE*

Right: Marie Nevins of New York City, the beauty (some say adventuress) who lured young Jamie Blaine into marriage only eighteen days after they met in Augusta—a marriage sundered by a divorce court in, of all places, Deadwood, South Dakota, that awarded her their child and a liberal monetary settlement.
BOYD, *LIFE AND PUBLIC SERVICES OF JAMES G. BLAINE*

St. Leo's Church, had performed the ceremony because Marie was a Catholic and, in order to do so, had obtained a special dispensation from the archbishop of New York, since Jamie had been raised a Protestant. Vigorous protests from Blaine to the two prelates, citing the boy's age, the couple's taking money from a Maine bank account on a false pretense, and no contact with the family, fell on deaf ears. What was done was done.

The next year, Jamie and Marie had a son whom they named James. That the marriage didn't last long was not surprising. Jamie moved back to Augusta by himself. Then, at the beginning of 1892, divorce proceedings were filed by Marie Nevins who had moved to South Dakota and sought alimony and custody of their child.

By then, Blaine was back as secretary of state, battling not only crises like the Bering Strait fur seal fight and the near-war with Chile, but also headline-grabbing bouts of illness magnified by rumors that had him at death's door. Suddenly, headlines from South Dakota were broadcasting the Blaine family linen in equally sensational fashion as Marie Nevins and her mother claimed to the entire nation that Harriet Blaine, acting as a hateful mother-in-law, had viciously broken up her son's marriage, literally imprisoning him in Augusta. To his wife's defense, James G. Blaine came rushing knight-like with another of his finely honed arguments, point by point making his case, including an offer they'd made to the couple of room and board in Augusta, a yearly stipend of $2,500, servants, horse and carriage, etc., turned down by Marie who refused to live in Maine.

The "abandoned" single mother, though, received the court's sympathy, as headlines in Maine's rather gleeful Democratic newspapers reported. Nor did Jamie go out to Deadwood to argue his own case in person. Perhaps on purpose, the Blaines lost, delighted to be rid of a daughter-in-law they couldn't stand, although they would have been happy to have been given custody of the child. They lost little Jim, too, and Jamie was required to pay the plaintiff's court costs of $1,400 and provide $100 a month alimony until further notice.

All grief of this kind, assuredly, paled as they gathered to bury Emmons, and after the funeral, Anita and her baby came to stay with the Blaines at Bar Harbor. Gilbert A. Harrison writes, "She [Anita]...fastened finally on the thought that Emmons would have wished her to be near his despondent parents. Secretary Blaine, seriously ill with Bright's disease, had resigned from President Harrison's cabinet and her place was surely at his side.... Anita went with her baby to Bar Harbor. After spending several days in the Blaine house, she moved into a separate cottage nearby, one with a wide porch on which the child could play on sunny days."[3]

On the child's second birthday, a formal christening was held at Stanwood. There, he officially became Emmons Blaine, Jr. Anita's mother Nettie wrote her husband that the Blaines "received these two dear ones with hearts too full for words." A few friends of

Emmons's had been invited, and the ceremony took place in the drawing room. Anita held the baby, who wore a white dress to which his father's pearl stickpin had been attached. Mother and child, alone as they were, made a sad portrait. Again, to quote Harrison, "The ailing grandfather, who had through the ceremony seemed almost overwhelmed with emotion and was leaning with head bowed on the mantel, brought out a tiny, silver-encased book with a clasp and had all the witnesses inscribe their names."[4]

At the time of Emmons's death, a nice gesture had been made by the Democrats, who were simultaneously holding their national convention in Chicago. The meeting's activities were interrupted and a resolution offered, expressing the entire body's sympathy to the Blaine family. A few days later, at a Democratic rally, when Blaine's name happened to be mentioned, there was loud, spontaneous, and sustained applause. The person speaking quipped, "Blaine seems to have more friends here than he had at Minneapolis," and this offhand remark was followed by a shout from the crowd of, "We are all his friends," to more heartfelt applause.

It was true that Blaine always had admirers among even his most adamant political foes and that much of the harm to him had come from within his own party. "Blaine Democrats" were a well-known, publicly labeled force in Maine. Nationwide, he ran well in some Democratic districts, far better than he did where Mugwumps prevailed among the Republicans. Yet at this twilight of his life, in ill health, out of office, his career ostensibly finished, he remained unswervingly faithful to the G.O.P.—a party man to the very last. Grover Cleveland once more had been nominated by the Democrats, but it wouldn't have mattered who they'd run. It wasn't revenge against Cleveland that motivated Blaine on September 3, 1892, to pen a strong letter in support of the Republican campaign, emphasizing its three main issues—tariff, reciprocity, and a sound currency. In the middle of the race, he went on the stump and gave, as Gail Hamilton described it, "a powerful speech at Ophir Farm, the residence of Mr. Whitelaw Reid, before an audience of all sorts and combinations of men, assembled on the lawn."[5]

He had also prepared an article for the *North American Review*, scheduled for November, on "The Presidential Election of 1892," which Gail Hamilton noted was "distinguished by the magnanimity of its treatment of Mr. Harrison." More than speaking well of the incumbent president, it also praised heavily Blaine's own pet project of trade reciprocity, using Cuba as the best example of its value to the U.S. His State Department statistics showed that for 1892 the U.S. was on track to send 674,000 barrels of flour to Cuba following a reciprocity treaty with that island as against 28,000 barrels the year before, without reciprocity, a gain of $4 million for the U.S. versus $175,000 previously. Along with other items of the Cuban trade, the U.S. was now ahead by $8 million. Then, Miss Hamilton felt she had to add, "If these utterances had not all of the enthusiasm, the swing and vigor of former days, they were yet marvelous productions for a man on the spring of whose life-currents had already been placed the seal of death, whose heart was half-broken with sorrow and whose wise forecast told him that the defeat of his party was a foregone conclusion."[6]

True enough, Harrison lost to Cleveland. The Republicans lost badly, all along the line—the presidency, the Senate, the House. For the first time since 1856, the Democrats controlled the entire federal government.

By October the remaining Blaine family had returned to Washington and that "ill-starred" Seward House. The final act took place there. Blaine's Bright's disease, a kidney inflammation that most likely had been bothering him for years, had become chronic, and such chronic nephritis then was invariably fatal. In late January 1893, Blaine went for a drive with his daughter Harriet. The next day, he was unable to get out of bed and his temperature rose alarmingly. On this occasion, the rumors of his impending demise that so often had been dispelled by his reappearance in seeming good health now rang true. James G. Blaine, indeed, was dying.

His mind stayed sharp to the end. One of those last days, Harriet leaned over his bed and said, "Father, did you know today is Mr. Gladstone's birthday?" and he responded, "That is true. Gladstone is eighty-three today."

On the morning of January 27 his pulse grew very weak and his breathing difficult. Heart failure brought fluid into his lungs, which had already shown signs of tuberculosis. Nitroglycerin was

The last photograph of James G. Blaine
MAINE HISTORIC PRESERVATION COMMISSION

tried; it had worked in the past to stimulate his heart, but no longer did. Surrounding his bed were Harriet, young Harriet, Maggie, Jamie, and Gail Hamilton.

The *Brownsville Clipper* detailed his last moments in one of several pages of articles. "In silent, tearful sorrow they witnessed the closing scenes. The patient lay so quietly that even the doctors were hardly able to say when he died. No word of consciousness, no look of recognition passed. At 10:45 he lay so still that the window shades were raised to give more light, to enable the physicians to determine if life still lingered. Fifteen minutes later they proclaimed him dead."

From the White House that same January 27, 1893, Benjamin Harrison, still president until March, issued a proclamation that began: "It is my painful duty to announce to the people of the United States the death of James Gillespie Blaine, which occurred in this city today at eleven o'clock" All public buildings throughout the U.S. were to lower their flags to half mast and for thirty days, the Department of State would be draped in black. This, the first of a mountainous gush of laudatory tributes, also included: "His devotion to the public interests, his marked ability and his exalted patriotism have won for him the gratitude and affection of his countrymen and the admiration of the world."

Thomas Brackett Reed, Blaine's fellow Maine Republican and another former ex-speaker of the U.S. House, noted for his tart tongue, once notably said, "A statesman is a politician who is dead." That pithy phrase easily comes to mind as one reads over the reported panegyrics from all over the country that followed Blaine's death. Members of the cabinet started it off. Stephen B. Elkins, secretary of war, Blaine's one-time campaign manager, said, "He was one of the greatest statesmen and political leaders the country had ever produced and the most conspicuous leader of his time." William H. H. Miller, the attorney general, added, "He was a born leader of men and richly endowed by nature with all those qualities that make a great statesman." John Wanamaker, the postmaster general proclaimed, "As an all round statesman his name will be cherished with the ten greatest Americans," adding, as a Philadelphian, "Pennsylvania may well be proud of her brilliant son, clever as Henry Clay and eloquent as Daniel Webster."

Maine, as well, hurried to recognize its adopted son. Governor Henry Cleaves had his own announcement of the death out that same January 27, praising Blaine's "long, faithful, and distinguished service to his State and country" and "his noble life...filled with usefulness." U.S. Senator Eugene Hale addressed the U.S. Senate saying, "A very great man has passed from this earth" and in the purple prose typical of that era, went on, "He belonged, Mr. President, not to any one State, but to all the country; and Pennsylvania, which gave him birthplace and nurtured him; and Maine, where he made his home and where he became its first citizen, and which filled his lap with all the honors which she could bestow, mourn him no more today than do the dwellers by the shores of the great Gulf and in the cabins of the far Sierras."

On January 31, 1893, Maine's Sixty-sixth Legislature memorialized the man who had commenced his career within the confines of the very building where they were meeting—the state house in Augusta on Weston's Hill. The two most interesting speeches, departing from the general run of statesmanship-type plaudits, were given by two members from northernmost Aroostook County, Republican Llewellyn Powers of Houlton, and Democrat William Dickey of Fort Kent.

Powers, too, threw in bits of U.S. history. "No man since Abraham Lincoln has been more closely in touch with the hearts of the people and no man's death will be or has been more sincerely mourned than his.... He was a co-worker with Lincoln, with Grant and with Garfield.... In Congress, he was on a par with Thaddeus Stevens, Henry Winter Davis and Roscoe Conkling..." and then, comparing him to illustrious Mainers, "an Evans, a Fessenden, a Morrill, and a Hamlin, yet I sincerely doubt if any of them had so strong a hold on the hearts and feelings of the people as the adopted son whose death we this day mourn."

William Dickey's memories of Blaine were entirely personal. "When I first became acquainted with James G. Blaine he was sitting (pointing) at this reporter's desk and Chief Justice Fuller was there (pointing). That was about 36 years ago. We became very intimate as youngish men at that time...one of the most wonderful young men in conversation that I ever met. He was different from Fuller; Fuller was thoughtful and reserved, with a legal mind; Blaine aspired to political life, and was perhaps one of the most astute and wily politicians that Maine has ever produced, by adoption or by birth.... I called at his house almost every week when we have both been here.... Though we differed in politics, yet as men we never differed. There is no man that I ever became acquainted with whom I loved more.... He was much like Clay as I remember Clay in my younger days...by certain circumstances they were both defeated."

There was one other personal anecdote, coming from a Representative Fairbanks of Bangor, who told of being on a steamer with Blaine to Bar Harbor when a passenger presented his daughter to the famous man—"...a mere child. He took her by the hand and delighted her with his questions, full of sunshine from his great heart. As the boat neared the wharf, he sought out the little girl and bade her a sweet good-bye."

And on February 7, 1893, Representative Harris of East Machias presented a resolution to have Blaine's body buried in Maine, in Augusa.

The funeral was held with a pomp that Blaine had said he hadn't wanted. The president, the cabinet, senators and congressmen, members of the U.S. Supreme Court swelled the crowd that

The scene at Blaine's funeral in Washington, D.C., on January 31, 1893. The former secretary of state, House speaker, and U.S. senator was initially buried in Georgetown, but eventually his body and that of his wife Harriet were transferred to a site in Augusta, Maine, overlooking their home.
BOYD, *LIFE AND PUBLIC SERVICES OF JAMES G. BLAINE*

filled Washington's Church of the Covenant on the last day of January, 1893. Afterward, his body was taken to Oak Hill Cemetery in nearby Georgetown and buried alongside the graves of Walker and Alice.

Despite State Representative Harris's best intentions, Blaine was not interred in Maine—not then. When Harriet died ten years later, on July 27, 1903, she was buried next to him at Oak Hill. There the two of them remained until seventeen years later, when another resolution was presented to the Maine legislature in 1919 and stated, after a preamble of encomiums about Blaine, that "the State hereby requests of his family the privilege of bringing from Washington the remains of himself and his beloved wife and of placing them in the family plot near Forest Grove Cemetery in Augusta and of erecting thereon, with the approval of the family, an appropriate memorial."

Certainly this action was being orchestrated in conjunction with the surviving Blaine offspring. Young Harriet had just made a present of the family home to the state as a memorial, itself, to her son and only child, Walker Blaine Beale, a recent Harvard graduate, killed in action in World War I in France in 1918. Before his death, Walker Beale, who had owned his grandparents' house, bought for him by his own father Truxton Beale, had lent it to the state to use during the war. As the Blaine House, and sometimes called the Blaine Mansion, that property has since 1920 been the domicile of Maine's governors.

On June 13, 1920, the bodies of James G. Blaine and Harriet Stanwood Blaine were transported in a special train from Washington and reburied atop one of Augusta's most scenic hills. Tom Sherman, who was present, wrote: "It was a June of great beauty and the place chosen for the graves was on a high hill overlooking the town. Mr. Blaine had loved to walk there in his lifetime and had delighted in the sweeping view of the river and the distant countryside. Children and grandchildren and cousins had come, and many who even more than they were intimately connected with the past..."[7] including descendants of Eugene Hale and Joseph Manley, and the ceremony was conducted by the Reverend James Ecob, the Blaines' old local pastor. The graves rest in a small park called the Blaine Memorial, off Blaine Avenue, and the original landscaping was done by the famed Olmsted firm, designer of New York's Central Park, who also did plans for the grounds of the Blaine House.

There is no elaborate monument, no stone angels nor even an obelisk, like that marking the graves of Blaine's mother and father in Pennsylvania. Engraved dark grey metal plates lie over the two bodies, bearing inscriptions, and they are simple and matter of fact. For Blaine, it is a recitation mostly of his accomplishments in public life, plus birth date, death date, parents' names; for Harriet, very, very simply: "His wife Harriet Stanwood Blaine, 1827–1903."

One thus learns that she was three years older than her husband.

Despite the gorgeous view, all the way to the Kennebec River and beyond, it is a lonely spot, not often visited.

---

1. Russell, p. 426.
2. Gilbert A. Harrison. *A Timeless Affair: The Life of Anita McCormick Blaine* (Chicago: University of Chicago Press, 1979), p. 170.
3. Ibid., p. 75.
4. Ibid., p. 76.
5. Hamilton, p. 710.
6. Ibid., p. 712.
7. Sherman, p. 150.

EPILOGUE

TOM SHERMAN, Blaine's longtime private secretary, includes in his 1928 book about his employer, an appendix written by Harriet Blaine Beale, the youngest of the Blaine children. She starts her essay, which she originally did for the Maine Writers Research Club, by stating a truism: "The eternal problem for all historians is how to make historic characters into living beings...." And then she proceeds to try to humanize her father.

Her mother had already done a good deal of that in her letters, later collected by the younger Harriet and published in two volumes. So had her Cousin Abby, "Gail Hamilton," particularly in the invaluable assortment of letters with which she peppered her voluminous biography of Blaine. Mostly Harriet Beale's memories were those of a child growing up in the household of a father whose name was a household word throughout the United States. That was a problem for her, as she said, "I was troubled because my father was so much in the public eye, and I hated to have him make speeches." Because he had once told her he was never sure until he heard his own voice that he could speak, Harriet admitted that after any political meeting he addressed, she would "conscientiously but secretly" look at the newspapers to see if he'd been struck dumb on the stage.

Harriet Beale also writes of Blaine's absent-mindedness—"...have you ever noticed that an absent-minded person is always lovable and never mean?" and how he was extremely careless about money. If Mrs. Blaine wasn't there when he left the house, he had to be inspected by the children's nurse, whose name was Maggie. "Now remember, Maggie," Harriet quotes her mother as saying, "a clean handkerchief for Mr. Blaine and at least two dollars in his pocket. I will leave the money here." His checks would often not be deposited and his own check book, which he kept separately from his wife's, was rarely in good order. Once, he found himself overdrawn and made a huge fuss, using his wife's nickname of Hat, which he reserved for very serious moments, "It cannot be, Hat! It is monstrous!" and repeating this mantra until one of the children reported there were undeposited checks beneath a clock in Hat's room—and there were—three of his congressional paychecks, which were promptly banked.

Her father's "terrific energy" and intense curiosity were other facets of Blaine's character that had struck Harriet. One famous incident illustrating these traits occurred in Boston when the family was on a rug-buying quest and Blaine asked so many questions about business aspects of a store that the proprietor became suspicious the customer, whose identity he didn't know, was a rival rug merchant.

Harriet, although very young, retained memories of the "Great State Steal" in Augusta, not only of the danger, the armed men, the continual excitement and the house full of people, coming and going, but also one special memory of Daniel Davis—"Diarrhea Davis"—who eventually became the governor, "spending a happy morning pasting green worsted onto the oaken bucket of my little well to make it look like real moss."

She remembered that "campaign summers were great times for us children." Maine's U.S. Senators Frye and Hale were frequent guests and Hale's father-in-law, old Senator Chandler of Michigan, came once and blasted the Greenbackers with the line, "A greenback is a promise to pay nobody nothing nowhere." Their cousin, General Thomas Ewing, Jr., the Democrat, visiting them, was mistakenly taken for a well-known speaker named T. E. Wing, so that everyone in the house kidded Ewing by calling him Mr. Wing. Robert Ingersoll, of the "Plumed Knight" speech fame, was particularly liked by the children because he "carried marshmallows always in the pockets of his prodigious frock coat." Senator Cameron of Pennsylvania was another favorite, since he gave out handfuls of candy, and the visits of dignitaries like Whitelaw Reid and even General Grant, who spent the night, were seared in Harriet's memory. Some lesser, more local celebrities were likewise recalled, such as her father's friend in Farmington, Maine, known as "Camp Meeting John Allen," whose granddaughter, Lillian Norton, became the distinguished world-famous opera singer, Madame Nordica.

Harriet remembered a trip, too, to Skowhegan to see Maine's richest man, Abner Coburn, and on the train trip back how they traveled in the baggage car and she stretched out on the mail bags while her father wrote and chatted with the brakemen.

To her, those were "such easy-going, happy days." She likened them to the nostalgic world portrayed in the novels of Booth Tarkington, who wrote about old-fashioned Indiana life but who had equally spent time in Maine. "Oh kind and generous Maine! Where did the idea ever arise that New Englanders are parsimonious?...Those were very tolerant days and our small lives were enriched by touching many slices of the life of the town about us."

Yet there were dark days, as well—Garfield's assassination and the loss in the 1884 election, where everyone was "white-faced and quiet" in the Blaine home, Joe Manley inconsolable, her mother breaking down, and the only person "perfectly cheerful and already planning ahead for the winter" was James G. Blaine, himself. The big disappointments, he could master easily, she indicated. The little stuff was often a problem. "He could storm like a child at small annoyances. He would think himself at the point of death when he had a cold."

Not dealt with were the terrible tragedies of the deaths of his children and her father's reaction to them. In the same stiff-upper-lip tradition, Harriet merely refers to her mother's "splendid courage that was so sorely tried."[1] From another source—oddly enough, Mrs. Bigelow Lawrence—one has a portrait of the widowed Mrs. James G. Blaine in Bar Harbor in 1896, wearing a long crepe veil and looking "so sad and changed" that her husband's former lady friend was moved to tears, remarking how the "poor soul" spoke pathetically of those days of old as "the happiest of her life."[2]

Harriet insisted that her father's greatest interest among all the issues with which he dealt in his career was the forging of "closer relations between our country and the South American states." She still carried a mental image, after the Arthur administration had killed his plan for a Pan-American congress, of how he was at home nursing an attack of gout and pulled out maps to show his little daughter trade routes to South America that were dominated by English shipping, which he believed could and should be supplanted by a beefed-up American merchant marine.

Harriet's final judgment was that no matter what the issue that might have faced him had he lived on and stayed in public life, "he would have headed the advance; he would never have sounded a retreat and no reactionary policy would ever have received any sympathy from his courageous heart."[3]

A daughter's estimation of her illustrious father is one thing. But just how illustrious was James G. Blaine? As one answer, take the case of Maine's Joshua Chamberlain, who could easily be seen as a rival to Blaine and whom Blaine, in their lifetimes, certainly thwarted and outshone. Thanks in part to the movie, *Gettysburg*, which may have owed some of its focus on Chamberlain to John J. Pullen's book, *The Twentieth Maine*, this Civil War hero has been rediscovered.[4] The town of Brunswick, Maine, where he lived most of his life, has erected a statue of him and books about him appear regularly. Meanwhile, in the twenty-first century, James G. Blaine languishes in anonymity, even in the State of Maine, statueless, his name unheralded except through the Blaine House in Augusta and a very small town called Blaine in Aroostook County, and his presence in his native Pennsylvania commemorated merely by a roadside marker. No president of the United States attended the funeral of Joshua Chamberlain, nor came to his deathbed, as Harrison did to Blaine's. While Maine mourned her ex-governor, former Bowdoin College president, and Congressional Medal of Honor winner, all of the United States mourned James G. Blaine and even the international press took note. The *London Times* pronounced Blaine "greater than a President." He was ranked with Gladstone and Bismarck, as well as Clay and Webster. John J. Pullen wrote of Chamberlain, who died in 1914, "Quickly thereafter the name of Joshua Chamberlain slipped into shadow. Overwhelmed by World War I, the Great Depression and World War II, Americans completely forgot him"[5] and yet, at the present time, this author is able to add, "thousands visit his home, now a museum. Here the register shows names and addresses from all over the country and the world."[6] This, and all the tributes to his memory at the Twentieth Maine monument in Gettysburg and on his grave in Brunswick—what a contrast with the all-but-ignored gravesite in Augusta!

In the late 1920s and early 1930s when a brief flurry of biographies of Blaine appeared, Charles Edward Russell tried to plumb the reasons for his lack of staying power as a figure in American history. The hardened political reporter identified what he called "the two cardinal omissions in his make-up for greatness." First cited were, in Russell's opinion, a sort of dialectic of character weaknesses; not having a single "great cause" to which he was dedicated, but at the same time, the one thing that might supply this lack, a huge egotism pushing him to overcome all obstacles, was also missing. Secondly, as Russell saw it, Blaine "had none of the stern and rugged fidelity to truth for its own sake and principle for its own sake that has made so many small men great. He was congenitally for compromise...."[7]

Added to these two notions was a summing-up series of condemnations of Blaine that were impressively devastating. "Of all this truly extraordinary endowment, this powerfully grasping mind, this phenomenal memory, this gift to see into the heart of a matter, this rare voice, this impressive presence, this fluent eloquence, this universal reading, this power to win confidence, this natural command—of the whole unequaled enginery, the sum at last was the sum of nothing. He had failed in his great ambition, but that was nothing to us. Infinitely more impressive and more pathetic is this, that he failed to leave anything but the record of an almost incredible popularity starting with little and ending in naught. There remained only a name that began at once to fade and is now all but forgotten. No other man in our annals has filled so large a space and left it so empty. No "cause of humanity was the better or stronger for his service to it; aside from the mild endorsement he gave to the anti-slavery protest, nothing was gained from his pilgrimage here...."[8]

Yet one has the impression that Russell, as he wrote these lines, regretted doing so, that he really liked Blaine but had been disillusioned by the "Slippery Jim" aspects of his career. That journalists—good journalists like Russell—are always looking for purity in politicians and end up almost universally being disappointed speaks more to the nature of the political profession than anything else. Russell's own hero, whom he contrasts to Blaine, was Wendell Phillips, the abolitionist whose statue stands in the Boston Public Garden, holding the broken chains of slaves. "Nobody will ever erect to the memory of James G. Blaine a statue holding broken chains," Russell wrote. I wonder if Russell would appreciate the irony that Wendell Phillips was a lifelong friend, admirer and political supporter of James G. Blaine.

So did other highly principled men stick with him, such as John Greenleaf Whittier and John Hay, whose best friend was the Blaine-hating Henry Adams, and nothing better illustrates this dichotomy versus the "Magnetic Man" than a bit of recorded dialogue between William Dean Howells, the distinguished novelist and editor and *his* close friend, Mark Twain, discussing their choices in the upcoming 1884 election. Twain, who had co-authored a statement that Blaine's "defeat may save our party by freeing it from the control of the camp followers and office seekers…" pleaded with Howells not to vote for Blaine and to support Grover Cleveland. The response from Howells, related to the Maria Halpin incident, was he "would not vote for a man guilty of what society sends a woman to hell for." Twain railed back against seeing "grown men…seriously arguing against a bachelor's fitness for President because he had private intercourse with a widow…" But Howells capped the argument by declaring, "I shall vote for Blaine. I do not believe he is guilty of the things they accuse him of and I know they are not proved against him."[9]

Thirteen years previously, Twain and another writer, Charles Dudley Warner, had published their satirical novel, *The Gilded Age*, whose title, outlasting the book's rather thin contents, gave its name to a whole era and a style of politics then overtaking the American scene. The backcover text on the Penguin Classic's reprint speaks of "an age of corruption, of national optimism and of crooked land speculators, ruthless bankers and dishonest politicians voraciously taking advantage of that new optimism."[10]

In this regard, an exchange of letters two years afterward, in 1875, between Twain, writing as Samuel Clemens, and Blaine provides a curious background. It began with an inquiry from Twain in Hartford, asking about a man referred to only as N., who had appeared presumably in the "Nook Farm" community where Twain resided, with a letter of recommendation signed by Speaker Blaine. The novelist was doing his due diligence. Twain wrote" "All who have met him here think the man is a fraud, but if he isn't, I want to right the wrong I have done him."

Blaine's candid reply was that N. was a Southerner who had fought for the Union, had come to D.C. looking for a job in government and that he had given him a letter to the secretary of state about a dispatch carrier's position, but didn't know he had written "so gushingly" as Twain had reported. Following which, the speaker was really blunt. "But alas! My real convictions are that N. in all his pitiful poverty belongs to that innumerable caravan of dead beats whose headquarters are in Washington. It does my very soul good to know that Hartford is getting its share.... And if the advent of N. teaches you Hartford saints no other lesson, let it deeply impress on your minds a newer, keener, fresher appreciation of the trials and the troubles, the beggars, the bores, the swindlers and the scalawags wherewith the average Congressman is evermore afflicted."[11]

One might think that the two were completely on the same page in their attitudes toward government. What made Twain change his mind and put Blaine into the same category as the outrageously prevaricating, unscrupulous anti-hero of *The Gilded Age*, Colonel Beriah Sellers, is hard to say. The "Mulligan Letters," perhaps? By 1884 he was obviously firm in his conviction that Blaine, himself, was among the "swindlers and the scalawags." Charles Dudley Warner, his co-satirist, by the way, resolutely stuck with Blaine in 1884.

Trying to determine how Blaine could have forfeited the confidence of someone like Mark Twain, whom he seemed to match in intelligence and even wit if the above letter is any indication, requires considerable thought. Start, perhaps, with the premise of

Blaine, the rising young Maine politician, trying to do his job—and do it in the light of his own personal political heritage—as a Whig, a hero worshipper of Henry Clay, turned into a Republican over the slavery issue. Two stories are told in Augusta of how, in keeping with the Whig notion of using government resources to further economic development and build infrastructure, he "brought the bacon home" to his district. One project was a dam across the Kennebec to produce power for local manufacturing industries and the other, the conversion of an unsuccessful resort complex into the Veterans Hospital in nearby Togus, Maine, which still exists to this day. Blaine found himself in government, first state, then national, when there was an explosion of opportunities for gain, and in a role that had become perfectly legitimate for an elected official, he worked hard at satisfying his constituents, who eventually grew to include the whole population of the country. His big mistake was that along the way, he tried to find—as seemed to be the thing to do—means of making all this effort worth his own while simultaneously.

A particular case in point was the most telling case against him in the Little Rock and Fort Smith Railroad situation. It was not so much that he supposedly received a "sweetheart deal" to sell the company's stocks and bonds; after all, he claimed he lost money and embarrassed himself with friends who bought from him. No, the most serious charge was that he had used his position as speaker to rule for the railroad. A closer look at that action reveals the sort of dilemma that from time to time faces a public official—getting in the middle between two rivals, in this instance, those who were trying to revive the Little Rock and Fort Smith's charter and a competing group who wanted to put them out of business. When pro-Little Rock legislators sought Blaine's advice, he told them, "Ask me if the amendment is pertinent to the bill." Since it wasn't, his ruling against it was perfectly legitimate. However, he then went one step further and told those he had helped, "See how useful I've been. Now, what can you do for me?" Fatal flaw.

There were enough of these instances, magnified by his enemies, to cast him forever as the "Continental Liar" and blacken his reputation to such an extent that no matter what his accomplishments, his gifts, his vision, he was eternally open to suspicion.

That sort of ambiguity he could never dodge and possibly part of its origin was his very being, the fact he was the product of a mixed religious marriage, not at all common in an era of fierce sectarianism among Christians. He could never disown the Catholic roots of his mother, although insisting on his own loudly professed Protestantism. It was ironic that he should come to Maine, which was the first state, at least in WASP New England, to have a Catholic governor, Edward Kavanagh, who served a brief term in the 1840s. But by the 1850s, when Blaine arrived, Down East was a hotbed of Know-Nothingism and Blaine, to his discredit, pandered to it in his efforts to build up the budding Republican Party. What that did to his inner conscience—how he rationalized such intellectual dishonesty—is a better study for a psychologist than a historian, but glibness of that ilk leads right into the making of "Slippery Jim."

What can be said of his lasting achievements, if any? Should much weight be given to his trailblazing as an expansionist secretary of state? To be trumpeted as the "Father of American Imperialism" doesn't exactly have a nice ring these days, yet there is also his success at having organized the American states for purposes of peace and conflict resolution, even if some suspicious Latinos saw his moves also as a front for gringo business penetration.

On the national level, we still today have his Blaine Amendment, not the one he attached to the Fourteenth Amendment, but the one to keep public funds from going to Catholic schools, and now under severe attack. There is also his heritage of linking the Republican Party to big business—how he changed the dynamic in opposition to Roscoe Conkling, who gathered power so he could threaten businesses if they didn't help the G.O.P. while Blaine said, "help us and we'll help you." The extent to which that symbiosis has mushroomed in our day and age might astonish him. Whether it would dismay him is another matter.

Professor Muzzey has stated that one of Blaine's Achilles heels was his utter devotion to the Republican Party, that in his eyes it could do no wrong. He also has referred to Blaine as the "Alcibiades of American Politics," a reference to the notorious Athenian "statesman and general" who ended his career as seemingly a scheming betrayer of his people yet by others seen as falsely accused and misunderstood.

Another factor must be mentioned in Blaine's career. John F. Kennedy once said that a successful politician must not only be skilled, but lucky. And James G. Blaine, while quick to take advantage of opportunities, seemed over and over again to encounter stretches of rotten luck, down to the horrendous, Old Testament-like tragedies that decimated his family at the very end.

Years after his death, those who knew him still told fond stories about James G. Blaine. Walter Damrosch, speaking to a commencement at Washington and Jefferson College in the 1930s, saw fit to include in his address an anecdote about his father-in-law, the school's most famous alumnus, who had a funny story for every occasion, and used one once to tease the noted musician about his German respect for order. Blaine's joke concerned an old German caught with a stolen horse in the American West. "Vat are you going to do mit me?" the old German asked. The sheriff answered, "We are going to hang you." The old German then replied, "Vell, vateffer is der rule." And Damrosch added, "I wish I could tell it to you in that inimitable way in which Mr. Blaine told his funny stories" and that Blaine would start chuckling even before he got to a punch line.

With human touches like those appearing throughout this man's outstanding life, it is hard to reconcile a chuckling, joke-telling statesman with the sense one has, in those final years of his, of a figure of doom, stark as any struck-down hero of a Greek tragedy, punished for hubris, or even a Biblical sufferer like Job, tested through one horrible ordeal after another.

Charles Edward Russell may be right. James Gillespie Blaine might not have left behind him anything of note in the public arena. Yet withal, in his story, told here again in biographical detail more than seventy years after the last publications in the early 1930s, with added attention to its Maine setting, there is a vitality and color that reflects a key extended moment in American history. It was a second *time that tried men's souls*—the Civil War, that is—and it determined if the great experiment of the United States could continue, and when that answer was yes, forged the manner in which it would progress. James G. Blaine was a colossus in the heart of this turmoil that stretched from the 1850s through to almost the twentieth century.

We have no idea of what kind of president he would have made, how much our country's path might have differed had he reached the White House. Robert G. Ingersoll was one of those highly principled Republicans who stuck with Blaine. What did he see in the "Magnetic Man"? Ingersoll, in an 1880 speech, outlined *his* ideas of what his party stood for: "Republicanism means justice in politics. Republicanism means progress in civilization. Republicanism means that every man shall be an educated patriot and a gentleman...." [12] Did he believe that Blaine would adhere to such standards if he reached the White House? In 1879, in an article Blaine wrote for the *North American Review* on the question of Negro Enfranchisement, he had stated if that issue were to return to Congress, "I would vote for suffrage in the light of experience with more confidence than I voted for it in the light of an experiment?" Would the U.S. have had a civil rights activist at its head? The office often changes the man. Lincoln had been considered a lightweight by many, practically purely a cracker of jokes. Would Blaine have sloughed off the snakeskin of *slipperiness* had he reached the highest heights? Would he have left us a legacy that, praised as it was at the time of his death, would, as they say, have *had legs*? It's impossible to tell and probably inexpedient to speculate.

Somehow, while I was researching the life of this complex and engaging man, I could not help but think of the movie *Citizen Kane* and what Orson Welles might have done with a character like Blaine who was every bit as fascinating, lively and quirky as William Randolph Hearst, who also wanted to be president and failed. On a big screen, at any rate, here would have been a slice of Americana, seen through the prism of one of its most important players, even if he is not remembered as the giant he was then.

James G. Blaine, "Continental Liar," or whatever, was a quintessential American, warts and all.

1. Beale, Vol. 1, p. v.
2. Beale, Vol. 2, p. 287.
3. Gemmill, p. 239.
4. John J. Pullen. *Joshua Chamberlain: A Hero's Life and Legacy* (Mechanicsburg, PA: Stackpole Books, 1999),
5. Ibid., p. 166.
6. Ibid., p. 172.
7. Russell, p. 432.
8. Ibid., pp. 432–33
9. Kenneth R. Andrews. *Nook Farm: Mark Twain's Hartford Circle* (Cambridge, MA: Harvard University Press, 1950), pp. 114–16.
10. Mark Twain and Charles Dudley Warner. *The Gilded Age: A Tale of Today* (New York: Penguin Books, reprint), 2001.
11. Hamilton, p. 377.
12. Robert G. Ingersoll. *What's God Got to Do with It?*, edited by Tim Page (Hanover, NH: Steerforth Press, 2005), p. 73.

BIBLIOGRAPHY

Berman, Miriam. *Madison Square: The Park and Its Celebrated Landmarks* (Salt Lake City: Gibbs-Smith Publisher, 2001).

Blaine, James G. *Memoir of Luther Severance* (Augusta, ME: Kennebec Journal, 1856).

_____. "Ought The Negro to Be Disenfranchised? Ought He to Have Been Enfranchised?" *North American Review,* March 1875.

_____. "The Presidential Election of 1892," *North American Review,* November 1892.

_____. *Political Discussions: Legislative, Diplomatic, and Popular, 1856–1886* (Norwich, CT: Henry Bill Publishing Company, 1887).

_____. *Twenty Years Of Congress,* Volumes I and II (Norwich, CT: The Henry Bill Publishing Company, 1886). Blaine's alleged masterpiece, a best-seller that earned him a good deal of money. Very didactic and unrevealing, although the man has a smooth style of writing.

Blaine, Margaret. Diaries (Washington, D.C.: Library of Congress, James G. Blaine Collection, Madison Building).

Boyd, James P. *Life and Public Services of James G. Blaine* (Publishers Union, 1893).

Brodsky, Alyn. *Grover Cleveland: A Study in Character* (New York: St. Martin's Press, 2000).

Brown, Fern G. *Franklin Pierce: 14th President of the United States* (Ada, OK: Garrett Educational Corporation, 1989).

Bunker, Benjamin. *Bunker's Text Book, Political Deviltry, A Record of Maine's Small Bore Politicians and Political Bosses, with Jack-Knife Illustrations by the Author* (Waterville, ME: Printed at the Kennebec Democrat Office, 1889). This is a funky nineteenth-century bit of Down East spoofing, cartooning, and serious venting of grievances by a frustrated Democrat and Blaine-hater, who does not spare his own party, either, while railing against the Maine political process at the time.

Burlin, Paul. "Harold Marsh Sewall and the Truculent Pursuit of Empire, Samoa, 1887–1890," *Maine History*, Volume 39, Summer 2000.

Byrne, Frank L. *Prophet of Prohibition: Neal Dow and His Crusade* (Madison, WI: University of Wisconsin, 1961).

Chaffin, Tom. *Pathfinder: John Charles Fremont and the Course of Empire* (New York: Hill and Wang, 2002).

Chidsey, Donald Barr. *The Gentleman from New York: A Life of Roscoe Conkling* (New Haven, CT: Yale University Press, 1935).

Christianson, Stephen G. *Facts About Congress* (New York and Dublin: H. W. Wilson Company, 1961).

Clark, Calvin Montague, D.D. *American Slavery and Maine Congressionals* (Bangor, ME: published by the author, 1940).

Clifford, Philip Greely. *Nathan Clifford, Democrat* (New York: G. P. Putnam's Sons, 1922).

Coffman, Tom. *Nation Within: The Story of America's Annexation of Hawaii* (Kame'ohe, HI: Epicenter, no date). An extremely good book for understanding the unlikely link between Maine's Kennebec Valley and Hawaii and the role played by Maine people in acquiring our fiftieth state.

Conwell, Russell. *Life and Public Service of James G. Blaine* (Augusta, ME: E. C. Allen and Company, 1884). The "official" campaign biography after Blaine received the G.O.P. nomination, written by the president of Temple University, a minister who was one of the most popular lecturers in the country. It is still a puff piece, hurriedly put together and published by an opportunistic Augusta Democratic businessman.

Cooper, Thomas V. *Campaign of 1884: Biographies of James G. Blaine and John A. Logan* (Chicago: Baird and Dillon, 1884).

Corry, John A. *A Rough Ride To Albany: Teddy Runs for Governor* (New York: John A. Corry, 2000).

Coulter, E. Merton. "Amnesty for All Except Jeff Davis: The Hill-Blaine Debate of 1876," *Georgia Historical Quarterly,* Volume LVI, Winter 1972, Number 4.

Craig, Hugh. *The Biography and Public Service of Honorable James G. Blaine* (New York and Chicago: H. S. Goodspeed and Company, 1884).

Crapol, Edward P. *James G. Blaine: Architect of Empire* (Wilmington, DE: SR [Scholarly Resources] Inc. Books, 2000). The latest look at James G. Blaine's policies as secretary of state. Useful as an outline.

Cressey, E. K. *Pine to Potomac: The Life of James G. Blaine with a Sketch of the Life of General John A. Logan* (Boston: James H. Earle Publisher, 1884).

Current, Richard Nelson. *Those Terrible Carpetbaggers: A Reinterpretation* (New York and Oxford, UK: Oxford University Press, 1988).

Davis, Richard Dewey. "National Problems, 1885-1897," *The American Nation: A History,* edited by Albert Bushnell Hart, Volume 24 (New York: Harper and Brothers Publishers, 1907).

Davis, William C. *Look Away: A History of the Confederate States of America* (New York: Free Press, 2002). Well done and objective.

de Hegermann-Lindencrone, Lillie L. *The Sunny Side of Diplomatic Life* (New York: Harper and Brothers, 1914). This delightful memoir of an American woman married to a Danish diplomat was discovered by chance on the Internet. Unfortunately, her husband's service in Washington, D.C., during the Blaine years was brief, but there are portraits of Blaine that are found nowhere else. The former Lillie Greenlough was also close to Blaine's friend Mrs. Bigelow Lawrence and her beauteous sister Fannie, who was the secret mistress of Blaine's political enemy Carl Schurz.

Dennett, Tyler. *John Hay: From Poetry To Politics* (New York: Dodd, Mead and Company, 1933).

Desmond, Jerry R. "The Attempt to Repeal Maine's Personal Liberty Laws," *Maine History,* Spring 1998.

Destler, Chester McArthur. *American Radicalism, 1865–1901* (Chicago: Quadrangle Books, 1966, reprint, original 1946).

Dow, Neal. *The Reminiscences of Neal Dow: Recollections of Eighty Years* (Portland, ME: Evening Express Publishing Company, 1898).

Dusinberre, William. *Slavemaster President: The Double Career of James Polk* (Oxford, UK: Oxford University Press, 2003).

Eckenrode, H. J. *Rutherford B. Hayes: Statesman of Reunion* (New York: Dodd, Mead and Company, 1930).

Flexner, James Thomas. *Washington: The Indispensable Man* (Boston: Little, Brown and Company, 1969).

Ford, Trowbridge H. Article in *Mid-America: An Historical Review,* Volume 57, Chicago, Loyola University, Institute of Jesuit History. This comment on the election results of 1884 posits a complicated plot by E. L. Godkin, editor of *The Nation,* a leader of the anti-Blaine Mugwump forces, to actually support Blaine in his pro-Irish independence stance but then changing his mind. If true, an upshot of this was Blaine's loss of significant Irish backing even before "Rum, Romanism and Rebellion."

Ford, Worthington Chauncy. *Letters of Henry Adams (1859–1891)* (Boston: Houghton Mifflin Company, 1930).

Fry, James B. *Conkling and Blaine-Fry Controversy in 1866* (New York: Press of A. G. Sherwood and Company, 1893).

Garraty, John A. *The New Commonwealth, 1877-1890* (New York: Harper and Row Publishers, 1968).

Gay, Janet. "Harrison, Blaine. and Cronyism," *Alaska Journal,* Volume 3, Number 1, Winter, 1973.

Gemmill, Helen Hartman. *EL The Breadbox Papers: The High Life of a Dazzling Victorian Lady* (Doylestown, PA: Tower Press, 1983). This biography of Elizabeth Chapman, Mrs. Bigelow Lawrence, sheds some—but not very much—light about the "mystery woman" in Blaine's life. It is called "The Breadbox Papers" because some of her documents were discovered in a breadbox.

Ginger, Ray. *Age of Excess: The United States from 1877 to 1914* (New York: MacMillan Company, 1965).

Gottlieb, Howard B. "A Revealing Letter by James G. Blaine [to John A. Logan]," *Colby Library Quarterly,* Series IV, Number 15, August 1958.

Green, Steven K. "The Blaine Amendment Reconsidered," *The American Journal of Legal History,* Volume XXXVI, January 1992, Number 1.

Hale, Richard Waldron. *The Story of Bar Harbor* (New York: Ives, Washburn, Inc., 1949).

Haley, John W. *The Rebel Yell and The Yankee Hurrah: The Civil War Journal of a Maine Volunteer,* edited by Ruth Silliker (Camden, ME: Down East Books, 1985). Haley, an outspoken irreverent Saco, Maine, recruit, is always fun to read. He's included here because of his pungent remarks about Blaine's friend, Governor Abner Coburn, the richest man in Maine.

Hamilton, Gail (Mary Abigail Dodge). *Biography of James G. Blaine* (Norwich, CT: Humphrey Bill Publishing Company, 1895). This is the blockbuster of all books about Blaine, more than 800 pages from "Cousin Abby," the bosom friend and relative of Blaine's wife, literally a member of their household and a secretary and ghostwriter for the great man, himself. A one-time school teacher, she was also a nationally known author and feminist. Her book is a jumbled treasure trove of letters and documents stuffed into a hero-worshipping framework; it appeared two years after Blaine's death and not long before her own.

Hamlin, Charles Eugene. *The Life and Times of Hannibal Hamlin by His Own Grandson* (Cambridge, MA, Riverside Press, 1899, published by subscription).

Harrison, Gilbert A. *A Timeless Affair: The Life of Anita McCormick Blaine* (Chicago: University of Chicago Press, 1979).

Hatch, Alden. *The Lodges of Massachusetts* (New York: Hawthorn Books, Inc., 1973).

Healy, David. *James G. Blaine and Latin America* (Columbia, MO: University of Missouri Press, 2001).

Hendrick, Burton J. *The Life of Andrew Carnegie* (Garden City, NY: Doubleday, Doran and Company, Inc., 1932).

Hibben, Payton. *Henry Ward Beecher: An American Portrait* (New York: George H. Doran Company, 1927).

Hinkley, Sue C. *The Life and Times of Luther Severance* (Livermore, ME: Washburn-Norlands, 1987).

Holt, Michael F. *The Political Crisis of the 1850s* (New York: John Wiley and Sons, 1978).

Howard, Oliver Otis. *The Autobiography of O. O. Howard* (New York: Baker and Taylor Company, two volumes, 1907).

Hunt, Gaillard. "Israel, Elihu. and Cadwallader Washburn," *American Biography* (New York: MacMillan Company, 1925).

Hunt, H. Draper. *The Blaine House: Home of Maine's Governors* (Augusta, ME: Friends of the Blaine House, 1994). A very readable volume about the building and grounds that constitute the State of Maine's most visible monument to James G. Blaine.

_____. *Hannibal Hamlin of Maine: Lincoln's First Vice President* (Syracuse, NY: Syracuse University Press, 1969).

Ingersoll, Robert G. *What's God Got to Do with It?,* edited by Tim Page (Hanover, NH: Steerforth Press, 2005).

Jellison, Charles A. *Fessenden of Maine: Civil War Senator* (Syracuse, NY: Syracuse University Press, 1962).

Johnson, Willis Fletcher. *The Plumed Knight* (Philadelphia: Atlantic Publishing Company Press of Alfred W. Slocum, 1893).

Jones, James Pickett. *John A. Logan: Stalwart Republican from Illinois* (Carbondale and Edwardville, IL: Southern Illinois University Press, 2001).

Karabell, Zachary. *Chester Alan Arthur* (New York: New York Times Books, Henry Holt and Company, 2004).

Katz, Irving. *August Belmont: A Political Biography* (New York: Columbia University Press, 1968).

Kelsey, Kerck. *Israel Washburn. Jr.: Maine's Little Known Giant of the Civil War* (Rockport, ME: Picton Press, 2004). Author Kelsey, who has been working on biographies of Maine's extraordinary Washburn family, most graciously shared with me writings by ex-Governor and Congressman Israel Washburn, Jr., in which Washburn expressed his true unhappy feelings toward James G. Blaine, with whom he had worked so closely during the Civil War.

King, Willard C. *Melville W. Fuller: Chief Justice of the United States, 1888–1910* (New York: MacMillan Company, 1950).

Kingsbury, Henry D. and Simeon L. Dexo. *Illustrated History of Kennebec County, 1625–1892* (New York: H. W. Blacke and Company, 1893).

Klinkhamer, Sister Mary Carolyn. "The Blaine Amendment of 1875: Private Motives for Political Action," *Catholic Historical Review,* Volume XLII, Number 1, April 1956.

Larson, Henrietta M. *Jay Cooke, Private Banker* (Cambridge, MA: Harvard University Press, 1936).

Livezy, William E. *Mahan on Sea Power* (Norman, OK: University of Oklahoma Press, 1947).

Marszalek, John F. *Sherman: A Soldier's Passion for Order* (New York: Vintage Books, 1993).

Martí, José. *The America of José Martí: Selected Writings of José Martí,* translated by Juan de Onis (New York: Noonday Press, 1953). Here's a real surprise—Cuba's national hero. But remember, he was a journalist in exile in New York City and writing about events and personalities in the United States. One of his essays was about Roscoe Conkling and includes Mart"s perspicacious remarks on the Conkling-Blaine blow-up in Congress.

Mason, Edward G. "The Presidential Campaign of 1884 in Mr. Blaine's Home City," *New England Magazine,* May 1901. Thanks to Earle G. Shettleworth, Jr., director of the Maine Historic Preservation Commission, I was able to use this marvelously vivid description of what happened in Augusta when Blaine won the G.O.P. presidential nomination in 1884.

Massachusetts Avenue Architecture, Volume II, Washington, D.C., 1975. This technical magazine number carried a detailed article on the elaborate home Blaine built near Dupont Circle but barely used.

Mayer, Grace M. *Once Upon A City* (New York: MacMillan Company, 1958).

McCall, Samuel W. *The Life of Thomas Brackett Reed* (Boston: Houghton Mifflin Company, 1914).

McCullough, David. *Mornings on Horseback* (New York: Simon and Schuster, 1981).

McFarland, Gerald W. "Blaine Men: Butlerites and Mugwumps in 1884," *Connecticut Historic Society Bulletin,* Volume 49, Number 2, Spring 1984.

Mead, Walter Russell. *Special Providence: American Foreign Policy and How It Changed the World* (New York: Alfred A. Knopf, 2001).

Morgan, H. Wayne, editor. *The Gilded Age* (Syracuse, NY: Syracuse University Press, 1963).

———. *Unity and Culture: The United States, 1877–1900* (Middlesex, UK: Penguin Books, 1971).

Mulkearn, Lois and Edwin V. Pugh. *A Traveler's Guide to Western Pennsylvania* (Pittsburgh: University of Pittsburgh Press, 1954).

Muzzey, David Saville. *James G. Blaine: A Political Idol of Other Days* (New York: Dodd, Mead and Company, 1934). The last full biography of James G. Blaine, written by a Columbia University professor. The subtitle gives away the fact that even seventy-plus years ago, Blaine was being forgotten. Muzzey's work is almost totally focused on Blaine's national political career.

Nash, Howard P., Jr. *Stormy Petrel: The Life and Times of General Benjamin Butler, 1818–1893* (Rutherford, NJ: Fairleigh Dickinson University Press, 1969).

Nelson, William Javier. *Almost a Territory: America's Attempt to Annex the Dominican Republic* (Newark, DE: University of Delaware Press, 1990).

North, James W. *The History of Augusta* (Somersworth, NH: reprint of 1870 edition, 1981).

Northrup, Henry Davenport. *The Life and Public Services of Honorable James G. Blaine* (Philadelphia: Acme Bible House Publishing Company, 1893).

Oberholtzer, Ellis Paxson. *A History of the United States Since the Civil War, Volume IV, 1878-1888* (New York: MacMillan Company, 1931).

O'Connor, Richard. *Gould's Millions* (Garden City, NY: Doubleday, 1962).

Paine, Albert Bigelow. *Thomas Nast: His Period and His Pictures* (New York: Harper and Brothers, 1904).

Parkman, Francis. *The Conspiracy of Pontiac: The Indian War After the Conquest of Canada* (Boston: Little, Brown and Company, 1969, reprint). Parkman is still always fun to read, even if he is criticized by more punctilious modern-day historians. The action here involves Blaine's own home area of western Pennsylvania and a "Lieutenant Blane" who was most likely his great-grandfather.

Peck, Henry Thurston. *Twenty Years of the Republic, 1885-1905* (New York: Dodd Mead and Company, 1906).

Perry, Mark. *Conceived in Liberty: Joshua Chamberlain, William Oates, and the American Civil War* (New York: Viking Press, 1997).

Peskin, Allan. *Garfield* (Kent, OH: Kent State University Press, 1978). A very thorough biography.

Peters, Ronald M., Jr. *The American Speakership in Historical Perspective* (Baltimore: Johns Hopkins University Press, 1997).

Phillips, David Graham. *The Treason of the Senate* (Chicago: Quadrangle Books, reprint, 1964, original 1906). A famous bit of muckraking journalism, today considered significantly overblown.

Phillips, Kevin. *William McKinley* (New York: New York Times Books, Henry Holt and Company, 2003).

Pullen, John J. *Joshua Chamberlain: A Hero's Life and Legacy* (Mechanicsburg, PA: Stackpole Books, 1999). The author, almost singlehandedly through his writings, helped revive interest in the hero of Gettysburg.

Ramsdell, H. J. *Life and Services of Honorable James G. Blaine* (Philadelphia: Hubbard Brothers Publishers, 1884). Another campaign biography, this one by a leading Washington, D.C., reporter, who was a close friend of Blaine's. It is fairly readable, for one of these thrown-together puff pieces.

Rehnquist, William H. *Centennial Crisis: The Disputed Election of 1876* (New York: Alfred A. Knopf, 2004). The late chief justice of the United States as a political historian. It has been claimed he wrote this book before his death to cover his actions in the "disputed election" of 2000.

Ridpath, John Clark. *Life and Works of James G. Blaine* (Philadelphia: Historical Publishing Company, 1893).

Ritchie, Donald. *Press Gallery: Congress and the Washington Correspondents* (Cambridge, MA: Harvard University Press, 1991). An interesting work by the director of the U.S. Senate Historical Office, who is an expert on the interaction of the D.C. press corps and Congress.

Rolde, Neil. "How Augusta Became and Stayed the State Capital," address at the Maine State House, 1982.

Russell, Charles Edward. *Blaine of Maine: His Life and Times* (New York: Cosmopolitan Book Corporation, 1931). The next-to-last major biography of Blaine. Russell was a Washington reporter who had covered him on many occasions and liked Blaine, in spite of himself. Russell was a Socialist who twice ran for governor of New York on the Socialist ticket and once for mayor of New York City. He declined to be the Socialist candidate for U.S. president in 1916. His tone in regard to Blaine is always one of regret that the "Plumed Knight" did not put his considerable talent and charm to better use.

Samuels, Ernest. *Henry Adams: The Middle Years* (Cambridge, MA: Belknap Press of Harvard University Press, 1958).

Scoggins, Mark. *Hannibal Hamlin: The Life of Abraham Lincoln's First Vice President* (Lanham, MD: Union Press of America, Inc., 1994).

Seitz, Don C. *The Dreadful Decade* (Indianapolis: Bobbs Merrill Company, 1926).

Sewell, Mike. "Political Rhetoric and Policy Making: James G. Blaine and Britain," *Cambridge University Journal of American Studies,* Volume 24, Number 1, April 1990.

Shank, William H. *Indian Trails to Super Highways* (York, PA: American Canal and Transportation Center, 1988).

Sherman, Thomas H. *Twenty Years with James G. Blaine* (New York: Grafton Press, 1928). More insights into Blaine as a person and, in this case, as an employer, by his longtime private secretary who thought the world of him.

Spetter, Allan. "Harrison and Blaine: Foreign Policy, 1889–1893," *Indiana Magazine of History,* Volume LXV, Number 3, September 1969.

Stanwood, Edward. *James Gillespie Blaine* (Boston: Houghton, Mifflin and Company, 1905). Another intimate and even critical look at Blaine by a close friend and cousin of Harriet Blaine.

Stevens, John L. and W. B. Oleson. *Picturesque Hawaii* (New York: Union Publishing House, 1894). A collector's item (it cost me a small fortune at a secondhand bookstore on the island of Hawaii) written by Blaine's colleague John L. Stevens, whom he had made ambassador to the Hawaiian Kingdom. No one was more responsible for the overthrow of that kingdom than Stevens. The language of the book is redolent with Anglo-Saxon supremacy ideas and contempt for the native Hawaiian culture.

Stowe, Harriet Beecher. *Uncle Tom's Cabin* (New York: Penguin Books, reprint, original 1852). This classic novel, written in Maine, helps vivify the issues that led the United States into a civil war. Mrs. Stowe and her husband, Bowdoin professor Calvin Stowe, were faithful supporters of Blaine. Mrs. Stowe's brother, the famed Reverend Henry Ward Beecher, was an adamant foe.

Summers, Mark Wahlgren. *Rum, Romanism, and Rebellion* (Chapel Hill, NC: University of North Carolina Press, 2000).

Swethan, George. *Pittsylvania Country* (New York: Duell, Sloan, and Pearce, 1951).

Taylor, John M. *William Henry Seward: Lincoln's Right Hand* (New York: Harper Collins Publishers, 1991).

Trefousse, Hans L. *Thaddeus Stevens: Nineteenth-Century Egalitarian* (Chapel Hill, NC: University of North Carolina Press, 1997).

_____. *The Radical Republicans: Lincoln's Vanguard for Social Justice* (New York: Alfred A. Knopf, 1969).

Twain, Mark and Charles Dudley Warner. *The Gilded Age: A Tale of Today* (New York: Penguin Books, 2001 reprint). The title has lived on, but the book, too much of a caricature, does not have the oomph of other Twain works.

Tyler, Alice Felt. *The Foreign Policy of James G. Blaine* (Minneapolis: University of Minnesota Press, 1927).

Van Deusen, Glyndon G. *The Life of Henry Clay* (Boston: Little, Brown and Company, 1937).

Vidal, Gore. *1876* (New York: Ballantine Books, 1976). Part of a trilogy by the well-known novelist, this book was issued in conjunction with the U.S. bi-centennial. Blaine, as envisaged by Vidal, plays a large role in it.

Vivian, Cassandra. *A Walking and Driving Tour of Historic Brownsville* (Brownsville, PA: Brownsville Area Revitalization Corps, 1994).

Waugh, John C. *Re-Electing Lincoln: The Battle for the 1864 Presidency* (New York: Crown Publishers, Inc., 1997).

Westcott, Richard R. *New Men, New Leaders: The Formation of the Republican Party in Maine* (Portland, ME: Maine Historical Society, 1986).

Westsylvania Stories (magazine) Summer 2004, Hollidaysburg, PA.

Weymouth, Lally. *America in 1876: The Way We Were* (New York: Vintage Books, 1976).

Whalon, Michael Winters. "Maine Republicans: A Study in Growth and

Political Power" (Lincoln, NE: University of Nebraska, dissertation). Well-done thesis.

Whiteside, Thomas. "James G. Blaine As a Political Leader," thesis for honors in American History, 1932.

Wilkins, Thurman, *Clarence King: A Biography* (Albuquerque, NM: University of New Mexico Press, 1988).

Willey, Reverend Austin. *The History of the Anti-Slavery Cause* (Portland, ME: Brown, Thurston, Hoyt, Fogg, and Dunham, 1886).

Williams, Charles Richard. *The Life of Rutherford B. Hayes,* two volumes (Boston: Houghton Mifflin, 1914).

Williams, John Hoyt. *A Great and Shining Road: The Epic Story of the Transcontinental Railroad* (Lincoln, NE: University of Nebraska Press, 1988).

Williams, T. Harry, editor. *Hayes: The Diary of a President, 1875–1888* (New York: David McKay Company, Inc., 1964).

Williamson, Harold Francis. *Edward Atkinson: The Biography of an American Liberal, 1827–1905* (Boston: Old Corner Bookstore, 1934).

Woodward, C. Vann. *Reunion and Reaction: The Compromise of 1877 and the End of Reconstruction* (Boston: Little, Brown and Company, 1951).

Young, Marilyn Blair. *American Expansionism: The Critical Issues* (Boston: Little, Brown and Company, 1973).

Zimmerman, Warren. *First Great Triumph* (New York: Farrar, Straus and Giroux, 2002).

INDEX